Foundations in Accountancy

MA2
MANAGING COSTS AND FINANCE

BPP Learning Media is an **ACCA Approved Content Provider** for the Foundations in Accountancy qualification. This means we work closely with ACCA to ensure this Interactive Text contains the information you need to pass your exam.

In this Interactive Text, which has been reviewed by the **ACCA examining team**, we:

- **Highlight** the **most important elements** in the syllabus and the **key skills** you need

- **Signpost** how each chapter links to the syllabus and the study guide

- **Provide** lots of **exam focus points** demonstrating what the examining team will want you to do

- **Emphasise key points** in regular **fast forward summaries**

- **Test your knowledge** in **quick quizzes**

- **Examine your understanding** in our **practice question bank**

- **Reference all the important topics** in our full index

BPP's **Practice & Revision Kit** also supports the MA2 syllabus.

INTERACTIVE TEXT

FOR EXAMS FROM 1 SEPTEMBER 2022 TO 31 AUGUST 2023

BPP LEARNING MEDIA

First edition November 2011
Eleventh edition March 2022

ISBN 9781 5097 4617 0
(Previous ISBN 9781 5097 3778 9)
e-ISBN 9781 5097 4667 5

British Library Cataloguing-in-Publication Data
A catalogue record for this book
is available from the British Library

Published by

BPP Learning Media Ltd
BPP House, Aldine Place
London W12 8AA

www.bpp.com/learningmedia

Printed in the United Kingdom

Your learning materials, published by BPP Learning
Media Ltd, are printed on paper obtained from
traceable sustainable sources.

We are grateful to the Association of Chartered Certified
Accountants for permission to reproduce past
examination questions and extracts from the syllabus.
The suggested solutions in the practice answer bank
have been prepared by BPP Learning Media Ltd, except
where otherwise stated.

Contents

Helping you to pass

BPP Learning Media – ACCA Approved Content Provider

As an ACCA **Approved Content Provider**, BPP Learning Media gives you the **opportunity** to use study materials reviewed by the ACCA examining team. By incorporating the examining team's comments and suggestions regarding the depth and breadth of syllabus coverage, the BPP Learning Media Interactive Text provides excellent, **ACCA-approved** support for your studies.

These materials are reviewed by the ACCA examining team. The objective of the review is to ensure that the material properly covers the syllabus and study guide outcomes, used by the examining team in setting the exams, in the appropriate breadth and depth. The review does not ensure that every eventuality, combination or application of examinable topics is addressed by the ACCA Approved Content. Nor does the review comprise a detailed technical check of the content as the Approved Content Provider has its own quality assurance processes in place in this respect.

BPP Learning Media does everything possible to ensure the material is accurate and up to date when sending to print. In the event that any errors are found after the print date, they are uploaded to the following website: www.bpp.com/learningmedia/Errata.

The PER alert!

To become a Certified Accounting Technician or qualify as an ACCA member, you not only have to pass all your exams but also fulfil a **practical experience requirement** (PER).To help you to recognise areas of the syllabus that you might be able to apply in the workplace to achieve different performance objectives, we have introduced the '**PER alert**' feature. You will find this feature throughout the Interactive Text to remind you that what you are **learning in order to pass** your Foundations in Accountancy and ACCA exams is **equally useful to the fulfilment of the PER requirement**.

Tackling studying

Studying can be a daunting prospect, particularly when you have lots of other commitments. The **different features** of the Interactive Text, the **purposes** of which are explained fully on the **Chapter features** page, will help you whilst studying and improve your chances of **exam success**.

Developing exam awareness

Our Interactive Texts are completely **focused** on helping you pass your exam.

Our advice on **Studying MA2** outlines the **content** of the exam, the **recommended approach to studying** and any **brought forward knowledge** you are expected to have.

Exam focus points are included within the chapters to highlight when and how specific topics might be examined.

Testing what you can do

Testing yourself helps you develop the skills you need to pass the exam and also confirms that you can recall what you have learnt.

We include **Questions** – lots of them – both within chapters and in the **Practice Question Bank**, as well as **Quick Quizzes** at the end of each chapter to test your knowledge of the chapter content.

BPP LEARNING MEDIA

Chapter features

Each chapter contains a number of helpful features to guide you through each topic.

Topic list		Tells you what you will be studying in this chapter and the relevant section numbers, together with ACCA syllabus references.
Introduction		Puts the chapter content in the context of the syllabus as a whole.
Study Guide		Links the chapter content with ACCA guidance.
	Fast Forward	Summarises the content of main chapter headings, allowing you to preview and review each section easily.
EXAMPLE		Demonstrates how to apply key knowledge and techniques.
	Key Term	Definitions of important concepts that can often earn you easy marks in exams.
	Exam Focus Point	Tell you how specific topics may be examined.
	Formula	Formulae which have to be learnt.
	PER Alert	This feature gives you a useful indication of syllabus areas that closely relate to performance objectives in your Practical Experience Requirement (PER).
	Question	Gives you essential practice of techniques covered in the chapter.
Chapter Roundup		A full list of the Fast Forwards included in the chapter, providing an easy source of review.
Quick Quiz		A quick test of your knowledge of the main topics in the chapter.
Practice Question Bank		Found at the back of the Interactive Text with more exam-style chapter questions. Cross referenced for easy navigation.

Studying MA2

How to use this Interactive Text

Aim of this Interactive Text

To provide the knowledge and practice to help you succeed in the examination for MA2 *Managing Costs and Finance.*

To pass the examination you need a thorough understanding in all areas covered by the syllabus and teaching guide.

Recommended approach

(a)   To pass you need to be able to answer questions on **everything** specified by the syllabus and teaching guide. Read the Text very carefully and do not skip any of it.

(b)   Learning is an **active** process. Do **all** the questions as you work through the Text so you can be sure you really understand what you have read.

(c)   After you have covered the material in the Interactive Text, work through the **Practice Question Bank**, checking your answers carefully against the **Practice Answer Bank**.

(d)   Before you take the exam, check that you still remember the material using the following quick revision plan.

   (i)   Read through the **chapter topic list** at the beginning of each chapter. Are there any gaps in your knowledge? If so, study the section again.

   (ii)   Read and learn the **key terms**.

   (iii) Look at the **exam focus points**. These show the ways in which topics might be examined.

   (iv) Read the **chapter roundups**, which are a summary of the **fast forwards** in each chapter.

   (v)   Do the **quick quizzes** again. If you know what you're doing, they shouldn't take long.

This approach is only a suggestion. You or your college may well adapt it to suit your needs. Remember this is a **practical** course.

(a)   Try to relate the material to your experience in the workplace or any other work experience you may have had.

(b)   Try to make as many links as you can to other Applied Knowledge and Applied Skills modules.

For practice and revision, use BPP Learning Media's Practice & Revision Kit and Passcards.

BPP LEARNING MEDIA

What MA2 is about

The aim of this syllabus is to develop a knowledge and understanding of the principles and techniques used in recording, analysing and reporting costs and revenues for internal management purposes. It covers management information, cost recording, costing techniques, decision making and cash management.

Brought-forward knowledge

You will need to have a good knowledge of basic management accounting from MA1 *Management Information*. Brought-forward knowledge is identified throughout the Interactive Text. The examining team will assume you know this material and it may form part of an exam question.

Approach to examining the syllabus

MA2 is a two-hour computer-based examination. The questions in the computer-based examination are objective test questions – multiple choice, number entry and multiple response. (See page ix for frequently asked questions about computer-based examinations.)

The examination is structured as follows:

	Number of marks
50 compulsory questions of two marks each	100

Syllabus and Study guide

The complete MA2 syllabus and study guide can be found by visiting the exam resource finder on the ACCA website: www.accaglobal.com/uk/en/student/exam-support-resources.html

The computer-based examination

Computer-based examinations (CBEs) are available for all of the Foundations in Accountancy examinations. The CBE exams for the first seven modules can be taken at any time; these are referred to as 'exams on demand'. The Option exams can be sat in June and December of each year; these are referred to as 'exams on sitting'.

Computer-based examinations must be taken at an ACCA CBE Licensed Centre.

How do On Demand CBEs work?

*   Questions are displayed on a monitor.

*   Candidates enter their answer directly onto the computer.

*   Candidates have two hours to complete the examination.

*   Candidates sitting exams on demand are provided with a Provisional Result Notification showing their results before leaving the examination room.

*   The CBE Licensed Centre uploads the results to the ACCA (as proof of the candidate's performance) within 72 hours.

How do On Sitting CBEs work?

*   Candidates sitting the Option exams will receive their results approximately five weeks after the exam sitting once they have been expert marked.

*   Candidates can check their exam status on the ACCA website by logging into myACCA.

For more information on computer-based exams, visit the ACCA website.
www.accaglobal.com/gb/en/student/exam-entry-and-administration/computer-based-exams.html

Tackling multiple choice questions

MCQs are part of all Foundations in Accountancy exams.

The MCQs in your exam contain four possible answers. You have to **choose the option that best answers the question**. The incorrect options are called distracters. There is a skill in answering MCQs quickly and correctly. By practising MCQs you can develop this skill, giving you a better chance of passing the exam.

You may wish to follow the approach outlined below, or you may prefer to adapt it.

Step 1	Skim read all the MCQs and identify what appear to be the easier questions.
Step 2	Attempt each question – **starting with the easier questions** identified in Step 1. Read the question **thoroughly**. You may prefer to work out the answer before looking at the options, or you may prefer to look at the options at the beginning. Adopt the method that works best for you.
Step 3	Read the options and see if one matches your own answer. Be careful with numerical questions as the distracters are designed to match answers that incorporate common errors. Check that your calculation is correct. Have you followed the requirement exactly? Have you included every stage of the calculation?
Step 4	You may find that none of the options match your answer. • Re-read the question to ensure that you understand it and are answering the requirement • Eliminate any obviously wrong answers • Consider which of the remaining answers is the most likely to be correct and select the option
Step 5	If you are still unsure make a note and continue to the next question.
Step 6	Revisit unanswered questions. When you come back to a question after a break you often find you are able to answer it correctly straight away. If you are still unsure have a guess. You are not penalised for incorrect answers, so **never leave a question unanswered!**

After extensive practice and revision of MCQs, you may find that you recognise a question when you sit the exam. Be aware that the detail and/or requirement may be different. If the question seems familiar read the requirement and options carefully – do not assume that it is identical.

Tempting though it might be, don't try to predict where the correct answers might fall based on any kind of pattern you think you might perceive in this section. The distribution of the correct answers do not follow any predictable pattern in this exam!

part

A

Management information

Management information

Cost and management accounting systems provide information to managers to help them make decisions about their business. This introductory chapter explains the **purpose of management information**, the **nature of the decision-making process** and the **qualities that management information should have** to be of value.

Management information may come from sources within the organisation or from external sources, and it may be **financial or non-financial** in nature. Accountants specialise in providing financial information. This chapter explains the role of the **trainee accountant** in providing management information and the main elements of information about costs. These will be described in more detail in later chapters.

|
|

Study Guide	Intellectual level
A Management information	
1 Management information requirements	
(a) Describe the purpose of management information: planning, control and decision making	K
(b) Describe the features of useful management information	K
(c) Describe the nature, source and importance of both financial and non-financial information for managers	K
(d) Describe management responsibilities for cost, profit and investment and their effect on management information and performance measurement	K
(f) Explain the role of the trainee accountant	K
2 Cost accounting systems	
(a) Explain the relationship between the cost/management accounting system and the financial accounting/management information systems (including interlocking and integrated bookkeeping systems)	K
(c) Identify the documentation required, and the flow of documentation, for different cost accounting transactions	S
(d) Explain and illustrate the use of codes in categorising and processing transactions (including sequential, hierarchical, block, faceted and mnemonic coding methods)	K
(e) Explain and illustrate the concept of cost units	S
(f) Describe the different methods of costing final outputs and their appropriateness to different types of business organisation	S

1   Management information

The purpose of management information is to help managers to manage resources efficiently and effectively, by planning and controlling operations and by allowing informed decision making.

1.1 Purpose of management information

It is useful to understand the difference between data and information.

Data is a 'scientific' term for facts, figures, and measurements. Data are the raw materials for data processing.

Information is data that has been processed in such a way as to be meaningful to the person who receives it. Information is anything that is communicated.

The successful management of any organisation depends on information. For example, consider the following problems and what management information would be useful in solving these problems.

Problem 1

> A company wishes to launch a new product. The company's pricing policy is to set the price at total cost + 20%. What should the price of the product be?

> In order to make the pricing decision, management need information about the cost of the product.

Problem 2

> A company's bottle making machine has a fault and the company has to decide whether to repair the machine, to buy a new machine or to hire a machine. If the company aims to minimise costs, which decision should management take?

> In order to decide which decision to make, management need cost information about for each alternative.

Problem 3

> A company is trying to plan its production schedule for the next year with the aim of holding as little inventory as possible but still meeting sales demand. How many products should the company plan to make each month?

> In order to plan production, management need information about:
> - Sales volume per month
> - Trends in sales volumes for the past few years
> - Maximum production output per month

Problem 4

> Budgeted production costs for January were as follows:
>
> | | $ |
> |---|---|
> | Raw materials | 100,000 |
> | Labour | 50,000 |
> | Overheads | 15,000 |
> | Total | 165,000 |
>
> Budgeted production volume 700,000 units
>
> In order to meet profit targets, the actual production costs cannot be more than 5% more than the budgeted cost. How can management control production costs to make sure they are in line with budget?

> In order to control production costs, management need information about:
> - Actual production volume
> - Actual costs for raw materials, labour and overheads

In solving these and a wide variety of other problems, management need **information**.

Management require information to help them to **plan** and **control** operations and to make informed **decisions**.

1.1.1 Planning

Planning involves establishing an **objective** or identifying a problem and then choosing a **strategy** to achieve the objective or alleviate the problem.

In a most basic sense, planning means **formulating ways of proceeding**.

There are four steps in the planning process.

Step 1	Establish an objective or identify a problem.
Step 2	Develop solutions or strategies which might contribute towards achieving the objective or alleviating the problem.
Step 3	Collect and analyse relevant data about each alternative solution or strategy.
Step 4	Make a decision about which strategy or solution to take. State the expected outcome of the decision and then check that the expected outcome meets the objective or alleviates the problem in Step 1.

- An objective is the aim or goal of an organisation.

- A strategy is a possible course of action that might enable an organisation to achieve its objectives.

Management have to **plan for both the short term and the long term**. A long-range plan is necessary in order to anticipate any future needs or opportunities that require action to be taken either now or in the future. For example, management may need to consider building a new factory to meet anticipated increased demand for a product. Management should constantly be **thinking ahead**. They should **never be surprised by any gradual developments**. Planning therefore involves **converting the organisation's long-term objectives into a succession of short-term plans**. One such short-term plan is the **annual budget**.

1.1.2 Control

Control is the action of monitoring something in order to keep it on course.

Control is the action of monitoring something in order to keep it on course. Most companies will set out a plan for a future period (for example, a **budget**) and then compare the actual results during the period with the budget. Any deviations from the budget can then be identified and corrected as necessary. Such deviations are known as **variances**.

1.1.3 Decision making

Decision making means choosing between various alternatives. Decision making and planning are linked: you decide to plan in the first place and the plan you make is a collection of decisions.

Managers at all levels within an organisation take decisions. Decision making always involves a **choice between alternatives** and it is the role of the trainee accountant to provide information so that management can reach an informed decision. It is therefore useful if trainee accountants understand the decision-making process so that they can supply the appropriate type of management information.

Decision-making process

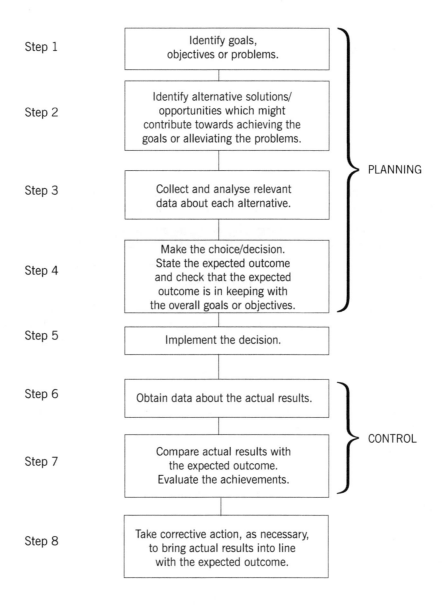

 # QUESTION

Planning and control

Mr and Mrs Average need to go to the supermarket to buy food and other household items. They make a list beforehand which sets out all the things they need. As they go round the supermarket they tick off the items on the list. If any particular item is not available they choose an alternative from the range on the shelves. They also buy a bottle of wine and two bars of chocolate. These were not on their original list.

(a)   What part or parts of this activity would you describe as planning?
(b)   There are several examples of decision making in this story. Identify three of them.
(c)   What part or parts of this activity would you describe as control?

ANSWER

We would describe making the list as planning, but making the list is also an example of decision making, since Mr and Mrs Average have to decide what items will go on the list. Ticking off the items is control and choosing alternatives is 'control action' involving further decision making.

You should be able to answer the various parts of this question without further help.

 BPP LEARNING MEDIA

1.2 The qualities of good management information

Good management information should be:

Accurate
Complete
Cost-beneficial
User-targeted
Relevant
Authoritative
Timely
Easy to use

Good management information helps managers make informed decisions. The **qualities of good information** are outlined below – in the form of a mnemonic 'accurate'.

Quality		Example
A	Accurate	Figures should **add up**, the degree of **rounding** should be appropriate, there should be **no mistakes**.
C	Complete	Information should include all relevant information – information that is correct but excludes something important is likely to be of little value. For example external data or comparative information may be required.
C	Cost-beneficial	It should not **cost more** to obtain the information than the **benefit** derived from having it.
U	User-targeted	The **needs of the user** should be borne in mind, for instance senior managers may require summaries.
R	Relevant	Information that is **not relevant** should be omitted.
A	Authoritative	The **source** of the information should be reputable and reliable.
T	Timely	The information should be available **when it is needed**.
E	Easy to use	Information should be **clearly presented**, **not excessively long**, and sent using the **right communication channel** (email, telephone, intranet, hard-copy report etc).

2 | Sources of management information

There are many **sources** of management information. Management information can come from sources **internal** or **external** to the organisation and can be both financial and non-financial.

2.1 Internal sources of management information

The main **internal sources of management information** within an organisation include the following.

- Accounting records – including the cost and management accounts
- Personnel records
- Production department records
- Detailed time records (especially in service organisations)

The **accounting records** include receivables ledgers, payables ledgers, general ledgers, cash books and so on. These records provide a detailed history of an organisation's monetary transactions.

Some of this information is of great value outside the accounts department, for example sales information for the marketing function.

To maintain the integrity of its financial accounting records, an organisation of any size will have systems for and controls over transactions. These also give rise to valuable information. An inventory control system is the classic example. Besides actually recording the monetary value of purchases and inventory in hand for external financial reporting purposes, the system will include purchase orders, goods received notes, goods returned notes and so on, and these can be analysed to provide management information about speed of delivery, say, or the quality of supplies.

Organisations also record information to allow them to carry out operations and administrative functions, such as the following.

(a) Information relating to **personnel** will be held, probably linked to the **payroll system**. Additional information may be obtained from this source if, say, a project is being costed and it is necessary to ascertain the availability and rate of pay of different levels of staff, or the need for and cost of recruiting staff from outside the organisation.

(b) Much information will be generated by the **production department** about machine capacity, fuel consumption, movement of people, materials, and work in progress, set up times, maintenance requirements and so on. A large part of the traditional work of cost accounting involves ascribing costs to the physical information produced by this source.

(c) Many **service** businesses – notably accountants and solicitors – need to keep detailed records of the **time spent** on various activities, both to justify fees to clients and to assess the efficiency of operations.

2.2 External sources of management information

An organisation's files are full of invoices, letters, advertisements and so on received from customers and suppliers. These documents provide information from an **external source**. There are many occasions when an active search outside the organisation is necessary.

(a) A **primary source** of information is, as the term implies, as close as you can get to the origin of an item of information: the eyewitness to an event, the place in question, the document under scrutiny.

(b) A **secondary source**, again logically enough, provides 'second-hand' information: books, articles, verbal or written reports by someone else.

2.3 Financial and non-financial information for management

Most organisations require the following types of information for management:

- Financial
- Non-financial
- A combination of financial and non-financial information

Suppose that the management of ABC Co have decided to provide a canteen for their employees.

(a) The **financial information** required by management might include the following:

- Canteen staff costs
- Costs of subsidising meals
- Capital costs
- Costs of heat and light

(b) The **non-financial information** might include the following:

- Management comment on the effect on employee morale of the provision of canteen facilities
- Details of the number of meals served each day
- Meter readings for gas and electricity
- Attendance records for canteen employees

BPP
LEARNING
MEDIA

ABC Co could now **combine financial and non-financial information** to calculate the **average cost** to the company of each meal served, thereby enabling them to predict total costs depending on the number of employees in the workforce.

Management accounting is concerned with non-financial as well as financial information. For example, managers of business organisations need to know whether employee morale has increased due to introducing a canteen, whether the bread from particular suppliers is fresh and the reason why the canteen staff are demanding a new dishwasher. This type of non-financial information will play its part in **planning, controlling** and **decision making** and is therefore just as important to management as financial information is.

Non-financial information must therefore be **monitored** as carefully, **recorded** as accurately and **taken into account** as fully as financial information. There is little point in a careful and accurate recording of total canteen costs if the recording of the information on the number of meals eaten in the canteen is uncontrolled and therefore produces inaccurate information.

While management accounting is mainly concerned with the provision of **financial information** to aid planning, control and decision making, the trainee accountant cannot ignore any **non-financial influences** which might be present.

3 Recording management information

- **Financial accounts** are prepared for individuals **external** to an organisation whereas **management accounts** are prepared for **internal** managers of an organisation. There are a number of differences between financial accounts and management accounts.

- **Cost accounting** produces information that is used for both financial accounting and management accounting.

3.1 Financial accounts and management accounts

Management information provides a common source from which is drawn information for two groups of people.

(a) **Financial accounts** are prepared for individuals **external** to an organisation.

- Shareholders
- Customers
- Suppliers
- Tax authorities

(b) **Management accounts** are prepared for **internal** managers of an organisation.

The information used to prepare financial accounts and management accounts is the same. The differences between the financial accounts and the management accounts arise because the information is analysed in different ways.

Financial accounts	Management accounts
Financial accounts are prepared primarily for external use and detail the performance of an organisation over a defined period and the state of affairs at the end of that period.	Management accounts can be generated for any period of time, (eg hourly, daily, weekly) and are used to aid management plan and control the organisation's activities and to help the decision-making process.
Limited companies must, by law, prepare financial accounts.	There is no legal requirement to prepare management accounts.

Financial accounts	Management accounts
The format of published financial accounts is determined by law and by accounting standards. In principle the accounts of different organisations can therefore be easily compared.	The format of management accounts is entirely at management discretion; no strict rules govern the way they are prepared or presented. Each organisation can devise its own management accounting system and format of reports.
Financial accounts concentrate on the business as a whole, aggregating revenues and costs from different operations, and are an end in themselves.	Management accounts can focus on specific areas of an organisation's activities. Information may be produced to aid a decision rather than to be an end product of a decision.
Most financial accounting information is of a monetary nature.	Management accounts incorporate non-monetary measures. Management may need to know, for example tonnes of aluminium produced, monthly machine hours, or miles travelled by salespeople.
Financial accounts present an essentially historic picture of past operations.	Management accounts are both an historical record and a future planning tool.

3.2 Cost accounts

Cost accounting and management accounting are terms which are often used interchangeably. It is **not** correct to do so.

Cost accounting aims to capture an organisation's costs of operations, departments or products, and then classify and analyse this information to produce cost reports. Cost accounting produces information that is used for both financial accounting and management accounting.

The purpose of management accounting is to provide managers with whatever information they need to assist them in planning and controlling operations and in decision making.

Cost accounting is part of management accounting. Cost accounting provides a bank of data for the management accountant to use. Cost accounts aim to establish the following:

(a)   The **cost** of goods produced or services provided

(b)   The **cost** of a department or work section

(c)   What **revenues** have been

(d)   The **profitability** of a product, a service, a department, or the organisation in total

(e)   **Selling prices** with some regard for the costs of sale

(f)   The **value of inventories of goods** (raw materials, work in progress, finished goods) that are still held in store at the end of a period, thereby aiding the preparation of a statement of financial position of the company's assets and liabilities

(g)   **Future costs** of goods and services (costing is an integral part of budgeting (planning) for the future)

It would be wrong to suppose that cost accounting systems are restricted to manufacturing operations, although they are probably more fully developed in this area of work. **Service industries** and **government departments** can make use of cost accounting information. Within a manufacturing organisation, the cost accounting system should be applied not only to **manufacturing** but also to **administration, selling and distribution, research and development** and all other departments.

4 The role of the trainee accountant

You have now had a brief introduction to management information, cost accounting and management accounting. Let us now consider the role of the trainee accountant in a cost accounting system.

Remember that the trainee accountant will have access to a large amount of information which is all recorded in the cost accounting records. With so much information, it is inevitable that many people are going to want to ask the trainee accountant lots of questions!

So, what sort of questions is the trainee accountant going to provide answers for? Well, here are a few examples:

(a)   What has the cost of goods produced or services provided been?
(b)   What has the cost of operating a department been?
(c)   What have revenues been?

All of these questions may relate to different periods. For example, if someone wants to know what revenues have been for the past ten years, the trainee accountant will need to extract this information from the cost accounting records. It is important therefore that the cost accounting system is capable of **analysing** such information.

If the trainee accountant knows all about the costs incurred or revenues earned, they may also be asked to do the following types of task:

(a)   To assess how profitable certain products or departments are.

(b)   To review the costs of products.

(c)   To put a value to inventories of goods (such as raw materials) which are unsold at the end of a period. The valuation of inventory is a very important part of cost accounting.

In order for the trainee accountant to provide all of this information, the organisation must have a **cost accounting system** which is capable of analysing cost information quickly and easily.

The trainee accountant may also need to provide information on **future** costs of goods and services. This is an integral part of the **planning or budgeting process**.

By comparing current costs with budgeted costs, the trainee accountant should be able to highlight areas which show significant **variances**. These variances should then be investigated.

Most cost accounting systems should be capable of producing regular **performance statements**, though the trainee accountant himself is likely to be the person producing them, and distributing them to the relevant personnel.

The role of a trainee accountant in a cost accounting system is therefore fairly varied. The role is likely to include spending much time providing answers to the many questions which may be directed at the trainee accountant (such as those that we have considered here).

5 Costs in outline

Let us suppose that in your hand you have a red pen which you bought in the shop for 50c. Why does the shop owner charge 50c for it? In other words what does that 50c represent?

From the shop owner's point of view the cost can be split into two.

Price paid by shop owner to wholesaler	Z
Shop owner's 'mark-up'	Y
	50c

If the shop owner did not charge more for the pen than they paid for it (Z) there would be no point in selling it. The mark-up itself can be split into further categories.

Pure profit	X
Amount paid to shop assistants	X
Expenses of owning and operating a shop (rent, electricity, cleaning and so on)	$\dfrac{X}{\underline{\underline{Y}}}$

The shop owner's **profit** is the amount they personally need to live, it is like your salary. Different shops have different ideas about this: this is why you might pay 60c for an identical pen if you went into another shop. The shop's expenses are amounts that have to be paid, whether or not the shop sells you a pen, simply to keep the shop going. Again, if other shops have to pay higher rent than our shop, this might be reflected in the price of pens.

The amount paid to the wholesaler can be split in a similar way: there will be a profit element and amounts to cover the costs of running a wholesaling business. There might also be a cost for getting the pen from the wholesaler's premises to the shop and, of course, there will be the amount paid to the manufacturer.

The majority of the remainder of this Text takes the point of view of the **manufacturer of products** since their costs are the most diverse. If you understand the costing that a manufacturer has to do, you will understand the costing performed by any other sort of business. Let us go on to have a look at costs in detail.

6 Costs in detail

- A **cost unit** is a unit of product or service which has costs attached to it. The cost unit is the basic control unit for costing purposes.

- **Direct costs** can be traced directly to specific units of production.

- **Overheads (indirect costs)** cannot be identified directly with any one product because they are incurred for the benefit of all products rather than for any one specific product.

- **Cost centres** are the essential building blocks of a costing system. They act as a collecting place for overheads before they are analysed further.

Technical performance objective 11 is to 'record and analyse information relating to direct costs'. You can apply the knowledge you obtain from this chapter of the Text to help demonstrate this competence.

6.1 Production costs

Look at your pen and consider what it consists of. There is probably a red plastic cap and a little red thing that fits into the end, and perhaps a yellow plastic sheath. There is an opaque plastic ink holder with red ink inside it. At the tip there is a gold plastic part holding a metal nib with a roller ball.

Let us suppose that the manufacturer sells pens to wholesalers for 20c each. How much does the little ball cost? What share of the 20c is taken up by the little red thing in the end of the pen? How much did somebody earn for putting it there?

To elaborate still further, the manufacturer probably has machines to mould the plastic and do some of the assembly. How much does it cost, per pen, to run the machines, to set them up so that they produce the right shape of moulded plastic? How much are the production line workers' wages per pen? How much does the plastic cost?

BPP LEARNING MEDIA

These costs of materials or wages, known as **direct costs** because they can be traced directly to specific units of production, could be calculated and recorded on a unit cost card which records how the total cost of a unit (in this instance, a pen) is arrived at.

PEN – UNIT COST CARD	$	$
Direct materials		
Yellow plastic	X	
Red plastic	X	
Opaque plastic	X	
Gold plastic	X	
Ink	X	
Metal	X̲	
		X
Direct labour		
Machine operators' wages	X	
Manual assembly staff wages	X̲	
		X̲
		X
Direct expenses		
Machinery – depreciation	X	
– power and fuel costs	X̲	
		X̲
Total direct cost (or prime cost)		X
Overheads (production)		X̲
Manufacturing cost (or factory cost)		X
Overheads (administration, distribution and selling)		X̲
Total cost		X̲

Don't worry if you are a bit unsure of the meaning of some of the terms in the unit cost card above as we will be looking at them in detail as we work through the Text.

6.2 Cost units

A **cost unit** is a unit of product or service which has costs attached to it. The cost unit is the basic control unit for costing purposes.

The only difficult thing about this is that a cost unit is not always a single item. It might be a **batch** of 1,000 if that is how the individual items are made. In fact, a cost per 1,000 is often more meaningful information, especially if calculating a cost for a single item gives a very small amount such as 0.003c. Examples of cost units are a construction contract, a batch of 1,000 pairs of shoes, a passenger kilometre (in other words, the transportation of a passenger for a kilometre).

QUESTION   Cost units

Suggest suitable cost units which could be used to aid control within the following organisations.

(a)   A hotel with 50 double rooms and 10 single rooms
(b)   A hospital
(c)   A road haulage business

ANSWER

(a)   • Guest/night
      • Bed occupied/night
      • Meal supplied

(b)   • Patient/night
      • Operation
      • Outpatient visit

(c) • Tonne/kilometre
     • Kilometre

6.3 Cost centres

Cost centres are the essential 'building blocks' of a costing system. They are a production or service location, function, activity or item of equipment. They act as a collecting place for overheads before they are analysed further.

A cost centre might be a place such as a regional office, a function such as human resources, a person or an item of equipment such as a printing machine which incurs costs. Cost centres are whatever is most useful for a business in order to control costs and apportion them to cost units.

Cost centres may vary in nature, but what they have in common is that they **incur costs**. It is therefore logical to **collect costs initially** under the headings of the various different cost centres that there may be in an organisation. Then, when we want to know how much our products cost, we simply find out how many cost units have been produced and share out the costs incurred by that cost centre amongst the cost units.

EXAM FOCUS POINT

Many students confuse cost units and cost centres – don't make that mistake! Remember a cost centre is something that incurs costs as it operates (for example a factory). A cost unit is the ultimate product or service to which the cost centre costs are allocated.

Taking the factory cost centre example, cost units are the products that are manufactured in the factory and therefore have the factory costs allocated to them.

A cost centre is also known as a **responsibility centre**. A responsibility centre is a department or organisational function whose performance is the direct responsibility of a specific manager. Other responsibility centres found in an organisation are as follows.

(a) A **profit centre** is accountable for **costs and revenues**. Profit centre managers should normally have control over how revenue is raised and how costs are incurred. Often, several cost centres will comprise one profit centre.

(b) A **revenue centre** is accountable for **revenues only**. Revenue centre managers should normally have control over how revenues are raised.

(c) An **investment centre** is a profit centre with additional responsibilities for capital investment and possibly for financing, and whose performance is measured by its return on investment.

6.4 Overheads

> Technical performance objective 12 is to 'record and analyse information relating to indirect costs'. The knowledge you gain in this chapter will help you demonstrate your competence in this area.

Overheads (or **indirect costs**) include costs that go into the making of the pen that you do not see when you dismantle it. You can touch the materials and you can appreciate that a combination of humans and machines put them together. It is not so obvious that the manufacturer has had to lubricate machines and employ people to supervise the assembly staff. They also have to pay rent for the factory and for somewhere to house the inventory of materials, and they have to pay someone to buy materials, recruit labour and run the payroll. Other people are paid to deliver the finished pens to the wholesalers; still others are out and about persuading wholesalers to buy pens, and they are supported at head office by staff taking orders and collecting payments.

In addition certain costs that could be identified with a specific product are classified as overheads and not direct costs. Nails used in the production of a cupboard can be identified specifically with the cupboard. However, because the cost is likely to be relatively insignificant, the expense of tracing such costs does not justify the possible benefits from calculating more accurate direct costs. Instead of keeping complex and time consuming records which might enable us to trace such costs directly to specific units of production, we try to **apportion** them and other overheads (indirect costs) to each cost unit in as fair a way as possible.

Overheads are the biggest problem for cost accountants because it is not easy to tell by either looking at or measuring the product, what overheads went into getting it into the hands of the buyer. Overheads, or indirect costs, unlike direct costs, will not be identified with any one product because they are incurred for the benefit of **all** products rather than for any one **specific** product.

Make sure that you understand the distinction between direct and indirect costs, as it is a very important part of your studies.

6.5 Direct and indirect costs

To summarise so far, the cost of an item can be divided into the following cost elements:

(a)   Materials
(b)   Labour
(c)   Expenses

Each element can be split into two, as follows:

Materials	=	Direct materials	+	Indirect materials
+		+		+
Labour	=	Direct labour	+	Indirect labour
+		+		+
Expenses	=	Direct expenses	+	Indirect expenses
Total cost	=	Direct cost		Overhead

QUESTION

Costs

List all of the different types of cost that a large supermarket might incur. Arrange them under headings of labour, materials used and other expenses.

ANSWER

Labour	*Materials*	*Expenses*
Petrol station staff	Saleable inventories	Heating
Car park attendant	Carrier bags	Lighting
Check-out staff	Other packaging	Telephone

BPP
LEARNING
MEDIA

Labour	*Materials*	*Expenses*
Supervisors	Cleaning materials	Post
Delicatessen staff	Bakery ingredients	Stationery
Bakery staff		Rent
Shelf fillers		Business rates
Warehouse staff		Water rates
Cleaners		Vehicle running costs
Security staff		Advertising
Administrative staff		Discounts
Managers		Bank charges
Delivery staff		Waste disposal
Maintenance staff		

6.6 Fixed costs and variable costs

> Costs are either **variable** or **fixed**, depending upon whether they change when the volume of production changes.

One other important distinction is that between fixed costs and variable costs.

(a)   If you produce two identical pens you will use twice as many direct materials as you would if you only produced one pen. Direct materials are in this case a **variable cost**. They vary according to the volume of production.

(b)   If you oil your machines after every 1,000 pens have been produced, the cost of oil is also a variable cost. It is an indirect material cost that varies according to the volume of production.

(c)   If you rent the factory that houses your pen-making machines you will pay the same amount of rent per annum whether you produce one pen or 10,000 pens. Factory rental is an indirect expense and it is **fixed** no matter what the volume of activity is.

The examples in (b) and (c) are both indirect costs, or overheads, but (b) is a variable overhead and (c) is a fixed overhead. The example in (a) is a variable direct cost. Direct costs usually are variable although they do not have to be.

Students often get confused about this point. Variable cost is **not** just another name for a direct cost. The distinctions that can be made are as follows.

(a)   Costs are either variable or fixed, depending upon whether they change when the volume of production changes.

(b)   Costs are either direct or indirect, depending upon how easily they can be traced to a specific unit of production.

QUESTION   Fixed and variable costs

Are the following likely to be fixed or variable costs?
(a)   Wages for hourly paid temporary staff
(b)   Charges for broadband
(c)   Annual salary of the managing director
(d)   Accountant's subscription to their accountancy body
(e)   Cost of materials used to pack 20 units of product X into a box

ANSWER
(a)   Variable
(b)   Fixed
(c)   Fixed
(d)   Fixed
(e)   Variable

7 Product costing

Job, batch and process costing are methods used to cost end products.

7.1 Job costing

There are several different ways of arriving at a value for the different cost elements (material, labour and expenses) which make up a unit cost of production. The most straightforward case is where the thing to be costed is a **one-off item**. For example, a furniture maker may make a table, say, to a customer's specific requirements. From start to finish the costs incurred to make that table are identifiable. It will cost so much for the table top, so much for the legs, and so on. This form of costing is known as **job costing** (covered in more detail in Chapter 13).

7.2 Batch costing

An item like a pen, however, will be produced as one of a **batch** of identical items, because it would clearly be uneconomical to set up the machinery, employ labour and incur overheads to produce each pen individually. There might be a production run of, say, 5,000 pens. The cost of producing 5,000 pens would be calculated and if we wanted to know the cost of one pen we would divide this total by 5,000. The answer would however be a fraction of a cent and this is not very meaningful information.

This method of costing is called **batch costing** and it applies to many everyday items. So far as costing techniques are concerned, job and batch costing are much the same. Batch costing is covered in more detail in Chapter 13.

7.3 Process costing

Another approach can be used when the product results from a series of **continuous** or **repetitive** operations or processes, and is not distinguishable as a separate unit of product until the final stage. For example oil refining, brewing, sugar refining or chemical processing.

The **output** of one process becomes the **input** to the next until the finished product is made in the final process. It is not possible to build up cost records of the cost per unit of output because production in progress is an **indistinguishable homogenous mass**.

There is often a **loss in process** due to spoilage, wastage, evaporation and so on. Process costing is covered in more detail in Chapter 14.

7.4 Service costing

Service organisations do not make or sell **tangible** goods. **Service costing** is used by organisations operating in a service industry (for example electricians, hotels, rail companies) or by organisations wishing to establish the cost of services carried out by some of their departments (for example the staff canteen, computer department or distribution). Service costing is covered in more detail in Chapter 13.

7.5 Accounting for overheads

Whether job costing, batch costing or process costing is used, there is still a problem in attributing to units of product the overhead costs like factory rental, canteen costs and head office lighting. The pros and cons of trying to work out an amount per unit for such costs are open to debate. Most businesses actually do try to do this in practice, and one very good reason for doing so is to make sure that all costs are covered when prices are set. Apportionment of production overheads is required for inventory valuation.

This practice of working out an amount per unit for overheads is known as **absorption costing**. Absorption costing is a technique that is used in conjunction with the product costing methods described above. Absorption costing is covered in more detail in Chapters 10 and 11.

QUESTION

Costing methods

For each of the items listed below decide which type of costing method would be used. Mark an X in the appropriate column.

	Job	Batch	Process
Suit (off the peg)			
Suit (tailored)			
Soap			
Yoghurt			
House decoration			
Car alarm			
Paper			
Poster			
Audit			

ANSWER

	Job	Batch	Process
Suit (off the peg)		X	
Suit (tailored)	X		
Soap			X
Yoghurt			X
House decoration	X		
Car alarm		X	
Paper			X
Poster		X	
Audit	X		

Note. It is assumed that soap, yoghurt and paper runs are continuous. However, there could be a case for batch costing for different scents, flavours or sizes respectively.

In addition, one-off specialised posters for a specific customer could be job costing.

8 Cost codes

A cost code is a brief reference designed to help with the classification of items by assisting with entry, collection and analysis.

Once costs have been classified, a coding system can be applied to make it easier to manage the cost data, both in manual systems and in computerised systems.

A **cost code** is a brief reference designed to help with the classification of items by assisting with entry, collection and analysis.

Coding systems can take many forms, but an efficient and effective coding system should incorporate the following features:

(a) The code must be **easy to use and communicate**.

(b) Each item should have a **unique code**.

(c) The coding system must **allow for expansion**.

(d) The code should be **flexible** so that small changes in a cost's classification can be incorporated without major changes to the coding system itself.

(e)   The coding system should provide a **comprehensive** system, whereby every recorded item can be suitably coded.

(f)   The coding system should be **brief**, to save clerical time in writing out codes and to save storage space in computer memory and on computer files. At the same time codes must be **long enough** to allow for the suitable coding of all items.

(g)   The likelihood of **errors** going undetected should be minimised.

(h)   Code numbers should be **issued from a single central point**. Different people should not be allowed to add new codes to the existing list independently.

(i)   Codes should be **uniform** (that is, have the same length and the same structure) to assist in the detection of missing characters and to facilitate processing.

(j)   The coding system should avoid problems such as confusion between I and 1, O and 0 (zero), S and 5 and so on.

(k)   The coding system should, if possible, be **significant** (in other words, the actual code should signify something about the item being coded).

(l)   If the code consists of alphabetic characters, it should be derived from the item's description or name (that is, **mnemonics** should be used).

8.1 Types of code

There are many different types of code that can be used.

(a)   **Sequential (or progressive) codes**

Numbers are given to items in ordinary numerical sequence, so that there is no obvious connection between an item and its code. For example:

000042	4 cm nails
000043	Office stapler
000044	Hand wrench

(b)   **Block (group classification) codes**

These are an improvement on simple sequences codes, in that a digit (often the first one) indicates the classification of an item. For example:

4NNNNN	Nails
5NNNNN	Screws
6NNNNN	Bolts

Note. 'N' stands for another digit; 'NNNNN' indicates there are five further digits in the code.

(c)   **Mnemonic codes**

Meaning of mnemonic is a learning technique to aid the memory. Under this type of coding the code means something, it may be an abbreviation of the object being coded. A well-known example of this type of code is the three letter coding used for airports. For example:

LAX	Los Angeles	SIN	Singapore
CAI	Cairo	LHR	London Heathrow

(d)   **Hierarchical codes**

In a hierarchical coding system each digit represents a classification, and each digit further to the right represents a smaller subset than those to the left. For example:

3	=	Screws	32	=	Round headed screws
31	=	Flat headed screws	322	=	Steel (round headed) screws

(e) **Faceted codes**

These are a refinement of group classification codes, in that each digit of the code gives information about an item. For example:

(i) The first digit:
1 Nails
2 Screws
3 Bolts
etc

(ii) The second digit:
1 Steel
2 Brass
3 Copper
etc

(iii) The third digit:
1 50mm
2 60mm
3 75mm
etc

A 60 mm steel screw would have a code of 212.

Unlike a simple hierarchical system, faceted classification gives users the ability to find items based on **more than one criteria**. For example, users shopping for building materials may be most interested in browsing by a particular type of item (screws, nails) while others are more interested in browsing by a particular material (steel, brass, copper).

A coding system does not have to be structured entirely on any one of the above systems. It can mix the various features according to the items which need to be coded.

8.2 Simple example

An illustration of the use of a four digit code to apply code numbers to consumable stores might be as follows.

Department 2

	1	2	3	4
Cost centre				
Consumable stores	2109	2209	2309	2409

The four-digit codes above indicate the following.

- The first digit, 2, refers to department 2.
- The second digit, 1, 2, 3 or 4, refers to the cost centre which incurred the cost.
- The last two digits, 09, refer to 'materials costs, consumable stores'.

QUESTION

Codes

Using the above code, describe the expenditure that is represented by the code number 6209.

ANSWER

- The first digit, 6, refers to department 6.
- The second digit, 2, refers to cost centre 2.
- The last two digits, 09, refer to 'material costs, consumable stores'.

Therefore the code number 6209 depicts the use of consumable stores which are to be charged to cost centre 2 within department 6.

8.3 Example: Numerical coding account system

Each account in use needs to be classified by the use of coding. A suggested computer-based four-digit numerical coding account system is set out as follows.

Basic structure		Code number	Allocation
(a)	First division	1000 – 4999	This range provides for cost accounts and is divided into four main departmental sections with ten cost centre subsections in each department, allowing for a maximum of 99 accounts in each cost centre
	Second division	1000 – 1999	Department 1
		2000 – 2999	Department 2
		3000 – 3999	Department 3
		4000 – 4999	Department 4
	Third division	000 – 099	Facility for ten cost centres in each department
		100 – 199	
		200 – 299	
		and so on	
	Fourth division		Breakdown of costs in each cost centre
		01 – 39	Direct costs
		40 – 79	Indirect costs
		80 – 99	Spare capacity
(b)		5000 – 5999	This range provides for the following:
			(i) Revenue accounts
			(ii) Work in progress accounts
			(iii) Finished goods accounts
			(iv) Cost of sales accounts
			(v) General expenses accounts
			(vi) Statement of profit or loss (Income statement)
(c)		6000 – 6999	This range provides for individual stores items
(d)		7000 – 7999	This range provides for individual receivable accounts
(e)		8000 – 8999	This range provides for individual payable accounts
(f)		9000 – 9999	This range is used for statement of financial position accounts including the following:
			(i) Stores control account
			(ii) Receivables' control account
			(iii) Payables' control account

An illustration of the coding of direct labour (grade T) might be as follows:

Department 2

Cost centre	1	2	3	4
Direct labour (grade T)	2109	2209	2309	2409

The four digit code is explained as follows:

(a)   The first digit, 2, refers to department 2.
(b)   The second digit 1, 2, 3 or 4 refers to the cost centre which incurred the cost.
(c)   The last two digits, 09, refer to 'direct labour costs, grade T'.

Obviously systems that you come across in practice will exhibit different features. The above describes only broad characteristics that are likely to be typical of all such systems.

8.4 The advantages of a coding system

(a)   A code is usually **briefer** than a description, thereby saving clerical time in a manual system and storage space in a computerised system.

(b)   A code is **more precise** than a description and therefore **reduces ambiguity**.

(c)   Coding **facilitates data processing**.

CHAPTER ROUNDUP

↳ The purpose of management information is to help managers to manage resources efficiently and effectively, by planning and controlling operations and by allowing informed decision making.

↳ **Planning** involves establishing an **objective** or identifying a problem and then choosing a **strategy** to achieve the objective or alleviate the problem.

↳ **Control** is the action of monitoring something in order to keep it on course.

↳ Good management information should be **A**ccurate, **C**omplete, **C**ost-beneficial, **U**ser-targeted, **R**elevant, **A**uthoritative, **T**imely, **E**asy to use.

↳ There are many **sources** of management information. Management information can come from sources **internal** or **external** to the organisation and can be both financial and non-financial.

↳ **Financial accounts** are prepared for individuals **external** to an organisation whereas **management accounts** are prepared for **internal** managers of an organisation. There are a number of differences between financial accounts and management accounts.

↳ **Cost accounting** produces information that is used for both financial accounting and management accounting.

↳ A **cost unit** is a unit of product or service which has costs attached to it. The cost unit is the basic control unit for costing purposes.

↳ **Direct costs** can be traced directly to specific units of production.

↳ **Overheads (indirect costs)** cannot be identified directly with any one product because they are incurred for the benefit of all products rather than for any one specific product.

↳ **Cost centres** are the essential building blocks of a costing system. They act as a collecting place for overheads before they are analysed further.

↳ Costs are either **variable** or **fixed**, depending upon whether they change when the volume of production changes.

↳ **Job**, **batch** and **process costing** are methods used to cost end products.

↳ A cost code is a brief reference designed to help with the classification of items by assisting with entry, collection and analysis.

QUICK QUIZ

1 Define the terms **data** and **information**.

2 The eight main qualities of good information are:

- ....
- ....
- ....
- ....
- ....
- ....
- ....
- ....

3 Secondary sources of information include documents or reports written for a specific purpose.
- O True
- O False

4 In terms of cost accounting, information is most likely to be used for (1) ...., (2) .... or (3) ....

5 What is a cost unit?

6 Which cost elements make up overheads?

7   Sources of useful data may be:

1   External
2   Internal
3   Financial
4   Non-financial

Which of the above sources may be used by a trainee accountant?

○   1, 2 and 3 only
○   2, 3 and 4 only
○   2 and 3 only
○   1, 2, 3 and 4

8   Which TWO of the following statements about cost and management accounting are true?

☐   Cost accounting cannot be used to provide inventory valuations for external financial reporting.

☐   There is a legal requirement to prepare management accounts.

☐   The format of management accounts may vary from one business to another.

☐   Management accounting provides information to help management make business decisions.

9   Which of the following are features of an efficient and effective cost coding system?

1   Codes need to be complex to include all items.
2   Each code must have a combination of alphabetic and numeric characters.
3   Codes for a particular type of item should be consistent in length and structure.

○   1 only
○   3 only
○   1 and 2
○   2 and 3

ANSWERS TO QUICK QUIZ

1   **Data** is the raw material for data processing. **Information** is data that has been processed in such a way as to be meaningful to the person who receives it. **Information** is anything that is communicated.

2
- Accurate
- Complete
- Cost-beneficial
- User-targeted
- Relevant
- Authoritative
- Timely
- Easy to use

3   False. Secondary information sources would include items that have not been prepared for a specific purpose (these would be primary information sources).

4   (1)   Planning
    (2)   Control
    (3)   Decision making

5   A unit of product which has costs attached to it. The cost unit is the basic control unit for costing purposes.

6
- Indirect materials
- Indirect labour
- Indirect expenses

7   1, 2, 3 and 4

8   The format of management accounts may vary from one business to another.

    Management accounting provides information to help management make business decisions.

9   3 only

Now try ...

Attempt the questions below from the **Practice Question Bank** at the back of this Text

Number

Q1

Q2

Q3

Q4

Q5

BPP LEARNING MEDIA

CHAPTER

02

Information technology (IT) is used extensively for **collecting**, **analysing** and **communicating** data and management information. This chapter explains **the role of IT and the main IT elements in a management information system**. Much of the content of this chapter may well be familiar to you already.

The role of information technology

1 Role of information technology

Computers are widely used for data processing because they have certain advantages over humans.

- Speed
- Accuracy
- Volume and complexity
- Access to information

Here is a very simple example of a **data processing model**.

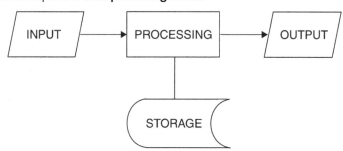

The processing of business data can be illustrated by a person working at their desk dealing with matters from their in-tray.

(a) A person receives **input from the in-tray**, which must be dealt with.

(b) The person may have a procedures manual or have learned a set of rules which are applied to do the work. Tools such as a calculator or a PC may also be used.

(c) To process data from the in-tray, it may be necessary to refer to other information held on file (either paper or computer-based files).

(d) As a result of doing the work, the person may:

(i) Produce **output**, perhaps a report or a completed routine task
(ii) Add to the information held on file, or change the information to bring it up to date

Data processing is essentially the same, no matter whether it is done manually or by computer. The **input, process, output,** storage steps apply to manual and computerised processing.

1.1 Advantages of computers

Computers are widely used for data processing because they have certain advantages over humans.

(a) **Speed**. Computers can process data much more quickly than a human. This means that using a computer to process large volumes of data should be cheaper than doing the work manually. As computer costs have fallen, this cost advantage of the computer has increased.

The ability to process data more quickly means that a computer can produce more timely information, when information is needed as soon as possible.

(b) **Accuracy**. If set up and programmed correctly, computers are generally accurate, whereas humans are prone to error. Errors in computer processing occur if the people involved inputting data or programming software have made errors, or if faults are present in the computer hardware.

(c) **Volume and complexity**. As businesses grow and become more complex, their data processing requirements increase in volume and complexity too. More managers need better quality information. More transactions have to be processed. The volume of processing required is beyond the capability of even the largest clerical workforce to do manually. Clearing banks, for example, would be unable to function without electronic data processing to ease the demands on their workforce.

(d) **Access to information**. The use of databases and the ability to link a number of users via some form of network improves the distribution of information within and beyond the organisation.

However, the 'manual' or 'human' method of data processing is more suitable when human judgement is involved in the work. For example, the human brain stores a lifetime of experiences and emotions that influence decisions and it is capable of drawing on them and making connections between them when making decisions.

2 Capturing and processing cost and management accounting data

Stages of **data input**:

- Origination of data
- Transcription of data
- Data input

The collection of data and its subsequent input to the computer can be a time-consuming and costly task. The computer will only accept data which is in machine-sensible form, data held on a source document must be manually input to produce a computer file.

The stages of data input are as follows.

(a) **Origination** of data (transactions giving rise to data which needs to be recorded and processed)

(b) **Transcription** of data onto a paper document suitable for operators to refer to while keying in data

(c) Data **input**

The ideal methods of data collection and input are those which minimise the following.

- The time needed to record the original data, and transmit, prepare and input the data to the computer

- Costs

- Errors

2.1 Direct data entry with a keyboard

The principal method of direct data entry is by means of a keyboard.

2.1.1 Keyboard layout and functions

A basic keyboard includes the following.

- **Ordinary typing keys** used to enter data or text
- A **numeric key pad** for use with the built-in calculator
- **Cursor control keys** (basically up/down/left/right keys to move the cursor)
- A number of **function keys** for use by the system and application software

In addition to the function keys, there are special keys that are used to communicate with the operating programs, to let the computer know that you have finished entering a command, that you wish to correct a command and so on. Nothing appears at the cursor point when these keys are used, but they affect operations on screen.

2.2 The visual display unit (VDU)

A **VDU** (or monitor) **displays text** and **graphics** and serves a number of purposes.

- It allows the operator to carry out a visual check on what he or she has keyed in.
- It helps the operator to input data by providing 'forms' on the screen for filling in.
- It displays output such as answers to file enquiries.
- It gives messages to the operator.

Graphical user interfaces (GUI) have become the principal means by which humans communicate with machines. Features include the following:

(a) **Windows**. This basically means that the screen can be divided into sections or 'windows' of flexible size which can be opened and closed. This enables two or more documents to be viewed and edited together, and sections of one to be inserted into another. This is particularly useful for word processed documents and spreadsheets, which are too large for the VDU screen.

(b) **Icons**. An icon is an image of an object used to represent an abstract idea or process. In software design, icons may be used instead of numbers, letters or words to identify and describe the various functions available for selection, or files to access. A common icon is a waste paper bin to indicate the deletion of a document.

(c) **Mouse**. This is a device used with on-screen graphics and sometimes as an alternative to using the keyboard to input instructions. It can be used to pick out the appropriate icon (or other option), to mark out the area of a new window, mark the beginning and end of a block for deletion/insertion and so on. It also has a button to execute the current command.

(d) **Pull-down menu**. An initial menu (or 'menu-bar') will be shown across the top of the VDU screen. Using the mouse to move the pointer to the required item in the menu, the pointer 'pulls down' a subsidiary menu, somewhat similar to pulling down a window blind in a room of a house. The pointer and mouse can then be used to select the required item on the pulled-down menu.

(e) **Graphical widgets.** Many GUIs (such as Microsoft Windows) also display dialogue boxes, buttons, sliders, check boxes, and a plethora of other graphical widgets that let you tell the computer what to do and how to do it.

2.3 Automatic input devices

In the following paragraphs we explain some of the most common document reading methods. Document reading methods reduce the manual work involved in data input. This **saves time and money** and also **reduces errors**.

(a) **Magnetic ink character recognition (MICR)** involves the recognition by a machine of special formatted characters printed in magnetic ink. The characters are read using a specialised reading device.

The main advantage of MICR is its speed and accuracy, but MICR documents are expensive to produce. The main commercial application of MICR is in the banking industry – on cheques and deposit slips.

(b) **Optical mark reading** involves the marking of a pre-printed form with a ballpoint pen or typed line or cross in an appropriate box. The card is then read by an OMR device which senses the mark in each box using an electric current and translates it into machine code. Applications in which OMR is used include **Lotto** entry forms, and answer sheets for multiple choice questions.

(c) A **scanner** is device that can **read text or illustrations printed on paper** and translate the information into a **form the computer can use**. A scanner works by digitising an image, the resulting matrix of bits is called a **bit map**.

To edit text read by an optical scanner, you need **optical character recognition (OCR)** software to translate the image into text. Most optical scanners sold today come with OCR packages. Businesses may use a scanner and OCR to obtain 'digital' versions of documents they have only paper copies of. For good results the copy must be of good quality.

(d) **Bar codes** are groups of marks which, by their spacing and thickness, indicate specific codes or values.

Large retail stores have Electronic Point of Sale (EPOS) devices, which include bar code readers. This enables the provision of immediate sales and stock level information.

(e) Most retailers have **EFTPOS systems (Electronic Funds Transfer at the Point of Sale)**. An EFTPOS terminal is used with a customer's credit card or debit card to pay for goods or services. The customer's credit card account or bank account will be debited automatically. EFTPOS systems combine point of sale systems with electronic funds transfer.

2.4 Card reading devices

(a) The standard **magnetic stripe card** contains machine-sensible data on a thin strip of magnetic recording tape stuck to the back of the card. The magnetic card reader converts this information into directly computer-sensible form. The widest application of magnetic stripe cards is as bank credit or service cards.

(b) A **smart card** is a plastic card in which is embedded **a microprocessor chip**. A smart card would typically contain a **memory** and a **processing capability**. The information held on smart cards can therefore be updated (eg using a PC and a special device).

2.5 Touch screens

A **touch screen** is a display screen that enables users to make selections by touching areas of the screen. Sensors, built into the screen surround, detect which area has been touched. These devices are widely used in vending situations, such as the selling of train tickets.

2.6 Voice recognition

Computer software has been developed that can convert speech into computer-sensible form via a microphone. Users are required to speak clearly and reasonably slowly.

3 Storing cost and management accounting data

Data can be **stored** on hard disks, DVDs or memory sticks.

3.1 Hard disks

Disks offer **direct access** to data. Almost all PCs have an **internal hard disk** to store software and data.

3.2 CD-ROM (Compact Disc – Read Only Memory)

The **speed** of a CD-ROM drive is relevant to how fast data can be retrieved: an **eight speed** drive is quicker than a **four speed** drive.

CD recorders are now available for general business use with blank CDs (CD-R) and **rewritable disks** (CD-RW) are now available.

3.3 DVD (Digital Versatile Disc)

Digital Versatile Disc (DVD) technology was encouraged by the advent of multimedia files with video graphics and sound – requiring greater disk capacity.

3.4 Memory stick or 'pen drive'

A memory stick or pen drive is a physically small external storage device usually connected via a USB port.

4   Outputting cost and management accounting data

Data is usually output via printers or a VDU.

4.1 Printers

Laser printers print a whole page at a time, rather than line by line. The **quality** of output is very **high**. Laser printers are relatively expensive to purchase, but compared with inkjet printers, running costs are relatively low.

Inkjet printers are small and reasonably cheap. They work by sending a jet of ink on to the paper to produce the required characters.

4.2 The VDU or monitor

Screens are generally used together with computer keyboards for **input**. It should also be clear that they can be used as an **output** medium, primarily where the output **volume is low** (for example a single enquiry) and **no permanent output** is required (for example the current balance on an account).

4.3 The choice of output medium

As with choosing an input medium, choosing a suitable output medium depends on a number of factors, which you should bear in mind when we go on to consider each type of output in turn. These factors are as follows.

(a) **Is a 'hard' copy of the output required**; in other words, is a printed version of the output needed? If so, what quality must the output be?

    (i) If the output includes documents that are going to be used as OCR turnround documents, the quality of printing must be good.

    (ii) If the information will be used as a working document with a short life or limited use (eg a copy of text for type-checking) then a low quality output on a printer might be sufficient.

(b) **The volume of information produced**. For example, a VDU screen can hold a certain amount of data, but it becomes more difficult to read when information goes 'off-screen' and can only be read a bit at a time.

(c) **The speed at which output is required**. For example, to print a large volume of data, a high speed printer might be most suitable to finish the work more quickly (and release the CPU for other jobs).

(d) **The suitability of the output medium to the application** – ie the purpose for which the output is needed.

(i)   A VDU is well suited to interactive processing with a computer.

(ii)   A graph plotter would be well suited to output in the form of graphs.

(iii) Output on to a magnetic disk would be well suited if the data is for further processing.

(iv)   Large volumes of reference data for human users to hold in a library might be held on microfilm or microfiche, and so output in these forms would be appropriate.

(e) **Cost**. Some output devices would not be worth having because their advantages would not justify their cost, and so another output medium should be chosen as 'second best'.

5 Management information systems

> A **management information system** is the hardware and software used to drive a database system which provides useful information for management.

5.1 Introduction

A **management information system** (MIS) is defined as a collective term for the hardware and software used to drive a database system with the outputs, both to screen and print, being designed to provide easily assimilated information for management.

Management information is by no means confined to accounting information, but until relatively recently accounting information systems have been the most formally constructed and well-developed part of the overall information system of a business enterprise.

An alternative definition of a management information system is 'an information system making use of available resources to provide managers at all levels in all functions with the information from all relevant sources to enable them to make timely and effective decisions for planning, directing and controlling the activities for which they are responsible'.

A management information system is therefore **a system of disseminating information which will enable managers to do their job**. Since managers must have information, there will always be a management information system in any organisation.

Most management information systems are not designed, but grow up **informally**, with each manager making sure that he or she gets all the information considered necessary to do the job. It is virtually taken for granted that the necessary information flows to the job, and to a certain extent this is so. Much accounting information, for example, is easily obtained, and managers can often get along with frequent face-to-face contact and co-operation with each other. Such an informal system works best in **small organisations**.

However, some information systems are **specially designed**, often because the introduction of computers has forced management to consider its information needs in detail. This is especially the case in **large** companies.

5.2 The need for formal planning

Management should try to develop/implement a management information system for their enterprise with care. If they allow the MIS to develop without any formal planning, it will almost certainly be **inefficient** because data will be obtained and processed in a random and disorganised way and the communication of information will also be random and hit-and-miss.

(a) Some managers will prefer to keep **data in their heads** and will not commit information to paper. When the manager is absent from work, or is moved to another job, their stand-in or successor will not know as much as they could and should about the work because no information has been recorded to help them.

(b) The organisation will not collect and process all the information that it should, and so valuable information that ought to be available to management will be missing from **neglect**.

(c)   Information may be available but not **disseminated** to the managers who are in a position of authority and so ought to be given it. The information would go to waste because it would not be used. In other words, the wrong people would have the information.

(d)   Information is **communicated late** because the need to communicate it earlier is not understood and appreciated by the data processors.

The consequences of a poor MIS might be **dissatisfaction** amongst employees who believe they should be told more, a **lack of understanding** about what the targets for achievement are and a **lack of information** about how well the work is being done.

5.3 Essential characteristics

Whether a management information system is formally or informally constructed, it should therefore have certain essential characteristics.

(a)   The functions of individuals and their areas of responsibility in achieving company objectives should be defined.

(b)   Areas of control within the company (eg cost centres, investment centres) should also be clearly defined.

(c)   Information required for an area of control should flow to the manager who is responsible for it.

An organisation's cost accounting system will be part of the overall management information system. It will both provide information to assist management with planning, control and decision making as well as accumulating historical costs to establish inventory valuations, profits and statement of financial position items.

CHAPTER ROUNDUP

↳ Computers are widely used for data processing because they have certain advantages over humans.
  – Speed
  – Accuracy
  – Volume and complexity
  – Access to information

↳ Stages of **data input**:
  – Origination of data
  – Transcription of data
  – Data input

↳ Data can be **stored** on hard disks, CD-ROMS, DVDs or memory sticks.

↳ Data is usually output via printers or a VDU.

↳ A **management information system** is the hardware and software used to drive a database system which provides useful information for management.

QUICK QUIZ

1 List four advantages that computers have over humans.

2 List four things that a basic keyboard includes.

3 What is the main function of a graphical user interface?

4 What sort of automatic input device is issued on Lotto entry forms?

5 Which TWO of the following are characteristics of management accounting information?

☐ Non-financial as well as financial

☐ Used by all stakeholders

☐ Concerned with cost control only

☐ Not legally required

ANSWERS TO QUICK QUIZ

1 • Speed
  • Accuracy
  • Volume and complexity
  • Access to information

2 • Ordinary typing keys
  • Numeric key pad
  • Cursor control keys
  • A number of function keys

3 To enable humans to communicate with machines

4 Optimal Mark Reading (OMR) which involves the marking of a pre-printed form with a ball point pen or typed line or cross in an appropriate box. The card is then read by an OMR device which senses the mark in each box using an electronic current and translates it into machine code.

5 Non-financial as well as financial.

  Not legally required.

Now try ...

Attempt the questions below from the **Practice Question Bank**

Number

Q6

Q7

Q8

Q9

Q10

03

In this chapter, we begin to look at **cost accounting systems** and the ways in which costs may be classified. **Costs are classified in a variety of different ways**, according to purpose for which the management information is required.

The chapter also introduces two basic building blocks of costing systems: **cost centres** and cost **units**.

Knowledge of the various classifications of cost, as well as cost centres and cost units, are important for an understanding of cost and management accounting methods and techniques, which will be described in subsequent chapters.

Cost classification

Study Guide	Intellectual level
A **Management information**	
3 **Cost classification**	
(a) Describe the variety of cost classifications used for different purposes in a cost accounting system, including by responsibility, function, direct/indirect, behaviour	K
B **Cost recording**	
2 **Accounting for labour**	
(c) Distinguish between direct and indirect labour costs	K

1 Cost classifications in a cost accounting system

The **total cost** of making a product or providing a service consists of **material** costs, **labour** costs and **other expenses** such as rent and rates.

The total cost of making a product or providing a service consists of the following.

(a)   Cost of **materials**

(b)   Cost of the **wages** and **salaries** (labour costs)

(c)   Cost of **other expenses**
- Rent and rates
- Electricity and gas bills
- Depreciation

2 Direct costs and indirect costs

- A **direct cost** is a cost that can be traced in full to the product or service being costed.

- An **indirect cost** (or overhead) is a cost that is incurred in the course of making a product or providing a service, but which cannot be traced directly and in full to the product or service.

- **Prime cost** = direct material cost + direct labour cost + direct expenses.

Technical performance objective 11 is to 'record and analyse information relating to direct costs'. The knowledge you gain in this chapter will help you demonstrate your competence in this area.

Materials, labour costs and other expenses can be classified as either **direct costs** or **indirect costs**.

As we saw in Chapter 1, **total expenditure** may therefore be **analysed** as follows.

Materials cost	=	Direct materials cost	+	Indirect materials cost
+		+		+
Labour cost	=	Direct labour cost	+	Indirect labour cost
+		+		+
Expenses	=	Direct expenses	+	Indirect expenses
Total cost	=	Direct cost/prime cost	+	Overhead cost

2.1 Direct costs

A **direct cost** is a cost that can be traced in full to saleable cost units (products or services) that are being costed. The sum of the direct costs is known as the **prime cost**.

Direct costs are therefore **directly attributable to cost units**.

(a) **Direct material costs** are the costs of materials that are known to have been used in making and selling a product (or providing a service).

(b) **Direct labour costs** are the specific costs of the workforce used to make a product or provide a service. Direct labour costs are established by measuring the time taken for a job, or the time taken in 'direct production work'.

(c) **Direct expenses** are those expenses that have been incurred in full as a direct consequence of making a product, or providing a service.

2.1.1 Direct material

Direct material is all material becoming part of the product (unless used in negligible amounts and/or having negligible cost).

Direct material costs are charged to the product as part of the **prime cost**. Examples of direct material are as follows.

(a) **Raw materials** that go in to the product

(b) **Component parts**, specially purchased for a particular job, order or process

(c) **Part-finished work** which is transferred from department one to department two becomes finished work of department one and a direct material cost in department two

(d) **Primary packing materials** like cartons and boxes

Materials used in negligible amounts and/or having negligible cost can be grouped under indirect materials as part of overhead.

2.1.2 Direct labour

Direct labour costs are the specific costs of the workforce used to make a unit of product or provide a service. Direct labour costs are calculated by quantifying the cost of the time taken for a job, or the time taken in 'direct production work'.

Direct wages costs are charged to the product as part of the prime cost.

Examples of groups of labour receiving payment as direct wages are as follows.

(a) Workers engaged in altering the condition, conformation or composition of the product
(b) Inspectors, analysts and testers specifically required for such production

Two **trends** may be identified in **direct labour costs**.

(a) The ratio of direct labour costs to total product cost is falling as the use of machinery increases, and hence depreciation charges increase.

(b) Skilled labour costs and sub-contractors' costs are increasing as direct labour costs decrease.

2.1.3 Direct expenses

Direct expenses are any expenses which are incurred on a specific product other than direct material cost and direct wages.

Direct expenses are charged to the product as part of the **prime** cost. Examples of direct expenses are as follows:

- The cost of special designs, drawings or layouts
- The hire of tools or equipment for a **particular** job

Direct expenses are also referred to as **chargeable expenses**.

2.2 Indirect costs/overhead

An indirect cost or overhead is a cost that is incurred in the course of making a product or providing a service, but which cannot be traced directly and in full to the product or service.

Technical performance objective 12 is to 'record and analyse information relating to indirect costs'. The knowledge you gain in this chapter will help you demonstrate your competence in this area.

Indirect costs are therefore **not directly attributable** to the product or service.

Examples of indirect costs might be the cost of supervisors' wages on a production line, cleaning materials and buildings insurance for a factory.

QUESTION

Prime costs

Which of the following costs would be charged to the product as a prime cost?

1   Component parts
2   Part-finished work
3   Primary packing materials
4   Supervisor wages

O   1 and 2 only
O   1, 2, 3 and 4
O   1, 2 and 3 only
O   3 and 4 only

ANSWER

1, 2 and 3 only

These are all examples of direct material costs. The prime cost includes direct material, direct labour and direct expenses. Supervisor wages is an indirect labour cost.

2.2.1 Production overhead

Production (or factory) overhead includes all indirect material cost, indirect wages and indirect expenses **incurred in the factory from receipt of an order for a product until the product's completion**, including:

(a) **Indirect materials** which cannot be traced in the finished product.

Consumable stores, eg material used in negligible amounts

(b)   **Indirect wages**, meaning all wages not charged directly to a product.

Salaries of non-productive personnel in the production department, eg supervisor

(c)   **Indirect expenses** (other than material and labour) not charged directly to production.

(i)   Rent, rates and insurance of a factory
(ii)   Depreciation, fuel, power and maintenance of plant and buildings

2.2.2 Administration overhead

Administration overhead is all indirect material costs, wages and expenses **incurred in the administration of an undertaking**, including:

- **Depreciation** of office equipment
- **Office salaries**, including the salaries of secretaries and accountants
- Rent, rates, insurance, telephone, heat and light cost of general offices

2.2.3 Selling overhead

Selling overhead is all indirect materials costs, wages and expenses **incurred in promoting sales and retaining customers**, including:

- **Printing** and **stationery**, such as catalogues and price lists
- **Salaries** and **commission** of sales representatives
- **Advertising** and **sales promotion**, market research
- Rent, rates and insurance for sales offices and showrooms

2.2.4 Distribution overhead

Distribution overhead is all indirect material costs, wages and expenses **incurred in making the packed product ready for despatch and delivering it to the customer**, including:

- Cost of packing cases
- Wages of packers, drivers and despatch clerks
- Depreciation and running expenses of delivery vehicles

3 Classification by function

Classification by function involves classifying costs as production/manufacturing costs, administration costs or marketing/selling and distribution costs.

In a 'traditional' costing system for a manufacturing organisation, costs are classified as follows:

(a)   **Production** or **manufacturing costs.** These are costs associated with the factory.

(b)   **Administration costs.** These are costs associated with general office departments.

(c)   **Marketing, or selling and distribution costs.** These are costs associated with sales, marketing, warehousing and transport departments.

Classification in this way is known as **classification by function.** Expenses that do not fall fully into one of these classifications might be categorised as **general overheads** or even listed as a classification on their own (for example research and development costs).

In costing a small product made by a manufacturing organisation, direct costs are usually restricted to some of the production costs. A commonly found build-up of costs is therefore as follows:

	$
Production costs	
Direct materials	A
Direct wages	B
Direct expenses	C
Prime cost	A+B+C
Production overheads	D

	$
Full production cost	A+B+C+D
Administration costs	E
Selling and distribution costs	F
Full cost of sales	A+B+C+D+E+F

Functional costs include the following:

(a) **Production costs** are the costs which are incurred by the sequence of operations beginning with the supply of raw materials, and ending with the completion of the product ready for warehousing as a finished goods item. Packaging costs are production costs where they relate to 'primary' packing (boxes, wrappers and so on).

(b) **Administration costs** are the costs of managing an organisation, that is, planning and controlling its operations, but only insofar as such administration costs are not related to the production, sales, distribution or research and development functions.

(c) **Selling costs** sometimes known as marketing costs, are the costs of creating demand for products and securing firm orders from customers.

(d) **Distribution costs** are the costs of the sequence of operations with the receipt of finished goods from the production department and making them ready for despatch and ending with the reconditioning for reuse of empty containers.

(e) **Research costs** are the costs of searching for new or improved products, whereas **development costs** are the costs incurred between the decision to produce a new or improved product and the commencement of full manufacture of the product.

(f) **Financing costs** are costs incurred to finance the business such as loan interest.

QUESTION

Cost classification

Within the costing system of a manufacturing company the following types of expense are incurred.

Reference number

1	Cost of oils used to lubricate production machinery
2	Motor vehicle licences for lorries
3	Depreciation of factory plant and equipment
4	Cost of chemicals used in the laboratory
5	Commission paid to sales representatives
6	Salary of the secretary to the finance director
7	Trade discount given to customers
8	Holiday pay of machine operatives
9	Salary of security guard in raw material warehouse
10	Fees to advertising agency
11	Rent of finished goods warehouse
12	Salary of scientist in laboratory
13	Insurance of the company's premises
14	Salary of supervisor working in the factory
15	Cost of typewriter ribbons in the general office
16	Protective clothing for machine operatives

Required

Complete the following table by placing each expense in the correct cost classification.

Cost classification	Reference number					
Production costs						
Selling and distribution costs						
Administration costs						
Research and development costs						

Each type of expense should appear only once in your answer. You may use the reference numbers in your answer.

ANSWER

Cost classification	Reference number					
Production costs	1	3	8	9	14	16
Selling and distribution costs	2	5	7	10	11	
Administration costs	6	13	15			
Research and development costs	4	12				

4 Classification by behaviour

 A different way of analysing and classifying costs is into **fixed costs** and **variable costs**. Many items of expenditure are part-fixed and part-variable and hence are termed **semi-fixed** or **semi-variable**. This is also known as **classification by behaviour**.

Costs can be classified according to how they vary in relation to the level of activity. This is known as classification by behaviour.

- A fixed cost is a cost which is incurred for a particular period of time and which, within certain activity levels, is **unaffected by changes in the level of activity**.
- A variable cost is a cost which tends to **vary** with the **level of activity**.

Examples of fixed and variable costs are as follows:

(a) Direct material costs are **variable costs** because they rise as more units of a product are manufactured.

(b) Sales commission is often a fixed percentage of sales turnover, and so is a **variable cost** that varies with the level of sales.

(c) Telephone call charges are likely to increase if the volume of business expands, and so they are a **variable overhead cost**.

(d) The rental cost of business premises is a constant amount, at least within a stated time period, and so it is a **fixed cost**.

Some items of expenditure are part-fixed and part-variable. In cost accounting, **semi-fixed** or **semi-variable costs** may be divided into their fixed and variable elements.

5 Classification by responsibility

 Costs and revenues must be traced to the individuals who are responsible for incurring them. This is known as **responsibility accounting**.

The three common responsibility centres are **cost centres**, **profit centres** and **investment centres**. We looked at each of these centres in Chapter 1.

Costs and revenues allocated to responsibility centres should be classified according to whether they are **controllable** or **non-controllable** by the manager of the respective responsibility centre.

From a **motivational** point of view this is important because it can be very demoralising for managers who feel that their performance is being judged on the basis of something over which they have no influence.

It is also important from a **control** point of view in that control reports should ensure that information on costs is reported to the manager who is able to take action to control them.

A controllable cost is a cost which can be controlled, typically by a cost, profit or investment centre manager.

5.1 The controllability of variable costs

Most **variable costs** within a department are thought to be **controllable in the short term** because managers can influence the efficiency with which resources are used, even if they cannot do anything to raise or lower price levels.

A cost which is not controllable by a junior manager might be controllable by a senior manager. For example, there may be high direct labour costs in a department caused by excessive overtime working. The junior manager may feel obliged to continue with the overtime to meet production schedules, but his/her senior may be able to reduce costs by hiring extra full-time staff, thereby reducing the requirements for overtime.

A cost which is not controllable by a manager in one department may be controllable by a manager in another department. For example, an increase in material costs may be caused by buying at higher prices than expected (controllable by the purchasing department) or by excessive wastage (controllable by the production department) or by a faulty machine producing rejects (controllable by the maintenance department).

Some costs are **non-controllable**, such as increases in expenditure items due to inflation. Other costs are **controllable, but in the long term rather than the short term**. For example, production costs might be reduced by the introduction of new machinery and technology, but in the short term, management must attempt to do the best they can with the resources and machinery at their disposal.

5.2 The controllability of fixed costs

It is often assumed that all fixed costs are non-controllable in the short run. This is not so.

(a) **Committed fixed costs** are those costs arising from the possession of plant, equipment, buildings and an administration department to **support the long-term needs of the business**. These costs (depreciation, rent, administration salaries) are largely **non-controllable in the short term** because they have been committed by longer-term decisions affecting longer-term needs. When a company decides to cut production drastically, the long-term committed fixed costs will be reduced, but only after redundancy terms have been settled and assets sold.

(b) A **discretionary cost** is a cost whose amount, within a particular time period, is **determined by**, and can be **altered by**, the **budget holder**. **Discretionary fixed costs**, such as advertising and research and development costs, are incurred as a result of a top management decision, but could be **raised or lowered at fairly short notice** (irrespective of the actual volume of production and sales).

EXAM FOCUS POINT

This chapter has introduced a number of new terms and definitions. The topics covered in this chapter are very important and are likely to be tested in the MA2 *Managing Costs and Finance* examination that you will be facing.

CHAPTER ROUNDUP

↳ The **total cost** of making a product or providing a service consists of **material** costs, **labour** costs and **other expenses** such as rent and rates.

↳ A **direct cost** is a cost that can be traced in full to the product or service being costed.

↳ An **indirect cost** (or overhead) is a cost that is incurred in the course of making a product or providing a service, but which cannot be traced directly and in full to the product or service.

↳ **Prime cost** = direct material cost + direct labour cost + direct expenses.

↳ **Classification by function** involves classifying costs as production/manufacturing costs, administration costs or marketing/selling and distribution costs.

↳ A different way of analysing and classifying costs is into **fixed costs** and **variable costs**. Many items of expenditure are part-fixed and part-variable and hence are termed **semi-fixed** or **semi-variable**. This is also known as **classification by behaviour**.

↳ Costs and revenues must be traced to the individuals who are responsible for incurring them. This is known as **responsibility accounting**.

QUICK QUIZ

1   Give two examples of direct expenses.

2   Give an example of an administration overhead, a selling overhead and a distribution overhead.

3   What are functional costs?

4   What is the distinction between fixed and variable costs?

5   Which of the following would be classified as a fixed cost in the operation of a motor vehicle?

    O   Oil change every 10,000 kilometres
    O   Petrol
    O   Insurance
    O   Tyre replacement

6   What is a controllable cost?

ANSWERS TO QUICK QUIZ

1
- The hire of tools or equipment for a particular job
- Maintenance costs of tools, fixtures and so on

2
- **Administration overhead** = Depreciation of office equipment, buildings and machinery
- **Selling overhead** = Printing and stationery (catalogues, price lists)
- **Distribution overhead** = Wages of packers, drivers and despatch clerks

3   Functional costs are classified as follows.
- **Production** or **manufacturing costs**
- **Administration costs**
- **Marketing** or **selling and distribution costs**

4   A **fixed cost** is a cost which is incurred for a particular period of time and which, within certain activity levels, is unaffected by changes in the level of activity.

A **variable cost** is a cost which tends to vary with the level of activity.

5   Insurance.

6   A **controllable cost** is a cost which can be controlled, typically by a cost, profit or investment centre manager.

Now try ...

Attempt the questions below from the **Practice Question Bank**

Number

Q11

Q12

Q13

Q14

04

Cost behaviour

This chapter describes the way that the cost of items of expense varies with changes in the volume of activity, such as the level of production or sales. It describes the **cost behaviour** of individual items of expense, but goes on to explain that it is often reasonable to assume that costs in total are either **fixed**, **variable** or a **combination of fixed and variable**.

Costs that are **semi-fixed** and **semi-variable** can be divided into fixed and variable elements using a simple technique called the **high-low method**.

The analysis of cost behaviour provides an essential basis for the application of several cost and management accounting techniques, such as marginal costing, CVP analysis and relevant costing, which are the subject of later chapters.

TOPIC LIST	SYLLABUS REFERENCE
1 Cost behaviour	A3 (d)
2 Cost behaviour patterns	A3 (b), (e)
3 The high-low method	A3 (c)

Study Guide	Intellectual level
A **Management information**	
3 **Cost classification**	
(b) Explain and illustrate the nature of variable, fixed, stepped fixed and mixed (semi-variable) costs	S
(c) Use the high-low method to separate semi-variable costs into their fixed and variable elements	S
(d) Use variable, fixed and semi-variable costs in cost analysis	S
(e) Analyse the effect of changing activity levels on unit costs	S

1 Cost behaviour

Cost behaviour is the way in which costs are affected by changes in the **volume of output** and is important for planning, control and decision making.

Cost behaviour is the way in which costs are affected by changes in the volume of output.

1.1 Cost behaviour and levels of activity

There are many factors which may influence costs. The major influence is **volume of output**, or the **level of activity**. The level of activity may refer to one of the following.

- Value of items sold
- Number of items sold
- Number of units of electricity consumed
- Number of invoices issued
- Number of units produced

1.2 Basic principles of cost behaviour

The basic principle of cost behaviour is that **as the level of activity rises, costs will usually rise**. It will cost more to produce 2,000 units of output than it will cost to produce 1,000 units.

This principle is common sense. The problem for the accountant, however is to determine for each item of cost, the way in which costs rise and by how much as the level of activity increases. For our purposes here, the level of activity for measuring cost will generally be taken to be the **volume of production**.

1.3 Example: Cost behaviour and activity level

Hans Bratch Co has a fleet of company cars for sales representatives. Running costs have been estimated as follows.

(a) Cars cost $12,000 when new, and have a guaranteed trade-in value of $6,000 at the end of two years. Depreciation is charged on a straight-line basis.

(b) Petrol and oil cost 15 cents per kilometre.

(c) Tyres cost $300 per set to replace; replacement occurs after 30,000 kilometres.

(d) Hans Bratch has an agreement with a local garage to perform routine maintenance on each car each year. Routine maintenance costs $200 per car in the first year and $450 in the second year.

(e)   Repairs average $400 per car over two years and are thought to vary with the number of
        kilometres travelled. The average car travels 25,000 kilometres per annum.

(f)   Tax, insurance, membership of motoring organisations and so on cost $400 per annum per car.

Required

Calculate the average cost per annum of cars which travel 10,000 kilometres per annum and 40,000
kilometres per annum.

Solution

Costs may be analysed into fixed, variable and stepped cost items, a stepped cost being a cost which is
fixed in nature but only within certain levels of activity.

(a)   **Fixed costs**

	$ per annum
Depreciation $(12,000 − 6,000) ÷ 2	3,000
Routine maintenance $(200 + 450) ÷ 2	325
Tax, insurance etc	400
	3,725

(b)   **Variable costs**

	Cents per km
Petrol and oil	15.0
Repairs ($400 ÷ 50,000 kilometres)	0.8
	15.8

(c)   **Stepped-fixed costs** are tyre replacement costs, which are $300 at the end of every 30,000
        kilometres.

        (i)   If the car travels less than or exactly 30,000 kilometres in 2 years, the tyres will not be
                changed. Average cost of tyres per annum = $0.

        (ii)   If a car travels more than 30,000 kilometres and up to (and including) 60,000 kilometres
                in 2 years, there will be 1 change of tyres in the period. Average cost of tyres per annum
                = $150 ($300 ÷ 2).

        (iii)   If a car exceeds 60,000 kilometres in 2 years (up to 90,000 kilometres) there will be 2
                tyre changes. Average cost of tyres per annum = $300 ($600 ÷ 2).

The estimated costs per annum of cars travelling 10,000 kilometres per annum and 40,000 kilometres
per annum would therefore be as follows.

	10,000 kilometres per annum $	*40,000 kilometres per annum* $
Fixed costs	3,725	3,725
Variable costs (15.8c per km)	1,580	6,320
Tyres	−	150
Cost per annum	5,305	10,195

2 Cost behaviour patterns

- Costs which, in total, are not affected by the level of activity are **fixed** costs or **period** costs.
- **Stepped-fixed costs** are fixed within a certain range of activity.
- **Variable costs** increase or decrease in total with the level of activity. It is usually assumed that there is a linear relationship between cost and activity.
- **Semi-variable, semi-fixed** or **mixed costs** are costs which are part fixed and part variable.

2.1 Fixed costs

A **fixed cost** is a cost which tends to be unaffected in total by increases or decreases in the volume of output.

Fixed costs are a **period charge**, in that they relate to a span of time; as the time span increases, so too will the fixed costs. A graph of a total fixed cost would look like this.

Graph of total fixed cost

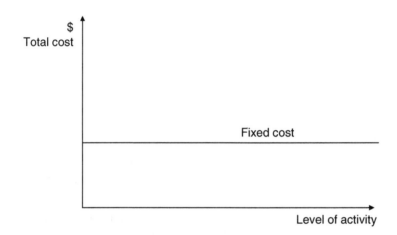

Examples of a fixed cost are as follows:

- The salary of the managing director (per month or per annum)
- The rent of a single factory building (per month or per annum)
- Straight line depreciation of a single machine (per month or per annum)

Because the total fixed costs remain the same for all levels of activity, the fixed cost per unit decreases as more units are produced.

Graph of fixed cost per unit

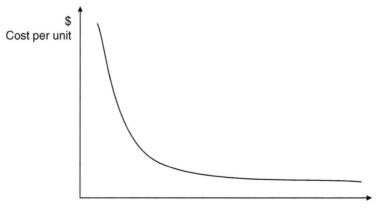

2.2 Stepped-fixed costs

A **stepped-fixed cost** is a cost which is fixed in nature but only within certain levels of activity.

Consider the depreciation of a machine which may be fixed if production remains below 1,000 units per month. If production exceeds 1,000 units, a second machine may be required, and the cost of depreciation (on two machines) would go up a step. A graph of a total stepped-fixed cost could look like this.

Graph of total stepped-fixed cost

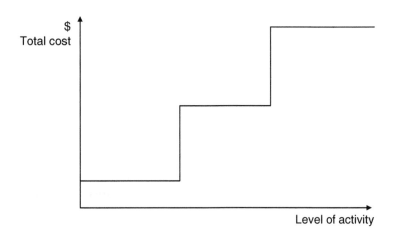

Graph of stepped-fixed cost per unit

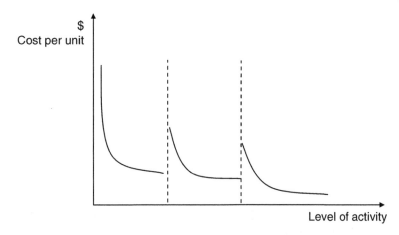

Other examples of stepped-fixed costs are as follows:

(a) **Rent**, where accommodation requirements increase as output levels get higher.

(b) **Supervisor salaries**. One supervisor may be able to supervise a maximum of ten employees. When the number of employees increases above a multiple of ten an extra supervisor will be required.

2.3 Variable costs

A **variable cost** is a cost which tends to vary in total directly with the volume of output. The variable cost per unit is the same amount for each unit produced.

Total variable costs will increase or decrease in **proportion** to any change in activity. This can be shown in a graph like this.

Graph of total variable cost

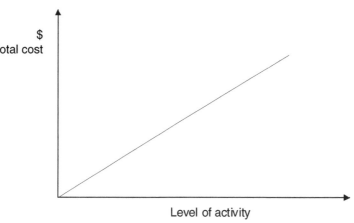

The cost will be the same for each unit produced giving the following graph for variable cost per unit.

Graph of variable cost per unit

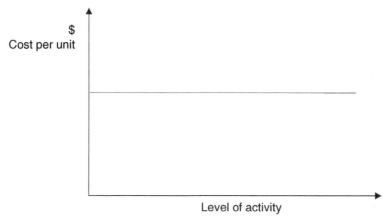

A constant variable cost per unit implies that the price per unit of say, material purchased is constant, and that the rate of material usage is also constant.

Examples of a variable cost are as follows.

(a)   The **cost of raw materials** is variable in relation to the level of production.

(b)   **Sales commission** is variable in relation to the volume or value of sales.

(c)   **Bonus payments** for productivity to employees might be variable once a certain level of output is achieved, as the following diagram illustrates.

Graph of total variable cost (2)

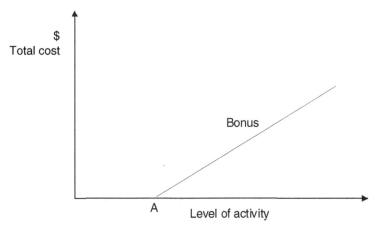

Up to output A, no bonus is earned.

2.4 Semi-variable costs

A **semi-variable/semi-fixed/mixed cost** is a cost which contains both fixed and variable components and so is partly affected by changes in the level of activity.

Examples of these costs include the following:

(a)   **Electricity and gas bills**
   •   Fixed cost = standing charge
   •   Variable cost = charge per unit of electricity used

(b)   **Salesman's salary**
   •   Fixed cost = basic salary
   •   Variable cost = commission on sales made

(c)   **Costs of running a car**
   •   Fixed cost = road tax, insurance
   •   Variable costs = petrol, oil, repairs (which vary with kilometres travelled)

A graph of a total semi-variable cost would look like this.

Graph of total semi-variable cost

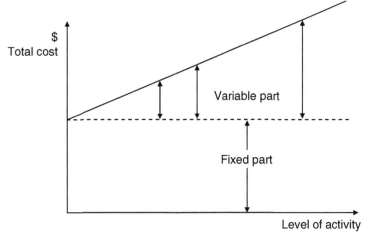

Graph of semi-variable cost per unit

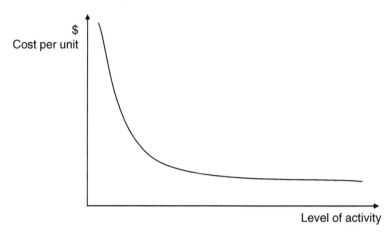

Examples of these costs can include utility bills, if there is a standing basic charge plus a variable charge per unit of consumption.

QUESTION

Cost behaviour

Are the following likely to be fixed, variable or semi-variable costs?

(a)   Telephone bill
(b)   Annual salary of the chief accountant
(c)   The accountant's annual membership fee to ACCA (paid by the company)
(d)   Cost of materials used to pack 20 units of product X into a box
(e)   Wages of warehouse workers

ANSWER

(a)   Semi-variable
(b)   Fixed
(c)   Fixed
(d)   Variable
(e)   Variable

2.5 Other cost behaviour patterns

Other cost behaviour patterns may be appropriate to certain cost items. Examples of two other cost behaviour patterns are shown below.

(a)   *Cost behaviour pattern (1)*

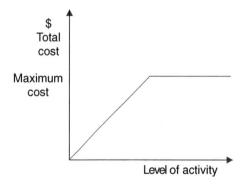

(b)   *Cost behaviour pattern (2)*

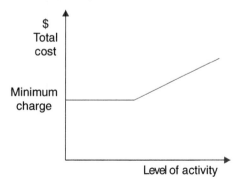

(i) Graph (a) represents an item of cost which is variable with output up to a certain maximum level of cost. This kind of cost behaviour could occur, for example, when an engineer is called to fix a photocopier. The company may have an agreement with the engineer that each visit to fix the photocopier is fixed at $75, up to a maximum total charge of $225 per month, the equivalent of three visits per month. If the engineer were to visit once in a month, the cost would be $75, twice in a month and the cost would be $150. However if they were to visit three or more times in a month the cost would be fixed at $225.

(ii) Graph (b) represents a cost which is variable with output, subject to a minimum (fixed) charge. Again thinking about the photocopier engineer, the engineer may have a different agreement with a different company to fix the photocopiers. In this agreement, they charge $20 per hour, subject to a minimum total charge of $40, for each visit to fix the photocopier. If the engineer takes an hour or two hours to fix the photocopier, the charge will be $40, however if the engineer takes more than two hours, the charge increases depending on the time taken.

(c) *Cost behaviour pattern (3)*

(d) *Cost behaviour pattern (4)*

(i) Graphs (c) and (d) represent direct costs that are not proportionately variable. Graph (c) shows a scenario in which, up to a given level of activity, the purchase price of raw material per unit is constant. After that point, a quantity discount is given so the price per unit is lower for further purchases and also retrospectively to all units already purchased.

(ii) Graph (d) represents a scenario in which, up to a given level of activity, the cost of labour per unit is constant. After that level of output, employees may be entitled to overtime (if worked at the specific request of a customer to complete an order or if overtime is worked regularly in the normal course of operations). This means that any further production incurs higher labour costs per unit.

2.6 Cost behaviour and cost analysis

Management decisions will often be based on how costs and revenues vary at different activity levels. Knowledge of cost behaviour is obviously essential for the tasks of **budgeting**, **decision making** and **control accounting**.

Management decisions will often be based on how costs and revenues vary at different activity levels. Examples of such decisions are as follows:

* What should the **planned activity level** be for the next period?
* Should the **selling price** be reduced in order to sell more units?
* Should a particular component be **manufactured internally** or **bought in**?
* Should a **contract** be undertaken?

Knowledge of cost behaviour is obviously essential for the tasks of **budgeting**, **decision making** and **control accounting**.

An important task in budgeting is to estimate what costs will be in the budgeted period. Reliable estimates of expected costs require some knowledge of cost behaviour, and what the costs will be at the expected volume of activity, output or sales.

(a)   In a company where employees are paid fixed wages or salaries, it may be necessary to identify whether additional employees will be required for the budgeted level of activity, and if so what the extra (stepped) costs will be.

(b)   Similarly, if it is expected that some overtime working may be required, it will be necessary to estimate the level of activity above which overtime hours will be needed, and what the overtime payments will be.

(c)   For organisations that incur large costs for energy or water consumption, reliable budget estimates of cost will require an understanding of the fixed and variable elements of these expense items.

When management are trying to decide whether it will be profitable to undertake a particular task or job, they need to know what the extra costs will be and whether the benefits will exceed these costs. Understanding cost behaviour is essential for making reliable estimates of the additional costs.

Control accounting involves the comparison of actual costs with what costs should have been. This too calls for knowledge of cost behaviour, in order to assess the expected costs.

In practice it is often much too difficult and time-consuming to estimate the expected costs for each item of expenditure, and simplifying assumptions are made. In particular, it may be assumed that at normal levels of activity, all costs are either fixed, variable or a combination of fixed and variable (semi-fixed, semi-variable).

3 The high-low method

The fixed and variable elements of semi-variable costs can be determined by the **high-low method**.

3.1 Assumptions about cost behaviour

Assumptions about cost behaviour include the following.

(a)   Within the normal or **relevant range** of output, costs are often assumed to be either **fixed**, **variable** or **semi-variable** (mixed).

(b)   Within the normal or relevant range of output, costs often rise in a straight line as the volume of activity increases. Such costs are said to be **linear**.

The **high-low method** of determining fixed and variable elements of mixed costs relies on the assumption that mixed costs are linear. We shall now go on to look at this method of cost determination.

3.2 High-low method

Follow the steps below to estimate the fixed and variable elements of semi-variable costs.

Step 1	Review records of activity and costs in previous periods.
	• Select the period with the **highest** activity level
	• Select the period with the **lowest** activity level

Step 2	Determine the following:
	• Total cost at highest activity level
	• Total costs at lowest activity level
	• Total units at highest activity level
	• Total units at lowest activity level

Step 3	Calculate the following:

$$\frac{\text{Total cost at highest activity level} - \text{total cost at lowest activity level}}{\text{Total units at highest activity level} - \text{total unit at lowest activity level}}$$

= variable cost per unit (v)

Step 4	The fixed costs can be determined as follows. (Total cost at highest activity level) – (total units at highest activity level × variable cost per unit)

Alternatively, the fixed costs can be determined using the lowest activity level: (Total cost at lowest activity level) – (total units at lowest activity level × variable cost per unit)

The following graph demonstrates the high-low method. 'a' is the variable cost per unit.

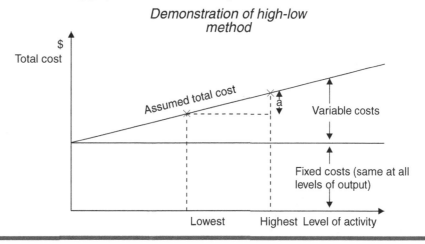

Demonstration of high-low method

3.2.1 Example: The high-low method

DG Co has recorded the following total costs during the last five years.

Year	Output volume Units	Total cost $
20X0	65,000	145,000
20X1	80,000	165,000
20X2	90,000	170,000
20X3	60,000	140,000
20X4	75,000	155,000

Required

Calculate the total cost that should be expected in 20X5 if output is 85,000 units.

BPP
LEARNING
MEDIA

Solution

Step 1	•	Period with highest activity = 20X2
	•	Period with lowest activity = 20X3

Step 2	•	Total cost at highest activity level = 170,000
	•	Total cost at lowest activity level = 140,000
	•	Total units at highest activity level = 90,000
	•	Total units at lowest activity level = 60,000

Step 3 Variable cost per unit

$$= \frac{\text{Total cost at highest activity level} - \text{total cost at lowest activity level}}{\text{Total units at highest activity level} - \text{total units at lowest activity level}}$$

$$= \frac{170,000 - 140,000}{90,000 - 60,000} = \frac{30,000}{30,000} = \$1 \text{ per unit}$$

Step 4 Fixed costs = (total cost at highest activity level) – (total units at highest activity level × variable cost per unit)

= 170,000 – (90,000 × 1) = 170,000 – 90,000 = $80,000

Therefore the costs in 20X5 for output of 85,000 units are as follows.

		$
Variable costs	(85,000 × $1)	85,000
Fixed costs		80,000
		165,000

QUESTION

The Valuation Department of a large firm of surveyors wishes to develop a method of predicting its total costs in a period. The following past costs have been recorded at two activity levels.

	Number of valuations (V)	Total cost (TC)
Period 1	420	82,200
Period 2	515	90,275

The total cost model for a period could be represented as follows:

○ TC = $46,500 + 85V
○ TC = $42,000 + 95V
○ TC = $46,500 – 85V
○ TC = $51,500 – 95V

ANSWER

TC = $46,500 + 85V

Although we only have two activity levels in this question we can still apply the high-low method.

	Valuations V	Total cost $
Period 2	515	90,275
Period 1	420	82,200
Change due to variable cost	95	8,075

∴ Variable cost per valuation = $8,075/95 = $85.

Period 2: fixed cost = $90,275 – (515 × $85)

= $46,500

Using good MCQ technique, you should have managed to eliminate TC = $46,500 – 85V and TC = $51,500 – 95V as incorrect options straightaway. The variable cost must be added to the fixed cost, rather than subtracted from it. Once you had calculated the variable cost as $85 per valuation (as shown above), you should have been able to select TC = $46,500 + 85V without going on to calculate the fixed cost (we have shown this calculation above for completeness).

CHAPTER ROUNDUP

- ⤷ **Cost behaviour** is the way in which costs are affected by changes in the volume of output and is important for planning, control and decision making.

- ⤷ Costs which, in total, are not affected by the level of activity are **fixed** costs or **period** costs.

- ⤷ **Stepped-fixed costs** are fixed within a certain range of activity.

- ⤷ **Variable costs** increase or decrease in total with the level of activity. It is usually assumed that there is a linear relationship between cost and activity.

- ⤷ **Semi-variable, semi-fixed** or **mixed costs** are costs which are part fixed and part variable.

- ⤷ Management decisions will often be based on how costs and revenues vary at different activity levels. Knowledge of cost behaviour is obviously essential for the tasks of **budgeting**, **decision making** and **control accounting**.

- ⤷ The fixed and variable elements of semi-variable costs can be determined by the **high-low method**.

QUICK QUIZ

1   Cost behaviour is ....

2   The basic principle of cost behaviour is that as the level of activity rises, costs will usually ....

3   Fill in the gaps for each of the graph titles below.

(a)

$ Total cost / Activity

Graph of a ....cost

Example:

(b)

$ Total cost / Activity

Graph of a ....cost

Example:

(c)

$ Total cost / Activity

Graph of a ....cost

Example:

(d)

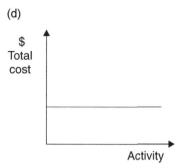

Graph of a ....cost

Example:

Activity

4   Costs are assumed to be either fixed, variable or semi-variable within the normal or relevant range of output.
     O   True
     O   False

5   The costs of operating the canteen at 'Eat a lot Company' for the past three months is as follows.

Month	Cost $	Employees
1	72,500	1,250
2	75,000	1,300
3	68,750	1,175

Variable cost (per employee per month) =

Fixed cost per month =

6   The following shows the cost per unit of an item of expense at different levels of activity:

Activity Units	Cost per unit $
1	10,000
50	200
100	120
150	80

What is the correct behavioural classification for the expense item?

     O   Fixed cost
     O   Semi-variable cost
     O   Stepped-fixed cost
     O   Variable cost

7   A particular cost is classified as being semi-variable.

What is the effect on the cost per unit if activity increases by 10%?

     O   Decrease by 10%
     O   Decrease by less than 10%
     O   Increase by less than 10%
     O   Remain constant

8   Production costs have been estimated at two levels of output:

	50,000 units	55,000 units
Prime costs	$430,000	$473,000
Overheads	$330,000	$339,000

What are the estimated production costs per unit at an output level of 54,000 units?
     O $14.76
     O $14.84
     O $15.20
     O $17.00

BPP LEARNING MEDIA

ANSWERS TO QUICK QUIZ

1   The variability of input costs with activity undertaken.

2   Rise

3   (a)   Stepped-fixed cost. Example: rent, supervisors' salaries
      (b)   Variable cost. Example: raw materials, direct labour
      (c)   Semi-variable cost. Example: electricity and telephone
      (d)   Fixed. Example: rent, depreciation (straight-line)

4   True

5   Variable cost = $50 per employee per month
     Fixed costs = $10,000 per month

	Activity	Cost
		$
High	1,300	75,000
Low	1,175	68,750
	125	6,250

     Variable cost per employee = $6,250/125 = $50

     For 1,175 employees, total cost = $68,750

     Total cost   = variable cost + fixed cost
     $68,750   = (1,175 × $50) + fixed cost
     ∴ Fixed cost = $68,750 – $58,750
                   = $10,000

6   Stepped-fixed cost

7   Decrease by less than 10%

     If a cost is semi-variable then it is part fixed and part variable. The total fixed element is **unaffected** by activity level, but the total variable element **is affected** by the activity level. The best way to answer this type of question is to make up some numbers to test what happens.

     Say the variable element is $10 per unit and the fixed cost is $100. If the level of activity is 200 units then the total cost will be $100 + ($10 × 200) = $2,100 and so the cost per unit will be $2,100 / 200 = $10.50.

     If the activity level increases by 10%, the fixed element of the total cost will be unaffected but the total variable cost will be affected.

     10% increase in activity level = 200 × 110% = 220 units

     Cost per unit at 220 units =

     $$\frac{100 + (220 \times \$10)}{220 \, units} = \$10.45$$

     The decrease in cost is $0.05 per unit. $0.05 / $10.50 = 0.48% ie less than 10%.

8    $14.84

Activity	Cost
	$
55,000	812,000
50,000	760,000
5,000	52,000

     Variable cost per unit = $52,000/5,000 = $10.40

     For 50,000 units, total cost = $760,000

     Total cost = variable cost + fixed cost

$760,000 = (50,000 × $10.40) + fixed cost

Fixed cost = $760,000 – $520,000		= $240,000
Cost at an output of 54,000 units		= $240,000 + (54,000 × $10.40)
		= $801,600
Cost per unit = $801,600/54,000		= $14.84

Now try ...

Attempt the questions below from the **Practice Question Bank**

Number

Q15

Q16

Q17

Q18

Q19

05

In this chapter we discuss how managers make comparisons between actual data and other data. In doing so they can assess the **significance** of the actual data for the period. Comparing current results with other data can make the information more useful. Comparisons may also help to show up any errors that have occurred. Differences between actual figures and the budget are called **variances**. **Variance reporting** is the reporting of differences between budgeted and actual performance.

Information for comparison

Study Guide	Intellectual level
A Management information	
4 Information for comparison	
(a) Explain the purpose of making comparisons	K
(b) Identify relevant bases for comparison: previous period data, corresponding period data, forecast/budget data	S
(c) Explain the forecasting/budgeting process and the concept of feed forward and feedback control	K
(d) Explain and illustrate the concept of flexible budgets	S
(e) Use appropriate income and expenditure data for comparison	S
(f) Calculate variances between actual and historical/forecast data which may or may not be adjusted for volume change (note: standard costing is excluded)	S
(g) Identify whether variances are favourable or adverse	S
(h) Identify possible causes of variances	S
(i) Explain the concept of exception reporting	K
(j) Explain factors affecting the decision whether to investigate variances	K

1 Types of comparison

Comparing actual results with **other information** helps to put them in context and may show up errors.

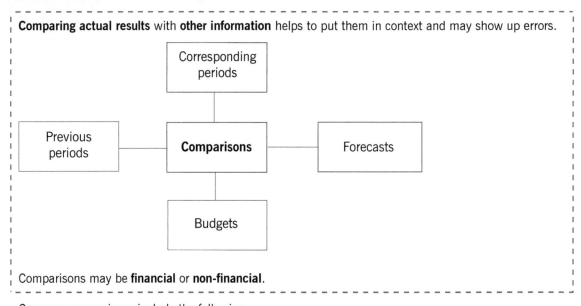

Comparisons may be **financial** or **non-financial**.

Common comparisons include the following.

1.1 Comparisons with previous periods

The most common comparison of a previous period is when **one year's final figures** are **compared** with the **previous year's**. A business's statutory financial accounts contain comparative figures for the previous year as well as the figures for the actual year. As financial accounts are sent to shareholders, this comparison is obviously of great interest to them.

For management accounting purposes, however, year-on-year comparisons are insufficient by themselves. Management will wish to pick up problems a lot sooner than the end of the financial year. Hence comparisons are often made for management accounting purposes **month-by-month** or **quarter-by-quarter**. This can either be a comparison with the previous period (eg comparing June 20X2 with May 20X2), or with the corresponding period (eg comparing June 20X2 with June 20X1).

Making comparisons month-by-month or quarter-by-quarter is most useful when you expect figures to be reasonably even over time. However demand for many products fluctuates **season-by-season**.

1.2 Example: seasonal fluctuations

A company making Christmas decorations had sales for the quarter ended 31 December that were considerably greater than sales for the previous quarter ended 30 September. For the quarter ended the following 31 March its sales decreased significantly again. Should its managers be concerned?

Based on the information given, we cannot tell. All the information tells us is that most people buy Christmas decorations in the three months leading up to Christmas. Comparing the December quarter's sales with the quarters either side is not very useful, because we are not comparing like with like. People are far more likely to buy Christmas decorations in the December quarter.

A far more meaningful comparison would therefore be to compare the December quarter's sales with those of the December quarter of the previous year, since the demand conditions would be similar.

This example demonstrates where comparisons with corresponding periods can be very useful, in businesses where the trade is **seasonal** (you would expect significant variations between adjacent periods).

Another example is heating bills. If the heating bill for the summer quarter is less than that for the winter quarter, the difference does not tell you anything about organisational performance, only about the weather.

1.3 Comparisons with forecasts

Businesses make forecasts for a number of purposes. A very common type of forecast is a **cash flow forecast**.

1.4 Example: Cash flow forecast

GEORGE CO: CASH FLOW FORECAST FOR FIRST QUARTER

	Jan $	Feb $	Mar $
Estimated cash receipts			
From credit customers	14,000	16,500	17,000
From cash sales	3,000	4,000	4,500
Proceeds on disposal of non-current assets	–	2,200	–
Total cash receipts	17,000	22,700	21,500
Estimated cash payments			
To suppliers of goods	8,000	7,800	10,500
To employees (wages)	3,000	3,500	3,500
Purchase of non-current assets	–	12,500	
Rent and rates	–	–	1,000
Other overheads	1,200	1,200	1,200
Repayment of loan	2,500	–	–
	14,700	25,000	16,200
Net surplus/(deficit) for month	2,300	(2,300)	5,300
Opening cash balance	1,200	3,500	1,200
Closing cash balance	3,500	1,200	6,500

The purpose of making this forecast is for the business to be able to see how likely it is to have problems **maintaining** a **positive cash balance**. If the cash balance becomes negative, the business will have to obtain a loan or overdraft and have to pay interest costs.

At the end of the period management will **compare** the **actual figures** with the **forecast figures**, and try to assess why they differ. Differences are likely to be a sign that some of the **assumptions** made when

BPP
LEARNING
MEDIA

drawing up the original forecast were **incorrect**. Hence management, when making forecasts for future periods, may wish to change the assumptions that are made.

1.5 Non-financial comparisons

As well as being made in **financial terms** (costs and revenues), you may make comparisons in other ways. For example you may compare units produced or sold. Other possible comparisons include measures of quality/customer satisfaction, time taken for various processes etc.

1.6 Example: A hospital casualty department

A hospital casualty department will aim to deal with incoming patients quickly, efficiently and effectively but numbers and types of patients are hard to predict. Comparing waiting times or cases dealt with per day will be misleading if one day includes the victims of a serious train crash and another covers only minor injuries. Long term comparisons might give a clearer picture and help to identify usage patterns (for example busy Saturday nights). Comparisons with other casualty departments might be even more revealing.

EXAM FOCUS POINT

You must be able to compare sets of data for the exam and be able to draw conclusions such as the fact that there were greater profits or higher levels of efficiency in one period versus the other.

1.7 Comparison with budgets

Most organisations have long-term goals which can be divided into:

- **Objectives** (measurable steps towards achieving their goals)
- **Action plans** (detailed steps for achieving their objectives)

The action plans are often expressed in money and provide:

- An overall view for management
- Assurance that different departments' plans co-ordinate with each other

The financial plan is usually called a **budget**.

A budget is an organisation's plan for a forthcoming period, expressed in monetary terms.

Budget comparisons are popular because they show whether budget holders are **achieving** their **targets**.

Budget reports may be **combined** with **other information** such as non-financial information, ratios etc.

Budgets, like forecasts, represent a view of the future. However the two are not identical. Forecasts represent a prediction of what is **likely to happen**, the most likely scenario. Budgets may be a **target** rather than a prediction. The target may be a very stiff one and it may be far more likely that the business fails to reach the target than that it does achieve the target. However management may feel that setting a stiff target may keep staff 'on their toes'.

You can use budgets to check that the organisation's financial plan is working by **comparing** the **budgeted results** for the day, week, month or year to date **with** the **actual results**. Differences between these are known as **variances**.

The ways in which managers use budgets is a part of a continuous process of planning, monitoring performance and taking action on variances. This is sometimes called the **control cycle** and can be illustrated as follows.

1.8 The control cycle

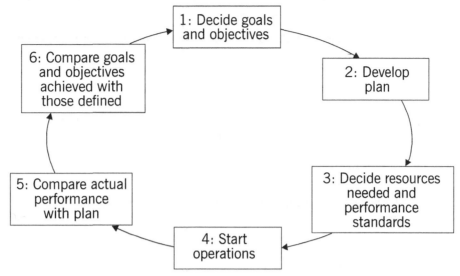

Stages of the control cycle is what we are looking at here.

2 Identifying differences

2.1 Flexible budgets

2.1.1 Fixed budgets versus flexible/flexed budgets

- A **fixed budget** is a budget which is set for a single activity level.

- A **flexible budget** is a budget which recognises different cost behaviour patterns and is designed to change as volume of activity changes.

- A flexible budget is designed at the planning stage to vary with activity levels. A **flexed** budget is a revised budget that reflects the actual activity levels achieved in the budget period.

2.1.2 Advantages of flexible budgets

A **flexible budget** has two advantages.

(a) At the **planning** stage, it may be helpful to know what the effects would be if the actual outcome differs from the prediction. For example, a company may budget to sell 10,000 units of its product, but may prepare flexible budgets based on sales of, say, 8,000 and 12,000 units. This would enable **contingency plans** to be drawn up if necessary.

(b) At the end of each month or year, actual results may be compared with the relevant activity level in the flexible budget as a **control** procedure.

2.1.3 Preparation of flexible budgets

Step 1	The first step in the preparation of a flexible budget is the **determination of cost behaviour patterns**, which means **deciding whether costs are fixed, variable or semi-variable**.
	• Fixed costs are easy to spot. They remain constant as activity levels change.
	• For non-fixed costs, divide each cost figure by the related activity level. If the cost is a variable cost, the cost per unit will remain constant. If the cost is a semi-variable cost, the unit rate will reduce as activity levels increase.

Step 2	The second step in the preparation of a flexible budget is to calculate the **budget cost allowance** for each cost item.

Budget cost allowance = budgeted fixed cost* + (number of units × variable cost per unit)**

* nil for variable cost
** nil for fixed cost

Semi-variable costs therefore need splitting into their fixed and variable components so that the budget cost allowance can be calculated.

Budget flexing involves 'flexing variable costs from original budgeted levels to the allowances permitted for actual volume achieved while maintaining fixed costs at original budget levels' (CIMA Official Terminology).

2.1.4 Splitting semi-variable costs

One method for splitting semi-variable costs is the high/low method, which we covered in Chapter 4. Attempt the following question to make sure you remember how to do this.

QUESTION
Cost estimation

The cost of factory power has behaved as follows in past years.

	Units of output produced	Cost of factory power $
20X1	7,900	38,700
20X2	7,700	38,100
20X3	9,800	44,400
20X4	9,100	42,300

Budgeted production for 20X5 is 10,200 units.

Ignoring inflation, the cost of factory power which will be incurred is estimated to be $ _____.

ANSWER

The cost of factory power is estimated to be $ | 45,600 |.

Workings

	Units	$
20X3 (highest output)	9,800	44,400
20X2 (lowest output)	7,700	38,100
	2,100	6,300

The variable cost per unit is therefore $6,300/2,100 = $3.

The level of fixed cost can be calculated by looking at any output level.

	$
Total cost of factory power in 20X3	44,400
Less variable cost of factory power (9,800 × $3)	29,400
Fixed cost of factory power	15,000

An estimate of costs is 20X5 is as follows.

	$
Fixed cost	15,000
Variable cost of budgeted production (10,200 × $3)	30,600
Total budgeted cost of factory power	45,600

Now you are ready to prepare a flexible budget.

2.1.5 Example: preparing a flexible budget

(a) Prepare a budget for 20X6 for the direct labour costs and overhead expenses of a production department flexed at the activity levels of 80%, 90% and 100%, using the information listed below.

(i) The direct labour hourly rate is expected to be $3.75.

(ii) 100% activity represents 60,000 direct labour hours.

(iii) Variable costs

Indirect labour	$0.75 per direct labour hour
Consumable supplies	$0.375 per direct labour hour
Canteen and other welfare services	6% of direct and indirect labour costs

(iv) Semi-variable costs are expected to relate to the direct labour hours in the same manner as for the last five years.

Year	Direct labour hours	Semi-variable costs $
20X1	64,000	20,800
20X2	59,000	19,800
20X3	53,000	18,600
20X4	49,000	17,800
20X5	40,000 (estimate)	16,000 (estimate)

(v) *Fixed costs*

	$
Depreciation	18,000
Maintenance	10,000
Insurance	4,000
Rates	15,000
Management salaries	25,000

(vi) Inflation is to be ignored.

(b) Calculate the budget cost allowance (ie expected expenditure) for 20X6 assuming that 57,000 direct labour hours are worked.

Solution

(a)

	80% level 48,000 hrs $'000	90% level 54,000 hrs $'000	100% level 60,000 hrs $'000
Direct labour	180.00	202.50	225.0
Other variable costs			
Indirect labour	36.00	40.50	45.0
Consumable supplies	18.00	20.25	22.5
Canteen etc	12.96	14.58	16.2
Total variable costs ($5.145 per hour)	246.96	277.83	308.7
Semi-variable costs (W)	17.60	18.80	20.0
Fixed costs			
Depreciation	18.00	18.00	18.0
Maintenance	10.00	10.00	10.0
Insurance	4.00	4.00	4.0
Rates	15.00	15.00	15.0
Management salaries	25.00	25.00	25.0
Budgeted costs	336.56	368.63	400.7

BPP
LEARNING
MEDIA

Working

Using the high/low method:

	$
Total cost of 64,000 hours	20,800
Total cost of 40,000 hours	16,000
Variable cost of 24,000 hours	4,800
Variable cost per hour ($4,800/24,000)	$0.20

	$
Total cost of 64,000 hours	20,800
Variable cost of 64,000 hours (× $0.20)	12,800
Fixed costs	8,000

Semi-variable costs are calculated as follows.

		$
60,000 hours	(60,000 × $0.20) + $8,000	20,000
54,000 hours	(54,000 × $0.20) + $8,000	18,800
48,000 hours	(48,000 × $0.20) + $8,000	17,600

(b) The budget cost allowance for 57,000 direct labour hours of work would be as follows.

		$
Variable costs	(57,000 × $5.145)	293,265
Semi-variable costs	($8,000 + (57,000 × $0.20))	19,400
Fixed costs		72,000
		384,665

EXAM FOCUS POINT

You must be able to analyse the fixed and variable elements of semi-variable costs in order to be able to produce a flexible budget.

2.2 Variances and flexed budgets

Variances can be calculated by comparing the budget with the actual results (total variance) or comparing the flexed budget with the actual results (efficiency of usage and price variance).

You should report differences in such a way that managers can **understand them** and pick out **vital information easily**. Comparisons should not be cluttered with irrelevant information or too much detail.

There are two ways of looking at variances. The first way is to compare the budget figures to the actual figures achieved and this is called a total cost variance (or total sales variance).

For example, XYZ Co produces a product M. The following information is available for June.

	Budget	Actual	Variance
Material cost	$5,000	$7,000	$2,000 (adverse)

The total cost variance comparing budget to actual cost is $2,000 adverse.

The problem with this type of variance calculation is that the volume of production may be different from the budgeted volume. This means that variance may not be very helpful for management making decisions on the product M.

In the example above, more was spent on materials than were budgeted for so there is an adverse variance. At first sight this may seem like a bad thing and management may decide product M is costing too much. However, it turns out that there was such a large demand for product M in June that twice as many units of M were produced and sold. The materials were bought from an alternative supplier and cost only 35c per unit instead of 50c per unit. This means that XYZ Co produced and sold more units and paid less per unit for the materials than budgeted. This is a good thing!

To make a useful comparison between the actual and budgeted figures for direct/variable costs we can use the second type of variance calculation. We can **adjust** or **flex** the budget to reflect the same production levels as was actually achieved. As you know from the paragraph above, the new budget, flexed to the actual production level is known as the **flexed budget.** The differences between the actual figures and the new flexed budget give us variances which we will study later on.

Flexed budgets take out the effects of volume changes between actual and budget, and focus instead on the variances resulting from changes in the efficiency with which resources are used, and from the price of the resources.

Flexed budgets should be used for comparison of direct/variable costs if the actual level of production is different from the original budget.

2.3 Example: Flexed budget

Here is a production cost report for week 32 for the department making cartons.

	Actual	Budget	Variance	
Production (units)	5,000	4,800		
	$	$	$	
Direct materials	1,874	1,850	24	Adverse
Direct labour	825	810	15	Adverse
Prime cost	2,699	2,660	39	Adverse
Fixed overheads	826	840	14	Favourable
Total cost	3,525	3,500	25	Adverse

Required

Prepare a flexed budget for week 32 for the department making cartons.

Solution

The figures above illustrate how easy it is to gain a misleading picture of performance if like is not compared with like. At first glance, it would seem that the results are generally worse than expected. An adverse difference, or variance, indicates that the actual cost was more than expected, and this was the case for direct costs, and the overall cost.

But if you were reminded that the budget was for a production level of 4,800 units, whilst 5,000 units were actually produced, this would change the picture. We might now suspect that the performance was better than expected, but to quantify and confirm that suspicion, we need to flex the original budget and make a new comparison.

All variable costs, such as direct materials and direct labour, will change in line with the change in production level, but fixed costs will remain the same.

	Actual	Flexed budget		Variance	
Production (units)	5,000	5,000			
	$	$		$	
Direct materials	1,874	1,927	$\left(\dfrac{1,850 \times 5,000}{4,800}\right)$	53	Favourable
Direct labour	825	844	$\left(\dfrac{810 \times 5,000}{4,800}\right)$	19	Favourable
Prime cost	2,699	2,771		72	Favourable
Fixed overheads	826	840		14	Favourable
Total cost	3,525	3,611		86	Favourable

Comparisons with budget are an extremely important aspect of management accounting, and need to be considered in more detail.

QUESTION

Flexed budgets

Here is a production cost report for MWR Co for the three month period January–March 20X2.

	Actual	Budget
Production and sales (units)	3,000	2,000
	$	$
Sales revenue	30,000	20,000
Direct materials	8,500	6,000
Direct labour	4,500	4,000
Fixed overheads		
– Depreciation	2,200	2,000
– Rent and rates	1,600	1,500
Total cost	16,800	13,500
Profit	13,200	6,500

Required

Prepare a flexed budget for MWR Co for the three month period January–March 20X2.

ANSWER

FLEXED BUDGET MWR CO JANUARY–MARCH 20X2

	Actual	Flexed budget	Variance	
Production and sales (units)	3,000	3,000		
	$	$	$	
Sales revenue	30,000	30,000		
Direct materials (W1)	8,500	9,000	500	Favourable
Direct labour (W2)	4,500	6,000	1,500	Favourable
Fixed overheads (W3)				
– Depreciation	2,200	2,000	200	Adverse
– Rent and rates	1,600	1,500	100	Adverse
Total cost	16,800	18,500	1,700	Favourable
Profit	13,200	11,500	1,700	Favourable

Workings

1 *Direct materials*

$$\text{Cost per unit} = \frac{\$6,000}{2,000 \text{ units}} = \$3 \text{ per unit}$$

Therefore 3,000 units = 3,000 × $3 = 9,000

2 *Direct labour*

$$\text{Cost per unit} = \frac{\$4,000}{2,000 \text{ units}} = \$2 \text{ per unit}$$

Therefore 3,000 units = 3,000 × $2 = $6,000

3 *Fixed overheads*

The flexed budget for fixed overheads will be the same as the original budget as overheads are **fixed costs**.

QUESTION

Flexible budgets

Which of the following best describes a flexible budget?

O   A budget which is designed to be easily updated to reflect recent changes in unit costs or selling prices

O   A budget which can be flexed when actual costs are known, to provide a realistic forecast for the forthcoming period

O   A budget which, by recognising different cost behaviour patterns, is designed to change as the volume of activity changes

O   A budget which is prepared on a spreadsheet, with the flexibility to add new cost items to prepare new forecasts as circumstances change during the year

ANSWER

A budget which, by recognising different cost behaviour patterns, is designed to change as the volume of activity changes.

A flexible budget identifies fixed costs separately from variable costs. The allowance for variable costs can be flexed to derive a realistic target in the light of the actual activity level achieved.

2.4 Other uses of comparisons with budgets

Businesses obviously need to be **co-ordinated**. For example you cannot increase sales if you do not have the goods available, or increase inventories if you don't have the money to pay for them. Variance reporting is important in alerting management to unplanned changes in one area of the business which may affect another. For example an unplanned decrease in production will affect future sales unless it can be made up.

3 | Calculating variances

Variance reports help budget holders to perform their function of **control**. The reports are especially useful if they separate controllable from non-controllable variances.

Variances are:

*   **Favourable** if the business has more money as a result
*   **Adverse** if the business has less money as a result

Favourable variances are not always good for the organisation. For example failure to recruit necessary staff will result in a favourable variance (less wages). It may, however, mean that business does not reach its production targets.

Reporting variances to the appropriate person draws attention to areas which are not running according to plan.

3.1 Example: Calculation of variances as a percentage

Here is an extract from a monthly cost report for a residential care home.

	Budgeted	Actual	Variance	Variance
	$	$	$	%
Laundry	1,000	1,045	45 (A)	4.5
Heat and light	1,500	1,420	80 (F)	5.3
Catering	8,500	8,895	395 (A)	4.6
Nursing staff	7,000	6,400	600 (F)	8.6
Ancillary staff	10,600	10,950	350 (A)	3.3

$$\text{Variance \%} = \frac{\text{Actual costs} - \text{Budgeted costs}}{\text{Budgeted costs}} \times 100\%$$

The difference between the actual figures and the flexed budget give us variances. The flexed budget enables the total cost variance to be divided into two sub variances called the activity variance and the price/efficiency variance.

4 Sales revenue variance calculations

There are **three types** of **sales revenue variance**. These are the total sales revenue variance, the activity (or volume) variance and the selling price variance.

4.1 Introduction

Total sales revenue variance = activity variance + selling price variance.

Now we will look at the variance calculations using fixed and flexed budgets.

4.2 Total sales revenue variance

The total sales revenue variance measures the combined effect of the following:

- The actual selling price being different to standard selling price
- The actual sales volume being different to budgeted sales volume

The following example will illustrate how the total sales revenue variance is calculated.

4.3 Example

The following budgeted cost and selling price data relate to SM Co's single product.

	$ per unit	$ per unit
Selling price		21.00
Direct cost	12.25	
Overhead cost	1.75	
		14.00
Budgeted profit		7.00

Data for last period were as follows.

Budgeted sales units	740
Actual sales units	795
Actual sales revenue	$16,200

Solution

	$
Sales revenue should have been (740 × $21)	15,540
Sales revenue actually was	16,200
	660 (F)

 QUESTION   Total sales revenue variance

Jasper Co has the following budget and actual figures for 20X4.

	Budget	Actual
Sales units	600	620
Selling price per unit	$30	$29

Budgeted full cost of production = $28 per unit.

Calculate the total sales revenue variance.

ANSWER

	$
Sales revenue should have been (600 × $30)	18,000
Sales revenue actually was (620 × $29)	17,980
Total sales revenue variance	20 (A)

4.4 Activity (or volume) variance

As mentioned in 4.2, the total sales revenue variance measures the combined effect of a difference in selling price and a difference in quantity sold. The activity (or volume) variance looks at the difference in quantity sold.

Remember that when we looked at flexed budgets, it was to take into account that the activity level was different from budgeted. In effect we were removing the variance which arose because of a difference in the quantity sold. This means that a comparison between actual figures and flexed budget figures gives us the price variance only.

4.5 Example

The budgeted sales of SM Co were 740 units at a selling price of $21. The actual sales were 795 units at a total sales revenue of $16,200. What is the activity variance?

Solution

	Units
Budgeted sales volume	740
Actual sales volume	795
Activity variance in units	55 (F)
× Budgeted sales price per unit	× $21
Activity variance	$1,155 (F)

QUESTION   Activity variance

Jasper Co has the following budget and actual figures for 20X4.

	Budget	Actual
Sales units	600	620
Selling price per unit	$30	$29

Calculate the activity (or volume) variance.

ANSWER

	Units
Budgeted sales volume	600
Actual sales volume	620
Activity variance in units	20 (F)
× Budgeted sales price per unit	× $30
Activity variance	$600 (F)

4.6 Selling price variance

The selling price variance is shown in the example below. Note that the total sales revenue variance is the activity variance added to the selling price variance.

4.7 Example

The budgeted sales of SM Co were 740 units at a selling price of $21 per unit. The actual sales were 795 units at a total sales revenue of $16,200.

What was the selling price variance?

Solution

	$
Sales revenue from 795 units should have been (× $21)	16,695
But was	16,200
Selling price variance	495 (A)

The total sales revenue variance calculated in example 4.3 was $660 favourable. The activity (quantity) variance calculated in example 4.5 was $1,155 favourable. The selling price variance calculated in example 4.7 was $495 adverse.

Note that $660 (F) = $1,155 (F) + $495 (A).

QUESTION

Selling price variance

Jasper Co has the following budget and actual figures for 20X4.

	Budget	Actual
Sales units	600	620
Selling price per unit	$30	$29

Calculate the selling price variance.

ANSWER

	$
Sales revenue from 620 units should have been (× $30)	18,600
But was	17,980
Selling price variance	620 (A)

5 Cost variance calculations

There are **three types** of **cost variance**. These are the total direct cost variance, the activity variance and the purchase price/efficiency of usage variance.

5.1 Total direct cost variance

Total direct cost variance = activity variance + purchase price/efficiency of usage variance

The total direct cost variance measures the combined effect of the following:

- The actual quantity produced being different to budgeted production volume
- The actual cost price being different to budgeted cost price
- The actual efficiency in which resources are used being different to budgeted efficiency

5.2 Example

The budgeted materials for CTF Co were 800 units at a cost of $20 each. Actual material costs for the month were $17,600.

Solution

	$
Materials should have cost (800 × $20)	16,000
But did cost	17,600
Total direct cost variance	1,600 (A)

QUESTION

Total cost variance

The budgeted materials for HMF Co were 500 units at a cost of $15 each. Actual material costs for the month were $5,000.

Calculate the total direct cost variance.

ANSWER

	$
Materials should have cost (500 × $15)	7,500
But did cost	5,000
Total direct cost variance	2,500 (F)

5.3 Activity (or volume) variance

The activity (or volume) variance looks at the difference in the quantity produced.

It is worth mentioning again that when we looked at flexed budgets, it was to take into account the fact that the activity level was different from budgeted. In effect we were removing the variance which arose because of a difference in quantity produced. This means that a comparison between actual figures and flexed budget figures gives us the price/efficiency variance only.

5.4 Example

The budgeted materials for CTF were 800 units at a cost of $20 each. Actual materials costs for the month were $17,600 and 820 units were produced.

Solution

	Units
Budgeted production volume	800
Actual production volume	820
Activity variance in units	20 (A)
× Budgeted cost per unit	× $20
Activity variance	$400 (A)

QUESTION

Volume variance

The budgeted materials for HMF Co were 500 units at a cost of $15 each. Actual material costs for the month were $5,000 and 550 units were produced.

Calculate the activity variance.

ANSWER

	Units
Budgeted production volume	500
Actual production volume	550
Activity variance in units	50 (A)
× Budgeted cost per unit	× $15
Activity variance	$750 (A)

5.5 Purchase price/efficiency of usage variance

This variance is shown in the example below. Note that the total cost variance is the activity variance added to the purchase price variance efficiency of usage variance (for direct materials) or the rate of pay/efficiency variance (for direct labour).

5.6 Example: Materials

The budgeted materials for CTF Co were 800 units at a cost of $20 each. Actual materials costs for the month were $17,600 and 820 units were produced. Calculate the price/efficiency variance.

Solution

	$
Production of 820 units should have cost (× $20)	16,400
But did cost	17,600
Price/efficiency variance	1,200 (A)

QUESTION

Purchase price variance

The budgeted materials for HMF Co were 500 units at a cost of $15 each. Actual material costs for the month were $5,000 and 550 units were produced.

Calculate the price/usage variance.

ANSWER

	$
Production of 550 units should have cost (× $15)	8,250
But did cost	5,000
Price/efficiency variance	3,250 (F)

Note that:

Total direct cost variance = Activity variance + purchase price/usage variance.

Using examples 5.2, 5.4 and 5.6, the variances are $1,600 adverse, $400 adverse and $1,200 adverse.

$1,600(A) = $400(A) + $1,200(A)

5.7 Example: Labour

The budgeted labour cost for Blob Co was $10.20 per unit for 20,000 units. Actual labour costs were $10.50 per unit for 22,000 units. Calculate the rate/efficiency variance and the activity variance.

Solution

	$
Production of 22,000 units should have cost (× $10.20)	224,400
But did cost	231,000
Rate/efficiency variance	6,600 (A)

	Units
Budgeted production volume	20,000
Actual production volume	22,000
Activity variance in units	2,000 (A)
× budgeted cost per unit	× $10.20
Activity variance	$20,400 (A)

Note again that:

Total direct cost variance = Activity variance + rate/efficiency variance
= $20,400 (A) + $6,600 (A)
= $27,000 (A)

You can check this by calculating the total direct cost variance as follows:

Should have cost	($10.20 × 20,000 units)	204,000
But did cost	($10.50 × 22,000 units)	231,000
		27,000 (A)

6 The reasons for cost variances

There are a wide range of **reasons** for the occurrence of adverse and favourable cost **variances**.

The following is not an exhaustive list and an exam question might suggest other possible causes. You should review the information provided and select any causes that are consistent with the reported variances.

Variance	Favourable	Adverse
(a) Material price	Unforeseen discounts received More care taken in purchasing	Price increase Careless purchasing
(b) Material usage	Material used of higher quality than standard More effective use made of material Errors in allocating material to jobs	Defective material Excessive waste Theft Stricter quality control Errors in allocating material to jobs
(c) Labour rate	Use of apprentices or other workers at a rate of pay lower than standard	Wage rate increase Use of higher grade labour
(d) Labour efficiency	Output produced more quickly than expected because of work motivation, better quality of equipment or materials, or better methods Errors in allocating time to jobs	Lost time in excess of standard allowed Output lower than standard set because of deliberate restriction, lack of training, or sub-standard material used Errors in allocating time to jobs

7 Exception reporting and investigating variances

Exception reporting highlights variances which might need investigating.

7.1 Exception reporting

Budgets are also used to allocate financial responsibility to individual managers. For example, the training manager will be responsible for expenditure on training. These responsible people are called **budget holders** and will have to decide what action to take if costs are higher or revenues lower than forecast. Reporting to them is sometimes called **responsibility accounting**.

Budget holders need to be informed of any variances that require investigation. They need not be pestered with immaterial variances, but they will need to look at larger variances. They should also investigate variances which are showing a worrying trend. For this reason, many businesses operate a system of **exception reporting**.

Exception reporting is the reporting only of those variances which exceed a certain amount or %.

7.2 Investigating variances

The decision to investigate a variance can also depend on whether it is **controllable** or **non-controllable**.

- **Controllable**: can be rectified by managers
- **Non-controllable:** are due to external factors beyond the managers' control

Budget holders may be required to explain why either type of variance has occurred and should take whatever action is needed. If the variance is controllable, management can take action to rectify problems. If the variance is non-controllable, management may wish to revise their plan. Either way budget holders are not necessarily to **blame** for the variance.

Finally, a variance will only be investigated if the cost of the investigation is to be outweighed by the benefits.

EXAM FOCUS POINT

You may need to be able to distinguish between controllable and non-controllable variances.

7.3 Example: Investigation of variances

A manufacturer of copper pipes has budgeted for expenditure of $25,000 on copper in month 6 but actual expenditure is $28,000. Possible reasons for this $3,000 adverse variance include:

(a) **Price increase** by supplier. This may be controllable. The purchasing officer should try alternative suppliers.

(b) **World price rise** for copper. This is non-controllable. The budget may need revising for the rest of the year.

(c) **Higher factory rejection rate** of finished pipes. This is probably controllable but needs investigation. Is the raw material quality satisfactory? (if not, is this due to supplier, purchasing, warehousing?) Is the factory process at fault? (if so why? Poor supervision? Inadequate training? Machinery wearing out? – find out from the factory supervisors/managers).

You can see that reporting variances puts managers on the alert but only gives clues as to where the real problems lie.

Variances can be **interdependent**.

It is important to understand that variances can be **interdependent**, with a single factor affecting more than one variance. Two examples are given below:

(a) Buying a better quality of material may increase the cost of materials due to its higher price, but usage of the material may be improved as there is less wastage. It could also decrease the labour cost for a given level of production as fewer hours may be needed to process the material if it is easier to work with, or fewer rejects are produced.

(b) Using unskilled labour rather than skilled labour for a particular task may cut the cost of labour in terms of rate of pay, but they may take longer to complete the job which will increase the labour cost again. Unskilled workers may also use more material than skilled labour, causing an adverse material variance.

To summarise, significant variances will be reported to the manager responsible who will then investigate the cause of the variance and act by either correcting an operational problem if the variance is controllable, or adjusting the budget if it is non-controllable and expected to continue. This system is known as **feedback control**.

Sometimes, if a variance is foreseen, the manager might take corrective action in advance of the problem in order to avoid a variance. This is known as **feedforward control**.

QUESTION

Favourable variances

A hospital decides to cut costs by reducing the number of cleaners employed by 10%. This results in a favourable variance in the budget reports. Is it good for the hospital?

Helping hand. Think of any other impacts a drop in a number of cleaners might have.

ANSWER

Helping hand. This illustrates not only the importance of non-financial objectives, but also how failure to meet non-financial objectives may impact upon financial objectives.

This is only good if the necessary standards of cleanliness can be maintained. If they can be, then there were probably too many cleaners before. If standards fall, there will be other effects (like more patient infections) which will cost more in the long term and damage the chief goal of improving health.

QUESTION

Controllable and non-controllable variances

Here is an extract from a sales report for Region 3 in month 4 of the budget year.

		$ actual	$ budgeted
Salesperson	Green	8,500	8,000
	Brown	7,600	8,000

Brown is more junior than Green, and has attended fewer training courses. The more 'difficult' customers are shared between the two salespeople.

Brown's variance for month 4 is:

O   Favourable and controllable
O   Adverse and controllable
O   Favourable and non-controllable
O   Adverse and non-controllable

ANSWER

Adverse and controllable.

Brown's actual sales were $400 less than the budget which is an adverse variance. The information in the question leads us to the conclusion that the variance is controllable as he has been given the same target as the more experienced salesperson. Brown could be sent on more training courses.

QUESTION

Controllable costs

A ward sister in a private hospital has the following changes in ward costs reported as exceptional.

	Actual $	Budget $	Variance $	
Nursing salaries	4,500	4,750	250	Favourable
Drugs and dressings	237	370	133	Favourable

Which of these costs do you think the sister can control?

O   Nursing salaries
O   Drugs
O   Dressings
O   None of the costs

ANSWER

Dressings

Helping hand. The key to this activity is determining who makes the decisions about which costs.

(a) Nursing salaries would probably be centrally controlled by the hospital and therefore not under the control of the sister. Drugs would be determined by a doctor and administered by a nurse. Dressings are probably the only item the ward sister has any control over.

(b) The $300 drugs cost for March looks quite different from the normal pattern of cost. You should look at the ledger account and purchase documents to see if it is correct.

(c) Combining drugs and dressings costs does not seem helpful in a ward report since only one is likely to be a controllable cost for the ward sister.

QUESTION

Performance reports

A company produces the following performance report.

PERFORMANCE REPORT		
PRODUCTION COST CENTRES		
TOTAL COSTS – APRIL 20X1		
	YEAR TO DATE 30.04.X1	
	Actual	**Budget (flexed)**
	$	$
Materials	39,038	35,000
Labour	89,022	85,000
Expenses	18,781	15,000

Which cost variances would be brought to the attention of the production managers responsible, if the company reports by exception any variances that vary by more than 10% from budget?

O Materials only
O Materials and labour
O Expenses only
O Expenses and materials

ANSWER

Expenses and materials

<table>
<tr><td colspan="2">VARIANCE REPORT
PRODUCTION COST CENTRES
APRIL 20X1</td></tr>
<tr><td></td><td>Year to 30 April 20X1
$</td></tr>
<tr><td>Materials</td><td>4,038 (A)</td></tr>
<tr><td>Labour</td><td>4,022 (A)</td></tr>
<tr><td>Expenses</td><td>3,781 (A)</td></tr>
</table>

Comment

The significant variances which are more than 10% from budget are:

- Materials $4,038 (A) = 11.5% $\left(\dfrac{4,038}{35,000}\right)$

- Expenses $3,781 (A) = 25.2% $\left(\dfrac{3,781}{15,000}\right)$

The labour variance is not more than 10% from budget.

- Labour $4,022 (A) = 4.7% $\left(\dfrac{4,022}{85,000}\right)$

CHAPTER ROUNDUP

↳ **Comparing actual results** with **other information** helps to put them in context and may show up errors.

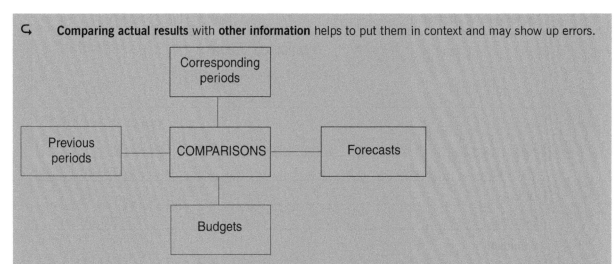

↳ Comparisons may be **financial** or **non-financial**.

↳ Budget comparisons are popular because they show whether budget holders are **achieving** their **targets**.

↳ Budget reports may be **combined** with **other information** such as non-financial information, ratios etc.

↳ Variances can be calculated by comparing the fixed budget with the actual results (total variance) or comparing the flexed budget with the actual results (efficiency of usage and price variance).

↳ You should report differences in such a way that managers can **understand them** and pick out **vital information easily**. Comparisons should not be cluttered with irrelevant information or too much detail.

↳ Flexed budgets should be used for comparison if the actual level of production is different from the original budget.

↳ **Variance reports** help budget holders to perform their function of **control**. The reports are especially useful if they separate controllable from non-controllable variances.

↳ There are **three types** of **sales revenue variance**. These are the total sales revenue variance, the activity (or volume) variance and the selling price variance.

↳ There are **three types** of **cost variance**. These are the total direct cost variance, the activity variance and the purchase price/efficiency of usage variance.

↳ There are a wide range of **reasons** for the occurrence of adverse and favourable cost **variances**.

↳ **Exception reporting** highlights variances which might need investigating.

↳ **Variances** can be **interdependent**.

↳ A **fixed budget** is a budget which is set for a single activity level.

↳ A **flexible budget** is a budget which recognises different cost behaviour patterns and is designed to change as volume of activity changes.

↳ A flexible budget is designed at the planning stage to vary with activity levels. A **flexed** budget is a revised budget that reflects the actual activity levels achieved in the budget period.

1 Which of the following options is a financial comparison?

- O   Number of units produced compared to last year
- O   Number of units sold compared to last year
- O   Profit compared to last month
- O   Customer satisfaction compared to last month

2 A budget is expressed in monetary terms. Is this true or false?

3 When are flexed budgets used?

- O   When the actual level of production is different from the original budget
- O   When the actual level of production is the same as the original budget
- O   Neither of the above

4 List possible non-financial comparisons that could be made by a manufacturing company.

5 A company selling Christmas trees has its sales figures for December. Which sales figures would provide the most meaningful comparison?

6 A difference between planned and actual results which results in the organisation having less money than forecast is called:

- O   A favourable variance
- O   An adverse variance
- O   A loss
- O   A profit

7 Statement 1   An adverse variance is always good for the business.
Statement 2   An adverse variance is always bad for the business.

- O   Both statements are false.
- O   Both statements are true.
- O   Statement 1 is true but statement 2 is false.
- O   Statement 1 is false but statement 2 is true.

8 Which of the following statements about exception reporting is false?

- O   It avoids information overload.
- O   It makes it easier for managers to spot important variances.
- O   It reports variances which exceed a certain amount or %.
- O   All variances highlighted should be investigated.

9 What is the name given when a variance is foreseen and the manager takes corrective action in advance of the problem to avoid a variance?

- O   Feedforward control
- O   Feedback control
- O   Neither of the above

10 Which of the following options describes an activity variance?

- O   The actual efficiency in which resources are used being different to budgeted efficiency
- O   The actual quantity produced being different to budgeted production volume
- O   The actual cost pricing being different to budgeted cost price
- O   The budgeted efficiency in which resources are used being different to actual efficiency

BPP
LEARNING
MEDIA

1   Profit compared to last month. Comparisons made in financial terms (costs and revenues) are financial comparisons. The other options are non-financial comparisons. Sometimes these are more difficult to compare, for example customer satisfaction may be hard to measure.

2   True   A budget is an organisation's plan, expressed in monetary terms.

3   When the actual level of production is different from the original budget. Flexed budgets should be used for comparison if the actual level of production is different from the original budget.

4   Your list may include: customer satisfaction measures, quality reports (eg number of defective units), units produced, units sold, time taken per production run, wastage.

5   December sales from the previous year are likely to provide the most meaningful comparison, since December will be the busiest month in terms of sales for this company.

6   This is an adverse variance.

7   Both statements are false. An adverse variance is not always good or not always bad. Whether it is good or bad depends on the reasons for the variance. For example, recruiting extra staff may result in an adverse labour variance but may mean that increased demand required higher levels of production (and higher revenue).

8   All variances highlighted should be investigated. Not all variances should necessarily be investigated. For example a variance should only be investigated if the cost of the investigation is to be outweighed by the benefits.

9   Feedforward control. Feedback control involves acting after the cause of the variance has been investigated.

10 The actual quantity produced being different to budgeted production volume. The activity (or volume) variance looks at the difference in the quantity produced.

Now try ...

Attempt the questions below from the **Practice Question Bank**

Number

Q20

Q21

Q22

Q23

Q24

06

This chapter looks at the **different ways** of communicating and presenting information. We also discuss when you should not communicate information – when you should keep it confidential.

Reporting management information

Study Guide	Intellectual level
A **Management information**	
5 **Reporting management information**	
(a) Identify suitable formats for the presentation of management information according to purpose	S
(b) Describe methods of analysing, presenting and communicating information	K
(c) Identify suitable formats for communicating management information according to purpose and organisational guidelines including: informal business reports, letter and email or memo	S
(d) Identify the general principles of distributing reports (eg procedures, timing, recipients) including the reporting of confidential information	K
(e) Interpret information presented in management reports	S

1 Deciding who needs what

Management information should be **relevant to** and **understood** by the individual who receives it.

Management information should be **relevant** to the organisation and the individual.

The person receiving management information should be able to **understand** it. Understandability can be helped by:

- Avoiding unexplained technical terms
- Cutting out unnecessary detail
- Using charts, diagrams, tables and good report layouts
- Asking the users' views on required information and presentation

In many organisations standard reports are issued regularly. The information system may produce the reports directly. Alternatively the reports may need special preparation. They will tell the managers responsible for various activities how they are performing. They may be used as a basis for extra rewards such as bonuses, promotions etc.

Ideally the reports should distinguish between **controllable** and **non-controllable** factors. This is not always easy in practice however.

Managers may also need **ad hoc** reports to help them with particular problems. For example they may want more detail than is given by the regular reports on a particular aspect of the business. If you have to provide this type of information you must understand **exactly what is required**, including the **format** required for presenting it.

2 Types of communication

Types of communication include:

- Letters
- Memos
- Emails
- Formal reports

It is important to choose the right one for a given purpose.

Most information is likely to be presented to managers in the form of a **report,** often as a Word document attached to an email, or sometimes within the email itself. In small organisations it is possible, however, that management information will be communicated less formally (orally or using informal reports/memos). We consider the different options for presenting management information below.

Choosing the right method of communication is important. Many organisations have standard sets of regular reports in prescribed formats. For example, BPP has a template for Powerpoint presentations to ensure consistency. Many organisations also have a standard **house style** for other documents, that is, a particular way of setting things out. The aim of this is to:

- Make it easier for employees to read, locate and produce information
- Present a consistent image to people outside the organisation

For example, BPP has a template for general communication emails that are sent to all employees. The heading is orange and says 'People update' and it begins with a short list of the topics to be covered in the email. There is then a heading for each topic and the information is contained under each heading.

Charts, graphs and tables can also be used to communicate management information. These will often be produced in Excel.

Different situations suit different methods of communication. Some relevant considerations are outlined in the following table.

Choosing a communication method	
Factor	**Considerations**
Time	How long will be needed to prepare the message, and how long will it take to transmit it in the chosen form? This must be weighed against the urgency with which the message must be sent.
Complexity	The method used for relaying a complex piece of information must be chosen carefully. A written document (eg email) may make it easier for the reader to take their time over digesting the information. On the other hand, a conversation would allow for instant clarification where necessary.
Distance	How far is the message required to travel? Must it be transmitted to an office on a different floor of the building, or across town, or to the other end of the country?
Written record	A written record may be needed as proof, confirming a transaction, or for legal purposes, or as an aid to memory. It can be sent to many recipients. It can be stored and later retrieved for reference and analysis as required.
Feedback/ interaction	How quickly is the feedback required? If an instant response is needed then a conversation may be appropriate. How many responses are required? If there are many responses needed then talking to each individual may take too long. One possible option is to send an email with voting options so that individuals can respond and a general consensus can be achieved.

Choosing a communication method	
Factor	**Considerations**
Confidentiality	Telephone calls may be overheard; emails can be read by whoever is near the recipient's computer screen; highly personal letters may be read by the recipient's secretary. On the other hand, a message may need to be spread widely and quickly to all staff: the notice-board, or a public announcement or the company newsletter/email may be more appropriate.
Recipient	It may be necessary to be reserved and tactful, warm and friendly, or impersonal, depending upon the desired effect on the recipient. If you are trying to impress them, a high quality document may be needed.
Cost	Cost must be considered in relation to all of the above factors. The aim is to achieve the best possible result at the least possible expense.

2.1 Letters

Many businesses no longer write letters, preferring emails instead, but some organisations, such as banks, still use letters to communicate with their customers. Most letters are automated rather than being hand written but they should be polite, accurate, clear, logical and concise. Spelling and punctuation should, of course, be impeccable! Also, if your company has a house style, your letter should conform to that.

QUESTION

Letters

If you begin a letter 'Dear Sir', you should sign the letter:

O   Yours sincerely
O   Yours faithfully
O   Yours truly
O   Yours gratefully

ANSWER

'Yours faithfully' is the formal ending if the recipient's name is not used. Option one would be used if the recipients name had been referred to, eg 'Dear Mr Jackson'. Options three and four are not generally used in business letters.

2.2 Memos

The **memorandum** or **memo** performs internally the same function as a letter does in communication externally. It can be used for any kind of communication that is best conveyed in writing such as reports, brief messages or notes.

Memos need less detail than a formal letter. Emails are more likely to be used in modern businesses.

QUESTION

Memorandums

A memorandum is:

O   Signed by the person sending it
O   Generally used for the communication of short messages between different organisations
O   Not used if important information is to be communicated
O   For any written communication within an organisation

ANSWER

For any written communication within an organisation. A memo can be used for internal communication of information that is presented in writing, so the second and third options are incorrect. The first option is incorrect as it does not have to be signed.

2.3 Emails

The main method of communication for management information is email. It is possible for emails to be used for documents to be signed electronically, or else for documents to be scanned, signed and then sent as email attachments.

2.3.1 Advantages of email

Email has the following **advantages**:

(a)   **Speed** (transmission, being electronic, is almost instantaneous). Email is far faster than post. It is a particular time-saver when communicating with people overseas.

(b)   **Economy** (no need for stamps etc).

(c)   **Efficiency** (a message is prepared once but can be sent to thousands of employees at the touch of a button).

(d)   **Security** (access can be restricted by the use of passwords).

(e)   Documents can be attached from **word-processing** and other packages.

(f)   Electronic **delivery and read receipts** can be requested.

2.3.2 Dangers of email

Email has the following dangers:

*   **Confidentiality** – passwords must be safeguarded
*   Used to **replace** other communications that may be more appropriate (eg conversation)
*   Too much going to **people who don't need it** as it is so easy to send to many recipients

2.4 Reports

Standard reports are a regular part of the management information system.

Ad hoc reports deal with a one-off issue or problem.

A formal **report** may be needed where a comprehensive investigation has taken place.

ELEMENTS OF A FORMAL REPORT	
Title	Subject of report
Terms of reference	Clarify what has been requested
Introduction	Who the report is from and to
	How the information was obtained
Main body	Divided into sections with sub-headings to aid reader
	Logical order
Conclusions	Summarises findings
Recommendations	Based on information and evidence
	May be combined with conclusion
Signature	Of writer
Executive summary	Saves time for managers receiving a long report
	No more than one page

Reports are often produced in Word and templates can be used to ensure consistency and ease of use. One example of a short formal report is shown below.

2.5 Example: Short formal report

REPORT ON PROPOSED UPDATING OF COMPANY POLICY MANUAL

To: Board of Directors, BCD Co
From: J Thurber, Opus Management Consultants
Status: Confidential
Date: 3 October 20X8

I   INTRODUCTION AND TERMS OF REFERENCE

This report details the results of an investigation commissioned by the Board on 7 September 20X8. We were asked to consider the current applicability of the company's policy manual and to propose changes needed to bring it into line with current practice.

II   METHOD

The following investigatory procedures were adopted:

1   Interview all senior staff regarding use of the policy manual in their departments
2   Observe working practices in each department

III   FINDINGS

The manual was last updated ten years ago. From our observations, the following amendments are now needed:

1   The policy section on computer use should be amended. It deals with safe storage of disks, which is no longer applicable as data is now stored on a server. Also, it does not set out the company's email policy.

2   The company's equal opportunities policy needs to be included.

3   The coding list in the manual is now very out of date. A number of new cost centres and profit centres have been set up in the last ten years and the codes for these are not noted in the manual.

4   There is no mention of the provisions of the Data Protection Act as they relate to the company.

IV CONCLUSIONS

We discovered upon interviewing staff that very little use is made of the policy manual. When it has been amended as above, it can be brought back into use, and we recommend that this should be done as soon as possible.

Signed J Thurber, Opus Management Consultants

2.6 Tables, charts and graphs

If you are preparing a report (or perhaps preparing slides for a presentation), you may need to use **visual aids** of some kind. Diagrams are useful in **conveying large amounts of data** more accessibly and in adding interest and appeal to a document. Tables, charts and graphs can be produced in Excel.

In addition to the numerical competences required to organise your data, there are some **key principles** of effective 'graphic' communication.

- Give each diagram or chart a concise and **meaningful title**.
- Cite the **source of the data**, where relevant.
- Clearly **label all elements of the diagram**, either on the diagram itself, or in a separate 'key' to the colours or symbols used.
- Keep **textual elements** (labels, explanatory notes) **brief**.
- Keep the presentation as **simple as possible**: cut down on unnecessary lines and elements, to avoid overcrowding, clutter and confusion.
- Make the **diagram large enough** so that it is easy to read.

Let's look briefly at some examples of visual elements you might use in an informal report.

2.6.1 Tables

Tables are a good way of **organising information**. The use of columns and rows allows the data to be classified under appropriate headings, clearly organised and labelled, totalled up in various ways (across rows or down columns) and so on.

You might use a table format to organise data about a list of trainees, say, as follows.

Staff member	Training undertaken	Training provider	Duration of training (days)	Cost of training
John				
Amy				
Fred				
			Total:	

2.6.2 Column and bar charts

Column and bar charts are useful for **showing** or **comparing magnitudes** or **sizes of items**. For example, sales revenue or expenditure on a month-by-month basis, or training costs per department.

- The diagram needs to be **labelled** to indicate what it shows.
- The **positions** of **the bars are labelled** to show what they represent (eg months or departments).
- The height/length of the bars, drawn against a specified scale, **indicate the magnitudes** of the different items (monetary value or number).
- The **bars can be subdivided** to show components of the total magnitudes (eg breakdown of monthly expenditure by department or category).

The main difference between column and bar charts is that bar charts present the information in a **horizontal bar** and **column charts** present the **information vertically** (like a column). The example below is a column chart.

BPP LEARNING MEDIA

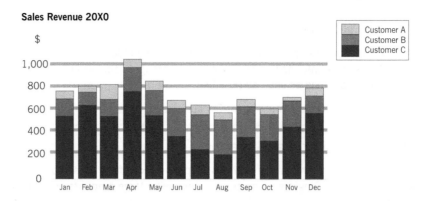

Sales Revenue 20X0

2.6.3 Pie charts

Pie charts are useful for showing the **relative sizes** of component elements of a total value or amount, represented by the 360° of the circle or 'pie'. An example might be showing the breakdown of the time you spend on different tasks during a day, or the breakdown of monthly sales revenue by product or customer. The slices of the pie have been calculated as:

Emails: 12.5% × 360 degrees =   45 degrees

Ledger tasks: 37.5% × 360 degrees =   135 degrees

Payroll tasks: 50% × 360 degrees =   180 degrees

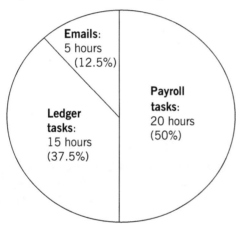

2.6.4 Line graphs

Line graphs are useful for **showing the relationship between two variables** (represented by the horizontal and vertical axes of the graph), by plotting points and joining them up with straight or curved lines. These are particularly useful for **demonstrating trends**, such as the increase in departmental output as more time/money is invested in training and development – or fluctuations in revenue or expenditure (or other values) over time.

Here's a very simple example.

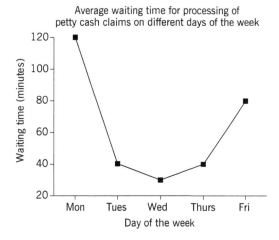

Such a graph could be used to highlight variations in work throughput.

2.6.5 Scatter diagrams

Scatter diagrams **take information**, often presented in a table, and use it to **plot points on a chart**. The chart has two axis, just like a line graph, but the points are not joined up. If enough points are plotted it will be possible to draw deductions about the relationship between the two series of data. For example, the following data is available regarding a factory.

The output at a factory each week for the last ten weeks, and the cost of that output, were as follows.

Week	1	2	3	4	5	6	7	8	9	10
Output (units)	10	12	10	8	9	11	7	12	9	14
Cost ($)	42	44	38	34	38	43	30	47	37	50

The data could be shown on a scatter diagram as follows.

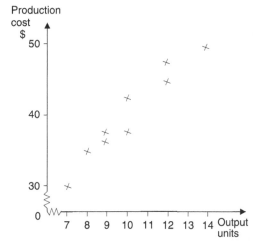

The cost depends on the volume of output. Volume is the independent variable and is shown on the x axis. You will notice from the graph that the plotted data, although scattered, lie approximately on a **rising trend line**, with higher total costs at higher output volumes. (The lower part of the axes have been omitted, so as not to waste space. The break in the axes is indicated by the jagged lines.)

BPP
LEARNING
MEDIA

QUESTION

Communication methods

In each of the cases below, select the form of communication which will generally be the most appropriate.

1   A complaint to a supplier about the quality of goods supplied.

    O   Letter
    O   Memo
    O   Formal report
    O   Email

2   A query to a supervisor about the coding of an invoice.

    O   Email
    O   Memo
    O   Face-to-face
    O   All of the above are equally suitable if available

3   An investigation into the purchasing costs of your company.

    O   Letter
    O   Memo
    O   Formal report
    O   Email

4   Notification to customers of a change of the company's telephone number.

    O   Letter
    O   Memo
    O   Email
    O   All of the above are equally suitable if available

5   Reply to an email.

    O   Letter
    O   Memo
    O   Email
    O   Face-to-face

6   Query to the sales department about an expenses claim.

    O   Memo
    O   Email
    O   Telephone
    O   All of the above are equally suitable if available

ANSWER

1   Letter or Email
2   All of the above are equally suitable if available
3   Formal report
4   Letter or Email
5   Email
6   All of the above are equally suitable if available

3 Confidentiality

Some information will be **confidential**, maybe because of the Data Protection Act or because of company policy. Access to it will be restricted.

Keeping some information confidential is an important **legal requirement**. It may also be part of your organisation's **policy**.

Some requirements are pure common sense. For example most of us would expect details of our wages, salaries, health etc to be kept confidential. Others are less obvious. For example some information about your organisation may be valuable to competitors. This is known as **commercially sensitive information**.

The **Data Protection Act 2018** aims to protect the rights of **individuals** in relation to information organisations hold about them.

3.1 Why is privacy an important issue?

In recent years, there has been a growing popular fear that **information** about individuals which was stored on computer files and processed by computer could be **misused**. In the UK the current legislation is the **Data Protection Act 2018** (TSO, 2018).

Privacy is the right of a person to be free of unwanted intrusion by others into their lives or activities.

3.2 The Data Protection Act 2018

The Data Protection Act 2018 (incorporating the General Data Protection Regulation (GDPR)) is an attempt to protect the **personal data** of an **individual**.

3.2.1 Definitions of terms used in the Act

(a) **Personal data** is any information that, either on its own or when combined with other data available to the business, can identify a specific individual, eg name, email address.

(b) **Data controller** is the person or entity that determines the purpose and manner in which personal data is processed.

(c) **Data processor** refers to any person or entity (other than an employee of a data controller) who processes personal data on behalf of the data controller.

(d) **Data processing** covers a wide range of activities including obtaining, recording or holding personal data or carrying out any operation on the personal data, such as organising, amending, disclosing, using, transmitting or otherwise making the personal data available.

(e) **Data subjects** are individuals on whom personal data is held.

BPP LEARNING MEDIA

3.2.2 The principles

(a) **Lawfulness, fairness and transparency of processing.** An organisation or business must only process personal data in accordance with a contract or applicable law, or with the consent of the individual.

(b) **Purpose limitation.** An organisation or business must only process personal data in accordance with the purposes for which it was collected. Data can't be collected for one reason and then used for an alternative purpose.

(c) **Data minimisation.** Only the minimum amount of data should be collected. No additional data should be collected.

(d) **Accuracy.** The organisation or business must ensure that the data it processes is both accurate and up-to-date.

(e) **Storage limitation.** Data must not be stored for longer than is necessary for the purpose it was collected.

(f) **Integrity and confidentiality.** Data must be processed in a way that ensures the security of that data from unlawful processing, disclosure or loss.

3.3 Internal requirements

Within an organisation, the policy manual will often lay down other confidentiality rules. For example some organisations forbid employees to talk to the press without authorisation, or to publish their research results. You can imagine that businesses planning large redundancies or the launch of a new product will not want the information to become public prematurely.

Paper files with **restricted access** should be:

- Listed
- Stored securely
- Only accessible by specific people

Computer systems often use **passwords** to restrict access to information that is held on computer. You should never divulge your password to an unauthorised person or keep it in view on your desk. Think of your password as needing as much secrecy as your bank PIN number.

Use of the **internet** can pose particular problems in maintaining confidentiality. Many companies have a policy on the purposes for which the Internet should and should not be used.

If you have access to restricted information in any form, you are responsible for protecting it to comply with company policy and the law. You should lock confidential papers away when you are not using them. You should not leave them lying around on your desk (or in the photocopier!).

You should also **not provide confidential information** to **others** outside your department without checking with a supervisor.

QUESTION
Confidential information

Your company's planning department asks for a copy of the monthly research cost reports for the last six months. Your computer password does not give you access to this information. What should you do?

O   Refer the query to your supervisor
O   Ask someone what the password is that will access the information
O   Ask for your password to be changed so that it will access the information
O   Try and find a hard copy of the information

ANSWER

Refer the query to your supervisor. Access to this information is restricted. The other options are therefore not appropriate.

CHAPTER ROUNDUP

- Management information should be **relevant to** and **understood** by the individual who receives it.

- **Types of communication** include:
  - Letters
  - Memos
  - Emails
  - Formal reports

  It is important to choose the right one for a given purpose.

- **Standard reports** are a regular part of the management information system.

- **Ad hoc reports** deal with a one-off issue or problem.

- Some information will be **confidential**, maybe because of the Data Protection Act or because of company policy. Access to it will be restricted.

- The **Data Protection Act 2018** aims to protect the rights of **individuals** in relation to information organisations hold about them.

QUICK QUIZ

1 Which of the following options would NOT help management information to be understood?

   O Avoiding unexplained technical terms
   O Using charts, diagrams and tables
   O Asking the users' view on required information and presentation
   O Lots of detail

2 Which of the following is NOT an aim of house style for documents?

   O To make it easier to read the documents
   O To make it easier to locate information
   O To control costs
   O To present a consistent image to people outside the organisation

3 Information about an organisation which may be valuable to competitors is known as which of the following?

   O Cost sensitive information
   O Commercially sensitive information
   O Commercially secure information
   O Cost secure information

4 Data users are individuals on whom personal data is held. Is this true or false?

5 List five considerations when choosing a communication method.

6 Which of the following is a possible disadvantage/danger of email?

   O Economy
   O Speed
   O Delivery and read receipts
   O Large volumes of information

7 What would be the most appropriate method of communication in each of the following circumstances?

   (a) Explaining to a customer that a cash discount that has been deducted was not valid, as the invoice was not paid within the discount period

   (b) Requesting customer balances from a colleague in the sales ledger department

   (c) Arranging your holiday period with the HR manager

   (d) A complaint to a supplier regarding the delivery times of goods, which are not as agreed

   (e) Information to be provided to the sales director regarding the breakdown of sales geographically for the last two years

BPP
LEARNING
MEDIA

ANSWERS TO QUICK QUIZ

1   Lots of detail. Cutting out unnecessary detail can greatly benefit understandability.

2   To control costs. Controlling costs is not one of the aims of house style.

3   This is known as commercially sensitive information.

4   False   Data subjects are individuals on whom personal data is held. Data users are organisations or individuals which use personal data.

5   Answers could include: time, complexity, distance, written record, feedback/interaction, confidentiality, recipient, and cost.

6   Large volumes of information. The danger with email is that too much information will go to people who don't need it because it is so easy to send to many recipients.

7   (a)   Telephone, followed-up in writing if required

    (b)   Note or email

    (c)   Email to request dates, perhaps followed-up by face-to-face discussion or phone call if negotiation is required

    (d)   Letter or email

    (e)   Email or possibly a more formal report

Now try ...

Attempt the questions below from the **Practice Question Bank**

Number

Q25

Q26

Q27

Q28

Q29

part

B

Cost recording

Materials

In many organisations, particularly manufacturing businesses, materials are a significant part of the total costs of operations. In a manufacturing company, most materials can be classified as **raw materials** and **bought-in components**, as **work in progress** (part-finished production) or as **finished goods** (completed items of production not yet sold).

This chapter explains the **procedures** and **documentation** that are used for purchasing and using materials, and the way that materials are accounted for within a cost accounting system. Materials costs, including wastage, need to be controlled. There must also be a method for giving a value to materials held in inventory at the end of an accounting period. This chapter goes into some detail about the system for **costing materials** and **controlling materials costs**.

TOPIC LIST	SYLLABUS REFERENCE
1 Types of material	B1 (a)
2 Buying materials	A2 (c), B1 (b), (e)
3 Valuing materials issues and inventories	B1 (c)
4 Inventory control	B1 (f), (g)
5 Inventory control levels	B1 (h), (i)
6 Computers and inventory control	B1 (j)

Study Guide	Intellectual level
A **Management information**	
2 **Cost accounting systems**	
(c) Identify the documentation required, and the flow of documentation, for different cost accounting transactions	S
B **Cost recording**	
1 **Accounting for materials**	
(a) Describe the main types of material classification	K
(b) Describe the procedures and documentation required to ensure the correct authorisation, coding, analysis and recording of direct and indirect material costs	K
(c) Explain, illustrate and evaluate the FIFO, LIFO and periodic and cumulative weighted average methods used to price materials issued from inventory	S
(e) Calculate material input requirements, and control measures, where wastage occurs	S
(f) Describe the procedures required to monitor inventory and to minimise discrepancies and losses	K
(g) Explain and illustrate the costs of holding inventory and of being without inventory	S
(h) Explain, illustrate and evaluate inventory control levels (minimum, maximum, re-order)	S
(i) Calculate and interpret optimal order quantities	S
(j) Explain the relationship between the materials costing system and the inventory control system	K

1 Types of material

> Materials can be **classified** according to the substances that make them up, how they are measured, or their physical properties.

1.1 Classifying materials

There are a number of different ways in which materials can be classified. The three main ways of classifying materials are as follows:

- They can be classified according to the **substances that make them up**.
- They can be classified according to **how they are measured**.
- They can be classified according to their **physical properties**.

Materials may be made of one or more substances. For example, when classifying materials according to the substances that make them up, they may be classified as either **wood, plastic, metal, wool** and so on. Many items may be made up of a **combination of substances**.

You may also classify materials according to how they are measured. Accounting text books could make it easy for you to believe that all materials come by the **litre, metre** or **kilogram**. In practice however, you will find that materials really come in **bags, packets** or **by the thousand**.

Finally, materials may also be classified by one or more of their physical properties. The same basic piece of material may be distinguished by one or more of the following features:

- Colour
- Shape
- Fire resistance
- Water resistance
- Abrasiveness
- Flexibility
- Quality

1.2 Raw materials

Raw materials are goods purchased for incorporation into products for sale. Raw materials are a direct cost.

Raw materials is a term which you are likely to come across often, both in your studies and your workplace. But what are raw materials?

Examples of raw materials are as follows:

- Clay for making terracotta garden pots
- Timber for making dining room tables
- Paper for making books

Raw materials are a direct cost of production as they are easily identifiable with a unit of production.

QUESTION   Raw materials

Without getting too technical, what are the main raw materials used in the manufacture of the following items?

(a) A car
(b) A box of breakfast cereal
(c) A house (just the basic structure)
(d) Your own organisation's products

ANSWER

(a) Metal, rubber, plastic, glass, fabric, oil, paint, glue.

(b) Cereals, plastic, cardboard, glue. You might have included sugar and preservatives and so on, depending upon what you eat for breakfast.

(c) Sand, gravel, cement, bricks, plaster, wood, metal, plastic, glass, slate.

(d) You will have to mark your own answer. If you work for a service organisation like a firm of accountants, you could view the paper of sets of accounts sent out to clients as raw materials, although in practice such materials are likely to be regarded as indirect costs.

1.3 Work in progress

Work in progress is a term used to represent an intermediate stage between the manufacturer purchasing the materials that go to make up the finished product and the finished product.

Work in progress is another term which you are likely to come across often, and valuing work in progress is one of the most difficult tasks in costing.

Work in progress means that some work has been done on the materials purchased as part of the process of producing the finished product, but **the production process is not complete**. Examples of work in progress are as follows:

(a)   Terracotta pots which have been shaped, but which have not been fired, and are therefore unfinished.

(b)   Dining room tables which have been assembled, but have not been polished, and are therefore not ready for sale.

(c)   Paper which has been used to print books, but which has not yet been bound. The books are therefore not yet assembled, and not yet ready for sale.

1.4 Finished goods

A **finished good** is a product ready for sale or despatch.

Did you notice how all of the examples of work in progress were items which were not ready for sale? It therefore follows that examples of finished goods are as follows.

*   Terracotta pots ready for sale or despatch
*   Dining room tables ready for sale or despatch
*   Books ready for sale or despatch

The examples in the previous paragraph show terracotta pots which have now been fired, dining room tables which have now been polished, and books which have now been bound. These final processes have transformed our **work in progress** into **finished goods**.

1.5 Direct and indirect materials costs

Materials are either a direct or indirect cost, depending upon how easily they can be traced to a specific unit of production.

*   **Direct materials** are materials that are **easily identifiable** with a specific unit of production, such as raw materials.

*   **Indirect materials** are materials that are **not easily identifiable** with a specific unit of production.

In general, indirect materials do not form part of the final product, but do make the manufacture of that product possible. There are some exceptions to this, for example, nails used in the production of a cupboard can be identified specifically with the cupboard and form part of the final product. However, because the cost is likely to be relatively insignificant, the expense of tracing such costs does not justify the possible benefits from calculating more accurate direct costs.

Indirect materials are often referred to as 'consumables' and include such things as cleaning products, oil and grease for machines, protective clothing, disposable tools and stationary supplies. Indirect material costs are an **overhead** cost.

QUESTION

Materials

(a)   Distinguish between raw materials, work in progress and finished goods.
(b)   Give three examples of indirect materials costs.

ANSWER

(a)   Raw materials are goods purchased for incorporation into products for sale, but not yet issued to production. Work in progress is the name given to the materials while they are in the course of being converted to the final product. Finished goods are the end products when they are ready to be sold.

(b)   Some examples of indirect materials costs are as follows:

    (i)   Oil for machine maintenance

    (ii)   Cleaning fluids and substances

    (iii)   Rags, dusters and the like

    (iv)   Glue if used in small quantities

    (v)   Secondary packaging, for example the sort of boxes you can pick up at the check-out in supermarkets

2 | Buying materials

Procedures and documentation are required for material purchases.

2.1 Purchasing procedures

All businesses have to buy materials of some sort, and this means that decisions have to be made and somebody has to be responsible for doing the **buying**.

Large businesses have specialist buying departments managed by people who are very skilled at the job. One of the reasons for the success of certain large companies is that they are expert at buying good quality goods at the best prices.

In spite of this, the essence of a buying transaction is simple and, in fact, familiar because you buy things every day and (mainly subconsciously) go through the following process.

- You need something.
- You find out where you can buy it.
- You identify the most suitable item (take into account cost, quality, and so on).
- You order the item, or perhaps several if you will need more in the future.
- You receive the item.
- You pay for the item.

In a business this process will be more involved, but only because those spending the money are likely to be different from those looking after the goods and those using them, and because none of those people will actually own the money spent. The following diagram illustrates who will be involved.

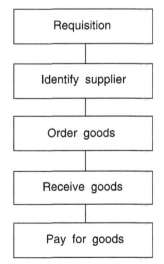

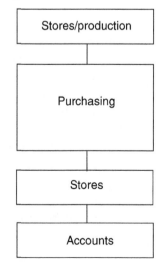

2.2 Purchasing documentation

Clearly there needs to be some means by which different departments can let each other know what they want and what is being done about it, and even the smallest business will need to keep records of some sort. We shall describe a manual system that might be used in a fairly large organisation. In reality it is likely that much of the procedure would be computerised, but this does not alter the basic principles or information flows.

2.2.1 Purchase requisition form

The first stage will be that the department requiring the goods will complete a **purchase requisition form** asking the **purchasing department** to carry out the necessary transaction. An example is shown below. Note that the purchase requisition will usually need some form of **authorisation**, probably that of a senior person in the department requiring the goods and possibly also that of a senior person in the finance department if substantial expense is involved.

	PURCHASE REQUISITION	Req. No.	
Department Suggested supplier:		Date Requested by: Latest date required:	
Quantity	Description	Estimated Cost	
		Unit	$
Authorised signature:			

2.2.2 Order form

Often the business will use a regular source of supply. The purchasing department may, however, be aware of special offers or have details of new suppliers: part of its job is to keep up to date with what is on the market. Thus once a **purchase requisition** is received in the purchasing department, the first task is to identify the most suitable **supplier**.

Often the requisitioning department will specify the goods they require but the buying department may have a choice (for example in deciding what quality paper will be ordered for stationery). Whatever the decision made, an **order form** is then completed by the purchasing department (again, it may have to be authorised by the finance department to ensure that budgets are not being over-stepped) and this is sent to the supplier. The order form, an example of which is shown below, will contain the following details:

(a)   The **name** and **address** of the ordering organisation
(b)   The **date** of order, and reference numbers for both ordering department and supplier
(c)   The **address** and **date**(s) for delivery (by road, rail, air and so on) or collection
(d)   **Details of goods/services**: quantity, code (if any), specification, unit costs and so on

An order form should be sent even if goods are initially ordered by telephone, to confirm that the order is a legitimate one and to make sure that the supplier does not overlook it.

Purchase Order/Confirmation		Fenchurch Garden Centre Pickle Lane Westbridge Kent			
Our Order Ref:		Date			
To					
⌐(Address)	⌐	Please deliver to the above address			
		Ordered by:			
		Passed and checked by:			
L	⌐	Total Order Value $			

Quantity	Code	Description/Specification		$	p
			Subtotal		
			Sales tax (@ 20%)		
			Total		

The **purchase order** is important because it provides a means by which the business can later check that the goods received are the same as those ordered. Copies can be sent to the person who requisitioned the goods so that he knows they are on their way and also to the stores so that they can arrange to accommodate the goods. Either now or later a copy can be sent to the accounts department so that they can see that goods invoiced were genuinely required and that the purchase was properly authorised.

2.2.3 Despatch note

Certain other documents may arise before the goods are actually received. The supplier may acknowledge the order and perhaps indicate how long it is likely to take to be fulfilled. A **despatch note** may be sent to warn that the goods are on their way.

2.2.4 Delivery note

We now move to the stores department. When the goods are delivered, goods inwards will be presented with a **delivery note** or **advice note** (although bear in mind that smaller suppliers may not go to these lengths). This is the supplier's document (a copy is signed by the person receiving the goods and returned to the supplier) and, as such, there is no guarantee that its details are correct. If the actual goods cannot be inspected immediately, the delivery note should be signed 'subject to inspection'.

BPP
LEARNING
MEDIA

2.2.5 Goods received note

Once the goods have been delivered they should be inspected as soon as possible. A **goods received note (GRN)** will be completed by goods inwards on the basis of a physical check, which involves counting the items received and seeing that they are not damaged.

ACCOUNTS COPY

GOODS RECEIVED NOTE WAREHOUSE COPY

DATE: __*7 March 20X5*__   TIME: ___*2.00 pm*____   NO 5565

ORDER NO: _____.

SUPPLIER'S ADVICE NOTE NO: _____ WAREHOUSE A

QUANTITY	CAT NO	DESCRIPTION
20	*TP 400*	*Terracotta pots, medium*

RECEIVED IN GOOD CONDITION: *L. W.*   (INITIALS)

A copy of the GRN can be sent to the purchasing department so that it can be matched with the purchase order. This is to make sure that the correct number and specification of items have been received. Any discrepancies would be taken up with the supplier.

A copy of the GRN would also be sent to the accounts department so that it can be matched with the **purchase invoice** when it is received. The payment of the invoice is the end of the transaction (unless there is a mistake on the invoice or there was some problem with the delivery, in which case a **credit note** may later be received from the supplier).

2.3 Buying and costing

Clearly the buying department needs to retain cost information for the purpose of identifying suitable suppliers. This is likely to be in the form of catalogues and price lists.

The costing department is chiefly interested in the actual cost of materials as shown on the **invoice** and included in the accounting records as cash and credit transactions.

2.3.1 Example: Buying and costing

It is Amy Alexander's first day in the costing department and she has been told to calculate the materials cost of job 1234 which has just been completed. No invoice has yet been received for the main material used, which is known as LW32. Amy uses her initiative and pops down to the purchasing department to see if they can help. They are rather busy but someone hands her a very well-thumbed catalogue and a thick file of purchase orders, all relating to the supplier of LW32. There are many orders for LW32, one of which has today's date. How should Amy go about costing the LW32 used for job 1234?

Solution

The quickest thing to do would be to phone up the supplier and ask what price will be charged for the order in question, but there might be good reasons for not doing this (for example not wishing to prompt an earlier invoice than usual!) It seems likely that, in the absence of the actual information, the best way of ascertaining a price for LW32 is to consult the catalogue (assuming it is up to date) and to find the most recent purchase order that **has** been invoiced. If there is a discrepancy, previous invoices could be looked at to see if they show a price rise since the date of the catalogue. If the price fluctuates widely it might be better to calculate an average.

As Amy gets to know her way around the system she will learn which are the most reliable sources of information. Possibly some suppliers make frequent errors on invoices but quote correct unit prices on delivery notes. The moral is to always be on your guard for errors.

QUESTION
Materials purchase

Draw a flow diagram illustrating the main documents involved in a materials purchase, from its initiation up until the time of delivery.

ANSWER

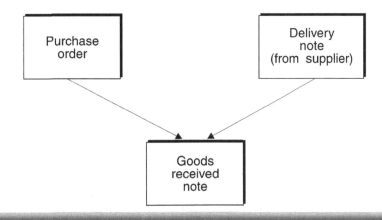

2.4 Material input requirements

Some organisations might need to buy 'extra' materials because wastage may occur as a matter of course in some production processes.

2.4.1 Example: Material input requirements

1 kg of Product A is manufactured from 1 kg of Material X in a process where wastage is equivalent to 3% of material input.

How many kg of Material X are needed in order to produce 100 kg of Product A?

100 kg of Material X will only produce 97 kg of Product A (and there will be 3 kg of Material X wasted).

100 kg of Material X = $(100 - 0.03) \times 100$ kg Product A
$= 0.97 \times 100$ kg of Product A
$= 97$ kg Product A

Therefore, in order to produce 100 kg of Product A, the company needs to buy 103.09 kg of Material X.

$$\frac{100 \text{ kg Material X}}{0.97} = 103.09 \text{ kg Material X}$$

	Kg
Material X input	103.09
Wastage (3% × 103.09 kg)	(3.09)
Product A output	100.00

QUESTION

Wastage

If JH Co produces 1 unit of Product L from 2 kg of Material W, and wastage equates to 5% of material input, how many kg of Material W should JH Co buy in order to produce 4,000 units of Product L? State your answer to the nearest kg.

ANSWER

4,000 units of Product L are produced from $\dfrac{8,000 \text{ kg*}}{0.95\text{**}}$ = 8,421 kg Material W

* Each unit of Product L is made from 2 kg of Material W

**(100% − 5% wastage)

Summary

	Kg
Material W input	8,421
5% wastage (5% × 8,421 kg)	(421)
Material W processed	8,000

If 8,000 kg of Material W are processed, they will produce 4,000 units of Product L (8,000 kg ÷ 2 kg = 4,000 units).

It is important, therefore, that any wastage is taken into account when calculating material input requirements and hence quantities of materials to be purchased.

2.5 Wastage and wastage control measures

When wastage levels are high they are an avoidable expense.

In the previous example, wastage of materials in production was an expected part of the production process. In some production systems, some wastage cannot be avoided.

On the other hand, wastage is an expense, and when wastage levels are unnecessarily high, they are an avoidable expense, reducing profit below what it should be. So what may be the causes of avoidable wastage? The most common causes of avoidable wastage are probably:

- Inefficiency, carelessness or other mistakes by workers, resulting in rejected items or wasteful usage of materials

- Badly maintained machinery or other equipment, causing unnecessary waste

- Poor quality of materials

- Failure to identify mistakes at an early stage in production and put them right before the wastage becomes excessive

- Holding materials in poor storage conditions, so that wastage occurs due to damage or deterioration

Improved materials usage might be achieved by **reducing levels of wastage**, where wastage is currently high.

2.5.1 Wastage control measures

Wastage can be measured in a number of ways. Typical measures include:

- **Input wastage.** Quantity of materials wasted as a percentage of the quantity of material used.
- **Output wastage.** Number of quality rejects as a percentage of total output.
- **Rework.** Rework costs as a percentage of production costs.

QUESTION

Reducing wastage

How can wastage be reduced?

ANSWER

Here are some suggestions.

(a)   Changing the specifications for cutting solid materials.

(b)   Introducing new equipment that reduces wastage in processing or handling materials.

(c)   Identifying poor quality output at an earlier stage in the operational processes.

(d)   Using better quality materials. Even though more expensive, better quality materials might save costs because they are less likely to tear or might last longer.

(e)   Better training and supervision of workers, to reduce the frequency of mistakes and inefficiencies in materials handling.

(f)   Where possible, re-working rejected items of output.

3   Valuing materials issues and inventories

Materials issued from inventory can be valued using FIFO, LIFO and weighted average methods.

3.1 Just-in-time inventory policy

The implicit assumption in the Amy Alexander example above was that materials were bought specifically for individual jobs and therefore that each order could be identified with a particular job. This is possible in practice. Certainly, keeping large quantities of inventory is something to be avoided in the modern business environment. Holding inventory means that you have to have somewhere to put it and so it takes up space that could be used for other purposes. Often it means employing somebody to look after it, perhaps 24 hours a day if it is very valuable.

Ideally, you should receive an order for so many items of the product in question, buy exactly the right quantity of materials to make that many items and be left with no inventories of finished goods, work in progress or raw materials. This is known as the **just-in-time (JIT) approach**, that is, the just-in-time purchasing of inventories to meet just-in-time production of goods ordered. From the point of view of costing, there is very little difficulty with the JIT approach. The materials costs of each production run are known because the materials used were bought specially for that run. There was no inventory to start with and there is none left over.

3.2 Buffer inventory

However the approach more common in practice is to keep a certain amount of inventory in reserve to cope with fluctuations in demand and with suppliers who cannot be relied upon to deliver the right quality and quantity of materials at the right time. This reserve of inventory is known as **buffer inventory** (or safety inventory). Buffer inventory may also be held when it is more economical to purchase inventory in greater quantities than required (in order to obtain bulk purchase discounts). The **valuation of buffer inventory** is one of the most important elements of your studies at this level.

3.3 Inventory valuation

3.3.1 The inventory valuation problem

Suppose, for example, that you have 50 litres of a chemical in inventory. You buy 2,000 litres to allow for the next batch of production. Both the opening inventory and the newly-purchased inventory cost $2 per litre.

	Litres	$
Opening inventory	50	100
Purchases	2,000	4,000
	2,050	4,100

You actually use 1,600 litres, leaving you with 450 litres. You know that each of the 1,600 litres used cost $2, as did each of the 450 litres remaining. There is no costing problem here.

Now suppose that in the following month you decide to buy 1,300 litres, but have to pay $2.10 per litre because you lose a 10c discount if buying under 1,500 litres.

	Litres	Cost per litre $	Total cost $
Opening inventory	450	2.00	900
Purchases	1,300	2.10	2,730
	1,750		3,630

For the next batch of production you use 1,600 litres, as before. What did the 1,600 litres used cost, and what value should you give to the 150 litres remaining in inventory?

We need to know the cost of the litres that we have used so that we know how much to charge for the final product and so that we can compare this cost with the equivalent cost in earlier or future periods. We also need to know the cost of closing inventory both because it will form part of the usage figure in the next period and for financial accounting purposes. Closing inventory is often a significant figure in the financial statements and it appears in both the statement of profit or loss (income statement) and the statement of financial position.

We therefore have to use a **consistent method** of pricing the litres which provides a reasonable approximation of the costs of the inventory.

3.3.2 Inventory valuation methods

There are a number of different methods of valuing inventory.

(a) **FIFO – First in, first out**

This method values issues at the prices of the oldest items in inventory at the time the issues were made. The remaining inventory will thus be valued at the price of the most recent purchases. Say, for example, ABC Co's inventory consisted of four deliveries of raw material in the last month:

	Units		
1 September	1,000	at	$2.00
8 September	500	at	$2.50
15 September	500	at	$3.00
22 September	1,000	at	$3.50

If on 23 September 1,500 units were issued to production, 1,000 of these units would be priced at $2 (the cost of the 1,000 oldest units in inventory), and 500 at $2.50 (the cost of the next oldest 500). 1,000 units of closing inventory would be valued at $3.50 (the cost of the 1,000 most recent units received) and 500 units at $3.00 (the cost of the next most recent 500).

(b) **LIFO – Last in, first out**

This method is the opposite of FIFO. Issues will be valued at the prices of the most recent purchases; hence inventory remaining will be valued at the cost of the oldest items. In the example above it will be 1,000 units of issues which will be valued at $3.50, and the other 500 units issued will be valued at $3.00. 1,000 units of closing inventory will be valued at $2.00, and 500 at $2.50.

(c) **Weighted average pricing methods**

There are two main weighted average pricing methods: **cumulative** and **periodic**.

(i) **Cumulative weighted average pricing**

With this method we calculate an **average cost** of all the litres in inventory whenever a new delivery is received.

(ii) **Periodic weighted average pricing**

The periodic weighted average pricing method involves calculating a new inventory value at the end of a given period (rather than whenever new inventory is purchased, as with the cumulative weighted average pricing method). The periodic weighted average pricing method is easier to calculate than the cumulative weighted average method, and therefore requires less effort, but it must be applied retrospectively since the costs of materials used cannot be calculated until the end of the period.

(d) **Standard cost**

Under the standard costing method, all issues are at a predetermined standard price. You will study standard costing in more detail if you go on to study for the FMA Management Accounting exam.

3.3.3 Example: FIFO, LIFO and weighted average pricing methods

The following transactions should be considered in order to demonstrate FIFO, LIFO and weighted average pricing methods.

TRANSACTIONS DURING MAY 20X3

	Quantity Units	Unit cost $	Total cost $	Market value per unit on date of transaction $
Opening balance, 1 May	100	2.00	200	
Receipts, 3 May	400	2.10	840	2.11
Issues, 4 May	200			2.11
Receipts, 9 May	300	2.12	636	2.15
Issues, 11 May	400			2.20
Receipts, 18 May	100	2.40	240	2.35
Issues, 20 May	100			2.35
Closing balance, 31 May	200			2.38
			1,916	

(a) **FIFO**

FIFO assumes that materials are issued out of inventory in the order in which they were delivered into inventory: issues are priced at the cost of the earliest delivery remaining in inventory.

Using FIFO, the cost of issues and the closing inventory value in the example would be as follows.

Date of issue	Quantity issued	Value		
	Units		$	$
4 May	200	100 o/s at $2	200	
		100 at $2.10	210	
				410
11 May	400	300 at $2.10	630	
		100 at $2.12	212	
				842
20 May	100	100 at $2.12		212
Cost of issues				1,464
Closing inventory value	200	100 at $2.12	212	
		100 at $2.40	240	
				452
				1,916 *

* The cost of materials issued plus the value of closing inventory equals the cost of purchases plus the value of opening inventory ($1,916).

The market price of purchased materials is rising dramatically. In a period of inflation, there is a tendency with FIFO for materials to be issued at a cost lower than the current market value, although closing inventories tend to be valued at a cost approximating to current market value.

(b)   **LIFO**

LIFO assumes that materials are issued out of inventory in the reverse order to which they were delivered: the most recent deliveries are issued before earlier ones, and are priced accordingly.

Using LIFO, the cost of issues and the closing inventory value in the example above would be as follows.

Date of issue	Quantity issued	Valuation		
	Units		$	$
4 May	200	200 at $2.10		420
11 May	400	300 at $2.12	636	
		100 at $2.10	210	
				846
20 May	100	100 at $2.40		240
Cost of issues				1,506
Closing inventory value	200	100 at $2.10	210	
		100 at $2.00	200	
				410
				1,916

Notes

1   The cost of materials issued plus the value of closing inventory equals the cost of purchases plus the value of opening inventory ($1,916).

2   In a period of inflation there is a tendency with LIFO for the following to occur.

- Materials are issued at a price which approximates to current market value.
- Closing inventories become undervalued when compared to market value.

(c)   **Cumulative weighted average pricing**

The cumulative weighted average pricing method calculates a **weighted average price** for all units in inventory. Issues are priced at this average cost, and the balance of inventory remaining would have the same unit valuation. The average price is determined by dividing the total cost by the total number of units.

A new weighted average price is calculated whenever a new delivery of materials into store is received. This is the key feature of cumulative weighted average pricing.

In our example, issue costs and closing inventory values would be as follows:

Date	Received Units	Issued Units	Balance Units	Total inventory value $	Unit cost $	$
Opening inventory			100	200	2.00	
3 May	400			840	2.10	
			* 500	1,040	2.08	
4 May		200		(416)	2.08	416
			300	624	2.08	
9 May	300			636	2.12	
			* 600	1,260	2.10	
11 May		400		(840)	2.10	840
			200	420	2.10	
18 May	100			240	2.40	
			* 300	660	2.20	
20 May		100		(220)	2.20	220
						1,476
Closing inventory value			200	440	2.20	440
						1,916

*A new inventory value per unit is calculated whenever a new receipt of materials occurs.

Notes

1   The cost of materials issued plus the value of closing inventory equals the cost of purchases plus the value of opening inventory ($1,916).

2   In a period of inflation, using the cumulative weighted average pricing system, the value of material issues will rise gradually, but will tend to lag a little behind the current market value at the date of issue. Closing inventory values will also be a little below current market value.

(d)   **Periodic weighted average pricing**

Under the periodic weighted average pricing method, a retrospective average price is calculated for **all** materials issued during the period. The average issue price is calculated for our example as follows.

$$\frac{\text{Cost of all receipts in the period} + \text{Cost of opening inventory}}{\text{Number of units received in the period} + \text{Number of units of opening inventory}}$$

$$= \frac{\$1,716 + \$200}{800 + 100}$$

Issue price = $2.129 per unit

Closing inventory values are a balancing figure.

The issue costs and closing inventory values are calculated as follows:

Date of issue	Quantity issued Units	Valuation $
4 May	200 × $2.129	426
11 May	400 × $2.129	852
20 May	100 × $2.129	213
Cost of issues		1,491
Value of opening inventory plus purchases		1,916
Value of 200 units of closing inventory (at $2.129)		425

EXAM FOCUS POINT

Getting to grips with these inventory valuation methods is a very important part of your studies at this stage.

3.3.4 Which method is correct?

This is a trick question, because there is no one correct method. Each method has **advantages** and **disadvantages**.

The advantages and disadvantages of the **FIFO** method are as follows:

(a) **Advantages**

  (i) It is a logical pricing method which probably represents what is physically happening, in practice the oldest inventory is likely to be used first.

  (ii) It is easy to understand and explain to managers.

  (iii) The closing inventory value can be near to a valuation based on the cost of replacing the inventory.

(b) **Disadvantages**

  (i) FIFO can be cumbersome to operate because of the need to identify each batch of material separately.

  (ii) Managers may find it difficult to compare costs and make decisions when they are charged with varying prices for the same materials.

The advantages and disadvantages of the **LIFO** method are as follows:

(a) **Advantages**

  (i) Inventories are issued at a price which is close to current market value. This is not the case with FIFO when there is a high rate of inflation.

  (ii) Managers are continually aware of recent costs when making decisions, because the costs being charged to their department or products will be current costs.

(b) **Disadvantages**

  (i) The method can be cumbersome to operate because it sometimes results in several batches being only part-used in the inventory records before another batch is received.

  (ii) LIFO is often the opposite of what is physically happening and can therefore be difficult to explain to managers.

  (iii) As with FIFO, decision making can be difficult because of the variations in prices.

The advantages and disadvantages of weighted **average pricing** are as follows:

(a) **Advantages**

  (i) Fluctuations in prices are smoothed out, making it easier to use the data for decision making.

  (ii) It is easier to administer than FIFO and LIFO, because there is no need to identify each batch separately.

(b) **Disadvantages**

  (i) The resulting issue price is rarely an actual price that has been paid, and can run to several decimal places.

  (ii) Prices tend to lag a little behind current market values when there is gradual inflation.

4 Inventory control

Inventory control is the regulation of inventory levels, which includes putting a value to the amounts of inventory issued and remaining. Inventory control also includes ordering, purchasing, receiving and storing goods.

The cost of materials are usually one of the largest costs faced by an organisation and, once obtained, inventory has to be carefully controlled and checked.

4.1 Locating inventory

You can probably picture a warehouse – a large room with rows and rows of high shelving, perhaps moveable ladders and maybe barrows or fork-lift trucks. Very modern 'highbay' warehouses have automatic guided vehicles (AGVs), stacker cranes and conveyors, all controlled by computer. All of this implies organisation; when they are brought into the warehouse inventories are not simply dumped in the nearest available space. There is a place for everything and everything is in its place. There is no point in keeping inventory at all if you don't know where to find it when it is needed.

Suppose, for example, that a warehouse were arranged as shown below, A to F representing rows of shelving and 1 to 7 the access bays between them. Suppose the shelves were 4 m high, 10 m long and 1 m wide and you needed to locate five 10 mm washers in stainless steel. (To put it another way, suppose you had a haystack and you were looking for a needle!) How would you go about organising the warehouse so that you could always find what you were looking for?

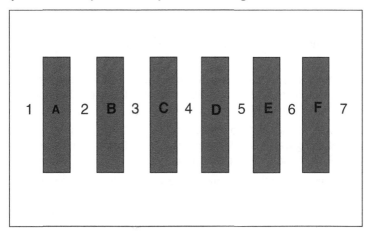

The solution is fairly obvious. You need to divide up the shelf-racks and give each section a code. A typical warehouse might organise its shelving as shown below.

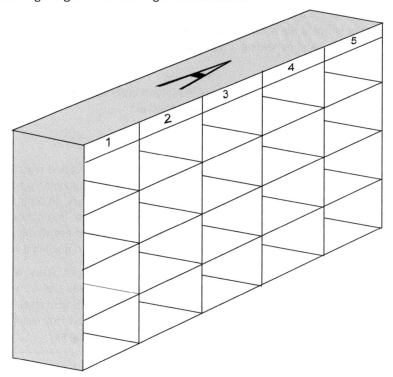

If you are reminded of a library, this is intentional: it is helpful to think of a warehouse as a library of materials.

You also need to keep a record which shows the whereabouts in the warehouse of all the different types of inventory, including the 10 mm washers in stainless steel. Suppose that the washers are listed as being kept in location A234.

The reference A234 would take you to Row A, bay 2, bin 3, shelf 4. Shelf 4 might contain a series of drawers containing washers of various sizes, each drawer being labelled with a precise part number (A234/1279, say) and a description of the item.

The term **bin** as it is used above may be new to you, but you need to get used to it meaning something other than the receptacle by your desk full of screwed up paper and apple cores! **Bin** simply means a receptacle. In warehouse terms it normally means a division of shelving (or simply one shelf) or some other container which can be located by a code letter or number. The term is in general usage but it does not have a precise meaning.

In the light of this you should understand what a **bin card** is. **In a manual inventory control system the bin card is kept with the actual inventory and is updated whenever items are removed or added** to provide an accurate record of the quantity in inventory for each stores item.

BIN CARD

Description ....   Bin No: ....
....   Code No: ....
Reorder Quantity ....   Maximum: ....
    Minimum: ....
    Re-order Level: ....

Receipts			Issues			Balance	Remarks
Date	G.R.N. No.	Quantity	Date	Req. No.	Quantity	Quantity	

Note that the bin card does not need to show any information about the cost of materials.

Organisations will also maintain what are known as **stores ledger accounts**, an example of an account being shown below.

STORES LEDGER ACCOUNT											

Material: .... Maximum Quantity: ....

Code: .... Minimum Quantity: ....

Date	Receipts				Issues				Inventory		
	G.R.N. No.	Quantity	Unit Price $	Amount $	Materials Req. No.	Quantity	Unit Price $	Amount $	Quantity	Unit Price $	Amount $

Details from GRNs and materials requisition notes (see later) are used to update stores ledger accounts, which then provide a record of the quantity and value of each line of inventory in the stores. The stores ledger accounts are normally kept in the cost department or in the stores office whereas the bin cards are written up and actually kept in the stores. There are two advantages to this procedure.

(a)   The accounting records can be maintained more accurately and in a better condition by a cost clerk or an experienced stores clerk than by a stores assistant.

(b)   A control check is provided. The balances on the bin cards in the stores can be compared with the balances on the stores ledger accounts.

The use of bin cards and stores ledger accounts ensures that every issue and receipt of inventory is recorded as it occurs so that there is a continuous clerical record of the balance of each item of inventory. This is known as a **perpetual inventory system**.

You may be thinking that the system we have described is rather over-complicated. Why not, for example, start at one end of the room and end at the other numbering each separate location in sequence and numbering each inventory item accordingly? The reasons are for practicality and flexibility. If item 1 is a 10 mm washer and item 2 is an exhaust pipe they are hardly going to fit into the same size drawer. If item 1 is a 10 mm washer and item 2 is a 15 mm washer, what happens when a new product needs 12 mm washers? If item 1 is used twice a year and item 10,001 is used every day the storekeeper will be collapsing with exhaustion by the end of the day if item 1 is the one nearest the issue point. If item 1 is a large heavy item and item 10,001 is also a large heavy item the storeman will be driving the fork-lift from one end of the warehouse to the other all day. It is therefore far better to have large heavy items in close proximity and to have frequently used items near to the issue point.

The last point is worth developing a little. Storekeeping involves a good deal of common sense and a considerable knowledge of the types of inventory held, and an effective storekeeping system should take the following points into account:

(a)   Heavy items should not be stored on high shelves (in case the shelves collapse and to make handling as safe and unstrenuous as possible).

(b)   Dangerous items (for example items with sharp edges) should not be stored above eye level.

(c)   Items liable to be damaged by flood (for example paper inventory) should not be stored on low shelves.

BPP
LEARNING
MEDIA

(d)   Special arrangements should be made for the storage and handling of chemicals and flammable materials.

(e)   Some inventories are sensitive to temperature or light and should be stored accordingly.

(f)   Other inventories may have special hygiene or 'clean air' requirements.

4.2 Coding of materials

Each item held in stores must be unambiguously identified and this can best be done by numbering them with inventory codes. The advantages of this are as follows:

(a)   **Ambiguity is avoided**. Different people may use different descriptions for materials. This is avoided if numbers are used.

(b)   **Time is saved**. Descriptions can be lengthy and time-consuming, particularly when completing written forms.

(c)   **Production efficiency is improved**. If the correct material can be accurately identified from a code number, production hold-ups caused by the issue of incorrect material can be avoided.

(d)   **Computerised processing** is made easier.

(e)   Numbered code systems can be designed to be **flexible**, and can be **expanded** to include more inventory items as necessary.

The digits in a code can stand for the type of inventory, supplier, location and so forth. For example inventory item A234/1279 might refer to the item of inventory kept in row A, bay 2, bin 3, shelf 4. The item might be identified by the digits 12 and its supplier might be identified by the digits 79.

4.3 Issuing materials

The sole point of holding inventories is so that they can be used to make products. This means that they have to be issued from stores to production. This transaction will be initiated by production who will complete a **materials requisition note** and pass it to the warehouse.

MATERIALS REQUISITION						
Material Required for: (Job or Overhead Account) Department:				No. Date:		
Quantity	Description	Code No.	Weight	Rate	$	Notes
Foreman:						

The stores department will locate the inventory, withdraw the amount required and update the bin card as appropriate. The stores ledger account will also be updated.

If the amount of materials required is overestimated the excess should be put back into store accompanied by a **materials returned note**. The form in our illustration is almost identical to a requisition note. In practice it would be wise to colour code the two documents (one white, one yellow, say) to prevent confusion.

MATERIALS RETURNED NOTE						
Material not needed for: (Job or Overhead Account) Department:					No. Date:	
Quantity	Description	Code No.	Weight	Rate $	$	Notes
Foreman:						

There may be occasions when materials already issued but not required for one job can be used for another job in progress. In this case there is no point in returning the materials to the warehouse. Instead a **materials transfer note** can be raised. This prevents one job being charged with too many materials and another with too little.

You will note that all of the forms shown above have spaces for cost information (that is, monetary values). This will be inserted either by the stores department or in costing, depending upon how the system is organised. We have already described the various bases which may be used to put a value on inventory – FIFO, LIFO or an average figure.

4.4 Stocktaking

Stocktaking involves counting the physical inventory on hand at a certain date and then checking this against the balance shown in the clerical records. There are two methods of carrying out this process.

- **Periodic stocktaking.** This is usually carried out annually and the objective is to count all items of inventory on a specific date.

- **Continuous stocktaking.** This involves counting and checking a number of inventory items on a regular basis so that each item is checked at least once a year, and valuable items can be checked more frequently. This has a number of advantages over periodic stocktaking. It is less disruptive, less prone to error, and achieves greater control.

4.5 Inventory discrepancies

There will be occasions when inventory checks disclose **discrepancies between the physical amount of an item in inventory and the amount shown in the inventory records**. When this occurs, the cause of the discrepancy should be investigated, and appropriate action taken to ensure that it does not happen again. Possible causes of discrepancies are as follows.

(a) Suppliers deliver a different quantity of goods than is shown on the goods received note. Since this note is used to update inventory records, a discrepancy will arise. This can be avoided by ensuring that all inventory is counted as it is received, and a responsible person should sign the document to verify the quantity.

(b) The quantity of inventory issued to production is different from that shown on the materials requisition note. Careful counting of all issues will prevent this.

(c) Excess inventory is returned from production without documentation. This can be avoided by ensuring that all movements of inventory are accurately documented – in this case, a materials returned note should be raised.

(d)   Clerical errors may occur in the inventory records. Regular checks by independent staff should detect and correct mistakes.

(e)   Inventory items may be wasted because, for example, they get broken. All wastage should be noted on the inventory records immediately so that physical inventory equals the inventory balance on records. (The cost of the wastage is then written off to the statement of profit or loss.)

(f)   Employees may steal inventory. Regular checks or continuous stocktaking will help to prevent this, and only authorised personnel should be allowed into the stores.

If the inventory discrepancy is found to be caused by clerical error, then the records should be rectified immediately. If the discrepancy occurs because units of inventory appear to be missing, the lost inventory must be written off. If actual inventory is greater than recorded inventory, extra units of inventory are added to the inventory records. The accounting transaction will be recorded by a stores credit note, where items of inventory have been lost, or a **stores debit note**, when there is more actual inventory than recorded.

A **stores credit note** may have the following format.

STORES CREDIT NOTE			
Quantity	Item code	Description	$

Continuous stocktaking report number...
Credit note authorised by...
Date...

4.6 Inventory costs

Inventory costs include **purchase costs**, **ordering costs**, **holding costs** and costs of **running out of inventory**. The purchase cost is the cost of the inventory itself.

4.6.1 Ordering costs

Ordering costs are the costs incurred when inventories are ordered. They include the following.

(a)   **Clerical and administrative costs** associated with purchasing, accounting for and receiving goods
(b)   **Transport costs**
(c)   **Production run costs**, if an organisation manufactures its own components

The more orders are placed, the higher the total ordering costs will be. So if a business chooses to place frequent orders for small amounts of inventory, the ordering costs will be higher than if it made less frequent orders for larger amounts of inventory. However, if larger amounts of inventories are ordered, the business will incur higher **holding costs** as the inventories will have to be stored until they are used.

4.6.2 Holding costs

Holding costs are the costs of storing inventories until they are used. Holding costs include the following.

(a)   **Costs of storage and stores operations**. Holding inventories requires storage space and staff and equipment to control and handle them while they are being stored. The larger the level of inventories, the higher the costs associated with storing and managing them will be.

(b)   **Interest charges**. Holding inventories involves the tying up of capital (cash) on which interest must be paid.

(c)   **Insurance costs**. The larger the value of inventories held, the greater insurance premiums are likely to be.

(d) **Obsolescence**. When materials or components become out-of-date and are no longer required, existing inventories must be thrown away and their cost must be written off to the statement or profit or loss (income statement).

(e) **Deterioration**. When materials in store deteriorate to the extent that they are unusable, they must be thrown away (with the likelihood that disposal costs would be incurred) and again, the value written off inventory plus the disposal costs will be a charge to the statement of profit or loss (income statement).

4.6.3 Stockout costs (costs of running out of inventory)

If too much inventory is held, holding costs will be incurred unnecessarily. But if too little inventory is held, the business may run out of inventory and incur stockout costs.

Stockout costs include:

- Lost contribution from lost sales
- Loss of future sales due to disgruntled customers
- Loss of customer goodwill as the product they require is not available
- Cost of production stoppages
- Labour inefficiency costs due to frustration over stoppages
- Extra ordering costs for urgent, small quantity orders

A business has to decide the **optimum amount of inventory** to hold so that the overall cost of inventory (purchase, ordering, holding and stockout costs) is minimised.

4.6.4 Other reasons for holding inventories

Businesses hold inventories to ensure sufficient goods are available to meet expected production requirements. Other reasons for holding inventories are as follows:

- To provide a buffer between processes
- To meet any future shortages
- To take advantage of bulk purchasing discounts
- To absorb seasonal fluctuations and any variations in usage and demand
- To allow production processes to flow smoothly and efficiently
- As a necessary part of the production process (such as when maturing cheese)
- As a deliberate investment policy, especially in times of inflation or possible shortages

5 | Inventory control levels

Inventory control levels can be calculated in order to maintain inventories at the **optimum level**. The three critical control levels are re-order level, minimum level and maximum level.

Based on an analysis of past inventory usage and delivery times, inventory control levels can be calculated and used to maintain inventory at their optimum level (in other words, a level which minimises costs). These levels will determine 'when to order' and 'how many to order'.

5.1 Re-order level

When inventories reach the re-order level, an order should be placed to replenish inventories. The re-order level is determined by considering:

- The maximum rate of consumption • The maximum lead time

The maximum lead time is the time between placing an order with a supplier, and the inventory becoming available for use.

FORMULA TO LEARN

Re-order level = maximum usage × maximum lead time

5.2 Minimum level

The minimum level is a warning level to draw management attention to the fact that inventories are approaching a dangerously low level and that stockouts are possible.

FORMULA TO LEARN

Minimum level = re-order level − (average usage × average lead time)

5.3 Maximum level

The maximum level also acts as a warning level to signal to management that inventories are reaching a potentially wasteful level.

FORMULA TO LEARN

Maximum level = re-order level + re-order quantity − (minimum usage × minimum lead time)

QUESTION
Maximum inventory level

A large retailer with multiple outlets maintains a central warehouse from which the outlets are supplied. The following information is available for Part Number SF525.

Average usage	350 per day
Minimum usage	180 per day
Maximum usage	420 per day
Lead time for replenishment	11–15 days
Re-order quantity	6,500 units
Re-order level	6,300 units

(a) Based on the data above, what is the maximum level of inventory?

    O 5,250   O 6,500   O 10,820   O 12,800

(b) Based on the data above, what is the approximate number of Part Number SF525 carried as buffer inventory?

    O 200   O 720   O 1,680   O 1,750

ANSWER

(a) 10,820

Maximum inventory level = re-order level + re-order quantity − (min usage × min lead time)
= 6,300 + 6,500 − (180 × 11)
= 10,820

You should have eliminated 5,250 immediately because the maximum inventory level cannot be less than the re-order quantity.

(b) 1,750

Buffer inventory = minimum level

Minimum level = re-order level − (average usage × average lead time)
= 6,300 − (350 × 13) = 1,750.

200 could again be easily eliminated. With minimum usage of 180 per day, a buffer inventory of only 200 would not be much of a buffer!

5.4 Re-order quantity

This is the quantity of inventory which is to be ordered when inventory reaches the re-order level. If it is set so as to minimise the total costs associated with holding and ordering inventory, then it is known as the economic order quantity.

5.5 Average inventory

The formula for the average inventory level assumes that inventory levels fluctuate evenly between the minimum (or safety) inventory level and the highest possible inventory level (the amount of inventory immediately after an order is received, ie safety inventory + re-order quantity).

FORMULA TO LEARN

Average inventory = safety inventory + ½ re-order quantity

QUESTION   Average inventory

A component has a safety inventory of 500, a re-order quantity of 3,000 and a rate of demand which varies between 200 and 700 per week. What is the approximate average inventory?

O 2,000   O 2,300   O 2,500   O 3,500

ANSWER

The correct answer is: 2,000

Average inventory   = safety inventory + ½ re-order quantity
                      = 500 + (0.5 × 3,000)
                      = 2,000

5.6 Economic order quantity (EOQ)

The **economic order quantity (EOQ)** is the order quantity which minimises inventory costs. The EOQ can be calculated using a table, graph or formula.

Economic order theory assumes that the average inventory held is equal to one half of the re-order quantity (although, if an organisation maintains some sort of buffer or safety inventory then average inventory = buffer inventory + half of the re-order quantity). We have seen that there are certain costs associated with holding inventory. These costs tend to increase with the level of inventories, and so could be reduced by ordering smaller amounts from suppliers each time.

On the other hand, as we have seen, there are costs associated with ordering from suppliers: documentation, telephone calls, payment of invoices, receiving goods into stores and so on. These costs tend to increase if small orders are placed, because a larger number of orders would then be needed for a given annual demand.

5.6.1 Example: Economic order quantity

Suppose a company purchases raw material at a cost of $16 per unit. The annual demand for the raw material is 25,000 units. The holding cost per unit is $6.40 and the cost of placing an order is $32.

We can tabulate the annual relevant costs for various order quantities as follows.

Order quantity (units)	Note	100	200	300	400	500	600	800	1,000
Average inventory (units)	1	50	100	150	200	250	300	400	500
Number of orders	2	250	125	83	63	50	42	31	25
		$	$	$	$	$	$	$	$
Annual holding cost	3	320	640	960	1,280	1,600	1,920	2,560	3,200
Annual order cost	4	8,000	4,000	2,656	2,016	1,600	1,344	992	800
Total relevant cost		8,320	4,640	3,616	3,296	3,200	3,264	3,552	4,000

Notes

1   Average inventory = Order quantity ÷ 2 (ie assuming no safety inventory)
2   Number of orders = annual demand ÷ order quantity
3   Annual holding cost = Average inventory × $6.40
4   Annual order cost = Number of orders × $32

You will see that the economic order quantity is 500 units. At this point the total annual relevant costs are at a minimum.

5.6.2 Example: Economic order quantity graph

We can present the information in the table above in graphical form. The vertical axis represents the relevant annual costs for the investment in inventories, and the horizontal axis can be used to represent either the various order quantities or the average inventory levels; two scales are actually shown on the horizontal axis so that both items can be incorporated. The graph shows that, as the average inventory level and order quantity increase, the holding cost increases. On the other hand, the ordering costs decline as inventory levels and order quantities increase. The total cost line represents the sum of both the holding and the ordering costs.

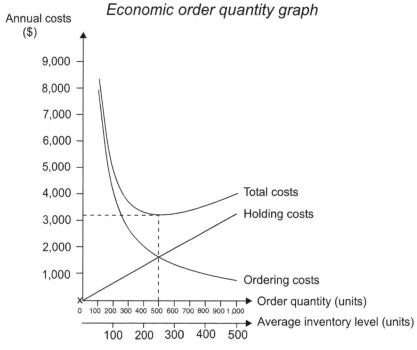

Economic order quantity graph

Note that the total cost line is at a minimum for an order quantity of 500 units and occurs at the point where the ordering cost curve and holding cost curve intersect. **The EOQ is therefore found at the point where holding costs equal ordering costs.**

5.6.3 EOQ formula

The EOQ formula is as follows.

FORMULA TO LEARN

$$\text{EOQ} = \sqrt{\frac{2C_o D}{C_H}}$$

where
C_H = cost of holding one unit of inventory for one time period
C_O = cost of ordering a consignment from a supplier
D = demand during the time period

QUESTION   EOQ

Use the formula to calculate the EOQ in the example in Paragraph 5.6.1 above.

ANSWER

$$\text{EOQ} = \sqrt{\frac{2 \times \$32 \times 25{,}000}{\$6.40}}$$

$$= \sqrt{250{,}000}$$

$$= 500 \text{ units}$$

QUESTION   EOQ and holding costs

A manufacturing company uses 25,000 components at an even rate during a year. Each order placed with the supplier of the components is for 2,000 components, which is the economic order quantity. The company holds a buffer inventory of 500 components. The annual cost of holding one component in inventory is $2.

What is the total annual cost of holding inventory of the component?

O $2,000   O $2,500   O $3,000   O $4,000

ANSWER

The correct answer is $3,000.

[Buffer inventory + (EOQ/2)] × Annual holding cost per component

= [500 + (2,000/2)] × $2

= $3,000

6 Computers and inventory control

Although the basic principles of inventory control are not difficult in themselves, you will appreciate by now that an effective system requires a good deal of administrative effort, even if only a few items of inventory are involved. There is therefore a good deal to be gained from computerisation of this function.

6.1 Computerised inventory files

A typical computerised **inventory** file would contain a record for each item, each record having fields (individual pieces of data) as follows:

(a) **Inventory code:** a unique inventory code to identify each item. This could be in bar code form for large organisations.

(b) **Description:** a brief description is helpful when perusing inventory records and probably essential when printing out lists of inventory for stocktaking purposes. Ideally the system will generate purchase orders which also require brief narrative details.

(c) **Supplier code:** this would match the code for the supplier in the purchase ledger.

(d) **Supplier's reference number:** again this information would be needed for purchase orders.

(e) **Quantity per unit:** this would specify how many individual items there were per 'unit'. This is sometimes called the 'factor'.

(f) **Cost price per item.**

(g) **Control levels:** there would be a field for each of the four control levels (minimum and maximum inventory, re-order level and re-order quantity).

(h) **Location:** a location code could be included if it were not part of the inventory code itself.

(i) **Movements history:** there could be fields for issues per day, per week, during the last month, in the last year and so on.

(j) **Job code:** there might be a field allowing costs to be linked to specific jobs. Inventories could be 'reserved' for jobs due to be started in the next week, say.

6.2 Inventory reports

A system with fields such as those above might be able to generate the following reports:

(a) **Daily listing:** a daily list of all items ordered, received, issued or placed on reserve. This might have 'exception reports' for unusual movements of inventory and for items that had reached the re-order level.

(b) **Inventory lists:** lists could be produced for stocktaking purposes, with inventory codes, descriptions and locations. This could be restricted to certain types of inventory, such as high value items or inventories with high turnover.

(c) **Inventory movements:** a report of inventory movements over time would help in setting control levels and in identifying 'slow-moving inventory' that is not really required.

(d) **Inventory valuations:** this would show current balances and place a value on inventories according to which calculation method (FIFO, LIFO, and so on) was in use.

(e) **Supplier analysis:** this would list all the items of inventory purchased from the same supplier, and might be useful for placing orders (several items could be ordered at the same time, cutting delivery costs).

6.3 Bill of materials

Many computerised inventory control systems have a **bill of materials facility**. This allows assembly records (sometimes called explosion records) to be compiled, containing details of the various assemblies that make up the final product. A CD player, for example may have three main assemblies – the motor mechanism, the electronics and the outer casing.

Each individual assembly could be further broken down into its constituent materials and components.

6.4 A common fallacy

It is sometimes assumed that computerising inventory records will guarantee they are 100% accurate. In fact discrepancies are just as likely to occur in a computerised as a non-computerised system. Stocktaking is thus equally important in a computerised inventory system as it is in a manual system.

CHAPTER ROUNDUP

↳ Materials can be **classified** according to the substances that make them up, how they are measured, or their physical properties.

↳ Procedures and documentation are required for material purchases.

↳ When wastage levels are high they are an avoidable expense.

↳ Materials issued from inventory can be valued using FIFO, LIFO and weighted average methods.

↳ **Inventory control** is the regulation of inventory levels, which includes putting a value to the amounts of inventory issued and remaining. Inventory control also includes ordering, purchasing, receiving and storing goods.

↳ **Inventory control levels** can be calculated in order to maintain inventories at the **optimum level**. The three critical control levels are re-order level, minimum level and maximum level.

↳ The **economic order quantity (EOQ)** is the order quantity which minimises inventory costs. The EOQ can be calculated using a table, graph or formula.

QUICK QUIZ

1 What are the three main ways of classifying materials?

2 What are raw materials?

3 What is work in progress?

4 List the five documents which you are likely to use when buying materials.

5 The goods received note is matched with two other documents in the buying process. What are they?

6 What are the advantages of FIFO?

7 What is a bin in warehouse terms?

8 Which documents are used to update the stores ledger account?

9 What are the two methods of stocktaking that are commonly used?

10 What are the main reasons for a company setting control levels with regard to inventory?

11 How would you calculate the minimum and maximum inventory control levels?

12 The raw materials issued to a job were overestimated and the excess is being sent back to the materials store.

What document is required?

O Stores credit note
O Stores debit note
O Materials returned note
O Materials transfer note

13 The inventory record of a raw material has the following details for a week:

Day	Cost ($ per unit)	Receipts (units)	Issues (units)
2	260	18	
3	270	12	
4			10
6			14

The first-in first-out (FIFO) method is used for pricing issues. There was no raw material at the start of Day 1.

Which was the value of the inventory on Day 5?

- O $5,200
- O $5,220
- O $5,320
- O $5,400

14 Average usage of a raw material is 200 kg per day, the average ordering lead time is 5 days, the re-order level is 1,600 kg and the re-order quantity is 2,800 kg.

What is the average raw material inventory?

- O   800 kg
- O   1,400 kg
- O   1,700 kg
- O   2,000 kg

ANSWERS TO QUICK QUIZ

1   According to the substances that make them up, how they are measured and their physical properties

2   Goods purchased for incorporation into products for sale

3   A term used to represent an intermediate stage between the purchase of raw materials and the completion of the finished product

4
- Purchase requisition form
- Order form
- Despatch note
- Delivery note
- Goods received note (GRN)

5   The purchase order and the supplier's invoice

6
- It is a logical pricing method.
- It is easy to understand.
- The closing inventory can be near to a valuation based on the cost of replacing the inventory.

7   A division of shelving or some other container which can be located by a code letter or number

8   Goods received notes and materials requisition notes

9   Periodic stocktaking and continuous stocktaking

10   To ensure it doesn't run out of inventory, and to ensure that it does not carry too much inventory

11   Minimum inventory control level = re-order level – (average usage × average lead time)

Maximum inventory control level = re-order level + re-order quantity – (minimum usage × minimum lead time)

12   Materials returned note

13    $5,320   (8 units × $260/unit) + (12 units × $270/unit)

14   2,000 kg

Minimum inventory control level = 1,600 – (200 × 5) = 600 kg
Maximum inventory control level = 1,600 + 2,800 – (200 × 5)
= 3,400 kg
Average inventory level = (600 + 3,400)/2 = 2,000 kg

Now try ...

Attempt the questions below from the **Practice Question Bank**

Number

Q30

Q31

Q32

Q33

Q34

The previous chapter explained how materials costs are recorded and accounted for, and some methods for controlling materials costs.

Labour costs are another major cost for many organisations, and this chapter explains how labour costs are accounted for and how labour performance might be measured. The chapter also explains how, in a system of **absorption costing**, labour costs are analysed into **direct labour costs** and **indirect labour costs** (which are a part of overhead costs).

Labour

TOPIC LIST	SYLLABUS REFERENCE
1 Labour costs	B2 (a)
2 The payroll accounting system	A2 (c), B2 (b), (d), (e), (f)
3 Direct and indirect labour	B2, (c), (e)
4 Labour turnover	B2 (g)
5 Measuring labour efficiency and utilisation	B2 (h)

Study Guide	Intellectual level
A **Management information**	
2 **Cost accounting systems**	
(c) Identify the documentation required, and the flow of documentation, for different cost accounting transactions	S
B **Cost recording**	
2 **Accounting for labour**	
(a) Explain, illustrate and evaluate labour remuneration methods	S
(b) Describe the operation of a payroll accounting system	K
(c) Distinguish between direct and indirect labour costs	K
(d) Describe the procedures and documentation required to ensure the correct coding, analysis and recording of direct and indirect labour	K
(e) Describe and illustrate the accounting for labour costs	S
(f) Explain the relationship between the labour costing system and the payroll accounting system	K
(g) Explain the causes and costs of, and calculate, labour turnover	S
(h) Describe and illustrate measures of labour efficiency and utilisation (efficiency, capacity utilisation, production volume and idle time ratios)	S

1 Labour costs

> **Labour costs** can be determined according to some prior agreement, the amount of time worked or the quantity or quality of work done.

1.1 What are labour costs?

Labour costs could be said to include any or all of the following items:

- The gross amount due to an employee
- Employer benefit contributions (payments made by an employer towards employees' pensions and other benefits)
- Amounts paid to recruit labour
- Amounts paid for staff welfare
- Training costs
- The costs of benefits like company cars

Labour costs are the amounts paid to any employee, including supervisors, office staff and managers. We will distinguish between **direct labour** and **indirect labour**, but even then you must not assume that this is necessarily a manual/clerical distinction (hopefully you are beginning to realise that direct costs and indirect costs differ in that they are accounted for differently).

1.2 Determining labour costs

There are three ways in which labour costs can be determined:

(a) According to some prior agreement

(b) According to the amount of time worked

(c) According to the amount and/or quality of work done ('piecework' or performance based remuneration)

Payment for most occupations is by a combination of methods (a) and (b). There will be a **basic wage** or **salary** which is agreed when the appointment is made. There will be a set number of hours per week during which the employee is expected to be available for work. There will be extra payments for time worked over and above the set hours, or deductions for time when the employee is not available beyond an agreed limit.

2 The payroll accounting system

Labour attendance time is recorded on an attendance record or a clockcard. **Job time** may be recorded on daily time sheets, weekly time sheets, jobcards or route cards depending on the circumstances.

Records of labour costs fall into three categories.

- Records of agreed basic wages and salaries
- Records of time spent working
- Records of work done

There are a number of ways in which this can be organised, but basically the information flow will be as follows.

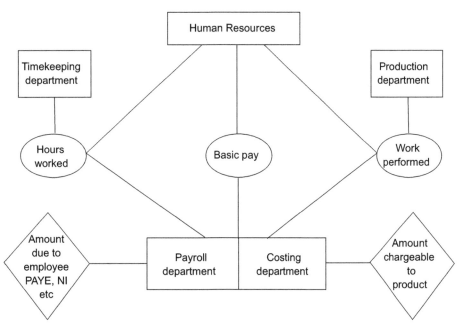

In practice, timekeeping would probably be a sub-function of production or of Human Resources. Alternatively, Human Resources may keep records of hours spent on the premises and available for work, while the production department keeps records of time spent doing different tasks. The system used will depend upon the nature of the job and the bases chosen for paying employees on the one hand and for costing products on the other.

All the information may, in practice, be given first to payroll, who would then pass it on for costing analysis, or vice versa. (Remember that in some organisations payroll administration is contracted out to a third party.) The main point is that both payroll and costing need the same information, but they analyse it differently, payroll asks **who**, and costing asks **what**.

BPP
LEARNING
MEDIA

2.1 Basic pay

Levels of basic pay are ultimately decided by senior management who will take into account what other employers are paying for similar work, what they consider the work to be worth, how easy it is to recruit labour and any agreements with trade unions.

The basic pay due to an individual worker will be mentioned in his or her **letter of appointment** and included in his or her **contract of employment**. The main on-going record, however, will probably be kept on an **employee record** held in the human resources computer system. This will also show subsequent increases in the wage rate or salary level and much other information. An example of an employee record is shown below.

2.1.1 Example: Employee record

EMPLOYEE RECORD

NAME: OTHER, A.N.

PERSONAL DETAILS

SURNAME	OTHER
FORENAMES	ALBERT NEIL
SEX	M (F)
Nationality	British
Social Security Number	WD 48 47 41C
Date of Birth	1 June 20V9
Marital Status	Single (Married) Separated Divorced Widowed
Dependants	None
Disabilities	None

ADDRESS: 94 Bootsale House, Antique Street, Old Salum, MERSEY ME5
Telephone 01973 89521

1ST CHANGE ADDRESS: 17 Newton Close, Brookeside, MERSEY ME1
Telephone 01973 12221

2ND CHANGE ADDRESS

Pension Scheme: Eligible 20X9 January, Joined 20X9 January

Professional Qualifications: Certified Accountant 20X9

Educational Details
Higher Education
A levels: Economics (C)
BTec: Computer Services
GCSE: n/a
O levels: 3
CSEs: 4
Other: City & Guilds Photography

IN EMERGENCY CONTACT
Name: Other, Noreen Olga — Wife
Address: 17 Newton Close, Brookeside, MERSEY ME1
Telephone (h) 01973 12221
Telephone (wk) 01973 51443

EMPLOYMENT HISTORY

Years of Service (12 months to 31 December)
1 2 3 4 5 6 7 8 9 10 11 12 13 14 15 16 17 18 19 20 21 22

FROM	TO	TITLE	DEPT	REASON	PAY
1/1/X8	31/3/X8	Junior Clerk	Sls Ledger	1st job here	£6,500
1/4/X8	30/6/X8			Probation period over	£7,000
1/7/X8				Annual payrise 5%	£7,350
1/X9		Senior Clerk	Pur Ledger	Got ACCA Quals & promoted	£9,000
7/X9				10% pay rise	£9,900
7/Y0				10% (8% + 2% merit)	£10,890
12/Y0		Asst Technician	Payroll	Transfer	£10,890

Training History

Course Code	
0713/I	Induction to new employees

Special Details

Leave Entitlement: 20 days

Much of the information on the employee record is confidential and there is no need for staff in the payroll department or the costing department to know about it.

In a computerised wage system, the basic rates are usually part of a database, and payroll and costing are only able to access information that is relevant to their tasks. Costing, for example, does not need to know the names of individual employees: in fact it is more efficient for workers to be coded according to the department they work in and the type of work that they do.

2.2 Attendance time

The bare minimum record of employees' time is a **simple attendance record** showing days absent because of holiday, sickness or other reason. Employees are usually required to book their annual leave in advance. For absence due to sickness, employees are usually required to let their line manager know as soon as they can. Line managers are usually responsible for contacting the human resources department, who will record the absence in the system. The typical attendance tracker is shown below.

Employee attendance tracker

| KEY | W | Working | H | Holiday | S | Sick | O | Other leave |

JANUARY	SUN	MON	TUES	WEDS	THURS	FRI	SAT	SUN	MON	TUES	WEDS	THURS	FRI	MONTHLY TOTALS			
EMPLOYEE NAME	1	2	3	4	5	6	7	8	9	10	11	12	13	W	H	S	O
Employee 1	W	W	W	S	S			W	W	W				6	0	2	0
Employee 2	W	H	W											2	1	0	0
Employee 3			W	O	W	S			W	W				4	0	1	1

Some businesses may record time of arrival, time of breaks, and time of departure, using employee swipe cards.

2.3 Job time

Job cards are often used in the construction industry to record the labour time spent on a particular project. Cards are prepared for each job or batch. When an employee works on a job, they record on the job card the time spent on that job. Job cards are therefore likely to contain entries relating to numerous employees. On completion of the job, it will contain a full record of the times and quantities involved in the job or batch.

Sometimes they are used to send job details to workers and workers fill them in (usually online) showing the work done. For example, a boiler repair service business may use this system for its engineers. The job card will show details of the job, such as the address and information about the problem to be fixed. The engineer updates the system with the status of the job, recording the work done and the time spent.

2.3.1 Salaried labour

Salaried staff are paid a set amount per month. The amount of the salary is usually set out in a contract of employment, along with the expected working hours. This is in contrast to receiving a wage, where the employee is paid on the basis of an hourly rate or a rate per item produced. Even though salaried staff are paid a set amount per month, they may be required to prepare time sheets. The reasons are as follows.

(a)   Time sheets provide management with information (eg product costs).

(b)   Time sheet information may provide a basis for billing for services provided (eg service firms where clients are billed based on the number of hours work done).

(c)   Time sheets are used to record hours spent and so **support claims for overtime payments** by salaried staff.

Service firms are chiefly in the business of selling the time and expertise of their employees to clients. This means that if an employee spends an hour working for a particular client, the client will be billed for one hour of the employee's time. A time sheet is necessary so that clients will be charged for the correct amount of time that has been spent doing their work.

Some systems automatically track time spent by the employee relating to a particular client. The employee (eg a lawyer or an accountant) clicks on a 'clock' relating to the client before they start work and clicks on it again when they stop work relating to that client.

2.3.2 Idle time

In many jobs there are times when, through no fault of their own, employees cannot get on with their work. A machine may break down or there may simply be a temporary shortage of work.

Idle time has a cost because employees will still be paid their basic wage or salary for these unproductive hours and so there should be a record of idle time. This may simply comprise an entry on time sheets coded to 'idle time' generally, or separate idle time cards may be prepared. A supervisor might record the time of a stoppage, its cause, its duration and the employees made idle.

2.4 Coding of job costs

By now you will appreciate that to analyse labour costs effectively it is necessary to be able to link up different pieces of information in various ways. Most organisations therefore develop a series of codes to facilitate analysis for each of the following:

(a) **Employee number** and perhaps a team number

(b) **Pay rate**, for example 'A' for $5 per hour, 'B' for $6 per hour and so on

(c) **Department** and/or **location** if the organisation has different branches or offices

(d) **Job** or **batch type**, for example different codes for audit, accounts preparation and tax in a firm of accountants, or for bodywork and mechanical repairs in a garage

(e) **Job** or **batch number** to enable each successive example of the same type of work to be allocated the next number in sequence

(f) **Client number** so that all work done for the same client or customer can be coded to the same number

You might like to think of different ways in which different pieces of information could be grouped together. For example, combining (b), (c) and (d) would show you whether the workers in one location could do a certain type of work more cheaply than the workers in another location.

QUESTION   Labour costs of jobs

Below are shown some extracts from the files of Penny Lane Co. You are required to calculate the labour cost of jobs 249 and 250.

Human resources files

	George	Paul	Ringo	John
Grade	A	B	C	D

Payroll – Master file

Grade	Basic rate per hour
A	$8.20
B	$7.40
C	$6.50
D	$5.30

Production report – labour

Job	Employee	Hours
249	George	14
249	Paul	49
250	George	2
250	John	107
250	Ringo	74

ANSWER

Job 249

Employee	Hours	Rate $	Total $
George	14	8.20	114.80
Paul	49	7.40	362.60
			477.40

Job 250

Employee	Hours	Rate $	Total $
George	2	8.20	16.40
John	107	5.30	567.10
Ringo	74	6.50	481.00
			1,064.50

2.5 Overtime

If an employee works for more hours than the basic daily requirement many organisations pay an extra amount.

The overtime payment may simply be at the **basic rate**. If an employee earns $5 an hour he will get an extra $5 for every hour worked in addition to the basic hours. If he earns $10,000 a year an hourly rate can be calculated by multiplying the basic hours per day by the normal number of days worked per week by the 52 weeks in the year. For example 7 hours × 5 days × 52 weeks = 1,820 hours and the hourly rate is approximately $5.49.

Usually, however, overtime is paid at a **premium rate**. You will hear expressions like 'time and a third', 'time and a half' and so on. This means that the hourly rate for overtime hours is $(1 + 1/3) \times$ basic rate or $(1 + 1/2) \times$ basic rate.

2.5.1 Example: Overtime premium

Pootings Co pays overtime at time and a quarter. Jo's basic hours are 9 to 5 with an hour for lunch, but one particular Friday she worked until six o'clock. She is paid a basic wage of $5 per hour. How much did she earn on the Friday in question, and how much of this is overtime premium?

Solution

The most obvious way of calculating the amount earned is as follows.

	$
Basic time (7 × $5)	35.00
Overtime (1.25 × $5)	6.25
Total pay	41.25

It is wrong, however, to say that the overtime premium is $6.25. For costing purposes all of the hours worked, whether in basic time or outside it, are costed at the basic rate. The premium is the extra amount paid on top of the basic rate for the hours worked over and above the basic hours.

		$
Basic pay (8 × $5)		40.00
Overtime premium (0.25 × $5)		1.25
		41.25

The **overtime premium** is thus $1.25. This is an important point because overtime premium is usually treated as an **indirect cost**. This is quite reasonable if you think about it. If you and your colleague use identical calculators it is reasonable to suppose that they cost the same amount to produce. It might be that one was assembled at 10 o'clock in the morning and the other at 10 o'clock at night but this doesn't make the calculators different from each other. They should therefore have the same cost and so **most organisations treat overtime premium as an overhead** and do not allocate it to the products manufactured outside basic hours.

There are two exceptions to this rule:

(a)   If overtime is worked at the specific request of a customer to get their order completed, the premium is a **direct cost of the order**.

(b)   If overtime is worked regularly by a production department in the normal course of operations, the overtime paid to direct workers could be incorporated into an **average direct labour hourly rate** (though it does not need to be).

EXAM FOCUS POINT

If you have trouble remembering how to deal with overtime premiums, think how you would feel if you had to pay more for your new tablet than all of the others in the shop, simply because it was made after 5:30pm.

2.6 Incentives and bonuses

There are five main types of **incentive scheme**: piecework, time-saved bonus, discretionary bonus, group bonus scheme and profit-sharing scheme.

Overtime premiums are paid to encourage staff to work longer hours than normal (or at least to recognise and reward the personal sacrifice of doing so). **Incentives and bonuses** are paid to encourage staff to work harder whatever the time of day.

Incentive schemes include the following:

*   Piecework
*   Time-saved bonus
*   Discretionary bonus
*   Group bonus scheme
*   Profit-sharing scheme

2.6.1 Piecework

Pieceworking can be seen as an incentive scheme since the more output you produce the more you are paid. If you are paid 5c per unit produced and you want to earn $300 gross a week you know you have to produce 6,000 units that week.

The system can be further refined by paying a different rate for different levels of production (**differential piecework**). For example the employer could pay 3c per unit for output of up to 3,500 a week, 5c per unit for every unit over 3,500.

In practice, persons working on such schemes normally receive a guaranteed minimum wage because they may not be able to work because of problems outside their control.

2.6.2 Example: Piecework

An employee is paid $5 per piecework hour produced. In a 35 hour week he produces the following output.

	Piecework time allowed per unit
3 units of product A	2.5 hours
5 units of product B	8.0 hours

Required

Calculate the employee's pay for the week.

Solution

Piecework hours produced are as follows.

Product A	3 × 2.5 hours	7.5 hours
Product B	5 × 8 hours	40.0 hours
Total piecework hours		47.5 hours

Therefore employee's pay = 47.5 × $5 = $237.50 for the week.

2.6.3 Time-saved bonus

Suppose that a garage has calculated that it takes an average of 45 minutes for an engineer to perform an MOT test, but the job could be done competently in 30 minutes. It could encourage its engineers to do such work at the faster rate by paying **a bonus for every minute saved** on the job up to a maximum of 15 minutes.

There are problems with this approach. In the first place it is necessary to establish a standard time for all types of work, and this may not be easy. In the second place a less than competent engineer may rush the job and not do it properly.

2.6.4 Example: time-saved bonus

In the garage example above, the bonus is 50c for every minute saved. During one afternoon the engineer completes three MOTs in 48 minutes, 35 minutes, and 40 minutes respectively.

Required

Calculate the engineer's time-saved bonus.

Solution

Bonus = (10 + 5) × 50c
    = $7.50

2.6.5 Discretionary bonuses

It is not uncommon, especially in smaller businesses, for **employers to give their employees bonuses simply because they think they deserve one**. This is a possible approach if it is difficult to measure an employee's output. Many office workers fall into this category. If, however, there is no obvious connection between what a person does and whether or not a bonus is paid, the scheme is likely to be perceived as unfair.

2.6.6 Group bonus schemes

Sometimes it is not possible to measure individual effort because overall performance is not within any one person's control (for example railway workers). In such cases, however, it is possible to measure overall performance and **a bonus can therefore be paid to all those who contributed**.

BPP
LEARNING
MEDIA

2.6.7 Profit-sharing schemes

In a **profit-sharing scheme** employees receive **a certain proportion of their company's year-end profits** (the size of their bonus might also be related to level of responsibility and length of service).

2.7 Absence from work

An employee may be absent from work for a variety of reasons, the most usual being as follows.

- Holidays
- Sickness
- Maternity/paternity/adoption leave
- Training

The costs relating to absence through sickness, maternity/paternity/adoption leave and training are usually treated as an overhead rather than a direct cost of production. Although some organisations treat holiday pay as an overhead, the normal treatment is to regard it as a direct cost by charging an inflated hourly rate. Suppose an employee, Jai, is normally paid $4 an hour for a 35 hour week and is entitled to four weeks annual holiday. He will therefore receive $560 ($4 × 35 × 4) holiday pay. Assuming that Jai works the remaining 48 weeks, his attendance time will total 1,680 (48 × 35) hours. Dividing $560 by 1,680 hours gives an addition of approximately 33c per hour to the employee's hourly rate to ensure that holiday pay is recovered.

Time absent because of holidays is paid at the normal basic rate, as is absence on training courses as a rule. There are statutory minimum levels for maternity pay and sickness pay, but above these employers can be as generous (or otherwise) as they wish.

3 Direct and indirect labour

> **Direct labour costs** are the specific costs of the workforce used to make a unit of product or provide a service. Indirect labour costs are all other labour costs: these are not directly attributable to the product or service.

Remember that **direct labour** costs are the specific costs of the workforce used to make a unit of product or provide a service. **Indirect labour** costs are all other labour costs that are **not directly attributable** to the product or service.

For example, suppose a business makes and sells tables. The wages of the employees involved in physically making the tables are a direct labour cost. However, there are many other people employed in the business, performing all kinds of other necessary functions other than making physically making the tables. The wages and salaries of these employees are **indirect labour costs** or overheads of the business, and could include the following:

- Wages and salaries of non-productive personnel in the production department, eg a supervisor, stores manager, cleaner, maintenance staff

- Wages of packers, drivers and despatch clerks in the distribution department

- **Office salaries**, including the salaries of secretaries and accountants

- **Salaries** and **commission** of sales representatives

Have a go at the following questions about the classification of labour costs.

QUESTION

Labour costs

Classify the following labour costs as either direct or indirect.

- (a) The basic pay of direct workers (cash paid, tax and other deductions)
- (b) The basic pay of indirect workers
- (c) Overtime premium
- (d) Bonus payments
- (e) Employer benefit contributions

(f)   Idle time of direct workers

(g)   Work on installation of equipment

ANSWER

(a)   The basic pay of direct workers is a direct cost to the unit, job or process.

(b)   The basic pay of indirect workers is an indirect cost, unless a customer asks for an order to be carried out which involves the dedicated use of indirect workers' time, when the cost of this time would be a direct labour cost of the order.

(c)   Overtime premium paid to both direct and indirect workers is an indirect cost, except in two particular circumstances.

   (i)   If overtime is worked at the specific request of a customer to get their order completed, the overtime premium paid is a direct cost of the order.

   (ii)   If overtime is worked regularly by a production department in the normal course of operations, the overtime premium paid to direct workers could be incorporated into the (average) direct labour hourly rate.

(d)   Bonus payments are generally an indirect cost. If a bonus system accumulates the total standard time and hours worked for a particular period and then calculates a bonus based on these totals, the bonus cannot be traced to a specific job and will be treated as an indirect cost.

   Bonuses paid on an individual task basis can be clearly attributed to a particular task and so would be treated as a direct labour cost of the respective task.

(e)   Employer benefit contributions (which are payments made by the employer as a contribution towards employees' benefits) are normally treated as an indirect labour cost as they cannot be traced to a specific job.

(f)   Idle time caused by machine breakdowns and scheduling mix-ups is an indirect labour cost as it cannot be traced to a specific job. Machine breakdowns occur randomly and therefore it would be unfair to charge them to particular jobs.

(g)   The cost of work on capital equipment is incorporated into the capital cost of the equipment.

QUESTION

Direct and indirect costs

A direct labour employee's wage in week 5 consists of the following:

		$
(a)	Basic pay for normal hours worked, 36 hours at $4 per hour =	144
(b)	Pay at the basic rate for overtime, 6 hours at $4 per hour =	24
(c)	Overtime shift premium, with overtime paid at time-and-a-quarter	
	¼ × 6 hours × $4 per hour =	6
(d)	A bonus payment under a group bonus (or 'incentive') scheme –	
	bonus for the month =	30
Total gross wages in week 5 for 42 hours of work		204

Required

Establish which costs are direct costs and which are indirect costs.

ANSWER

Items (a) and (b) are direct labour costs of the items produced in the 42 hours worked in week 5.

Overtime premium, item (c), is usually regarded as an overhead expense, because it is 'unfair' to charge the items produced in overtime hours with the premium. Why should an item made in overtime be more costly just because, by chance, it was made after the employee normally clocks off for the day?

Group bonus scheme payments, item (d), are usually overhead costs, because they cannot normally be traced directly to individual products or jobs.

In this example, the direct labour employee costs were $168 in direct costs and $36 in indirect costs.

QUESTION

Overtime

Jaffa Co employs two types of labour: skilled workers, considered to be direct workers, and semi-skilled workers considered to be indirect workers. Skilled workers are paid $10 per hour and semi-skilled $5 per hour.

The skilled workers have worked 20 hours overtime this week, 12 hours on specific orders and 8 hours on general overtime. Overtime is paid at a rate of time and a quarter.

The semi-skilled workers have worked 30 hours overtime, 20 hours for a specific order at a customer's request and the rest for general purposes. Overtime again is paid at time and a quarter.

What would be the total overtime pay considered to be a direct cost for this week?

- O $275
- O $355
- O $375
- O $437.50

ANSWER

$355

		Direct cost $	Indirect cost $
Skilled workers			
Specific overtime	(12 hours × $10 × 1.25)	150	
General overtime	(8 hours × $10 × 1)	80	
	(8 hours × $10 × 0.25)		20
Semi-skilled workers			
Specific overtime	(20 hours × $5 × 1.25)	125	
General overtime	(10 hours × $5 × 1.25)		62.50
		355	82.50

If you selected $275, you forgot to include the direct cost of the general overtime of $80 for the skilled workers.

If you selected $375, you included the overtime premium for skilled workers' general overtime of $20.

If you selected $437.50, you calculated the total of direct cost + indirect cost instead of the direct cost.

4 Labour turnover

Labour turnover is the rate at which employees leave a company and this rate should be kept as low as possible. The cost of labour turnover can be divided into **preventative** and **replacement** costs.

4.1 The reasons for labour turnover

There are many reasons why employees will leave their job. It may be because they wish to go to work for another company or organisation. Alternatively it may be for one of the following unavoidable reasons:

- Illness or accidents
- A family move away from the locality
- Retirement or death

In addition to the above examples, other causes of labour turnover are as follows:

- Paying a lower wage rate than is available elsewhere
- Requiring employees to work in unsafe or highly stressful conditions
- Requiring employees to work unsociable hours
- Poor relationships between management and staff
- Lack of opportunity for career enhancement
- Requiring employees to work in inaccessible places
- Discharging employees for misconduct, bad timekeeping or unsuitability

4.2 Measuring labour turnover

- **Labour turnover** is a measure of the number of employees leaving/being recruited in a period of time (say one year) expressed as a percentage of the total labour force.

- Labour turnover rate = $\dfrac{\text{Replacements}}{\text{Average number of employees in period}} \times 100\%$

4.2.1 Example: Labour turnover

(a) Florence Co had a staff numbering 800 at the beginning of 20X1 and 1,200 at the end of that year. Four hundred employees resigned on 30 June, and were immediately replaced by 400 new employees on 1 July. 400 extra employees were also recruited at that time.

What is the labour turnover rate?

Rate = $\dfrac{400}{(800+1,200) \div 2} \times 100\% = 40\%$

(b) Rome Co had a staff of 2,000 at the beginning of 20X1 and, owing to a series of redundancies caused by the recession, 1,000 at the end of the year. Voluntary redundancy was taken by 1,500 staff at the end of June, 500 more than the company had anticipated, and these excess redundancies were immediately replaced by new joiners.

The labour turnover rate is calculated as follows.

Rate = $\dfrac{500}{(2,000+1,000) \div 2} \times 100\% = 33\%$

4.3 The costs of labour turnover

The costs of labour turnover can be large and management should attempt to keep labour turnover as low as possible so as to minimise these costs.

The **cost of labour turnover** may be divided into the following:

- Preventative costs
- Replacement costs

4.3.1 Replacement costs

These are the costs incurred as a result of **hiring new employees** and they include the following:

(a) Cost of selection and placement

(b) Inefficiency of new labour; productivity will be lower

(c) Costs of training; training costs will include formal training courses plus the costs of on-the-job instructors diverted from their own work to teach new recruits

(d) Loss of output due to delay in new labour becoming available

(e) Increased wastage and spoilage due to lack of expertise among new staff

(f)   The possibility of more frequent accidents at work

(g)   Cost of tool and machine breakages

4.3.2 Preventative costs

These are costs incurred in order to **prevent employees leaving** and they include the following.

(a)   Cost of human resources administration incurred in maintaining good relationships
(b)   Cost of medical services including check-ups, nursing staff and so on
(c)   Cost of welfare services, including sports facilities, laundry services and canteen meals
(d)   Pension schemes providing security to employees
(e)   Cost of providing training and offering career progression

4.4 The prevention of high labour turnover

Labour turnover will be reduced by the following actions.

- Paying satisfactory wages
- Offering satisfactory hours and conditions of work
- Creating good relations between fellow workers, supervisors and subordinates
- Offering good training schemes and a well-understood career or promotion ladder
- Improving the content of jobs to create job satisfaction
- Proper planning so as to avoid redundancies
- Investigating the cause of high labour turnover rates

5   Measuring labour efficiency and utilisation

Labour efficiency and utilisation can be measured using ratios.

5.1 Labour efficiency and utilisation

Labour costs are often a large proportion of the total costs incurred by many organisations. It is important therefore that the performance of the labour force is continually measured.

Labour performance is generally measured by comparing actual results for an organisation with budgets (for now you can think of a budget as a plan for the future (in money terms) and is therefore the result that we expect to get).

5.1.1 Efficiency, capacity utilisation and production volume ratios

The ways of measuring labour performance are:

- Efficiency ratio
- Capacity utilisation ratio
- Production volume ratio

- **Efficiency ratio** $= \dfrac{\text{Expected hours to make actual output}}{\text{Actual hours taken}} \times 100\%$

- **Capacity utilisation ratio** $= \dfrac{\text{Actual hours worked}}{\text{Hours budgeted}} \times 100\%$

- **Production volume ratio** $= \dfrac{\text{Expected hours to make actual output}}{\text{Hours budgeted}} \times 100\%$

These ratios are based on direct labour hours and are usually expressed as percentages.

Efficiency ratio × Capacity utilisation ratio = Production volume ratio

5.1.2 Example: Ratios

Rarney Bubble Co budgets to make 25,000 units of output (in four direct labour hours each) during a budget period of 100,000 direct labour hours.

Actual output during the period was 27,000 units which took 120,000 direct labour hours to make.

Required

Calculate the efficiency, capacity utilisation and production volume ratios.

Solution

(a) Efficiency ratio $\dfrac{(27,000 \times 4) \text{ hours}}{120,000} \times 100\% = 90\%$

(b) Capacity utilisation ratio $\dfrac{120,000 \text{ hours}}{100,000 \text{ hours}} \times 100\% = 120\%$

(c) Production volume ratio $\dfrac{(27,000 \times 4) \text{ hours}}{100,000} \times 100\% = 108\%$

These ratios may be used, therefore, to measure the performance of the labour force. At a later stage in your studies you will come across variances, in particular labour variances which are another means of measuring labour efficiency.

EXAM FOCUS POINT

Few candidates are able to correctly apply these ratios, don't be one of them!

5.1.3 Idle time

We considered idle time earlier. A useful ratio for the control of idle time is the **idle time ratio.**

Idle time ratio $= \dfrac{\text{Idle hours}}{\text{Total hours}} \times 100\%$

This ratio is useful because it shows the proportion of available hours which were lost as a result of idle time.

CHAPTER ROUNDUP

- **Labour costs** can be determined according to some prior agreement, the amount of time worked or the quantity or quality of work done.

- **Labour attendance time** is recorded on an attendance record or a clockcard. **Job time** may be recorded on daily time sheets, weekly time sheets, jobcards or route cards depending on the circumstances.

- There are five main types of **incentive scheme**: piecework, time-saved bonus, discretionary bonus, group bonus scheme and profit-sharing scheme.

- **Direct labour costs** are the specific costs of the workforce used to make a unit of product or provide a service. Indirect labour costs are all other labour costs: these are not directly attributable to the product or service.

- **Labour turnover** is the rate at which employees leave a company and this rate should be kept as low as possible. The cost of labour turnover can be divided into **preventative** and **replacement** costs.

- Labour efficiency and utilisation can be measured using ratios.

QUICK QUIZ

1   Name three ways in which labour costs can be determined.

2   Give three reasons why salaried staff may be required to fill in detailed timesheets.

3   What is idle time, and why may it occur?

4   List five types of incentive scheme.

5   What is the formula used to calculate the labour turnover rate?

6   List five methods used to reduce labour turnover.

7   Analysis of the gross wages in a factory reveals:

	Direct operatives	Indirect operatives
	$	$
Productive hours at basic rate	41,200	17,600
Overtime premium	1,100	450
Idle time	760	
Group bonuses	2,780	
Total gross pay	45,840	18,050

What amount would **normally** be accounted for as production overhead?

- O $18,050
- O $18,810
- O $21,590
- O $22,690

8   Which of the following are aspects of payroll systems?

1   Attendance records
2   Calculation of bonuses
3   Employee tax codes
4   Apportion of wages to cost centres

- O   1, 2 and 3 only
- O   2, 3 and 4 only
- O   1, 2 and 4 only
- O   All four items

9   The direct labour capacity utilisation ratio for a period was 104%.

What could have caused this?

- O   Actual hours worked being greater than budgeted hours
- O   Actual hours worked being less than budgeted hours
- O   Standard time for actual output being greater than budgeted hours
- O   Standard time for actual output being less than budgeted hours

ANSWERS TO QUICK QUIZ

1 Agreed basic wages and salaries, time spent, work done

2 • Time sheets assist in the creation of management information about product costs and profitability.

 • Time sheet information may have a direct impact on the revenue an organisation receives (eg solicitors, accountants).

 • Time sheet information may support overtime claims made by salaried staff.

3 Time during which employees cannot get on with their work (though it is not their fault). It occurs when a machine breaks down or when there is a temporary shortage of work.

4 Piecework, time-saved bonus, discretionary bonus, group bonus scheme, profit-sharing scheme

5 Labour turnover rate = $\dfrac{\text{Replacements}}{\text{Average number of employees in period}} \times 100\%$

6 • Paying satisfactory wages
 • Offering satisfactory hours and conditions of work
 • Offering good training schemes
 • Improving job content to create job satisfaction
 • Proper staff planning so as to avoid redundancies

7 $22,690 (17,600 + 450 + 760 + 2,780 + 1,100)

8 1, 2 and 3 only

9 Actual hours worked being greater than budgeted hours.

Now try ...

Attempt the questions below from the **Practice Question Bank**

Number

Q35

Q36

Q37

Q38

Q39

BPP
LEARNING
MEDIA

CHAPTER

09

The previous two chapters explained how materials and labour costs are analysed and recorded. Organisations also incur **other expenses**, such as depreciation on its non-current assets.

This chapter describes the nature of these expenses, and how they may be analysed into **direct** and **indirect expenses**, or **fixed** and **variable costs**. This chapter and the two preceding chapters on materials and labour costs, taken together, explain the basic features of the costs within a business organisation.

Expenses

TOPIC LIST	SYLLABUS REFERENCE
1 Expense distinctions	B3 (c)
2 Types of expense	B3 (a)
3 Depreciation	B3 (d)
4 Recording expenses	A2 (c), B3 (b), (e)

Study Guide | Intellectual level

A   Management information

2   Cost accounting systems

(c)   Identify the documentation required, and the flow of documentation, for different cost accounting transactions   S

B   Cost recording

3   Accounting for other expenses

(a)   Describe the nature of expenses by function   K

(b)   Describe the procedures and documentation required to ensure the correct authorisation, coding, analysis and recording of direct and indirect expenses   K

(c)   Describe and calculate asset and expenses items and illustrate the relevant accounting treatment   K

(d)   Calculate and explain depreciation charges using straight line, reducing balance, machine hour and product units methods   S

(e)   Explain the relationship between the expenses costing system and the expense accounting system   K

1   Expense distinctions

The total cost of a cost unit is made up of the following three **elements of cost**:

- **Materials**
- **Labour**
- **Other expenses**

We have now looked at materials costs and labour costs in some detail. Any other costs that might be incurred by an organisation are generally known as **expenses** or **other expenses**.

Like materials and labour costs, expenses can be also divided up into different categories. You should not find too much difficulty in distinguishing between the following.

- Direct expense costs (eg tool hire for a specific job)
- Indirect expense costs (eg factory insurance)
- Fixed expense costs (eg factory insurance)
- Variable expense costs (eg cost per advert)

1.1 Direct expenses and indirect expenses

- A **direct cost** is a cost that can be traced in full to the product or service that is being costed.

- **Direct expenses** are any expenses which are incurred on a specific product other than direct material cost and direct wages. Direct expenses are rare.

Direct expenses are charged to the product as part of the **prime** cost. Examples of direct expenses are as follows:

- The cost of **special** designs, drawings or layouts
- The **hire of tools** or equipment for a particular job

Direct expenses are also referred to as **chargeable expenses**.

Indirect expenses are also known as overheads.

2 Types of expense

Expenses other than materials and labour costs can arise for a number of different reasons.

(a) **Buildings costs**. The main types are rent, business rates and buildings insurance.

(b) **The costs of making buildings habitable**. Gas and electricity bills and water rates, repairs and maintenance costs and cleaning costs.

(c) **People-related costs**. These include expenditure on health and safety, the cost of uniforms, and the cost of staff welfare provisions like tea and coffee, canteen costs and staff training.

(d) **Machine operating costs**. Machines need fuel or power and they need to be kept clean and properly maintained. Machines also need to be insured. A proportion of the cost of the machines becomes an expense item in the form of depreciation (see later). Some machines are hired.

(e) **Information processing costs**. Associated with information processing are the costs of telephone, postage, fax, computer disks and stationery, as well as subscriptions to information sources, like trade journals.

(f) **Finance costs**. If there is a bank loan there will be interest and bank charges to pay, and if equipment is leased there will be lease interest. Dividends paid to shareholders, however, are not a cost, they are an appropriation of some of the income earned in excess of all costs.

(g) **Selling and distribution costs**. Selling expenses include advertising and the costs of providing customer service and after sales service. The organisation's finished product also has to be stored and then delivered to customers. Distribution expenses would therefore include warehouse charges, upkeep and running of delivery vehicles and carriage outwards.

(h) Finally there are the **costs of dealing with the outside world**. Fees paid to professionals like external auditors, surveyors or solicitors and the costs of marketing (such as market research) would all be collected under this heading.

A typical detailed statement of profit or loss might, therefore, have the following headings:

	$	$
Sales		X
Less cost of sales:		
Opening inventory	X	
Materials	X	
Labour	X	
Depreciation	X	
Power and fuel	X	
	X	
Less closing inventory	(X)	
Cost of sales		(X)
Gross profit		X
Less costs of administration, distribution and selling:		
Wages and salaries	X	
Rent	X	
Insurance	X	
Heat and light	X	
Depreciation of office equipment	X	
Repairs and maintenance	X	
Cleaning	X	
Telecommunications	X	
Printing, postage and stationery	X	
Hire of computer equipment	X	
Advertising	X	
Warehouse charges	X	
Carriage outwards	X	
Audit and accountancy fees	X	
Bank charges	X	
Interest	X	
		(X)
Profit before tax		X

The following paragraphs describe some of these expenses in more detail.

2.1 Rent

Rent is usually an annual charge payable quarterly in advance.

Rent is normally subject to a tenancy agreement and it may be fixed for a period of so many years, or reviewable annually, or there may be some other agreement.

2.2 Insurance costs

These comprise **premiums** paid to an insurance company to cover the risk, say, of damage to buildings or their contents by fire, flood, explosions, theft and so on. Buildings insurance is usually based on the cost of rebuilding the property with adjustments to take account of the property's particular location. It is an annual sum, payable either whenever the renewal date occurs or in instalments.

Other types of insurance are charged on a similar basis. Examples include employer's liability insurance (against the risk of harming employees), and vehicle insurance.

2.3 Electricity, gas and telecommunications

Electricity, gas and telecommunications charges normally have two elements, a fixed amount called a standing charge, generally payable quarterly, and a variable amount based on consumption. There are a number of rates depending on the status of the user (domestic/commercial/industrial) and the time of day the power is consumed or the calls are made.

2.4 Subscriptions

Subscriptions are generally paid annually, though not necessarily by calendar year. This category includes both subscriptions to publications like trade journals or information services and subscriptions for membership of Chambers of Commerce or professional or trade bodies.

2.5 Professional fees

Such charges are usually made on the basis of time spent attending to the client's business.

2.6 Hire charges

Hire charges are sometimes payable on a time basis. For example a cement mixer may be hired for, say, $10 a day. Sometimes an additional charge is made for usage. A photocopier, for example, might have a meter on it showing how many copies had been made. The meter would be read periodically by the hire company and the invoice would include a charge for the number of copies made in the period.

2.7 Discretionary costs

Discretionary costs are, as you might expect, costs that are incurred at somebody's discretion. Whereas an organisation has to pay a certain amount for, say, electricity simply so that the business can function, other costs are not crucial to the short-term continuance of operations. The main examples are research and development costs, staff training and advertising.

Before we go on to consider the way in which expenses are recorded for cost accounting purposes, we are going to look at one further type of expense.

3 Depreciation

- **Asset expenditure** is expenditure which results in the acquisition of non-current assets. Non-current assets are assets acquired to provide benefits in more than one accounting period. Asset expenditure is charged to the statement of profit or loss via a depreciation charge over a period of time.
- **Expense items** are incurred for the purpose of the trade of the business, or in order to maintain the existing earning capacity of non-current assets. Expense items are charged to the statement of profit or loss in the period to which they relate.
- **Depreciation** is a method of writing off asset expenditure. There are four methods used: **straight line**, **reducing balance**, **machine hour** and **product units**.

3.1 Expense items and asset expenditure

Expenditure may also be classified as either an **expense item** or as **asset expenditure**.

- **Asset expenditure** is expenditure which results in the acquisition of non-current assets, eg purchasing a new piece of equipment.
- **Non-current assets** are assets which are acquired to provide benefits in more than one accounting period and are not intended to be resold in the normal course of trade. Eg a new piece of equipment would be expected to bring benefits for many years.

Asset expenditure is **not** charged to the statement of profit or loss. A **depreciation charge** is instead charged to the statement of profit or loss in order to write the asset expenditure off over a period of time. The depreciation charge is therefore an expense in the statement of profit or loss.

For example, if an asset is bought for $20,000 and it is expected to last for 5 years, then for 5 years, $4,000 ($20,000 ÷ 5 years) will be charged to the statement of profit or loss in each accounting period.

The costs incurred in purchasing non-current assets result in the non-current assets appearing in the statement of financial position.

Expense items are charges incurred for one of the following reasons.

- For the purpose of the trade of the business, including administration expenses, selling and distribution expenses and finance charges
- In order to maintain the existing earning capacity of non-current assets

Expense items are charged to the statement of profit or loss in the period to which they relate.

3.1.1 Example: Expense items and asset expenditure compared

Let us look at an example which should help you to distinguish between **expense items** and **asset items**.

Suppose that Bevan Co purchases a building for $30,000. A few years later it adds an extension to the building at a cost of $10,000. The building needs to have a few broken windows mended, its floors polished, and some missing roof tiles replaced. These cleaning and maintenance jobs cost $900.

Which items of expenditure are expense items and which are asset expenditure?

Solution

The original purchase ($30,000) and the cost of the extension ($10,000) are asset expenditure because they are incurred to acquire and then improve a non-current asset. The other costs of $900 are expense items because they are maintaining the existing earning capacity of the building.

Expense items and asset items are therefore distinguished by the ways they are accounted for in the statement of profit or loss and the statement of financial position.

BPP
LEARNING
MEDIA

3.2 Expense items and asset expenditure and costing

Expense items are of more relevance to the costing of products than asset expenditure. Asset expenditure is only of relevance when it is turned into an expense item in the form of depreciation.

EXAM FOCUS POINT

It is important that you have a clear understanding of the differences between expense items and asset items of expenditure. In an examination, you may be asked to distinguish between these terms and to decide whether certain items are asset or expense items.

QUESTION

Asset and expense items

Distinguish between asset expenditure and expense items and give an example of each.

ANSWER

Asset expenditure is expenditure which results in the acquisition of non-current assets or an improvement in their ability to earn income. **Expense items** refers to expenditure which is incurred either for the purpose of the trade or to maintain the **existing** earning capacity of non-current assets.

For example:

Expense	Cost	Asset/Expense
Ford Transit van	$8,000	Asset
Sign-painting of company name, logo and telephone number on van	$500	Asset
Petrol for van	$500	Expense
New engine, replacing old one which blew up	$1,000	Expense

3.3 The objectives of depreciation accounting

If an asset is purchased for $8,000 at the beginning of the year and sold for $6,000 at the end of the year then it is reasonable to conclude that the cost of owning the asset for a year is $2,000. This $2,000 is a real cost and it is in addition to the costs of using the asset, like fuel and repairs costs.

If the business had not owned the asset it would not have been able to make its product. It is therefore reasonable that the $2,000 cost should be charged as a cost of the product (although we won't say how to do this, for now).

One of the objectives of depreciation accounting is therefore **to find some way of calculating this cost of ownership**.

Consider, however, the use of a machine that is constructed to do a specific job for a specific firm. It may last 20 years and yet be of no use to anybody else at any time in which case its resale value would be nil on the same day that it was bought. It is, however, hardly fair to charge the whole cost of the machine to the first product that it makes, or even to the first year's production. Very probably the products it is making in year 19 will be just as well made as the products made in year 1.

Thus a second objective of depreciation accounting is **to spread out the cost of the asset over as long a period as the asset is used**. In the example given there is a good case for spreading this cost in equal proportions over the whole 20 years.

3.4 Depreciation methods

There are four principal methods of depreciating an asset: the **straight line method**, the **reducing balance method**, the **machine hour method** and **product units**.

(a)   The **straight line method** charges an equal amount of depreciation each period.

(b)   The **reducing balance method** charges the largest amount of depreciation at the beginning of an asset's life. As the asset grows older the amount charged each period gets steadily smaller.

(c)   The **machine hour method** charges depreciation in proportion of hours used to expected usage.

(d)   In the **product units method** the useful life of the asset is expressed in terms of the total number of units expected to be produced.

These methods of depreciation are simply different ways of systematically writing off the cost of an asset over its **useful life**. An asset's useful life is either the period over which an asset is expected to be available for use by an entity or the number of production units expected to be obtained from the asset by an entity, depending on the depreciation method used.

3.4.1 Example: Straight line and reducing balance methods

Two assets are purchased for $8,000 each. Asset A is depreciated over four years using the straight line method and Asset B is depreciated at the rate of 25% per annum on the reducing balance. What is the value of each asset after four years and how much per year is charged to the statement of profit or loss?

Solution

	Asset A (straight line)		Asset B (reducing balance)	
	Statement of financial position balance	Statement of profit or loss charge	Statement of financial position balance	Statement of profit or loss charge
	$	$	$	$
Capital cost	8,000		8,000	
Year 1 charge	(2,000)	2,000	(2,000)	2,000
c/f	6,000		6,000	
Year 2 charge	(2,000)	2,000	1,500	1,500
c/f	4,000		4,500	
Year 3 charge	(2,000)	2,000	(1,125)	1,125
c/f	2,000		3,375	
Year 4 charge	(2,000)	2,000	(844)	844
Value after four years	-		2,531	

The statement of profit or loss charge for Asset A is calculated by splitting the $8,000 capital cost into four. For Asset B it is calculated by taking 25% of the opening balance each year. In theory Asset B could continue to be depreciated for evermore.

3.4.2 Example: Machine hour method

A lorry bought for a business cost $17,000. It is expected to last for five years and then be sold for scrap for $2,000. Usage over the five years is expected to be:

Year 1	200 days
Year 2	100 days
Year 3	100 days
Year 4	150 days
Year 5	40 days

Required

Work out the depreciation to be charged each year under the machine hour method.

Solution

Under the machine hour method, depreciation for each of the five years is calculated as follows:

Total usage (days) = 200 + 100 + 100 + 150 + 40 = 590 days

$$\text{Depreciation per day} = \frac{\$(17,000 - 2,000)}{590} = \$25.42$$

Year	Usage Days	Depreciation (days × $25.42) $
1	200	5,084.00
2	100	2,542.00
3	100	2,542.00
4	150	3,813.00
5	40	1,016.80
		14,997.80

Note. The answer does not come to exactly $15,000 because of the rounding carried out at the 'depreciation per day' stage of the calculation.

In order to decide which method is most appropriate we need to think a little more about why we are depreciating the asset at all.

3.4.3 Example: Product units method

Under the product units method, the useful life of the asset is expressed in terms of the total number of units expected to be produced.

$$\text{Annual depreciation expense} = \frac{\text{cost of non-current asset} - \text{residual value}}{\text{estimated total production}} \times \text{actual production}$$

Suppose, an asset has original cost $70,000, a residual value of $10,000, and is expected to produce 6,000 units.

Depreciation per unit = ($70,000−$10,000) / 6,000 = $10

$10 × actual production will give you the depreciation cost of the current year.

The table below illustrates the production units depreciation schedule of the asset.

Carrying value at beginning of year $	Units of production	Depreciation cost per unit $	Depreciation expense $	Accumulated depreciation $	Carrying value at end of year $
70,000	1,000	10	10,000	10,000	60,000
60,000	1,100	10	11,000	21,000	49,000
49,000	1,200	10	12,000	33,000	37,000
37,000	1,300	10	13,000	46,000	24,000
24,000	1,400	10	14,000	60,000	10,000 (scrap value)

Depreciation stops when carrying value is equal to the residual of the asset. In the end the sum of **accumulated depreciation** and **scrap value** equals to the original cost.

3.5 Depreciation in practice

In practice you may find that the depreciation method most often used is the straight line method because it is simple and gives a reasonable approximation (given that depreciation is at best an estimate).

Typical depreciation rates under the straight line method are as follows:

Freehold land	Not depreciated
Freehold buildings	2% per annum (50 years)
Leasehold buildings	Over the period of the lease
Plant and machinery	10% per annum (10 years)
Fixtures and fittings	10% per annum (10 years)
Motor vehicles	25% per annum (4 years)

Note that these are not rules. Businesses can choose whatever method or rate they think is most appropriate. Motor vehicles, for example, are often depreciated using the reducing balance method since it is well known that in reality they lose the largest proportion of their value in their first few years.

4 Recording expenses

- **Direct expenses** are recorded by coding them to the appropriate job or client.
- **Indirect expenses** are initially **allocated** to cost centres and **apportioned** or **absorbed** to reflect areas of the business (other cost centres, different products) that have utilised the resource.

In this chapter we are only going to deal with the initial stages of recording expenses. Much more detail will be found later on which explains how overhead costs are further analysed and attributed to cost units.

4.1 Direct expenses

Direct expenses (such as plant hire for a specific job or solicitor's fees for drawing up a contract to provide a service) can simply be coded to the appropriate job or client when the bill arrives and recorded together with other direct costs.

4.2 Indirect expenses

Allocation is the process by which whole cost items are charged to a cost centre.

Indirect expenses are initially allocated to the appropriate **cost centres**. A cost centre is a collecting place for costs which cannot be directly attributed to cost units – ie a collecting place for overheads. Cost are further analysed into cost units once they have been traced to cost centres.

When costs are incurred, they are generally allocated to a **cost centre**. Cost centres may include the following.

- A department
- A machine, or group of machines
- A project (eg the installation of a new computer system)

Cost centres are an essential 'building block' of a costing system.

The decision as to which cost centre is the appropriate one for an expense depends upon the type of expense. Some expenses will be solely related to a particular cost centre and so can easily be allocated to that cost centre. For example, if the cost centre is a group of specialised machines, the costs of purchasing specialised cleaning materials to clean those machines is an overhead that can be easily allocated to that cost centre.

Other expenses, however, will be shared between the various cost centres and so cannot be allocated directly to one particular cost centre. Other cost centres therefore have to be established for the **initial allocation** of such shared overhead costs. Examples of shared expenses include: rent, rates, heating and lighting, building maintenance and so on.

The shared general overhead expenses are then **apportioned** to the cost centre representing departments, projects and so on.

4.2.1 Example: Overhead allocation

The coding, analysis and recording of indirect expenses and other overheads at the initial stage may be demonstrated by the following example.

The weekly costs of Medlycott Co include the following.

Wages of supervisor of Department A	$1,000
Wages of supervisor of Department B	$1,200
Indirect materials consumed in Department A	$400
Rent of premises shared by Departments A and B	$1,500

Medlycott Co's cost accounting system includes the following cost centres.

Code
101   Department A
102   Department B
201   Rent

Show how the costs will be initially coded.

Solution

(a)

	$	Code
Wages of supervisor of Department A	1,000	101
Wages of supervisor of Department B	1,200	102
Indirect materials consumed in Department A	400	101
Rent of premises shared by Departments A and B	1,500	201

(b)   You may think that this is so obvious as not to be worth explaining. You will certainly not be surprised to be told that the next stage is to share the rent paid between the two departments. Why, you might ask, do we not split the cost of rent straightaway and not bother with cost centre 201?

(c)   To answer this question consider the following extract from the cost accounts of Medlycott Co, several months after the previous example. Cost centre 201 is no longer used because nobody could see the point of it.

	Cost centre	
	101	*102*
	$	$
Wages	1,172.36	1,415.00
Materials	73.92	169.75
Rent	638.25	1,086.75

You have just received an email telling you that starting from this month (to which the above figures relate), Department A is to pay 25% of the total rent for the premises shared with Department B and Department B is to be split into two departments, with the new department (C) paying 37% of the remaining rent charge. The manager of Department B is standing over you asking you how much their department's new monthly rent charge will be.

(d)   The answer is $815.06. More importantly the first thing you have to do to calculate the answer is to recreate the total cost information that used to be allocated to cost centre 201. This is not very difficult in the present example, but imagine that there were ten cost centres sharing premises. Do you think it would have been easy to spot that the monthly rent had increased to $1,725?

4.3 Documentation

There are several ways in which this initial allocation could be documented.

%	A/C	$	P
25.00%	101	431	25
47.25%	102	815	06
27.75%	103	478	69
TOTAL	201	1,725	00

Approved		Date	
Authorised		Date	
Posted		Date	

4.4 Apportionment and responsibility accounting

The last point raises another important question. It is unlikely that the managers of departments A, B and C have any control over the amount of rent that is paid for the building. They need to be made aware that their part of the building is not free but they are not responsible for the cost. The person responsible for controlling the amount of a cost such as this is more likely to be a separate manager, who looks after the interests of all of the company's buildings.

If cost centre 201 is maintained it can therefore be used to collect all the costs that are the responsibility of the premises manager. This approach is known as **responsibility accounting** and such cost centres can be called **responsibility centres**.

CHAPTER ROUNDUP

↳ The total cost of a cost unit is made up of the following three **elements of cost**:

- Materials
- Labour
- Other expenses

↳ **Asset expenditure** is expenditure which results in the acquisition of non-current assets. Non-current assets are assets acquired to provide benefits in more than one accounting period. Asset expenditure is charged to the statement of profit or loss via a depreciation charge over a period of time.

↳ **Expense items** are incurred for the purpose of the trade of the business, or in order to maintain the existing earning capacity of non-current assets. Expense items are charged to the statement of profit or loss in the period to which they relate.

↳ Depreciation is a method of writing off asset expenditure. There are four methods used: **straight line**, **reducing balance**, **machine hour** and **product units**.

↳ **Direct expenses** are recorded by coding them to the appropriate job or client.

↳ **Indirect expenses** are initially **allocated** to appropriate cost centres and **apportioned or absorbed** to reflect areas of the business (other cost centres, different products) that have utilised the resource.

QUICK QUIZ

1 What is asset expenditure?

2 What are expense items?

3 What is the main distinguishing feature of asset and expense items?

4 What are the two main methods of depreciating an asset?

5 What are the two main objectives of depreciation accounting?

6 What is responsibility accounting?

ANSWERS TO QUICK QUIZ

1   Expenditure resulting in the acquisition of non-current assets. It is not charged to the statement of profit or loss as an expense. Instead a depreciation charge is made to the statement of profit or loss which writes off the asset expenditure over a period of time.

2   Expense items are incurred for the purpose of the trade of the business, or in order to maintain the existing earning capacity of non-current assets. Expenses are charged to the statement of profit or loss in the period to which they relate.

3   The way that they are accounted for in the statement of profit or loss (see answers 1 and 2)

4   Straight line method and reducing balance method

5   To find a way of calculating the cost of ownership of non-current assets and to spread out the cost of the asset over its lifetime

6   When cost centre managers have responsibility for controlling the amount of the cost collected within certain cost centres, such cost centres are called responsibility centres.

Now try ...

Attempt the questions below from the **Practice Question Bank**

Number

Q40

Q41

Q42

Q43

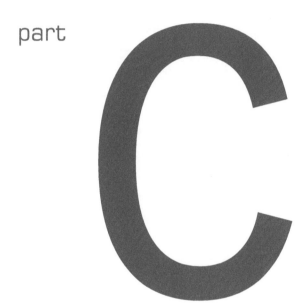

part

C

Costing techniques

10

Overheads and absorption costing

Costing systems are used to measure the **cost of output** (goods or services) and **profitability**, and to put a value to **closing inventories** of **work in progress** and **finished goods.** Traditionally, the techniques used to measure cost have applied mainly to manufacturing businesses, but similar techniques are used in service industries too.

For the purpose of the MA2 syllabus, you need to know about two costing techniques for measuring the cost of output: **absorption costing** and **marginal costing**.

This chapter explains the processes used in absorption costing. Absorption costing can seem quite complicated, because there is a three-stage process for dealing with overhead costs: **allocation, apportionment** and **absorption**. It is important to study this chapter carefully.

TOPIC LIST	SYLLABUS REFERENCE
1 What are overheads?	C1 (a)
2 What is absorption costing?	C1 (a)
3 Overhead apportionment – Stage 1	C1 (b), (c), (d)
4 Overhead apportionment – Stage 2	C1 (e)
5 Absorption of overheads	C1 (f), (g), (j)
6 Predetermined overhead absorption rates	C1 (g)
7 Over- and under-absorption	C1 (h), (g)
8 Non-production overheads	C1 (i), (j)

Study Guide	Intellectual level

C   Costing techniques

1   Absorption costing

(a)	Explain the rationale for absorption costing	K
(b)	Describe the nature of production and service cost centres and their significance for production overhead allocation, apportionment and absorption	K
(c)	Describe the process of allocating, apportioning and absorbing production overheads to establish product costs	K
(d)	Apportion overheads to cost centres using appropriate bases	S
(e)	Re-apportion service cost centre overheads to production cost centres using direct and step-down methods	S
(f)	Justify, calculate and apply production cost centre overhead absorption rates using labour hour and machine hour methods	S
(g)	Explain the relative merits of actual and predetermined absorption rates	K
(h)	Describe and illustrate the accounting for production overhead costs, including the analysis and interpretation of over/under-absorption	S
(i)	Describe and apply methods of attributing non-production overheads to cost units	S
(j)	Calculate product costs using the absorption costing method	S

1   What are overheads?

Overheads are the total of the indirect costs incurred in the course of making a product or providing a service. Overheads cannot be traced directly and in full to the product or service.

Now that we have completed our detailed study of direct materials, direct labour and direct expenses, we can move on to look in more depth at **indirect costs,** or **overheads**. Overheads may be dealt with in a number of different ways. In this chapter we will be looking at **traditional absorption costing**. The only other method that you need to have knowledge of is **marginal costing** which we will look at later on.

1.1 Overheads

An **indirect cost** or **overhead** is the cost incurred in the course of making a product or providing a service which cannot be traced directly and in full to the product or service.

Overheads are the total of the following:

*   Indirect materials
*   Indirect labour
*   Indirect expenses

One common way of categorising overheads is as follows:

*   Production overhead
*   Administration overhead
*   Selling overhead
*   Distribution overhead

2 What is absorption costing?

> Absorption costing is a method of sharing overheads between a number of different products or services on a fair basis. It involves **allocation**, **apportionment** and **absorption**.

2.1 The objective of absorption costing

The objective of absorption costing is to include in the total cost of a product or service an appropriate **share** of the organisation's total overhead. By an appropriate share we mean an amount that reflects the amount of time and effort that has gone into producing a unit or completing a service.

If an organisation only produced one identical unit then the total overheads would be divided among the total number of units produced. Life is, of course, never that simple. Absorption costing is a method of sharing overheads between a number of different products or services on a fair basis.

2.2 Practical reasons for using absorption costing

> The main reasons for using absorption costing are for **inventory valuations** and **establishing the profitability of different products**.

There are two main reasons for using absorption costing.

(a)   **Inventory valuations**. Production overheads are added to the cost of production to give the 'factory cost' or 'full cost of production'. **Full cost of production = prime cost + production overheads**.

The full cost of production is used to value inventories of finished goods. Inventories of finished goods must be valued for two reasons.

(i)   For the closing inventory figure in the statement of financial position

(ii)   For the cost of sales figure in the statement of profit or loss

The valuation of inventory will affect profitability during a period because of the way in which the cost of sales is calculated.

	The cost of goods produced
+	the value of opening inventories
−	the value of closing inventories
=	the cost of goods sold

(b)   **Establishing the profitability of different products or services**. If a company sells more than one product, it will be difficult to judge how profitable each individual product is unless the **total unit cost** of each product or service is known. To calculate the total unit cost, **all** overhead costs, including those relating to administration, sales and so on, as well as production overheads, are absorbed on a fair basis into the products.

2.3 Absorption costing procedures

In overview, the absorption costing process is to share out all of the **production overheads** amongst the cost centres that incur them and then to share their overheads amongst the products made in the cost centre.

However we have to recognise that not all of these cost centres are **production cost centres**, ie cost centres that actually produce goods. Some of the cost centres which incur overheads are **service cost centres**. These are areas of the business that provide necessary services to the production cost centres such as stores, maintenance and canteen.

The overheads incurred by the service cost centres must in turn be shared amongst the production cost centres until all of the overheads are within the production cost centres. Then finally the total overhead can be shared amongst the units which are made in each of the production cost centres.

BPP
LEARNING
MEDIA

The three steps involved in calculating the costs of overheads to be charged to cost units are:

- **Allocation**
- **Apportionment**
- **Absorption**

QUESTION

Absorption costing

(a)   What is absorption costing?
(b)   What are the three stages in accounting for overheads in absorption costing?

ANSWER

(a)   **Absorption costing** is a method of determining a product cost that includes a proportion of all production overheads incurred in the making of the product and possibly a proportion of other overheads such as administration and selling overheads.

(b)   - **Allocation** of costs to cost centres
        - **Apportionment** of shared costs between cost centres
        - **Absorption** of costs into cost units

EXAM FOCUS POINT

Candidates often demonstrate a lack of basic knowledge and understanding of the overhead absorption process. You need to make sure you fully understand the process of overhead allocation, apportionment and absorption (especially the last stage of the process).

2.4 Allocation of overhead costs

Allocation is the process of assigning whole items of cost to cost centres. It is the first stage in the absorption costing process.

It helps to think of a hierarchy of cost centres. At the top are cost centres for items of cost that are shared by all departments within the organisation, so that they cannot be allocated in full to production, administration or sales and distribution overheads. Examples are the costs of building occupancy, such as rent and heating costs, where all departments operate from the same premises. These shared costs (common costs) are allocated initially to a cost centre at the top level of the hierarchy.

We can think of the next stage in the hierarchy as costs centres for production, administration and sales and distribution. Some costs can be allocated directly to these cost centres. An example is the salary cost of the production manager, which can be allocated directly as a production overhead, or the salary of the sales and marketing manager, which can be allocated directly as a sales and marketing overhead cost.

Traditionally, absorption costing has been a costing system for manufacturing businesses. The next level in the hierarchy for production overhead costs are production departments that are engaged directly in production work (such as machining and product assembly) and production departments that provide support and assistance but are not directly engaged in production work – such as the production stores department, production planning department, repairs and maintenance department, and so on. These support departments are 'service cost centres'.

Some costs can be allocated directly to specific production cost centres or service cost centres. For example, the labour costs of employees in the repairs and maintenance section (all indirect labour) can be allocated directly to the repairs and maintenance service centre. Similarly, depreciation costs of machinery can be allocated directly to the cost centre where the machinery is located and used.

③ Overhead apportionment – Stage 1

In the first stage of overhead apportionment, costs that cannot be allocated directly to a production cost centre or a service cost centre (or to administration overheads or sales and distribution overheads) must be shared on a fair basis between these cost centres.

We shall now look at the first stage of **overhead apportionment**. Costs that cannot be allocated directly to a production cost centre or a service cost centre (or to administration overheads or sales and distribution overheads) must be apportioned, or shared on a fair basis between the cost centres that are lower down in the hierarchy.

Apportionment is a procedure whereby indirect costs (overheads) are spread between cost centres on a fair basis.

3.1 Sharing out common costs

Overhead apportionment follows on from overhead allocation. The first stage of overhead apportionment is to **identify all overhead costs** as production, administration, selling and distribution overhead. The common costs for heat and light, rent and rates, the canteen and so on (ie cost allocated to general overhead cost centres at the top of the cost centre hierarchy) must be shared out between the other cost centres.

3.2 Bases of apportionment

It is important that overhead costs are shared out on a **fair basis** using appropriate bases of apportionment. The bases of apportionment for the most usual cases are given below.

Shared overhead cost item	Basis of apportionment
Rent, rates, heating and light, repairs and depreciation of buildings	Floor area occupied by each cost centre
Insurance of equipment, where the same insurance policy covers equipment in different cost centres	Cost or carrying value of equipment
Heating, lighting (see above)	Volume of space occupied by each cost centre

3.2.1 Example: Bases of apportionment

Bravo Co incurred the following overhead costs.

	$
Depreciation of factory	1,000
Factory repairs and maintenance	600
Insurance of equipment	200
Heating	390
Lighting	100
	2,290

Information relating to the production and service cost centres in the factory is as follows.

	Production cost centres		Service cost centres	
	Production A	Production B	Service X	Service Y
Floor space (m²)	1,200	1,600	800	400
Volume (m³)	3,000	6,000	2,400	1,600
Carrying value of equipment	$30,000	$20,000	$10,000	$20,000

On what bases should the overhead costs be apportioned between the four cost centres? How much overhead would be apportioned to each cost centre?

Solution

Item of cost	Basis of apportionment	Total cost	A	B	To cost centre X	Y
		$	$	$	$	$
Factory depreciation	floor area	1,000	300	400	200	100
Factory repairs	floor area	600	180	240	120	60
Equipment insurance	carrying value	200	75	50	25	50
Heating	volume	390	90	180	72	48
Lighting	floor area	100	30	40	20	10
Total		2,290	675	910	437	268

Workings

Factory depreciation

Total floor space $= (1,200 + 1,600 + 800 + 400)\text{m}^2$
$$= 4,000 \text{ m}^2$$

Factory depreciation is apportioned to the different cost centres as follows.

Production cost centre A $= \dfrac{1,200}{4,000} \times \$1,000 = \$300$

Production cost centre B $= \dfrac{1,600}{4,000} \times \$1,000 = \$400$

Service cost centre X $= \dfrac{800}{4,000} \times \$1,000 = \$200$

Service cost centre Y $= \dfrac{400}{4,000} \times \$1,000 = \$100$

The same method can be applied in order to calculate the apportionments of the other overheads.

QUESTION
Apportionment (1)

Baldwin Co is preparing its production overhead budgets. Cost centre expenses and related information have been budgeted as follows.

	Total $	Machine shop A $	Machine shop B $	Assembly $	Canteen $	Maintenance $
Indirect wages	78,560	8,586	9,190	15,674	29,650	15,460
Consumable materials (inc. maintenance)	16,900	6,400	8,700	1,200	600	–
Rent and rates	16,700					
Buildings insurance	2,400					
Power	8,600					
Heat and light	3,400					
Depreciation of machinery	40,200					

Other information:	Total	Machine shop A	Machine shop B	Assembly	Canteen	Maintenance
Value of machinery ($)	402,000	201,000	179,000	22,000	–	–
Power usage – technical estimates (%)	100	55	40	3	–	2
Direct labour (hours)	35,000	8,000	6,200	20,800	–	–
Machine usage (hours)	25,200	7,200	18,000	–	–	–
Area (square metres)	45,000	10,000	12,000	15,000	6,000	2,000

Required

Calculate the overheads to be apportioned to the five cost centres. (In this example, you should assume that the depreciation costs for machinery have to be apportioned on a fair basis. In practice, depreciation costs are usually allocated directly to the cost centre using the machinery.)

ANSWER

	Total $	A $	B $	Assembly $	Canteen $	Maintenance $	Basis of apportionment
Indirect wages	78,560	8,586	9,190	15,674	29,650	15,460	Actual
Consumable materials	16,900	6,400	8,700	1,200	600	–	Actual
Rent and rates	16,700	3,711	4,453	5,567	2,227	742	Area
Insurance	2,400	533	640	800	320	107	Area
Power	8,600	4,730	3,440	258	–	172	Usage
Heat and light	3,400	756	907	1,133	453	151	Area
Depreciation	40,200	20,100	17,900	2,200	–	–	Value
	166,760	44,816	45,230	26,832	33,250	16,632	

Workings

1   Rent and rates, insurance, heat and light
    Floor area is a sensible measure to use as the basis for apportionment.

	Area Sq metres	Proportion total area	Share of rent & rates $	Share of insurance $	Share of heat & light $
Machine shop A	10,000	10/45	3,711	533	756
Machine shop B	12,000	12/45	4,453	640	907
Assembly	15,000	15/45	5,567	800	1,133
Canteen	6,000	6/45	2,227	320	453
Maintenance	2,000	2/45	742	107	151
	45,000		16,700	2,400	3,400

2   Power

	Percentage %	Share of cost $
Machine shop A	55	4,730
Machine shop B	40	3,440
Assembly	3	258
Maintenance	2	172
		8,600

3   Depreciation

In the absence of specific information about the non-current assets in use in each cost centre and the depreciation rates that are applied, this cost is shared out on the basis of the **relative value of each cost centre's machinery** to the total. In practice more specific information would (or should) be available.

4   Overhead apportionment – Stage 2

The second stage of production overhead apportionment is to **reapportion service centre costs** between production cost centres.

4.1 Reapportionment of service cost centre costs

The second stage of production overhead apportionment concerns the treatment of **service cost centres**.

A factory is usually divided into **several production cost centres** and also **many service cost centres**. Service cost centres might include the **stores** or the **canteen**.

Only the production cost centres are **directly involved** in the manufacture of the units. In order to be able to add production overheads to unit costs, it is necessary to have all the overheads charged to the production cost centres only.

The next stage in absorption costing is therefore to **apportion the overheads of service cost centres to the production cost centres**. This is sometimes called **reapportionment**.

4.2 Methods of reapportionment

The reapportionment of service cost centre costs can be done by a number of methods. You only need to know about the following two methods.

- Direct method of reapportionment
- Step-down method of reapportionment

Whichever method of reapportionment is used, **the basis of apportionment must be fair**. A different apportionment basis may be applied for each service cost centre. This is demonstrated in the following table.

Service cost centre	Possible basis of apportionment
Stores	Number or cost value of material requisitions
Maintenance	Hours of maintenance work done for each cost centre
Production planning	Direct labour hours worked in each production cost centre

4.2.1 Direct method of reapportionment

The **direct method of reapportionment** involves apportioning the costs of each service cost centre **to production cost centres only**.

This method is most easily explained by working through the following example.

4.2.2 Example: Direct method of reapportionment

Winfields Co incurred the following overhead costs.

| | Production cost centres | | Stores | Maintenance |
	P	Q	cost centre	cost centre
	$	$	$	$
Allocated costs	6,000	4,000	1,000	2,000
Apportioned costs	2,000	1,000	1,000	500
	8,000	5,000	2,000	2,500

Production cost centre P requisitioned materials to the value of $12,000. Cost centre Q requisitioned $8,000 of materials. The maintenance cost centre provided 500 hours of work for cost centre P and 750 hours for cost centre Q.

Required

Calculate the total production overhead costs of cost centres P and Q.

Solution

| | | | Cost centre | Cost centre |
Service cost centre	Basis of apportionment	Total cost	P	Q
		$	$	$
Stores	Value of requisitions (W1)	2,000	1,200	800
Maintenance	Maintenance hours (W2)	2,500	1,000	1,500
		4,500	2,200	2,300
Previously allocated and apportioned costs		13,000	8,000	5,000
Total overhead		17,500	10,200	7,300

Workings

1   *Stores cost centre overheads*

These are reapportioned as follows.

Total value of materials requisitioned   = $12,000 + $8,000
                                             = $20,000

Reapportioned to Cost centre P $= \dfrac{\$12,000}{\$20,000} \times \$2,000 = \$1,200$

Reapportioned to Cost centre Q $= \dfrac{\$8,000}{\$20,000} \times \$2,000 = \$800$

2   *Maintenance cost centre overheads*

These are reapportioned as follows.

Total hours worked = 500 + 750 = 1,250 hours

Reapportioned to Cost centre P $= \dfrac{500}{1,250} \times \$2,500 = \$1,000$

Reapportioned to Cost centre Q $= \dfrac{750}{1,250} \times \$2,500 = \$1,500$

The total overhead has now been shared, on a fair basis, between the two production cost centres.

BPP
LEARNING
MEDIA

QUESTION

Apportionment (2)

Carrying on from the question above, the table below shows the overheads apportioned to the five cost centres of Baldwin Co.

	Total $	Machine shop A $	Machine shop B $	Assembly $	Canteen $	Maintenance $
Indirect wages	78,560	8,586	9,190	15,674	29,650	15,460
Consumable materials	16,900	6,400	8,700	1,200	600	–
Rent and rates	16,700	3,711	4,453	5,567	2,227	742
Insurance	2,400	533	640	800	320	107
Power	8,600	4,730	3,440	258	–	172
Heat and light	3,400	756	907	1,133	453	151
Depreciation	40,200	20,100	17,900	2,200	–	–
	166,760	44,816	45,230	26,832	33,250	16,632

Other information:

	Total	Machine shop A	Machine shop B	Assembly	Canteen	Maintenance
Power usage – technical estimates (%)	100	55	40	3	–	2
Direct labour (hours)	35,000	8,000	6,200	20,800	–	–
Machine usage (hours)	25,200	7,200	18,000	–	–	–
Area (square metres)	45,000	10,000	12,000	15,000	6,000	2,000

Required

Using the bases which you consider to be the most appropriate, calculate overhead totals for Baldwin Co's three production cost centres, Machine Shop A, Machine Shop B and Assembly.

ANSWER

	Total $	A $	B $	Assembly $	Canteen $	Maintenance $	Basis of apportionment
Total overheads	166,760	44,816	45,230	26,832	33,250	16,632	
Reapportion (W1)	–	7,600	5,890	19,760	(33,250)	–	Dir labour
Reapportion (W2)	–	4,752	11,880	–	–	(16,632)	Mac usage
Totals	166,760	57,168	63,000	46,592	–	–	

Workings

1 Canteen overheads

Total direct labour hours = 35,000

Machine shop A $= \dfrac{8,000}{35,000} \times \$33,250 = \$7,600$

Machine shop B $= \dfrac{6,200}{35,000} \times \$33,250 = \$5,890$

Assembly $= \dfrac{20,800}{35,000} \times \$33,250 = \$19,760$

2 Maintenance overheads

Total machine hours = 25,200

Machine shop A $= \dfrac{7,200}{25,200} \times \$16,632 = \$4,752$

$$\text{Machine shop B} \quad = \frac{18,000}{25,200} \times \$16,632 = \$11,880$$

The total overhead has now been shared, on a fair basis, between the three production cost centres.

The direct method of reapportionment is simple, but it ignores the fact that there may be inter-service cost centre work occurring, for example, the stores department may do work for the maintenance department and vice versa.

4.2.3 Step-down method of reapportionment

The step-down method of reapportionment recognises the inter-service cost centre work. This method apportions the costs of service cost centres to other cost centres but once a service cost centre's costs have been apportioned, no subsequent costs are apportioned to it.

This method works as follows (where there are two service cost centres). The same principle is applied if there are more than two service cost centres.

Step 1	Reapportion one of the service cost centre's overheads to all of the other centres which make use of its services (production and service).

Step 2	Reapportion the overheads of the remaining service cost centre to the production cost centres only. The other service cost centre is ignored.

4.2.4 Example: Step-down method of reapportionment

A company has two production cost centres and two service cost centres (stores and maintenance). The following information about activity in a recent costing period is available.

	Production cost centres		Stores cost centre	Maintenance cost centre
	1	2		
Overhead costs	$10,030	$8,970	$10,000	$8,000
Value of material requisitions	$30,000	$50,000	–	$20,000
Maintenance hours used	8,000	1,000	1,000	–

The stores and maintenance cost centres do work for each other as shown in the table below

	Production cost centres		Stores cost centre	Maintenance cost centre
	1	2		
Stores work done (100%)	30%	50%	–	20%
Maintenance work done (100%)	80%	10%	10%	–

Required

Using the information given above, re-apportion the service cost centre overhead costs using the step-down method of apportionment, **starting with the stores cost centre**.

Solution

	Production cost centres		Stores cost centre	Maintenance cost centre
	1	2		
	$	$	$	$
Overhead costs	10,030	8,970	10,000	8,000
Apportion stores (30%/50%/20%)	3,000	5,000	(10,000)	2,000
				10,000
Apportion maintenance ($^8/_9$/$^1/_9$)	8,889	1,111	–	(10,000)
	21,919	15,081	–	–

Note. Maintenance costs are not apportioned to the stores cost centre because the stores costs have already been apportioned.

If the first apportionment had been the maintenance cost centre, then the overheads of $8,000 would have been apportioned as follows.

	Production cost centres 1 $	2 $	Stores cost centre $	Maintenance cost centre $
Overhead costs	10,030	8,970	10,000	8,000
Apportion maintenance (80%/10%/10%)	6,400	800	800	(8,000)
			10,800	–
Apportion stores ($^3/_8$/$^5/_8$)	4,050	6,750	(10,800)	
	20,480	16,520	–	–

Note. Notice how the final results differ, depending upon whether the stores cost centre or the maintenance cost centre is apportioned first.

If one service cost centre, compared with the other(s), has higher overhead costs and carries out a bigger proportion of work for the other service cost centre(s), then the overheads of this service centre should be reapportioned first.

QUESTION

Reapportionment

Elm Co has two service cost centres serving two production cost centres. Overhead costs allocated and apportioned to each cost centre are as follows.

Production 1 $	Production 2 $	Service 1 $	Service 2 $
97,428	84,947	9,384	15,823

Service 1 cost centre is expected to work a total of 40,000 hours for the other cost centres, divided as follows.

	Hours
Production 1	20,000
Production 2	15,000
Service 2	5,000

Service 2 cost centre is expected to work a total of 12,000 hours for the other cost centres, divided as follows.

	Hours
Production 1	3,000
Production 2	8,000
Service 1	1,000

Required

The finance director has asked you to reapportion the costs of the two service cost centres using the direct method of apportionment.

ANSWER

Direct apportionment method	Production 1 $	Production 2 $	Service 1 $	Service 2 $
	97,428	84,947	9,384	15,823
Apportion Service 1 costs (20:15)	5,362	4,022	(9,384)	–
	102,790	88,969	–	15,823
Apportion Service 2 costs (3:8)	4,315	11,508	–	(15,823)
	107,105	100,477	–	–

QUESTION

Step-down method

When you show the finance director how you have reapportioned the costs of the two service cost centres, he says 'Did I say that we used the direct method? Well, I meant to say the step-down method.'

Required

Prove to the finance director that you know how to use the step-down method. (**Note.** Apportion the overheads of service cost centre 1 first.)

ANSWER

Step-down method	Production 1	Production 2	Service 1	Service 2
	$	$	$	$
	97,428	84,947	9,384	15,823
Apportion Service 1 costs (20:15:5)	4,692	3,519	(9,384)	1,173
	102,120	88,466	–	16,996
Apportion Service 2 costs (3:8)	4,635	12,361	–	(16,996)
	106,755	100,827	–	–

---

5 Absorption of overheads

Once all of the production overheads have been apportioned to the production cost centres an **overhead absorption rate** is determined with which to absorb or include the overhead into the cost of each unit of production.

The final stage of the process now that all of the production overheads have been allocated and apportioned to the production cost centres is to find an absorption rate with which to absorb or include the overhead into the cost of each unit of production. This is done by finding a basis for absorption which will generally tend to be based upon the activity of the department.

5.1 Example: Absorption of overheads

Powertool Co needs to calculate the absorption rates for its assembly cost centre and its finishing cost centre. The assembly cost centre is a largely machine based cost centre whereas the finishing cost centre is largely labour based. The management of Powertool Co have decided that the assembly cost centre overheads should be absorbed on the basis of machine hours and that the finishing cost centre overheads should be absorbed on the basis of labour hours.

The machine hours in the assembly cost centre are 100,000 whereas the labour hours for the finishing cost centre are 20,000. The overheads for the assembly cost centre are $145,876 and the overheads for the finishing cost centre are $75,624.

What is the overhead absorption rate for each cost centre?

Solution

The overhead absorption rate is as follows:

Assembly $\dfrac{\$145,876}{100,000}$ = $1.46 per machine hour

Finishing $\dfrac{\$75,624}{20,000}$ = $3.78 per labour hour

QUESTION

Overhead absorption rate

A business has two production cost centres, manufacturing and packaging. The overheads and other details for these cost centres are as follows:

	Manufacturing	Packaging
Overhead	$154,000	$89,000
Labour hours	110,000	68,000
Machine hours	35,000	60,000

Management have decided that the overheads are to be absorbed on the basis of labour hours in the manufacturing cost centre and on the basis of machine hours in the packaging cost centre.

What is the overhead absorption rate per hour in each cost centre (to the nearest cent)?

	Manufacturing	Packaging
O	$1.40	$1.31
O	$1.40	$1.48
O	$4.40	$1.31
O	$4.40	$1.48

ANSWER

Manufacturing $= \dfrac{\$154,000}{110,000} = \$1.40$ per labour hour

Packaging $= \dfrac{\$89,000}{60,000} = \$1.48$ per machine hour

The **overhead absorption rate** is then used to cost each product depending upon how many relevant hours each product takes in each production cost centre.

For each product that is produced in the two cost centres a certain amount of overhead will be included in the cost of the product based upon the number of hours that the product spends in each production cost centre.

5.2 Example: Product costs

Continuing the example from above, one of the products of the Powertool Co is the Powerpuff. This product has direct material costs of $14.30 per unit and direct labour costs of $16.50 per unit. Each unit of the Powerpuff spends 6 machine hours in the assembly cost centre and 3 labour hours in the finishing cost centre. The absorption rates calculated above are as follows:

Assembly $1.46 per machine hour

Finishing $3.78 per labour hour

What is the full unit cost of production of the Powerpuff?

Solution

	$
Direct materials	14.30
Direct labour	16.50
Assembly overhead (6 hours × $1.46)	8.76
Finishing overhead (3 hours × $3.78)	11.34
Full production cost per unit	50.90

QUESTION   Total overhead per product

A business has two production departments, assembly and polishing. One of the products made in these departments is the Stun. Details for these departments and the Stun are as follows.

	Assembly	Polishing
Overhead	$94,800	$74,800
Labour hours	20,000	40,000
Machine hours	60,000	15,000
Stun – labour hours per unit	3 hours	5 hours
Stun – machine hours per unit	4 hours	2 hours

Overheads in the assembly department are to be absorbed on the basis of machine hours and in the polishing department on the basis of labour hours.

How much overhead in total would be included in the cost of a Stun?

O $3.45
O $8.48
O $10.06
O $15.67

ANSWER

$15.67

Assembly overhead absorption rate $= \dfrac{\$94,800}{60,000} = \$1.58$ per machine hour

Polishing overhead absorption rate $= \dfrac{\$74,800}{40,000} = \$1.87$ per labour hour

	$
Overhead to be absorbed	
Assembly $1.58 × 4 hours	6.32
Polishing $1.87 × 5 hours	9.35
Total overhead	15.67

5.3 Possible bases of absorption

The most common absorption bases are as follows.

- A rate per machine hour
- A rate per direct labour hour
- A percentage of direct labour cost
- A percentage of direct materials cost
- A percentage of total direct cost (prime cost)
- A rate per unit
- A percentage of factory cost (for administration overhead)
- A percentage of sales value or factory cost (for selling and distribution overhead)

The most appropriate basis for production overhead depends largely on the organisation concerned. As with apportionment it is a matter of being fair.

Many factories tend to use the **direct labour hour rate** or **machine hour rate** in preference to a rate based on a percentage of direct materials cost, wages or prime cost.

A **machine hour rate** would be used in cost centres where production is controlled or dictated by machines. A **direct labour hour basis** is more appropriate in a labour intensive environment.

BPP
LEARNING
MEDIA

5.4 The arbitrary nature of absorption costing

It should be obvious to you that, even if a company is trying to be 'fair', there is a great **lack of precision** about the way an absorption base is chosen.

This arbitrariness is one of the main criticisms of absorption costing, and if absorption costing is to be used then it is important that **the methods used are kept under regular review**. Changes in working conditions should, if necessary, lead to changes in the way in which work is accounted for.

For example, a **labour intensive cost centre** may become **mechanised**. If a direct labour hour rate of absorption had been used previous to the mechanisation, it would probably now be more appropriate to change to the use of a machine hour rate.

6   Predetermined overhead absorption rates

A **predetermined overhead absorption rate**, which is calculated using figures from the **budget**, is often used.

In practice, the absorption rate used is usually a **predetermined overhead absorption rate**, which is calculated using figures from the **budget**.

This predetermined overhead absorption rate is a sort of **expected cost** since it is based on figures representing what is supposed to happen (that is, figures from the budget). Using the **predetermined overhead absorption rate**, the **actual** cost of production can be established as follows.

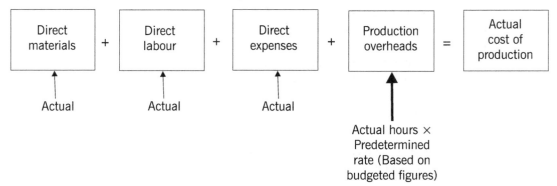

Using a predetermined overhead absorption rate means that the **actual** cost of production includes an element of cost which is based on a **budgeted rate**.

6.1 Calculating and using a predetermined overhead absorption rate

A predetermined overhead absorption rate for the forthcoming accounting period is calculated and used as follows.

Step 1	**Estimate the overhead** likely to be incurred during the coming period.
Step 2	**Estimate the activity level for the period.** This could be **total hours, units, or direct costs** or whatever measure of activity upon which the overhead absorption rates are to be based.
Step 3	**Divide the estimated overhead by the budgeted activity level.** This produces the predetermined overhead absorption rate. Predetermined overhead absorption rate = Total budgeted overheads for the cost based on machine hours centre/Total budgeted machine hours Predetermined overhead absorption rate = Total budgeted overheads for the cost based on direct labour hours centre/Total budgeted direct labour hours
Step 4	**Absorb** or **recover** the overhead into the cost unit by multiplying the calculated absorption rate by the **actual** activity: **predetermined absorption rate × actual hours**

EXAM FOCUS POINT

In some questions on this topic, predetermined absorption rates have to be calculated as part of the question requirements. Alternatively they may be given to you to use to calculate the overheads absorbed.

6.2 Example: Predetermined overhead absorption rates

Channel Co makes two products, the Jersey and the Guernsey. Jerseys take 2 direct labour hours each to make and Guernseys take 5 direct labour hours. Channel Co has budgeted for overhead of $50,000 and direct labour hours of 100,000.

Required

Calculate the overhead cost per unit for Jerseys and Guernseys respectively if overheads are absorbed on the basis of labour hours.

Solution

Step 1	Estimate the overhead likely to be incurred during the coming period. Channel Co estimates that the total overhead will be $50,000.
Step 2	Estimate the activity level for the period. Channel Co estimates that a total of 100,000 direct labour hours will be worked.
Step 3	Divide the estimated overhead by the budgeted activity level. Overhead absorption rate $= \dfrac{\$50,000}{100,000 \text{ hrs}} = \$0.50$ per direct labour hour

BPP
LEARNING
MEDIA

Step 4 Absorb the overhead into the cost unit by applying the calculated absorption rate.

	Jersey	Guernsey
Labour hours per unit	2	5
Absorption rate per labour hour	$0.50	$0.50
Overhead absorbed per unit	$1	$2.50

QUESTION

Overhead absorption rate

(a) If production overheads in total are expected to be $108,000 and direct labour hours are planned to be 90,000 hours costing $5 per hour, what is the overhead absorption rate per **direct labour hour**?

(b) If production overheads in total are expected to be $720,000 and direct machine hours are planned to be 50,000 hours, what is the overhead absorption rate per **machine hour**?

ANSWER

(a) **Overhead absorption rate** $= \dfrac{\text{Expected overheads}}{\text{Planned direct labour hours}}$

$\dfrac{\$108,000}{90,000} = \$1.20$ per direct labour hour

(b) **Overhead absorption rate** $= \dfrac{\text{Expected overheads}}{\text{Planned machine hours}}$

$\dfrac{\$720,000}{50,000} = \$14.40$ per direct machine hour

6.3 Predetermined versus actual absorption rates

An **actual absorption rate** is based on **actual** overheads incurred and **actual** machine or direct labour hours worked. But because actual overheads and actual hours are not known until the end of an accounting period, the actual absorption rate cannot be calculated until then. In effect then, the total cost of the product cannot be determined until the end of the period as well. This is too late for management planning and control purposes such as product pricing, production scheduling, product cost estimating and so on. It is also too late for routine accounting functions like invoicing.

In practice then, most organisations use **predetermined absorption rates**. The predetermined rate is set at the **beginning** of the accounting period, using **budgeted** overheads and **budgeted** machine or direct labour hours, so that overheads can be absorbed into actual production throughout the accounting period. However, as actual costs and actual hours worked are almost always not the same as budgeted costs and budgeted hours worked, using a predetermined absorption rate can mean that not all the actual overhead is absorbed (under-absorption) or that too much overhead is absorbed (over-absorption) into the product.

7 Over- and under-absorption

Under- or **over-absorption** of overheads occurs because the **predetermined overhead absorption rates** are based on forecasts (estimates).

- If actual overheads are greater than absorbed overheads, then overheads are **under-absorbed**.
- If actual overheads are less than absorbed overheads, then overheads are **over-absorbed**.

7.1 Under/over-absorption of overheads

The discrepancy between actual overheads incurred and the overheads absorbed is the **under-absorption** or **over-absorption** of overhead. This under/over-absorption is an inevitable feature of absorption costing using predetermined absorption rates because the rate is **predetermined from estimates of overhead cost and the expected volume of activity**. It is quite likely, therefore, that either one or both of the estimates will not agree with what actually occurs. When this happens, under- or over-absorption of overheads will arise.

7.2 Example: Under/over-absorption of overheads

The estimated overhead in a production cost centre is $80,000 and the estimated activity is 40,000 direct labour hours. The predetermined absorption rate (using a direct labour hour basis) is therefore $2 per direct labour hour ($80,000 ÷ 40,000 direct labour hours).

Actual overheads in the period are $84,000 and 45,000 direct labour hours are worked.

	$
Overhead incurred (actual)	84,000
Overhead absorbed (45,000 × $2)	90,000
Over-absorption of overhead	6,000

In this example, the cost of units produced has been charged with $6,000 more than was actually spent. An adjustment to reconcile the overheads charged to the actual overhead is necessary and the over-absorbed overhead will be **written off as a credit in the statement of profit or loss (income statement)** at the end of the accounting period.

QUESTION
Overhead absorption

The actual total production overhead expenditure of Nuthatch Co, was $176,533. Its actual activity, and the predetermined overhead absorption rates were as follows.

	Machine shop A	Machine shop B	Assembly
Direct labour hours	8,200	6,500	21,900
Machine usage hours	7,300	18,700	–
Predetermined overhead absorption rates	$7.94 per machine hr	$3.50 per machine hr	$2.24 per direct labour hr

Required

Calculate the under- or over-absorption of overheads.

ANSWER

		$	$
Actual expenditure			176,533
Overhead absorbed			
Machine shop A	7,300 hrs × $7.94	57,962	
Machine shop B	18,700 hrs × $3.50	65,450	
Assembly	21,900 hrs × $2.24	49,056	
			172,468
Under-absorbed overhead			4,065

8 Non-production overheads

For **internal reporting** purposes and for organisations which base the selling prices of their products on estimates of total cost, a **total cost per unit of output** may be required.

For **external reporting** (eg statutory accounts) it is not necessary to allocate non-production overheads to products.

For **internal reporting** purposes and for organisations which base the selling price of their product on estimates of **total** cost or even actual cost (such industries usually use a job costing system), a total cost per unit of output may be required. Builders, law firms and garages often charge for their services by adding a percentage profit margin to actual cost. For product pricing purposes and for internal management reports it may therefore be appropriate to allocate non-production overheads to units of output.

8.1 Bases for apportioning

Two possible methods of allocating such non-production overheads are as follows.

(a) **Choose a basis for the overhead absorption rate** which most closely matches the non-production overhead. However, allocation bases that are widely used by traditional costing systems such as direct labour hours and direct machine hours are not necessarily those that are closely related to non-manufacturing overheads.

(b) Use the **production cost as the basis** for allocating non-production costs to products.

The **overhead absorption rate** is calculated as follows.

$$\text{Overhead absorption rate} = \frac{\text{Estimated non-production overheads}}{\text{Estimated production costs}}$$

If, for example, budgeted distribution overheads are $200,000 and budgeted production costs are $800,000, the predetermined distribution overhead absorption rate will be 25% of production cost.

Other bases for absorbing overheads are as follows.

Types of overhead	Possible absorption base
Selling and marketing	Sales value
Research and development	Consumer cost (= production cost minus cost of direct materials) or added value (= sales value of product minus cost of bought in materials and services)
Distribution	Sales value
Administration	Full production cost

Absorption rates are usually stated as a percentage, such as a percentage of full production cost or a percentage of sales value.

The absorption rates are predetermined, based on budgeted figures; therefore there will be some over- or under-absorption of these overheads because actual overhead costs will differ from the amounts of cost absorbed into the cost of sale. Or actual production unit numbers will differ from budgeted production numbers.

8.2 Administration overheads

The administration overhead usually consists of the following:

- Executive salaries and wages/salaries of all staff in administration departments
- Office rent and rates
- Lighting
- Heating and cleaning the offices

Absorption rates for administration overheads are often stated as a percentage of **full production cost**.

8.3 Selling and distribution overheads

Selling and distribution overheads are often considered collectively as one type of overhead but they are actually quite different forms of expense.

(a)   **Selling costs** are incurred in order to obtain sales.
(b)   **Distribution costs** begin as soon as the finished goods are put into the warehouse and continue until the goods are despatched or delivered to the customer.

Selling overhead is therefore often absorbed on the basis of sales value.

Distribution overhead is more closely linked to production than sales and from one point of view could be regarded as an extra cost of production. It is, however, more usual to regard production cost as ending on the factory floor and to deal with distribution overhead separately. It is generally absorbed on a percentage of production cost but special circumstances, such as size and weight of products affecting the delivery charges, may cause a different basis of absorption to be used.

8.4 Example: Product costs

Continuing the previous example of the Powertool Co and the cost of the Powerpuff product. This product has a full production cost of $50.90 per unit.

Budgeted costs and revenue for the year were:

Production costs for all products	$600,000
Administration overheads	$120,000
Sales and distribution overheads	$400,000
Budgeted sales in total (all products)	$1,600,000

Sales price of the Powerpuff: $100 per unit

Administration overheads are absorbed as a percentage of production cost and sales and distribution costs are absorbed as a percentage of sales revenue.

What is the full unit cost of sales of the Powerpuff?

Solution

Overhead absorption rate for administration overheads: $120,000/$600,000 = 20% of full production cost.

Overhead absorption rate for sales and distribution overheads: $400,000/$1,600,000 = 25% of sales price

	$
Full production cost per unit	50.90
Administration overhead: 20% × $50.90	10.18
Sales and distribution overhead: 25% × $100	25.00
Full cost of sale per unit	86.08

BPP
LEARNING
MEDIA

In practice, an absorption costing system may be restricted to production costs only, without the absorption of administration and sales and distribution overheads to calculate a fully absorbed cost of sale. Instead of absorbing these overhead costs into product costs, the overheads are simply treated as a period charge against profit, and the actual overhead costs are included in the cost of sales.

EXAM FOCUS POINT

It is vital that you are happy with the contents of this chapter as it covers one of the most important topics in the MA2 syllabus.

CHAPTER ROUNDUP

⤷ **Overheads** are the total of the indirect costs incurred in the course of making a product or providing a service. Overheads cannot be traced directly and in full to the product or service.

⤷ Absorption costing is a method of sharing overheads between a number of different products or services on a fair basis. It involves **allocation, apportionment** and **absorption**.

⤷ The main reasons for using absorption costing are for **inventory valuations** and **establishing the profitability of different products**.

⤷ Allocation is the process of assigning whole items of cost to cost centres. It is the first stage in the absorption costing process.

⤷ In the first stage of overhead apportionment, costs that cannot be allocated directly to a production cost centre or a service cost centre (or to administration overheads or sales and distribution overheads) must be shared on a fair basis between these cost centres.

⤷ The second stage of production overhead apportionment is to **reapportion service centre costs** between production cost centres.

⤷ Once all of the production overheads have been apportioned to the production cost centres an **overhead absorption rate** is determined with which to absorb or include the overhead into the cost of each unit of production.

⤷ A **predetermined overhead absorption rate**, which is calculated using figures from the **budget**, is often used.

⤷ **Under-** or **over-absorption** of overheads occurs because the **predetermined overhead absorption rates** are based on forecasts (estimates).

– If actual overheads are greater than absorbed overheads, then overheads are **under absorbed**.
– If actual overheads are less than absorbed overheads, then overheads are **over absorbed**.

⤷ For **internal reporting** purposes and for organisations which base the selling prices of their products on estimates of total cost, a **total cost per unit of output** may be required.

QUICK QUIZ

1 What is overhead cost allocation?

2 Match the following overheads with the most appropriate basis of apportionment.

Overhead	Basis of apportionment
(a) Maintenance of equipment	(1) Direct machine hours
(b) Heat and light costs	(2) Number of employees
(c) Canteen	(3) Carrying value of equipment
(d) Insurance of equipment	(4) Floor area

3 Which of the following departments are directly involved in production?

Department	Involved in production (✓)
Finished goods warehouse	
Canteen	
Machining department	
Offices	
Assembly department	

BPP
LEARNING
MEDIA

4 In relation to calculating total absorption cost (full cost) or production, label the following descriptions in the correct order as Steps 1–5.

Description	Step
A Apportion overhead costs between cost centres	
B Establish the overhead absorption rate	
C Choose fair methods of apportionment	
D Apply the overhead absorption rate to products	
E Reapportion service cost centre costs	

5 How do the direct and step-down methods of service cost centre apportionment differ?

6 A direct labour hour basis of overhead absorption is most appropriate in which of the following environments?

- O Machine-intensive
- O Labour-intensive
- O When all units produced are identical
- O None of the above

7 Does over absorption occur when absorbed overheads are greater than or less than actual overheads?

- O Greater than
- O Less than

8 Consider the following statements, regarding the reapportionment of service cost centre overheads to production cost centres, where reciprocal services exist:

1 The direct method results in costs being reapportioned between service cost centres.

2 If the direct method is used, the order in which the service cost centre overheads are reapportioned is irrelevant.

3 The step-down method results in costs being reapportioned between service cost centres.

4 If the step-down method is used, the order in which the service cost centre overheads are reapportioned is irrelevant.

Which statement(s) is/are correct?

- O 1, 2 and 4
- O 1, 3 and 4
- O 2 only
- O 2 and 3

ANSWERS TO QUICK QUIZ

1   The process whereby whole cost items are charged direct to a cost unit or cost centre

2   (a)   (1) or (3), or possibly allocate costs of maintenance directly to cost centres on the basis of time sheets/maintenance work done

    (b)   (4)

    (c)   (2)

    (d)   (3)

3

Department	Involved in production (✓)
Finished goods warehouse	
Canteen	
Machining department	✓
Offices	
Assembly department	✓

4   A   =   2
    B   =   4
    C   =   1
    D   =   5
    E   =   3

5   The **direct method** is generally used when inter-service department work is not taken into account, ie the costs of each service cost centre are apportioned to production cost centres only. The **step-down method** involves the following.

    •   Apportioning one of the service cost centre's overheads to the cost centres using its services (production and service)

    •   Apportioning the overheads of the remaining service cost centre to the **production cost centres only**

6   Labour intensive

7   Greater than

8   2 and 3

Now try ...

Attempt the questions below from the **Practice Question Bank**

Number

Q44

Q45

Q46

Q47

Q48

CHAPTER

11

The previous chapter explained the processes used in absorption costing to measure the cost of output. This chapter describes marginal costing, which is an alternative costing technique. **Marginal costing** is a much simpler technique than absorption costing, because **fixed overhead costs are treated as an expense in the period they are incurred and are simply written off against profit**.

However the **profit reported by marginal costing will usually differ from the profit reported in a system of absorption costing, because of the different methods of measuring inventory values.** This chapter explains not only the process of marginal costing, but also how to reconcile the differences in reported profit using absorption and marginal costing.

Marginal costing and absorption costing

Study Guide	Intellectual level
C **Costing techniques**	
2 **Marginal costing**	
(a) Explain and illustrate the concept of contribution	S
(b) Prepare profit statements using the marginal costing method	S
(c) Prepare profit statements using the absorption costing method	S
(d) Compare and contrast the use of absorption and marginal costing for period profit reporting and inventory valuation	K
(e) Reconcile the profits reported by absorption and marginal costing	S
(f) Explain the usefulness of profit and contribution information respectively	K

1   Marginal costing

> **Marginal costing** is an alternative method of costing to absorption costing. In marginal costing, only variable costs are charged as a cost of sale and a **contribution** is calculated which is sales revenue minus the variable cost of sales.

1.1 Marginal cost

Marginal cost is the cost of a unit of a product or service which would be avoided if that unit were not produced or provided.

The marginal production cost per unit of an item usually consists of the following.

- Direct materials
- Direct labour
- Variable production overheads

Direct labour costs might be excluded from marginal costs when the work force is a given number of employees on a fixed wage or salary. Even so, it is not uncommon for direct labour to be treated as a variable cost, even when employees are paid a basic wage for a fixed working week. If in doubt, you should treat direct labour as a variable cost unless given clear indications to the contrary.

1.2 Contribution

Contribution is the difference between sales value and the marginal cost of sales.

Contribution is of fundamental importance in marginal costing, and the term 'contribution' is really short for 'contribution towards covering fixed overheads and making a profit'.

2 The principles of marginal costing

2.1 Principle 1

Period fixed costs are the same for any volume of sales and production (provided that the level of activity is within the 'relevant range'). Therefore, by selling an extra item of product or service the following will happen.

- Revenue will increase by the sales value of the item sold.
- Costs will increase by the variable cost per unit.
- Profit will increase by the amount of contribution earned from the extra item.

2.2 Principle 2

Profit measurement should be based on an analysis of total contribution. Since fixed costs relate to a period of time, and do not change with increases or decreases in sales volume, it is misleading to charge units of sale with a share of fixed costs. Absorption costing is therefore misleading, and it is more appropriate to deduct fixed costs from total contribution for the period to derive a profit figure.

2.3 Principle 3

When a unit of product is made, the **extra costs incurred in its manufacture are the variable production costs**. Fixed costs are unaffected, and no extra fixed costs are incurred when output is increased. It is therefore argued that the valuation of closing inventories should be at variable production cost (direct materials, direct labour, direct expenses (if any) and variable production overhead) because these are the only costs properly attributable to the product.

Before explaining marginal costing principles any further, it will be helpful to look at a numerical example.

2.4 Example: Marginal costing principles

Bain Painkillers Co makes a drug called 'Relief', which has a variable production cost of $6 per unit and a sales price of $10 per unit. At the beginning of June 20X1, there were no opening inventories and production during the month was 20,000 units. Fixed costs for the month were $45,000 (production, administration, sales and distribution). There were no variable non-production costs.

Required

Calculate the contribution and profit for June 20X1, using marginal costing principles, if sales were as follows.

(a)   10,000 Reliefs
(b)   15,000 Reliefs
(c)   20,000 Reliefs

Solution

The first stage in the profit calculation must be to identify the variable cost of sales, and then the contribution. Fixed costs are deducted from the total contribution to derive the profit. All closing inventories are valued at marginal production cost ($6 per unit).

	10,000 Reliefs		15,000 Reliefs		20,000 Reliefs	
	$	$	$	$	$	$
Sales (at $10)		100,000		150,000		200,000
Opening inventory	0		0		0	
Variable production cost	120,000		120,000			
					120,000	
	120,000		120,000			
					120,000	
Less value of closing inventory (at marginal cost)	60,000		30,000		–	
Variable cost of sales		60,000		90,000		120,000
Contribution		40,000		60,000		80,000
Less fixed costs		45,000		45,000		45,000
Profit/(loss)		(5,000)		15,000		35,000
Profit/(loss) per unit		$(0.50)		$1		$1.75
Contribution per unit		$4		$4		$4

The conclusions which may be drawn from this example are as follows.

(a) The **profit per unit varies** at differing levels of sales, because the average fixed overhead cost per unit changes with the volume of output and sales.

(b) The **contribution per unit is constant** at all levels of output and sales. Total contribution, which is the contribution per unit multiplied by the number of units sold, increases in direct proportion to the volume of sales.

(c) Since the **contribution per unit does not change**, the most effective way of calculating the expected profit at any level of output and sales would be as follows.

　(i) First calculate the total contribution.

　(ii) Then deduct fixed costs as a period charge in order to find the profit.

(d) In our example the expected profit from the sale of 17,000 Reliefs would be as follows.

	$
Total contribution (17,000 × $4)	68,000
Less fixed costs	45,000
Profit	23,000

2.5 Summary

(a) If total contribution exceeds fixed costs, a profit is made.

(b) If total contribution **exactly equals fixed costs**, no profit and no loss is made. This is known as the **breakeven point**.

(c) If total contribution is **less than fixed costs**, there will be a loss.

QUESTION
Marginal costing principles

Wong Co makes two products, the Ping and the Pong. Information relating to each of these products for August 20X1 is as follows:

	Ping		Pong
Opening inventory	nil		nil
Production (units)	15,000		6,000
Sales (units)	10,000		5,000
Sales price per unit	$20		$30
Unit costs	$		$
Direct materials	8		14
Direct labour	4		2
Variable production overhead	2		1
Variable sales overhead	2		3
Fixed costs for the month		$	
Production costs		40,000	
Administration costs		15,000	
Sales and distribution costs		25,000	

Required

(a) Using marginal costing principles, calculate the profit in August 20X1.

(b) Calculate the profit if sales had been 15,000 units of Ping and 6,000 units of Pong.

ANSWER

(a)

	$
Contribution from Pings (unit production = $20 – $(8 + 4 + 2 + 2) = $4 × 10,000)	40,000
Contribution from Pongs (unit production = $30 – $(14 + 2 + 1 + 3) = $10 × 5,000)	50,000
Total contribution	90,000
Fixed costs for the period ($40,000 + $15,000 + $25,000)	80,000
Profit	10,000

(b) At a higher volume of sales, profit would be as follows.

	$
Contribution from sales of 15,000 Pings (× $4)	60,000
Contribution from sales of 6,000 Pongs (× $10)	60,000
Total contribution	120,000
Less fixed costs	80,000
Profit	40,000

3 Marginal costing and absorption costing and the calculation of profit

3.1 Introduction

> **In marginal costing, fixed production costs are treated as period costs** and are written off as they are incurred. **In absorption costing, fixed production costs are absorbed into the cost of units** and are carried forward in inventory to be charged against sales for the next period. Inventory values using absorption costing are therefore greater than those calculated using marginal costing.

Marginal costing as a cost accounting system is significantly different from absorption costing. It is an **alternative method** of accounting for costs and profit, which rejects the principles of absorbing fixed overheads into unit costs.

Marginal costing	Absorption costing
Closing inventories are valued at marginal production cost.	Closing inventories are valued at full production cost.
Fixed costs are period costs.	Fixed costs are absorbed into unit costs.
Production cost of sales does not include a share of fixed overheads.	Production cost of sales does include a share of fixed overheads (see note below).

Note. The share of fixed overheads included in cost of sales are partly from the previous period (in opening inventory values). Some of the fixed overheads from the current period will be excluded by being carried forward in closing inventory values.

In **marginal costing**, it is necessary to identify the following:

- Variable costs
- Contribution
- Fixed costs

In **absorption costing** (sometimes known as **full costing**), it is not necessary to distinguish variable costs from fixed costs.

3.2 Example: Marginal and absorption costing compared

Look back at the information contained in the question entitled Marginal costing principles. Suppose that the budgeted production for August 20X1 was 15,000 units of Ping and 6,000 units of Pong, and production overhead is absorbed through the use of absorption costing using direct labour hours. The Ping requires two direct labour hours per unit and the Pong requires one direct labour hour per unit.

Assume the fixed costs and variable overheads referred to in the question are the budgeted and actual overheads.

Required

Calculate the profit if production was as budgeted, and sales were as follows.

(a)   10,000 units of Ping and 5,000 units of Pong
(b)   15,000 units of Ping and 6,000 units of Pong

Administration, sales and distribution costs should be charged as a period cost against profit.

Solution

Budgeted production overhead is calculated as follows:

		$
Fixed		40,000
Variable:	Pings (15,000 × $2)	30,000
	Pongs (6,000 × $1)	6,000
Total		76,000

The production overhead absorption rate would be calculated as follows:

$$\frac{\text{Budgeted production overhead}}{\text{Budgeted direct labour hours}} = \frac{\$76,000}{(15,000 \times 2) + 6,000} = \$2.1111 \text{ per direct labour hour}$$

(a)   If sales are 10,000 units of Ping and 5,000 units of Pong, profit would be as follows:

	Absorption costing		
	Pings	Pongs	Total
	$	$	$
Costs of production			
Direct materials	120,000	84,000	204,000
Direct labour	60,000	12,000	72,000
Overhead ($2.1111 × direct labour hours)	63,333	12,667	76,000
	243,333	108,667	352,000
Less closing inventories	(1/3) 81,111	(1/6) 18,111	99,222
Production cost of sales	162,222	90,556	252,778
Administration costs			15,000
Sales and distribution costs			
Variable			35,000
Fixed			25,000
Total cost of sales			327,778
Sales	200,000	150,000	350,000
Profit			22,222

Note. There is no under/over-absorption of overhead, since actual production is the same as budgeted production and budgeted and actual overheads are also equal.

The profit derived using absorption costing techniques is different from the profit ($10,000) using marginal costing techniques at this volume of sales (see earlier question).

(b)   If production and sales are exactly the same (15,000 units of Ping and 6,000 units of Pong) profit would be $40,000.

	$
Sales (300,000 + 180,000)	480,000
Cost of sales (352,000* + 15,000 + 48,000 + 25,000)	440,000
Profit	40,000

* No closing inventory if sales and production are equal.

This is the same as the profit calculated by marginal costing techniques in the earlier question.

3.3 Marginal costing versus absorption costing

(a)   In **marginal costing**, it is necessary to identify the following.

              Variable costs
              Contribution
              Fixed costs

(b)   In **absorption costing** it is not necessary to distinguish variable costs from fixed costs.

(c)   Marginal costing and absorption costing are different techniques for assessing profit in a period.

(d)   If there are changes in inventories during a period, so that opening inventory volumes are different to closing inventory volumes, marginal costing and absorption costing give different results for profit obtained.

(e)   If the opening and closing inventory volumes are the same, marginal costing and absorption costing will give the same profit figure. This is because the total cost of sales during the period would be the same, no matter how calculated.

3.4 The long-run effect on profit

In the long run, total profit for a company will be the same whether marginal costing or absorption costing is used. Different accounting conventions merely affect the profit of individual accounting periods.

3.4.1 Example: Comparison of total profits

To illustrate this point, let us suppose that a company makes and sells a single product. At the beginning of period 1, there are no opening inventories of the product, for which the variable production cost is $4 and the sales price $6 per unit. Fixed costs are $2,000 per period, of which $1,500 are fixed production costs.

	Period 1	Period 2
Sales	1,200 units	1,800 units
Production	1,500 units	1,500 units

There are no variable non-production costs.

Required

Determine the profit in each period using the following methods of costing.

(a)   Absorption costing. Assume output is 1,500 units per period.
(b)   Marginal costing.

Solution

It is important to notice that although production and sales volumes in each period are different (and therefore the profit for each period by absorption costing will be different from the profit by marginal costing), over the full period, total production equals sales volume, the total cost of sales is the same, and therefore the profit is the same by either method of accounting.

(a) **Absorption costing**

The absorption rate for fixed production overhead is $\dfrac{\$1,500}{1,500 \text{ units}} = \$1$ per unit.

Total unit cost for inventory valuation = $4 + $1 = $5

	Period 1		Period 2		Total	
	$	$	$	$	$	$
Sales		7,200		10,800		18,000
Production costs						
Variable	6,000		6,000		12,000	
Fixed	1,500		1,500		3,000	
	7,500		7,500		15,000	
Add opening inventory b/f	–		1,500			
	7,500		9,000			
Less closing inventory c/f						
(300 × $5)	1,500		–		–	
Production cost of sales	6,000		9,000		15,000	
Other costs	500		500		1,000	
Total cost of sales		6,500		9,500		16,000
Unadjusted profit		700		1,300		2,000
(Under-)/over-absorbed overhead		–		–		–
Profit		700		1,300		2,000

(b) **Marginal costing**

	Period 1		Period 2		Total	
	$	$	$	$	$	$
Sales		7,200		10,800		18,000
Variable production cost	6,000		6,000		12,000	
Add opening inventory b/f	–		1,200			
	6,000		7,200			
Less closing inventory c/f						
(300 × $4)	1,200		–		–	
Variable production cost of sales		4,800		7,200		12,000
Contribution		2,400		3,600		6,000
Fixed costs		2,000		2,000		4,000
Profit		400		1,600		2,000

Notes

1 The total profit over the two periods is the **same** for each method of costing, but the profit in each period is different.

2 In absorption costing, fixed production overhead of $300 is carried forward from period 1 into period 2 in inventory values, and becomes a charge to profit in period 2. In marginal costing all fixed costs are charged in the period they are incurred, therefore the profit in period 1 is $300 lower and in period 2 is $300 higher than the absorption costing profit.

3 There is no over- or under-absorption of overheads because production levels and overhead expenditure were as expected.

3.4.2 Example: Comparison of total profits when there is over- or under-absorption

Any over- or under-absorption of overheads does not affect the comparison of profits between absorption costing and marginal costing. This point is illustrated by the following example.

A company makes and sells a single product. During a budgeted period, there was no opening or closing inventory, and all units produced in the period were sold. Budgeted and actual data are as follows:

Budgeted data:

	$
Sales	800,000
Direct production costs	250,000
Budgeted production overheads	200,000
Budgeted other overheads	180,000

Actual data:

	$
Sales	750,000
Direct production costs ($70,000 variable, $160,000 fixed)	230,000
Actual production overheads (all fixed costs)	220,000
Actual other overheads ($25,000 variable, $150,000 fixed)	175,000

Required

Calculate the profit for the period using:

(a) Marginal costing

(b) Absorption costing, assuming that production overheads are absorbed at a predetermined rate and as a percentage of direct production costs, and that other overhead costs are written off as a period charge

Solution

(a) Marginal costing

	$	$
Sales		750,000
Variable costs:		
Production direct costs	70,000	
Other overheads	25,000	
Total variable cost of sales		95,000
Contribution		655,000
Fixed costs		
Production fixed direct costs	160,000	
Fixed production overhead costs	220,000	
Other fixed costs	150,000	
Total fixed costs		530,000
Profit		125,000

(b) Absorption costing

The absorption rate for production overheads is (200,000/250/000) 80% of direct production costs.

	$	$
Sales		750,000
Production costs:		
Production direct costs	230,000	
Production overheads absorbed (80% × 230,000)	184,000	
Full production cost of sales		(414,000)
		336,000
Under-absorbed overhead (220,000 − 184,000)		(36,000)
		300,000
Other overhead costs		(175,000)
Profit		125,000

The under-absorbed production overhead resulted in the recorded costs of production being $36,000 less than actual costs, but this is offset by the adjustment for the under-absorbed overheads. The profit reported by absorption costing and by marginal costing is the same.

The reported profits are different, however, when there are changes in inventory levels and values, between opening and closing inventory in the period.

4 Reconciling the profit figures given by the two methods

Reported profit figures using marginal costing or absorption costing will **differ** if there is any **change** in the level of inventories in the period. If production is **equal** to sales, there will be **no difference** in calculated profits using these costing methods.

4.1 Introduction

The difference in profits reported under the two costing systems is due to the **different inventory valuation methods used**.

If inventory levels increase between the beginning and end of a period, absorption costing will report the higher profit. This is because some of the fixed production overhead incurred during the period will be carried forward in closing inventory (which reduces cost of sales) to be set against sales revenue in the following period instead of being written off in full against profit in the period concerned.

If inventory levels decrease, absorption costing will report the lower profit because as well as the fixed overhead incurred, fixed production overhead which had been carried forward in opening inventory is released and is also included in cost of sales.

4.2 Example: Reconciling profits

The profits reported under absorption costing and marginal costing for period 1 in the example in Paragraph 3.4.1 would be reconciled as follows.

	$
Marginal costing profit ([$2 × 1,200] – [2,000])	400
Adjust for fixed production overhead in inventory:	
Inventory increase of 300 units × $1 per unit	300
Absorption costing profit	700

EXAM FOCUS POINT

If you have trouble reconciling the different profits reported under absorption costing and marginal costing, remember the following formula.

Marginal costing profit	X
Increase/(decrease) in inventory units × fixed production overhead absorption rate	Y
Absorption costing profit	Z

QUESTION

Profit reconciliation

Reconcile the profits reported under the two systems for period 2 of the example in Paragraph 3.4.1.

ANSWER

	$
Marginal costing profit	1,600
Adjust for fixed production overhead in inventory:	
Inventory decrease of 300 units × $1 per unit	(300)
Absorption costing profit	1,300

QUESTION

Absorption v Marginal costing

The fixed production overhead absorption rate for product X is $10 per machine hour. Each unit of product X requires five machine hours. Inventory of product X on 1.1.X1 was 150 units and on 31.12.X1 it was 100 units. What is the difference in profit between results reported using absorption costing and results reported using marginal costing?

- O   The absorption costing profit would be $2,500 less.
- O   The absorption costing profit would be $2,500 greater.
- O   The absorption costing profit would be $5,000 less.
- O   The absorption costing profit would be $5,000 greater.

ANSWER

The absorption costing profit would be $2,500 less.

Difference in profit = **change** in inventory levels × fixed production overhead absorption rate per unit = (150 − 100) × $10 × 5 = $2,500 **lower** profit, because inventory levels **decreased**.

---

5   Marginal costing versus absorption costing – which is better?

Absorption costing is most often used for routine profit reporting and must be used for financial accounting purposes. **Marginal costing** (contribution information) provides better management information for planning and decision making.

5.1 Usefulness of profit and contribution information

The main advantage of **contribution information** (rather than profit information) is that it allows an easy calculation of profit if sales increase or decrease from a certain level.

By comparing total contribution with fixed overheads, it is possible to determine whether profits or losses will be made at certain sales levels.

Profit information, on the other hand, does not lend itself to easy manipulation but note how easy it was to calculate profits using contribution information in the question above.

The following diagram summarises the arguments in favour of both marginal and absorption costing.

CHAPTER ROUNDUP

↳ **Marginal costing** is an alternative method of costing to absorption costing. In marginal costing, only variable costs are charged as a cost of sale and a **contribution** is calculated which is sales revenue minus the variable cost of sales.

↳ **In marginal costing, fixed production costs are treated as period costs** and are written off as they are incurred. **In absorption costing, fixed production costs are absorbed into the cost of units** and are carried forward in inventory to be charged against sales for the next period. Inventory values using absorption costing are therefore greater than those calculated using marginal costing.

↳ **Reported profit figures** using marginal costing or absorption costing will **differ** if there is any **change** in the level of inventories in the period. If production is **equal** to sales, there will be **no difference** in calculated profits using these costing methods.

↳ **Absorption costing** is most often used for routine profit reporting and must be used for financial accounting purposes. **Marginal costing** (contribution information) provides better management information for planning and decision making.

QUICK QUIZ

1 What is a period cost in marginal costing?

2 Sales value – marginal cost of sales = ...

3 What is a breakeven point?

4 Marginal costing and absorption costing are different techniques for assessing profit in a period. If there are changes in inventory during a period, marginal costing and absorption costing will report different profits.

Which of the following statements are true?

1 If inventory levels increase, marginal costing will report the higher profit.

2 If inventory levels decrease, marginal costing will report the lower profit.

3 If inventory levels decrease, marginal costing will report the higher profit.

4 If the opening and closing inventory volumes are the same, marginal costing and absorption costing will report the same profit figure.

O All of the above
O 1, 2 and 4
O 1 and 4
O 3 and 4

5 Which of the following are arguments in favour of marginal costing? Tick as appropriate.

☐ (a) Closing inventory is valued in accordance with accounting standards.

☐ (b) It is simple to operate.

☐ (c) There is no under or over absorption of overheads.

☐ (d) Fixed costs are the same regardless of activity levels.

☐ (e) The information from this costing method may be used for decision making.

6 A product has the following costs:

	$/unit
Variable production costs	4.80
Total production costs	7.50
Total variable costs	5.90
Total costs	10.00

11,400 units of the product were manufactured in a period during which 11,200 units were sold.

What is the profit difference using absorption costing rather than marginal costing?

○ The profit for the period is $540 lower.
○ The profit for the period is $540 higher.
○ The profit for the period is $820 lower.
○ The profit for the period is $820 higher.

ANSWERS TO QUICK QUIZ

1   A fixed cost

2   Contribution

3   It is the point at which total contribution exactly equals fixed costs, and when no profit and no loss is made.

4   3 and 4

5   ☐ (a)
    ☑ (b)
    ☑ (c)
    ☑ (d)
    ☑ (e)

6   The profit for the period is $540 higher. 200 units × ($7.50 – $4.80)/unit

Now try ...

Attempt the questions below from the **Practice Question Bank**

Number

Q49

Q50

Q51

Q52

Q53

12

The previous two chapters explained the processes used in absorption costing and marginal costing for measuring costs of output and profit. There has been no explanation yet of how costs are recorded. For either absorption costing or marginal costing systems, there has to be a system for recording costs – a **cost bookkeeping system**.

There are two cost bookkeeping systems, an **integrated accounts system** and an **interlocking accounts system**. The difference between the two systems relates to the connection between the cost accounting system and the financial accounting bookkeeping system. Both systems are explained in this chapter.

Cost bookkeeping

Study Guide	**Intellectual level**

A   Management information

2   Cost accounting systems

(a)   Explain the relationship between the cost/management accounting system and the financial accounting/management information systems (including interlocking and integrated bookkeeping systems)   K

(b)   Describe the process of accounting for input costs and relating them to work done   K

(d)   Explain and illustrate the use of codes in categorising and processing transactions (including sequential, hierarchical, block, faceted and mnemonic coding methods)   K

B   Cost recording

1   Accounting for materials

(d)   Describe and illustrate the accounting for material costs   S

(j)   Explain the relationship between the materials costing system and the inventory control system   K

2   Accounting for labour

(e)   Describe and illustrate the accounting for labour costs   S

(f)   Explain the relationship between the labour costing system and the payroll accounting system   K

3   Accounting for other expenses

(e)   Explain the relationship between the expenses costing system and the expense accounting system   K

C   Costing techniques

1   Absorption costing

(h)   Describe and illustrate the accounting for production overhead costs, including the analysis and interpretation of over/under-absorption   S

1   Accounting for costs and ledger accounting

> Cost records are a **detailed breakdown** of the information contained in the purchases account, the wages and salaries account and all the expense accounts in the general ledger.

1.1 Introduction

Previously, we have scrupulously avoided T-accounts, debits and credits, ledgers and bookkeeping. The cost records we have described so far are quite adequate for individual products or jobs, and it is not essential to go beyond this.

However, unless records of **totals** are maintained and checks of these records are made, there is no way of knowing whether all the costs that should have been recorded really have been recorded. The solution to this problem is **to link the cost records to the cash and credit transactions that are summarised in the general ledger**.

These are known as **control accounts** – they are simply summary accounts in the general ledger which then feed into the financial statements – the statement of profit or loss (often referred to as the income statement) and statement of financial position.

If you like you can think of accounting for costs as dealing with debits. Let us look at an example to illustrate what we mean.

We shall demonstrate how a single purchase of materials works through into the final accounts. The relevant double entries are:

			$	$
(a)	Debit	Materials	X	
	Credit	Cash		X

Being the buying of materials which are put into raw materials inventory

			$	$
(b)	Debit	Work in progress	X	
	Credit	Materials		X

Being the issue of materials to production for use in work in progress

			$	$
(c)	Debit	Finished goods	X	
	Credit	Work in progress		X

Being the issue of units that are now finished to finished goods inventory

			$	$
(d)	Debit	Cost of sales	X	
	Credit	Finished goods		X

Being the taking of units out of finished goods inventory and selling them

			$	$
(e)	Debit	Statement of profit or loss	X	
	Credit	Cost of sales		X

Being the closing off of ledger accounts and the drawing up of financial statements

Entry (e) would only be made at the end of a period.

1.2 Example: Basic cost accounting entries

Fred Stoneflint Co begins trading with $200 cash. $200 is initially spent on timber to make garden furniture. $100 worth of timber is left in store, whilst the other $100 is worked on to make garden chairs and tables. Before long, $50 worth of timber has been converted into garden furniture and this furniture is sold for $150. How will these events and transactions be reflected in the books?

Solution

CASH ACCOUNT

	$		$
Cash – opening balance	200	Purchase of materials	200
Sale of finished goods	150	Closing balance	150
	350		350

MATERIALS ACCOUNT

	$		$
Cash purchase	200	Transfer to WIP	100
	–	Closing balance	100
	200		200

WORK IN PROGRESS ACCOUNT

	$		$
Transfer from materials	100	Transfer to finished goods	50
	–	Closing balance	50
	100		100

FINISHED GOODS ACCOUNT

	$		$
Transfer from WIP	50	Transfer to cost of sales	50
	50		50

COST OF SALES ACCOUNT

	$		$
Transfer from finished goods	50	Shown in statement of profit or loss	50
	50		50

SALES ACCOUNT

	$		$
Shown in statement of profit or loss	150	Cash	150
	150		150

FRED STONEFLINT CO
STATEMENT OF PROFIT OR LOSS (INCOME STATEMENT)

	$
Sales	150
Cost of sales	50
Profit	100

FRED STONEFLINT CO
STATEMENT OF FINANCIAL POSITION

	$	$
Cash		150
Inventories: materials	100	
WIP	50	
		150
		300
Capital: b/f		200
profit		100
		300

The principle, as you can see, is very straightforward. We have not included entries for labour costs or direct expenses to keep things simple, but these are treated in the same way. Instead of amounts being debited initially to the materials account, they would be debited to the labour costs or direct expenses accounts (with cash being credited). They would then be transferred to work in progress and the other entries would be as for materials.

Note. The **materials account** may also be known as the **materials inventory account** or **stores ledger control account**.

1.3 Accounting for indirect materials

Direct materials are charged directly to the cost of production. Indirect materials, on the other hand, are overhead costs and should be accounted for accordingly. The materials account records the actual costs of all materials, direct and indirect. The accounting entry to record the cost of indirect materials if the materials are kept in stores and requisitioned when required is:

Debit	Overhead account (production, administration or sales and distribution overheads account)	X	
Credit	Materials account		X

Indirect materials relating to admin or sales and distribution may be written off to expense accounts directly and not held in central stores.

1.4 Example: Direct and indirect materials

During one month, a company incurred materials costs of $28,000. There were no opening or closing inventories at the beginning and end of the month. Direct material costs were $20,000 (all paid for in cash), and indirect materials costs were $1,000 for production, $5,000 for administration and $2,000 for sales and distribution. All materials are kept in stores and requisitioned when required. How will these transactions be reflected in the books?

Solution

MATERIALS ACCOUNT

	$		$
Cash purchases	28,000	Work in progress	20,000
		Production overheads account	1,000
		Admin overheads account	5,000
		Sales and dist'n overheads a/c	2,000
	–		
	28,000		28,000

WORK IN PROGRESS ACCOUNT

	$		$
Transfer from materials	20,000		
	20,000		

PRODUCTION OVERHEADS ACCOUNT

	$		$
Transfer from materials	1,000		
	1,000		

ADMINISTRATION OVERHEADS ACCOUNT

	$		$
Transfer from materials	5,000		
	5,000		

SALES AND DIST'N OVERHEADS ACCOUNT

	$		$
Transfer from materials	2,000		
	2,000		

1.5 Accounting for labour costs

Labour costs are either direct labour or indirect labour costs. In a manufacturing company, only production workers may be direct labour. The costs of all other employees are production overheads, administration overheads or sales and distribution overheads, depending on where the employees work.

Some of the costs of direct workers are also treated as production overhead costs. These include:

- The cost of any premium payments for overtime work (unless the work was done in overtime at the specific request of the customer, to complete a job more quickly)

- The cost of any idle time for direct workers

- The cost of sick pay for direct workers

The basic process for recording labour costs is similar to the process for recording materials costs:

(a)   **The wages control account** acts as a sort of **collecting place** for net wages paid and deductions made from gross pay. The actual gross pay for all employees is therefore debited to the wages control account or wages and salaries control account. (The corresponding double entry is a credit entry to Cash or the relevant Deductions from Pay account.)

(b)   Wages (and salaries) are then analysed between direct and indirect costs. These costs are debited to the work in progress account for direct labour costs, production overhead account for indirect production labour costs, and the administration overheads or sales and distribution overheads accounts.

BPP
LEARNING
MEDIA

WAGES CONTROL ACCOUNT

	$		$
Cash and deductions (= gross wages and salaries)	X	Work in progress (direct labour cost)	X
		Production overheads account (indirect production labour costs)	X
		Admin overheads account (costs of admin labour)	X
		Sales and dist'n overheads a/c (costs of sales and distribution labour)	X

WORK IN PROGRESS ACCOUNT

	$		$
Transfer from wages control (direct labour costs)	X		

PRODUCTION OVERHEADS ACCOUNT

	$		$
Transfer from wages control (indirect production labour costs)	X		

ADMINISTRATION OVERHEADS ACCOUNT

	$		$
Transfer from wages control (admin labour costs)	X		

SALES AND DIST'N OVERHEADS ACCOUNT

	$		$
Transfer from wages control (sales and distribution labour costs)	X		

1.6 Example: accounting for production labour costs

We will use an example to briefly review the principal bookkeeping entries for wages of production labour employees.

The following details were extracted from a weekly payroll for 750 employees at a factory in Trinidad.

Analysis of gross pay

	Direct workers $	Indirect workers $	Total $
Ordinary time	36,000	22,000	58,000
Overtime: basic wage	8,700	5,430	14,130
premium	4,350	2,715	7,065
Sick pay	950	500	1,450
Idle time	3,200	–	3,200
	53,200	30,645	83,845
Net wages paid to employees	$42,605	$22,220	$64,825

Required

Prepare the wages control account for the week for these production workers.

Solution

(a) The first step is to determine which wage costs are **direct** and which are **indirect**.

There are in fact only two items of direct wages cost in this example, the ordinary time ($36,000) and the basic overtime wage ($8,700) paid to direct workers. All other payments (including the overtime premium) are indirect wages.

(b)   The net wages paid are debited to the control account, and the balance then represents the deductions which have been made for income tax, national insurance, and so on.

WAGES CONTROL ACCOUNT

	$		$
Bank: net wages paid	64,825	Work in progress – direct labour	44,700
Deductions control accounts*		Production overhead control:	
($83,845 – $64,825)	19,020	Indirect labour	27,430
		Overtime premium	7,065
		Sick pay	1,450
		Idle time	3,200
	83,845		83,845

* In practice there would be a separate deductions control account for each type of deduction made (for example in the UK, PAYE and National Insurance).

1.7 Dealing with overheads

The bookkeeping entries for overheads are not as straight forward as those for materials and labour. We shall now consider the way in which overheads are dealt with in a cost accounting system.

Actual overhead costs incurred are recorded as a debit entry in the overhead control account. This should be the production overhead control account, the administration overhead control account or the sales and distribution overhead control account, depending on the nature of the overhead cost.

The corresponding credit entry should be to the materials account or materials account (for indirect materials costs), the wages control account (for indirect labour costs) or cash account (for indirect expenses).

For actual overhead costs incurred			$	$
(a)	Debit	Overhead control account	X	
	Credit	Materials account		X
	Credit	Wages control account		X
	Credit	Cash account (indirect expenses)		X

When an absorption costing system is used, the amount of overhead included in the cost of an item is absorbed at a predetermined rate. The amount absorbed is recorded by crediting the relevant overhead account and debiting work in progress (production overhead costs absorbed) or cost of sales account (for other overhead costs).

Production overhead costs absorbed			$	$
(a)	Debit	Work in progress account	X	
	Credit	Production overheads control account		X

Other overhead costs absorbed			$	$
(a)	Debit	Cost of sales account	X	
	Credit	Overheads control account		X

Note. In many costing systems, administration overhead costs and sales and distribution costs are not charged to cost of sales at a predetermined absorption rate, but are simply recorded at actual cost. In this case, the amount debited to cost of sales and credited to the overhead account is the actual overhead costs incurred.

As we saw earlier, it is highly unlikely that the actual amount and the absorbed amount will be the same. The difference is called **under- or over-absorbed overhead**. This is the difference between the amount on the debit side of the overhead account (= overhead costs incurred) and the credit side (= overhead costs absorbed). To deal with under- or over-absorbed overheads in the cost accounting books, we also need to have an account to collect under- or over-absorbed amounts for each type of overhead.

1.8 Example: The under-/over-absorbed overhead account

Gnocci Co absorbs production overheads at the rate of $0.50 per operating hour and administration overheads at 20% of the production cost of sales. Actual data for one month was as follows.

Administration overheads	$32,000
Production overheads	$46,500
Operating hours	90,000
Production cost of sales	$180,000

What entries need to be made for overheads in the ledgers?

Solution

	Debit	Credit
	$	$
	Production overheads	
Cash (actual overhead costs incurred)	46,500	
Absorbed into WIP (90,000 × $0.50)		45,000
Under-absorbed overhead		1,500
	46,500	46,500
	Administration overheads	
Cash (actual overhead costs incurred)	32,000	
To cost of sales (180,000 × 0.2)		36,000
Over-absorbed overhead	4,000	
	36,000	36,000
	Under-/over-absorbed overhead	
Production overhead	1,500	
Administration overhead		4,000
Balance to statement of profit or loss	2,500	
	4,000	4,000

Less production overhead has been absorbed than has been spent so there is under-absorbed overhead of $1,500. More administration overhead has been absorbed (into cost of sales, note, not into WIP) and so there is over-absorbed overhead of $4,000. The net over-absorbed overhead of $2,500 is a credit in the statement of profit or loss.

1.9 Accounting entries in a system of cost ledger accounts

The accounting entries in a system of cost ledger accounts can be confusing and it is important to keep in mind some general principles.

(a)   When **expenditure** is incurred on materials, wages or overheads, the actual amounts paid or payable are debited to the appropriate resources accounts. The credit entries (which in a financial accounting ledger would be in the cash or payables accounts) are in the cost ledger control account. The cost ledger control account appears in the financial accounting ledger where an interlocking bookkeeping system is maintained (separate ledgers for financial and costing records).

(b)   When production begins, **resources are allocated to work in progress**. This is recorded by crediting the resources accounts and debiting the work in progress account. In the case of production overheads, the amount credited to the overhead account and debited to work in progress should be the amount of overhead absorbed. If this differs from the amount of overhead incurred, there will be a difference on the overhead control account; this should be written off to an 'under-/over-absorbed overhead' account. (One other point to remember is that when indirect materials and labour are allocated to production, the entries are to credit the materials and wages accounts and debit production overhead account.)

(c)   As **finished goods** are produced, work in progress is reduced. This is recorded by debiting the finished goods control account and crediting the work in progress control account.

(d)   To establish the **cost of goods sold**, the balances on the administration overhead control account and the selling and distribution overhead control account are transferred to cost of sales control account. For a company with a full absorption costing system, the transfers from administration overhead and selling and distribution overhead accounts would be the amounts absorbed, rather than the amounts incurred. Any difference would again be written off to an 'under-/over-absorbed overhead' account. The balance of the **finished goods control account** is the finished goods inventory remaining. As goods are sold a transfer is made of the production cost of the goods sold, from the finished goods control account to the **production cost of sales account**.

(e)   **Sales** are debited to the cost ledger control account and credited to sales account.

(f)   **Profit** is established by transferring to the cost statement of profit or loss the balances on sales account, cost of sales account and under-/over-absorbed overhead accounts.

1.10 Accounting entries in absorption costing and marginal costing systems

The principles outlined above are illustrated for absorption costing and marginal costing systems in the diagrams on the following pages.

The following points should be noted:

(a)   In both diagrams the direct and indirect materials figures, and the direct and indirect labour figures, are extracted from the materials and wages analyses respectively.

(b)   In the diagram of an absorption costing system, the debit in respect of overheads to the WIP account is the absorbed overheads and is found by multiplying the total units of the basis for absorption (labour hours, machines hours and so on) for the period by the overhead absorption rate. For example, if 10,000 direct labour hours were booked to cost units and the overhead absorption rate was $2 per direct labour hour, then $20,000 would be debited to the WIP account for overheads.

(c)   In the diagram of the marginal costing system, only the variable overheads are debited to the WIP account. Fixed overheads are debited direct to the costing statement of profit or loss (income statement).

(d)   The final balance on the overhead account of the absorption costing system is the under- or over-absorbed overhead. There will be no such balance under a marginal costing system. However, there may be an over- or under-absorption of variable production overheads.

(e)   The closing balances on the WIP and finished goods accounts under absorption costing will be at absorbed cost, but will be at marginal cost under marginal costing.

(f)   Our diagrams are highly simplified versions of the full set of cost accounts used in practice.

Cost bookkeeping using absorption costing

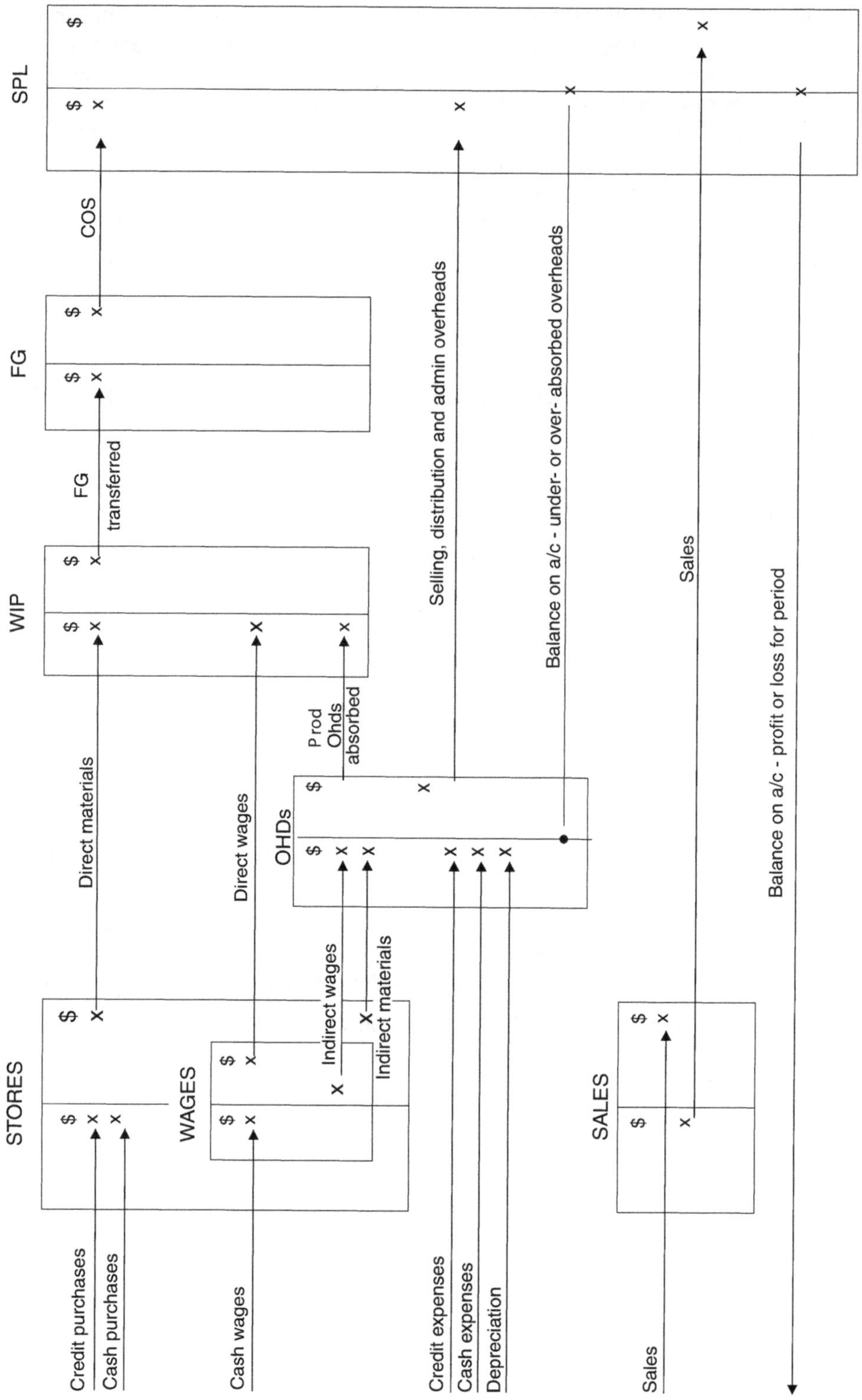

Cost bookkeeping using marginal costing

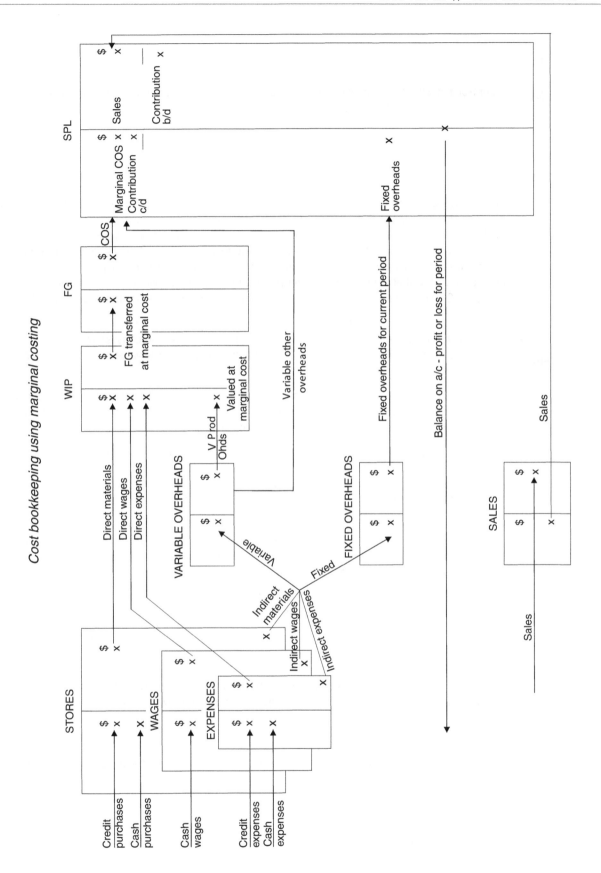

2 Control accounts

A **control account** is an account which records total cost, unlike an individual ledger account which records individual debits and credits.

TERM

A **control account** is an account which records total cost. In contrast, individual ledger accounts record individual debits and credits.

Previously, we kept things simple to avoid obscuring basic principles. For example, we have until now assumed that if $200 of materials are purchased the only entries made will be Debit Materials, Credit Cash. In practice, of course, this $200 might be made up of 20 different types of material, each costing $10, and if so each type of material is likely to have its own sub-account. These sub-accounts would be exactly like individual personal accounts in the payables' ledger or the receivables' ledger. You have probably guessed that we need to use **control accounts** to summarise the detailed transactions (such as how the $200 of materials is made up) and to maintain the double entry in the general ledger.

TERM

- A **materials account** (or **materials control account** or **stores ledger control account**) records the total cost of invoices received for each type of material (purchases) and the total cost of each type of material issued to various departments (the sum of the value of all materials requisition notes).

- A **wages control account** records the total cost of the payroll (plus employer's national insurance contributions) and the total cost of direct and indirect labour as recorded in the wages analysis sheets and charged to each production job or process.

- A **production overhead control account** is a total record of actual expenditure incurred and the amount absorbed into individual units, jobs or processes. Subsidiary records for actual overhead expenditure items and cost records which show the overheads attributed to individual units or jobs must agree with or reconcile to the totals in the control account.

- A **work in progress control account** records the total costs of direct materials, direct wages and production overheads charged to units, jobs or processes, and the cost of finished goods which are completed and transferred to the distribution department. Subsidiary records of individual job costs and so on will exist for jobs still in production and for jobs completed.

- A **finished goods control account** records the total cost of finished goods transferred from the production department to the distribution department.

- A **cost of sales control account** records the total cost of the finished goods sold.

The precise level of detail depends entirely upon the individual organisation. For example an organisation that makes different products might want a hierarchy of materials accounts as follows:

QUESTION
Stores ledger control

The following data relate to the materials account of Fresh Co, an air freshener manufacturer, for the month of April 20X2.

	$
Opening inventory	18,500
Closing inventory	16,100
Deliveries from suppliers	142,000
Returns to suppliers	2,300
Cost of indirect materials issued	25,200

Required

(a) Calculate the value of the issue of direct materials during April 20X2.
(b) State the double entry to record the issue of direct materials in the cost accounts.

BPP
LEARNING
MEDIA

ANSWER

(a)   Since we are given no information on the issue of direct materials we need to construct a materials account.

MATERIALS ACCOUNT

	$		$
Balance b/f	18,500	Payables/cash (returns)	2,300
Payables/cash	142,000	Overhead accounts	25,200
		WIP (balancing figure)	116,900
		Balance c/f	16,100
	160,500		160,500

The value of the issue of direct materials during April 20X2 was $116,900.

(b)   The issue of direct materials would therefore be recorded as follows.

Dr   WIP control account $116,900
Cr   Materials account $116,900

---

3   Cost bookkeeping systems

> There are two main cost bookkeeping systems, **interlocking systems** and **integrated systems**.

3.1 Introduction

There are two types of cost bookkeeping system, the **interlocking** and **integrated**. The main difference between the two systems is that interlocking systems require separate ledgers to be kept for the cost accounting function and the financial accounting function, which means that the cost accounting profit and financial accounting profit have to be reconciled. Integrated systems, on the other hand, combine the two functions in one set of ledger accounts.

Modern cost accounting systems (computerised) integrate cost accounting information and financial accounting information and are known as **integrated systems**. You are much more likely to deal with integrated systems in practice.

3.2 Interlocking systems

An **interlocking system** is a bookkeeping system where separate ledger accounts are kept for both the cost accounting function and the financial accounting function. Such a system necessitates the reconciliation of the profits produced by the separate statements of profit or loss. The cost accounts use the same basic cost data (purchases, wages and so on) as the financial accounts, but then provide the cost analysis linking the input costs with the output of products and services.

3.2.1 How an interlocking system works

An **interlocking system** features two ledgers.

(a)   The **financial ledger** contains asset, liability, revenue, expense and appropriation (eg dividend) accounts. The trial balance of an enterprise is prepared from the financial ledger.

(b)   The **cost ledger** is where cost information such as the build-up of work in progress is analysed in more detail.

3.2.2 The cost ledger control account

We mentioned the cost ledger control account briefly earlier. There are certain items of cost or revenue which are of no interest to the cost accountant because they are **financial accounting items**. These include the following:

- Interest or dividends received
- Dividends paid
- Discounts allowed or received for prompt payment of invoices

Some financial accounting items are **not** related to costs and profits such as:

- Cash
- Payables
- Receivables
- Revenue reserves

The items listed are **not** included in the separate cost accounting books, but are held in a **cost ledger control account**.

3.2.3 Principal cost accounts in a system of interlocking accounts

(a) The resources accounts
- Materials control account or stores control account
- Wages (and salaries) control account
- Production overhead control account
- Administration overhead control account
- Selling and distribution overhead control account

(b) Accounts which record the cost of production items from the start of production work through to cost of sales
- Work in progress control account
- Finished goods control account
- Cost of sales control account

(c) Sales account

(d) The costing statement of profit or loss (income statement)

(e) The under-/over-absorbed overhead account

(f) Cost ledger control account (in the cost ledger)

3.2.4 The financial bookkeeping system

The financial bookkeeping system consists of the financial ledger (or general ledger) and this is used to produce the financial statements for an organisation. The general ledger shows a complete record of an organisation's financial transactions. It shows debits and credits and may have subsidiary ledgers which show the detail pertaining to each transaction.

3.2.5 Notional costs

In some interlocking costing systems, there may be notional costs. These are costs that are introduced into a costing system in order to present a more realistic measure of the cost of an item. The most common types of notional cost are notional rent and notional interest.

(a) Notional rent may be charged to the cost of an item when the organisation owns its own premises, but it is considered appropriate to charge a notional commercial rent, as though the property is rented rather than owned.

(b) Notional interest may be charged on the capital invested in an item, to reflect the cost of the capital invested.

The purpose of notional costs is to make comparisons of cost between different items or different operations more realistic and fairer.

Notional costs must be recorded in the cost accounts. The 'actual' notional cost is recorded as a debit entry in the appropriate overhead account, and the corresponding credit entry is to the cost accounting statement of profit or loss (income statement).

3.3 Example: Interlocking accounts

Write up the cost ledger accounts of a manufacturing company for the latest accounting period. The following data is relevant.

(a)   There is no inventory on hand at the beginning of the period.

(b)   Details of the transactions for the period received from the financial accounts department include the following:

	$
Sales	420,000
Indirect wages:	
production	25,000
administration	15,000
sales and distribution	20,000
Materials purchased	101,000
Direct factory wages	153,200
Production overheads	46,500
Selling and distribution expenses	39,500
Administration expenses	32,000

(c)   Other cost data for the period includes the following.

Stores issued to production as indirect materials	$15,000
Stores issued to production as direct materials	$77,000
Cost of finished production	$270,200
Cost of goods sold at finished goods inventory valuation	$267,700
Standard rate of production overhead absorption	50c per operating hour
Rate of administration overhead absorption	20% of production cost of sales
Rate of sales and distribution overhead absorption	10% of sales revenue
Actual operating hours worked	160,000

Solution

The problem should be tackled methodically. The letters in brackets show the sequence in which the various entries are made. Any entries without a letter are merely transfers of closing balances.

COST LEDGER CONTROL (CLC)

	$		$
Sales (a)	420,000	Wages control (b)	213,200
Balance c/d	51,500	Materials control (c)	101,000
		Prod'n o'hd control (d)	46,500
		S & D o'hd control (e)	39,500
		Admin o'hd control (f)	32,000
		Cost statement of profit or loss	39,300
	471,500		471,500
		Balance b/d	51,500

MATERIALS CONTROL

	$		$
CLC (c) – purchases	101,000	Prod'n o'hd control (k) (indirect materials)	15,000
		WIP control (l) (issues to production)	77,000
		∴ Closing inventory c/d (balancing item)	9,000
	101,000		101,000
Closing inventory b/d	9,000		

WAGES CONTROL

	$		$
CLC (b)	213,200	Prod'n o'hd control (g)	25,000
		Admin o'hd control (h)	15,000
		S & D o'hd control (j)	20,000
		WIP control (m)(direct labour)	153,200
	213,200		213,200

PRODUCTION OVERHEAD CONTROL

	$		$
CLC (d)	46,500	WIP control (p)(160,000 × 50p)	
Wages control (g)	25,000	(overheads absorbed)	80,000
Materials control (k)	15,000	∴ O'hds under-absorbed	6,500
	86,500		86,500

ADMINISTRATION OVERHEAD CONTROL

	$		$
CLC (f)	32,000	Cost of sales control (q)	
Wages control (h)	15,000	(20% × $267,700)	53,540
∴ O'hds over-absorbed	6,540		
	53,540		53,540

SELLING AND DISTRIBUTION OVERHEAD CONTROL

	$		$
CLC (e)	39,500	Cost of sales control (r)(o/hds	
Wages control (j)	20,000	absorbed) (10% × $420,000)	42,000
		∴ O'hds under-absorbed	17,500
	59,500		59,500

WORK IN PROGRESS CONTROL

	$		$
Materials control (l)	77,000	Finished goods control (n)	270,200
Wages control (m)	153,200	(transfer of finished production)	
Prod'n o'hd control (p)	80,000	∴ Closing inventory of WIP c/d	40,000
	310,200		310,200
Balance b/d	40,000		

FINISHED GOODS CONTROL

	$		$
WIP control (n)	270,200	Cost of sales control (o)	267,700
		∴ Inventory of finished goods c/d	2,500
	270,200		270,200
Balance b/d	2,500		

COST OF SALES CONTROL

	$		$
Finished goods control (o)	267,700	Cost statement of profit or loss	363,240
Admin o'hd control (q)	53,540		
S & D o'hd control (r)	42,000		
	363,240		363,240

SALES

	$		$
Cost statement of profit or loss	420,000	CLC (a)	420,000

UNDER-/OVER-ABSORBED OVERHEAD

	$		$
Prod'n o'hd control	6,500	Admin o'hd control	6,540
S & D o'hd control	17,500	∴ Cost statement of profit or loss	17,460
	24,000		24,000

COST STATEMENT OF PROFIT OR LOSS (INCOME STATEMENT)

	$		$
Cost of sales control	363,240	Sales	420,000
Under-/over-absorbed o'hd	17,460		
CLC (profit for period)	39,300		
	420,000		420,000

Note how the trial balance can be extracted from the accounts.

TRIAL BALANCE

	Debit $	Credit $
Cost ledger control		51,500
Materials	9,000	
Work in progress	40,000	
Finished goods inventories	2,500	
	51,500	51,500

4 Advantages and limitations of interlocking and integrated cost accounting systems

4.1 Interlocking systems

The main advantage of interlocking systems is that they feature two ledgers, each of which fulfil different purposes. Having two sets of ledgers means that it is less likely that any conflict of needs will arise. This contrasts with integrated accounts, where one ledger is expected to fulfil two different purposes, and there may be conflicts between financial and cost accounting purposes, for example over valuation of inventory.

The main limitations of interlocking systems are as follows:

- Profits of separate cost and financial accounts must be reconciled.
- They require more administration time.
- They are more costly to run.

4.2 Integrated systems

The main **advantage** of integrated systems is the saving in administration time and costs. This is because only one set of accounts needs to be maintained instead of two. There is also no need to reconcile the profits of the separate cost and financial accounts.

The main limitation of integrated accounts is that one set of accounts is expected to fulfil two different purposes, the cost accounts provide internal management information and the financial accounts are used for external reporting. At times external reporting and internal management information may conflict. For example, for external reporting, inventories will be valued in accordance with accounting standards. Cost accountants may however prefer to value inventories at marginal cost. It is clear therefore that in some circumstances it is more advantageous to have two separate systems.

BPP
LEARNING
MEDIA

CHAPTER ROUNDUP

↳ Cost records are a **detailed breakdown** of the information contained in the purchases account, the wages and salaries account and all the expense accounts in the general ledger.

↳ A **control account** is an account which records total cost, unlike an individual ledger account which records individual debits and credits.

↳ There are two main cost bookkeeping systems, **interlocking systems** and **integrated systems**.

QUICK QUIZ

1 What is a control account?

2 What are the two types of cost bookkeeping system?

3 Where are direct expenses and overheads collected?

4 List four financial accounting items which are of interest to the cost accountant.

5 Where are the items referred to in 4 held?

6 What are the main limitations of interlocking systems?

ANSWERS TO QUICK QUIZ

1   An account which records total cost, as opposed to individual costs (which are recorded in individual ledger accounts)

2   Integrated and interlocking

3   In the work in progress control account

4   •   Cash
     •   Payables
     •   Receivables
     •   Revenue reserves

5   In the cost ledger control account

6   •   Profits of separate cost and financial accounts must be reconciled.
     •   They require more administration time.
     •   They are more costly to run.

Now try ...

Attempt the questions below from the **Practice Question Bank**

Number

Q54

Q55

Q56

Q57

Q58

Job, batch and service costing

This chapter explains how **cost units** are identified and the cost of cost units is measured in three different types of operation. Some businesses make non-standard items for customers, and for each customer there is a unique order or 'job': the costing system measures the cost of each job. Some businesses make a number of different standard products in batches – and make a batch of one product, then a batch of a different product, and so on. Service industries are also different: the aim of a costing system for services should be to measure the cost of a unit of service. This chapter explains how costs are recorded and measured in **job costing, batch costing** and **service costing**.

Absorption costing or marginal costing methods can be applied to all three types of costing.

TOPIC LIST	SYLLABUS REFERENCE
1 Job costing	A2 (b), (c), (f), C3 (a), (b), (c), (d)
2 Batch costing	A2 (b), (f), C3 (a), (b), (c), (d)
3 Service costing	A2 (b), C5 (a), (b), (c), (d), (e)

1 Job costing

Job costing is the costing method used where each job is separately identifiable as a cost unit.

1.1 Introduction

In this chapter we will be looking at three important costing systems.

- Job costing
- Batch costing
- Service costing

We will be looking at another important system, that of **process costing**, later on.

A costing system is a system of collecting costs which is designed to suit the way that goods are processed or manufactured or the way that services are provided.

Each organisation's costing system will have unique features but **costing systems of organisation's in the same line of business will have common aspects.** On the other hand, organisations involved in completely different activities, such as hospitals and car part manufacturers, will each use very different costing systems.

1.2 Aim of job costing

The aim of **job costing** is simply to collect the cost information shown below.

	$
Direct materials	X
Direct labour	X
Direct expenses	X
Direct cost	X
Production overhead	X
Total production cost	X
Administration overhead	X
Selling overhead	X
Cost of sales	X

A profit **'mark-up'** is added to the final figure and the total is the selling price of the job.

In other words, all we are doing is looking at one way of putting together the pieces of information that we have studied separately so far.

1.3 What is a job?

A **job** is a cost unit which consists of a single order or contract.

With other methods of costing it is usual to **produce for inventory**. Management therefore decide in advance how many units of each type, size, colour, quality and so on will be produced during the coming period. These decisions will all be taken without taking into account the identity of the individual customers who will eventually buy the products.

In job costing on the other hand, production is usually carried out in accordance with the **special requirements** of each customer. It is therefore usual for each job to **differ in one or more respects from every other job**, which means that a separate record must be maintained to show the details of a particular job.

The work relating to a job is usually carried out within a factory or workshop and moves through processes and operations as a **continuously identifiable unit**.

1.4 Procedure for the performance of jobs

The normal procedure in jobbing concerns involves the following:

(a)   The prospective customer approaches the supplier and indicates the **requirements** of the job.

(b)   A responsible official sees the prospective customer and agrees the **precise details of the items** to be supplied, for example the quantity, quality and colour of the goods, the date of delivery and any special requirements.

(c)   The estimating department of the organisation then prepares an **estimate** for the job. The total of these items will represent the **quoted selling price**.

(d)   At the appropriate time, the job will be 'loaded' on to the factory floor. This means that as soon as all materials, labour and equipment are available and subject to the scheduling of other orders, the job will be started.

1.5 Collection of job costs

Each job will be given a **number** to identify it. A separate record must be maintained to show the details of individual jobs. The process of collecting job costs may be outlined as follows:

(a)   Materials requisitions are sent to stores.

(b)   The materials requisition note will be used to cost the materials issued to the job concerned, and this cost may then be recorded on a job cost sheet.

(c)   The job ticket is passed to the worker who is to perform the first operation.

(d)   When the job is completed by the worker who performs the final operation, the job ticket is sent to the cost office, where the time spent will be costed and recorded on the job cost sheet.

(e)   The relevant costs of materials issued, direct labour performed and direct expenses incurred as recorded on the job cost sheet are charged to the job account in the work in progress ledger.

(f)   The job account is debited with the job's share of the factory overhead, based on the absorption rate(s) in operation.

(g)   On completion of the job, the job account is charged with the appropriate administration, selling and distribution overhead, after which the total cost of the job can be ascertained.

(h)   The difference between the agreed selling price and the total actual cost will be the supplier's profit (or loss).

1.6 Job account

Here is a proforma job account, which will be one of the accounts in the work in progress control account.

JOB ACCOUNT

	$		$
Materials issued	X	Finished jobs	X
Direct labour	X		
Direct expenses	X		
Production overhead at			
predetermined rate	X		
Other overheads	X		
	X		X

1.7 Job card

When jobs are completed, **job cards** are transferred from the **work in progress** category to **finished goods**. When delivery is made to the customer, the costs become a **cost of sale**.

1.7.1 Example: Job card

JOB CARD										Job No.				B641	
Customer		Mr J White			Customer's Order No.					Vehicle make				Peugot 205 GTE	
Job Description		Repair damage to offside front door								Vehicle reg. no.				G 614 SOX	
Estimate Ref.		2599			Invoice No.					Date to collect				14.6.XO	
Quoted price		$338.68			Invoice price		$355.05								

Material / Labour / Overheads

Material						Labour								Overheads			
Date	Req. No.	Qty.	Price	Cost $	Cost p	Date	Emp-loyee	Cost Ctre	Hrs.	Rate	Bonus	Cost $	Cost p	Hrs	OAR	Cost $	Cost p
12.6	36815	1	75.49	75	49	12.6	018	B	1.98	6.50	-	12	87	7.9	2.50	19	75
12.6	36816	1	33.19	33	19	13.6	018	B	5.92	6.50	-	38	48				
12.6	36842	5	6.01	30	05						13.65	13	65				
13.6	36881	5	3.99	19	95												
Total C/F				158	68	Total C/F						65	00	Total C/F		19	75

Expenses / Job Cost Summary

Expenses						Job Cost Summary	Actual $	Actual p	Estimate $	Estimate p
Date	Ref.	Description		Cost $	Cost p					
12.6	-	N. Jolley Panel-beating		50	-	Direct Materials B/F	158	68	158	68
						Direct Expenses B/F	50	00		
						Direct Labour B/F	65	00	180	00
						Direct Cost	273	68		
						Overheads B/F	19	75		
							293	43		
						Admin overhead (add 10%)	29	34		
						= Total Cost	322	77	338	68
						Invoice Price	355	05		
Total C/F				50	-	Job Profit/Loss	32	28		

Comments

Job Cost Card Completed by _____

1.8 Job costing and computerisation

Job cards exist in **manual** systems, but it is increasingly likely that in large organisations the job costing system will be **computerised**, using accounting software specifically designed to deal with job costing requirements.

Job costing systems may also be used to control the costs of **internal service departments**, eg the maintenance department.

1.9 Example: Job costing

Pansy Co is a company that carries out jobbing work. One of the jobs carried out in May was job 2409, to which the following information relates.

Direct material Y:	400 kilos were issued from stores at a cost of $5 per kilo.
Direct material Z:	800 kilos were issued from stores at a cost of $6 per kilo. 60 kilos were returned to stores.
Department P:	300 labour hours were worked, of which 100 hours were overtime.
Department Q:	200 labour hours were worked, of which 100 hours were overtime.

Overtime work is not normal in Department P, where basic pay is $6 per hour plus an overtime premium of $1 per hour. Overtime work was done in Department Q in May because of a request by the customer of another job to complete their job quickly. Basic pay in Department Q is $8 per hour and overtime premium is $1.50 per hour. Overhead is absorbed at the rate of $3 per direct labour hour in both departments.

Required

(a)   Calculate the direct materials cost of job 2409.
(b)   Calculate the direct labour cost of job 2409.
(c)   Calculate the full production cost of job 2409 using absorption costing.

Solution

(a)
	$
Direct material Y (400 kilos × $5)	2,000
Direct material Z (800 – 60 kilos × $6)	4,440
Total direct material cost	6,440

(b)
	$
Department P (300 hours × $6)	1,800
Department Q (200 hours × $8)	1,600
Total direct labour cost	3,400

Overtime premium will be charged to overhead in the case of Department P, and to the job of the customer who asked for overtime to be worked in the case of Department Q.

(c)
	$
Direct material cost	6,440
Direct labour cost	3,400
Production overhead (500 hours × $3)	1,500
	11,340

1.10 Cost plus pricing

Many organisations base the price of a product on simple **cost plus** rules which involves estimating costs and then adding a profit margin in order to set the price.

Cost plus pricing is a method of determining the sales price by calculating the full cost of a product and adding a percentage mark-up for profit.

TERM

BPP LEARNING MEDIA

The full cost may be a fully absorbed production cost only, or it may include some absorbed administration, selling and distribution overhead (non-production overheads).

1.11 Example: Cost plus pricing

A company budgets to have a variable cost of production of $4 per unit. Fixed production costs are $6,000 per month. A customer requests a job of 5,000 units. This will take exactly one month to produce. The selling price is to be 40% higher than full cost.

Required

Calculate the selling price of the job using the cost plus pricing method.

Solution

Full cost per unit = variable cost + fixed cost

Total variable cost = $4 × 5,000 = $20,000

Fixed cost = $6,000 per month

Full cost   = $26,000

$$\therefore \text{Selling price} \quad = \frac{140}{100} \times \$26,000$$

$$= \$36,400$$

EXAM FOCUS POINT

An exam question about job costing may ask you to determine a job price by adding a certain amount of profit. To do this, you need to remember the following crucial formula.

	%
Cost of job	100
+ profit	25
= price	125

Profit may be expressed either as a percentage of job cost (such as 25% 25/100 mark up) or as a percentage of price (such as 20% (25/125) margin).

QUESTION
Job costing

A curtain-making business manufactures quality curtains to customers' orders. It has three production departments (X, Y and Z) which have overhead absorption rates (per direct labour hour) of $12.86, $12.40 and $14.03 respectively.

Two pairs of curtains are to be manufactured for customers. Direct costs are as follows.

	Job TN8	Job KT2
Direct material	$154	$108
Direct labour	20 hours dept X	16 hours dept X
	12 hours dept Y	10 hours dept Y
	10 hours dept Z	14 hours dept Z

Labour rates per hour are as follows: $3.80 (X); $3.50 (Y); $3.40 (Z).

The firm quotes prices to customers that reflect a required profit of 25% on selling price.

Required

Calculate the total cost and selling price of each job.

ANSWER

Helping hand. Note that the profit margin is given as a percentage on selling price. If profit is 25% on selling price, this is the same as $33^{1}/_{3}\%$ (25/75) on cost.

		Job TN8 $		Job KT2 $
Direct material		154.00		108.00
Direct labour: dept X	(20 × 3.80)	76.00	(16 × 3.80)	60.80
dept Y	(12 × 3.50)	42.00	(10 × 3.50)	35.00
dept Z	(10 × 3.40)	34.00	(14 × 3.40)	47.60
Total direct cost		306.00		251.40
Overhead: dept X	(20 × 12.86)	257.20	(16 × 12.86)	205.76
dept Y	(12 × 12.40)	148.80	(10 × 12.40)	124.00
dept Z	(10 × 14.03)	140.30	(14 × 14.03)	196.42
Total cost		852.30		777.58
Profit		284.10		259.19
Quoted selling price		1,136.40		1,036.77

2 Batch costing

Batch costing is a form of specific order costing in which costs are attributed to batches of products. It is similar to job costing in that each batch of similar articles is separately identifiable. The **cost per unit** manufactured in a batch is the total batch cost divided by the number of units in the batch.

2.1 Introduction

Batch costing is used where common equipment is used to produce batches of different products for inventory. For example, in food production and paint manufacturing.

A **batch** is a cost unit which consists of a separate, readily identifiable group of product units which maintains its separate identity throughout the production process.

The procedures for **costing batches** are very similar to those for costing jobs.

> The batch is treated as a separate cost unit during production and the costs are collected as described earlier.

> Once the batch has been completed, the **cost per unit** can be calculated as the total batch cost divided by the number of units in the batch.

2.2 Example: Batch costing

A company manufactures model cars and has the following budgeted overheads for a period.

Department	Budgeted overheads $	Budgeted activity
Welding	6,000	1,500 labour hours
Assembly	10,000	1,000 labour hours

Selling and administrative overheads are 20% of production cost. Production of 250 model cars type XJS1, made as Batch 8638, incurred the following costs.

Materials $12,000
Labour 100 hours welding shop at $8/hour
200 hours assembly shop at $9/hour

The cost of hiring special X-ray equipment for testing the welds is $500.

Required

Calculate the cost per unit for Batch 8638.

Solution

The first step is to calculate the overhead absorption rate for the production departments.

Welding $= \dfrac{\$6,000}{1,500} =$ \$4 per labour hour

Assembly $= \dfrac{\$10,000}{1,000} =$ \$10 per labour hour

Total cost – Batch no 8638

	\$	\$
Direct material		12,000
Direct labour 100 × \$8 =	800	
200 × \$9 =	1,800	
		2,600
Direct expense		500
Prime cost		15,100
Overheads 100 × 4 =	400	
200 × 10 =	2,000	
		2,400
Production cost		17,500
Selling and administrative cost (20% of production cost)		3,500
Total cost		21,000

Cost per unit $= \dfrac{\$21,000}{250} =$ \$84

QUESTION

Batch costing

Lyfsa Kitchen Units Co crafts two different sizes of standard unit and a DIY all-purpose unit for filling up awkward spaces. The units are built in batches of around 250 (although the number varies according to the quality of wood purchased), and each batch is sold to NGJ Furniture Warehouses Co.

The costs incurred in May were as follows.

	Big unit	Little unit	All-purpose
Direct materials purchased	\$5,240	\$6,710	\$3,820
Direct labour			
Skilled (hours)	1,580	1,700	160
Semi-skilled (hours)	3,160	1,900	300
Direct expenses	\$1,180	\$1,700	\$250
Selling price of batch	\$48,980	\$43,125	\$25,660
Completed at 31 May	100%	80%	25%

The following information is available.

All direct materials for the completion of the batches have been recorded. Skilled labour is paid \$9 per hour, semi-skilled \$7 per hour. Administration expenses total \$4,400 per month and are to be allocated to the batches on the basis of direct labour hours. Direct labour costs, direct expenses and administration expenses will increase in proportion to the total labour hours required to complete the little units and the all-purpose units. On completion of the work the practice of the manufacturer is to divide the calculated profit on each batch 20% to staff as a bonus, 80% to the company. Losses are absorbed 100% by the company.

Required

(a) Calculate the profit or loss made by the company on big units.
(b) Project the profit or loss likely to be made by the company on little units and all-purpose units.

ANSWER

(a) **Big units**

	$	$
Direct materials		5,240
Direct labour		
Skilled 1,580 hours at $9	14,220	
Semi-skilled 3,160 hours at $7	22,120	
		36,340
Direct expenses		1,180
Administrative expenses		
4,740 hours at $0.50 (see below)*		2,370
		45,130
Selling price		48,980
Calculated profit		3,850
Divided: Staff bonus 20%		770
Profit for company 80%		3,080

*Administrative expenses absorption rate $= \dfrac{\$4,400}{8,800}$ per labour hour

$= \$0.50$ per labour hour

(b)

		Little units			All-purpose	
		$	$		$	$
Direct materials			6,710			3,820
Direct labour						
Skilled	1,700 hrs at $9	15,300		160 hrs at $9	1,440	
Semi-skilled	1,900 hrs at $7	13,300		300 hrs at $7	2,100	
Direct expenses		1,700			250	
Administration						
expenses:	3,600 hrs at	1,800		460 hrs at	230	
	$0.50			$0.50		
		32,100			4,020	
Costs to						
completion	20/80 × 32,100	8,025		75/25 × 4,020	12,060	
			40,125			16,080
Total costs			46,835			19,900
Selling price			43,125			25,660
Calculated						
profit/(loss)			(3,710)			5,760
Divided: Staff bonus 20%			–			1,152
(Loss)/profit for company			(3,710)			4,608

Note that whilst direct labour costs, direct expenses and administration expenses increase in proportion to the total labour hours required to complete the little units and the all-purpose units, there will be no further material costs to complete the batches.

2.3 Controlling costs in job and batch costing

One of the tasks of management is to control costs, and prevent unnecessary expenditures or inefficiencies. Some of the methods of controlling costs are the same in any type of organisation: economical purchasing, supervision and training of employees to maintain efficiency levels, controls over spending limits (departmental budgets) and so on.

However there are some aspects of cost control that differ between job costing and batch costing systems.

(a)   **Job costing**. Although many jobs may be similar, a feature of job costing systems is that each job is different, because each customer has different specific requirements. As a consequence:

   (i)   The materials obtained for a job may be non-standard, and there may be a tendency to over-purchase.

   (ii)   Similarly it may be difficult to estimate the time for a job with accuracy, and the total labour cost of a job will increase with the length of time required for completion.

   (iii) There may be special overhead costs for jobbing systems, with specialist staff employed to liaise with customers and to monitor the progress of individual jobs.

   Control over costs involves asking why particular expenses are necessary, why the job is taking so long to complete, or whether material costs are excessive, compared with the original job estimate.

(b)   **Batch costing**. Batch costing involves the production of a quantity of the same units. The units produced should be standard items, and unit costs should be easier to estimate than job costs.

   However, an important cost in batch costing is the cost of preparing for the next batch of a product, and the cost of cleaning up after one batch has been completed. Costs of cleaning up and setting up for the next batch are called 'set-up costs'. When the time between batches is long, set-up costs may be high.

   Set-up costs may be controlled by trying to ensure that the work is done as quickly as possible, but also by manufacturing batches in a suitable size. With larger batches, there will be fewer batches produced and therefore fewer 'set-ups' between jobs.

3 Service costing

Service costing can be used by companies operating in a service industry or by companies wishing to establish the cost of services carried out by different departments.

3.1 What are service organisations?

Service organisations **do not make or sell tangible goods**. Profit-seeking service organisations include accountancy firms, law firms, transport companies, banks and hotels. Almost all not-for-profit organisations – hospitals, schools, libraries and so on – are also service organisations.

Service costing differs from the other costing methods in the following ways:

(a)   In general, with service costing, the cost of direct materials consumed will be relatively small compared to the labour, direct expenses and overheads cost.

(b)   Indirect costs tend to represent a higher proportion of total cost compared with product costing.

(c)   The output of most service organisations is often intangible and it is therefore difficult to establish a measurable cost unit.

3.1.1 Characteristics of service organisations

(a)   **S**imultaneous

   The production and consumption of a service are simultaneous, and therefore it cannot be inspected for quality in advance.

(b)   **H**eterogeneous

   A service is heterogeneous. The service received will vary each time. Services are more reliant on people. People are not robots, so how the service is delivered will not be identical each time.

(c)   **I**ntangible

   A service is intangible. The actual benefit being bought cannot be touched.

(d)   **P**erishable

   Services are perishable, that is, they cannot be stored. For example, a hairdresser cannot do haircuts in advance and keep them stocked away for when demand increases.

This can be remembered using **SHIP**.

BPP
LEARNING
MEDIA

3.2 Cost units

A particular problem with service costing is the difficulty in defining a **realistic cost** unit that represents a suitable measure of the service provided. Frequently, a **composite cost unit** may be deemed more appropriate if the service is a function of two activity variables.

Typical composite cost units used by companies operating in a service industry are shown below.

Service	Cost unit
Road, rail and air transport services	Passenger-kilometre (cost per passenger per kilometre) Tonne-kilometre (cost per tonne per kilometre)
Hotels	Occupied room-night (cost per occupied room per night)
Hospitals	Patient-day (cost per patient per day)

Each organisation will need to ascertain the cost unit most appropriate to its activities. If a number of organisations within an industry use a common cost unit, valuable **comparisons** can be made between similar establishments. This is particularly applicable to hospitals, educational establishments and local authorities.

3.3 Example: Composite cost units

The following information is available for the Whiteley Hotel for the latest 30-day period.

Number of rooms available per night   40
Percentage occupancy achieved   65%
Room servicing cost incurred $3,900

Required

(a) Calculate the number of occupied room-nights.
(b) Calculate the room servicing cost per occupied room-night (to the nearest cent).

Solution

(a) Firstly, we need to calculate the number of occupied room-nights. We can do this as follows.

Number of occupied room-nights = 40 rooms × 30 nights × 65%
= 780

(b) In order to calculate the room servicing cost per occupied room-night we can use the following equation.

$$\text{Room servicing cost per occupied room-night} = \frac{\text{Total room servicing costs}}{\text{Number of occupied room-nights}}$$

$$= \frac{\$3,900}{780}$$

$$= \$5$$

FORMULA TO LEARN

$$\text{Cost per service unit} = \frac{\text{Total costs for period}}{\text{Number of service units in the period}}$$

QUESTION   Cost per tonne – kilometre

Carry Co operates a small fleet of delivery vehicles. Expected costs are as follows.

Loading   1 hour per tonne loaded
Loading costs:
     Labour (casual) $2 per hour
     Equipment depreciation $80 per week
     Supervision $80 per week

Drivers' wages (fixed)	$100 per man per week
Petrol	10c per kilometre
Repairs	5c per kilometre
Depreciation	$80 per week per vehicle
Supervision	$120 per week
Other general expenses (fixed)	$200 per week

There are two drivers and two vehicles in the fleet.

During a slack week, only six journeys were made.

Journey	Tonnes carried (one way)	One-way distance of journey Kilometres
1	5	100
2	8	20
3	2	60
4	4	50
5	6	200
6	5	300

Required

Calculate the average full cost per tonne – kilometre for a week.

ANSWER

The average full cost per tonne-kilometre for a week is $0.304

Workings

Variable costs

Journey	1	2	3	4	5	6
	$	$	$	$	$	$
Loading labour	10	16	4	8	12	10
Petrol (both ways)	20	4	12	10	40	60
Repairs (both ways)	10	2	6	5	20	30
	40	22	22	23	72	100

Total costs

	$
Variable costs (total for journeys 1 to 6)	279
Loading equipment depreciation	80
Loading supervision	80
Drivers' wages	200
Vehicles depreciation	160
Drivers' supervision	120
Other costs	200
	1,119

Journey	Tonnes	One-way distance Kilometres	Tonne-kilometres
1	5	100	500
2	8	20	160
3	2	60	120
4	4	50	200
5	6	200	1,200
6	5	300	1,500
			3,680

Cost per tonne-kilometre $\dfrac{\$1,119}{3,680} = \$0.304$

⤷ **Job costing** is the costing method used where each job is separately identifiable as a cost unit.

⤷ **Batch costing** is a form of specific order costing in which costs are attributed to batches of products. It is similar to job costing in that each batch of similar articles is separately identifiable. The **cost per unit** manufactured in a batch is the total batch cost divided by the number of units in the batch.

⤷ **Service costing** can be used by companies operating in a service industry or by companies wishing to establish the cost of services carried out by different departments.

1   Which of the following are not characteristics of job costing?

    1   Customer driven production
    2   Complete production possible within a single accounting period
    3   Homogeneous products

    O   1 and 2 only
    O   1 and 3 only
    O   2 and 3 only
    O   3 only

2   The cost of a job is $100,000.

    (a)   If profit is 25% of the job cost, the price of the job = $.................
    (b)   If there is a 25% margin, the price of the job = $....................

3   How would you calculate the cost per unit of a completed batch?

4   Match up the following services with their typical cost units.

Service		Cost unit
Hotels		Patient-day
Education	?	Meal served
Hospitals		Full-time student
Catering organisations		Occupied bed-night

5   A job cost estimate includes 630 productive labour hours. In addition, it is anticipated that idle time will be 10% of the total hours paid for the job. The wage rate is $12 per hour.

    What is the total estimated labour cost for the job?

    O $6,804
    O $7,560
    O $8,316
    O $8,400

6   A firm uses job costing. Details of the three jobs worked on during a period are:

	Job BA	Job DC	Job FE
	$	$	$
Opening work-in-progress	22,760	3,190	–
Direct materials in the period	4,620	11,660	14,335
Direct labour in the period	12,125	10,520	7,695

Overheads are absorbed at 40% of prime cost in each period. Jobs DC and FE remained incomplete at the end of the period.

What is the value of the closing work-in-progress?

O $61,894
O $65,084
O $66,360
O $68,952

7   A company has a delivery vehicle, which made three journeys in one week. Costs were $13,200.
Journey 1: One-way distance = 200 kilometres, weight of load carried 5 tonnes
Journey 2: One-way distance = 500 kilometres, weight of load carried 8 tonnes
Journey 3: One-way distance = 800 kilometres, weight of load carried 2 tonnes

What was the cost per tonne-kilometre?

O $1
O $2
O $8.80
O $88

8   A hospital has a ward with 15 beds. During April (30 days) average bed occupancy was 80%. The costs of operating the ward in the month were $810,000. What was the cost per patient day for the ward during April?

O $150
O $1,800
O $2,250
O $70,000

9   Which of the following would be appropriate cost units for a passenger coach company?

1   Vehicle cost per passenger kilometre
2   Fuel cost for each vehicle per kilometre
3   Fixed cost per kilometre

O   1 only
O   1 and 2 only
O   1 and 3 only
O   2 and 3 only

1 3 only

2 (a) $100,000 + (25% × $100,000) = $100,000 + $25,000 = $125,000

(b) Profit is 25% of the selling price, therefore selling price should be written as 100%:

	%
Selling price	100
Profit	25
Cost	75

∴ Price = $100,000 × 100/75 = $133,333.

3 $\dfrac{\text{Total batch cost}}{\text{Number of units in the batch}}$

4

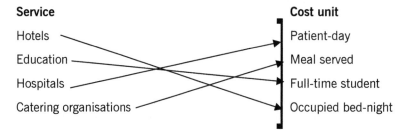

Service	Cost unit
Hotels	Patient-day
Education	Meal served
Hospitals	Full-time student
Catering organisations	Occupied bed-night

5 $8,400   (630 ÷ 0.9 hours) × $12/hour) = $8,400

6 $65,084   Job BA is completed so can be ignored.

Total costs = (11,660 + 10,520 + 14,335 + 7,695) × 1.4
= $61,894

Closing work in progress value = 61,894 + 3,190
= $65,084

7 $2

Tonne kilometres = (5 × 200) + (8 × 500) + (2 × 800) = 6,600

Cost per tonne-kilometre = $13,200/6,600 = $2

One-way distance only should be used, because no weight is carried on the return journey.

8 $2,250

Average number of patients per day = 80% × 15 = 12

Patient days in April = 12 × 30 = 360

Cost per patient day = $810,000/360 = $2,250

9 1 and 2 only

Measure 1 is appropriate for control purposes because it combines the distance travelled with the number of passengers carried, both of which affect costs.

Measure 2 can be useful for control purposes because it focuses on a particular aspect of the cost of operating each vehicle.

Now try ...

Attempt the questions below from the **Practice Question Bank**

Number

Q59

Q60

Q61

Q62

Process costing

The previous chapter described how unit costs are measured in systems of job costing, batch costing and service costing. This chapter looks at how unit costs are measured in a **manufacturing system where output is produced in a continuous process,** such as **chemicals production** and **oil refining**. There are several special features of **process manufacturing** and **process costing**. The production process may involve some **loss of materials during the process,** due to evaporation or unavoidable waste or loss. Another feature of process industries is that a process may produce not just one product, but several different **joint products** or **by-products**.

This chapter explains the techniques used to record costs in a system of process costing, and in particular the accounting treatment of loss in process, measuring the costs of joint products and the accounting treatment of by-products.

TOPIC LIST	SYLLABUS REFERENCE
1 Process costing features	C4 (a)
2 Losses and gains	C4 (b), (c), (d)
3 Accounting for scrap	C4 (e)
4 Joint products and by-products	C4 (f), (g), (h), (i)
5 Accounting for by-products	C4 (g), (h)
6 The further processing decision	C4 (j)

Study Guide	Intellectual level
C Costing techniques	
4 Process costing	
(a) Identify situations where the use of process costing is appropriate	K
(b) Explain and illustrate the nature of normal and abnormal losses/gains	S
(c) Calculate unit costs where losses are separated into normal and abnormal	S
(d) Prepare process accounts where losses are separated into normal and abnormal	S
(e) Account for scrap and waste	S
(f) Distinguish between joint products and by-products	K
(g) Explain the accounting treatment of joint products and by-products at the point of separation	K
(h) Apportion joint process costs using net realisable values and weight/volume of output respectively	S
(i) Discuss the usefulness of product cost/profit data from a joint process	K
(j) Evaluate the benefit of further processing	S

1 Process costing features

> **Process costing** is a costing method used where there are continuous processes. Process costs are attributed to the units produced in a period.

1.1 Introduction

We have now looked at three cost accounting methods: **job costing**, **batch costing,** and **service costing**. In this chapter we will consider another costing method, **process costing**. Process costing is applied when output consists of a continuous stream of **identical units**.

We will begin from basics and look at how to account for the most simple of processes. We will then move on to how to account for any **losses** which might occur, as well as what to do with any **scrapped units** which are sold.

EXAM FOCUS POINT

Process costing is a popular exam topic and so it is very important that you understand it.

1.2 Features of process costing

Process costing is a costing method used to determine the cost of units manufactured from a continuous process. It is common to identify process costing with **continuous production** such as the following:

- Oil refining
- Brewing
- Sugar refining
- Chemical processing

Features of process costing include the following:

(a)   The continuous nature of production in process costing means that it is not possible to calculate the cost per unit of output or the cost per unit of closing inventory.

(b)   There is often a **loss in process** due to spoilage, wastage, evaporation and so on.

(c)   The **output** of one process becomes the **input** to the next until the finished product is made in the final process.

(d)   Output from production may be a single product, but there may also be one or more **by-products** and/or **joint products**.

2   Losses and gains

TERM

> During a production process, a **loss** may occur due to wastage, spoilage, evaporation, and so on.

- **Normal loss** is the loss expected during a process. It is not given a cost.

- **Abnormal loss** is the extra loss resulting when actual loss is greater than normal or expected loss, and it is given a cost.

- **Abnormal gain** is the gain resulting when actual loss is less than the normal or expected loss, and it is given a 'negative cost'.

Since **normal loss is not given a cost**, the cost of producing these units is borne by the 'good' units of output.

Abnormal loss and gain units are valued at the same unit rate as 'good' units. Abnormal events do not therefore affect the cost of good production. Their costs are **analysed separately** in an **abnormal loss or abnormal gain account**.

2.1 Framework for dealing with process costing

Process costing is centred around **four key steps**. The exact work done at each step will depend on the circumstances of the question, but the approach can always be used. Don't worry about the terms used. We will be looking at their meaning as we work through the chapter.

Step 1	**Determine output and losses.** • Determine expected output. • Calculate normal loss and abnormal loss and gain.
Step 2	**Calculate cost per unit of output and losses.** Divide the process costs by the expected output.
Step 3	**Calculate total cost of output and losses.** Multiply the cost per unit by the units of output and abnormal loss/gain.

> **Step 4** **Complete accounts**.
> - Complete the process account.
> - Write up the other accounts required by the question.

2.2 Example: Normal loss

Suppose 2,000 units are input to a process. Normal loss is 5% of input and there are no opening or closing inventories.

Required

Calculate the normal loss.

Solution

Normal loss = 5% × 2,000 units
= 100 units

2.3 Example: Abnormal loss

Suppose 2,000 units are input to a process. Normal loss is 5% of input and there are no opening and closing inventories. Actual output was 1,800 units.

Required

Calculate the abnormal loss.

Solution

Normal loss   = 5% × 2,000 units
        = 100 units

Actual loss   = 2,000 – 1,800
        = 200 units

∴ Abnormal loss   = Actual loss – normal loss
        = 200 units – 100 units
        = 100 units

2.4 Example: Abnormal gain

Suppose 2,000 units are input to a process. Normal loss is 5% of input and there are no opening or closing inventories. Actual output was 1,950 units.

Required

Calculate the abnormal gain.

Solution

Normal loss   = 5% × 2,000 units
        = 100 units

Actual loss   = 2,000 units – 1,950 units
        = 50 units

Abnormal gain   = Actual loss – normal loss
        = 50 units – 100 units
        = 50 units

2.5 Example: Cost per unit (Step 2)

Jingles Co operates a single manufacturing process, and during March the following processing took place.

Opening inventory	nil	Closing inventory	nil
Units introduced	1,000 units	Output	900 units
Costs incurred	$4,500	Loss	100 units

Required

Determine the cost per unit in the following circumstances.

(a)   Expected or normal loss is 10% of input.
(b)   There is no expected loss, so that the entire loss of 100 units was unexpected.

Solution

(a) $$\frac{\text{Costs}}{\text{Expected output (90\% of 1,000)}} = \frac{\$4,500}{900\text{ units}}$$

$$\text{Cost per unit of output} = \frac{\$4,500}{900} = \$5$$

(b) $$\frac{\text{Costs incurred}}{\text{Expected output}} = \frac{\$4,500}{1,000\text{ units}}$$

Costs per unit = $4.50

2.6 Example: Total cost and process accounts (Steps 3 and 4)

Use the information from the example above.

Required

Determine the cost of output and produce the process accounts in the following circumstances.

(a)   Expected or normal loss is 10% of input.
(b)   There is no expected loss, so that the entire loss of 100 units was unexpected.

Solution

(a)   Cost of output   = $4,500

Normal loss is not given any cost, so that the process account would appear as follows.

PROCESS ACCOUNT

	Units	$		Units	$
Costs incurred	1,000	4,500	Normal loss	100	0
			Output units	900	4,500
	1,000	4,500		1,000	4,500

It helps to enter normal loss into the process 'T' account, just to make sure that your memorandum columns for units are the same on the debit and the credit sides of the account.

(b)   Cost of output   = $4,500

The process account and abnormal loss account would look like this.

PROCESS ACCOUNT

	Units	$		Units	$
Costs incurred	1,000	4,500	Abnormal loss	100	450
			Output units	900	4,050
	1,000	4,500		1,000	4,500

ABNORMAL LOSS ACCOUNT

	Units	$		Units	$
Process account	100	4 50	Statement of profit or loss	1 00	450

2.7 Example: Losses and gains a comprehensive example

Suppose 1,000 units at a cost of $4,500 are input to a process. Normal loss is 10% and there are no opening or closing inventories.

Required

(a) Complete the process account and the abnormal loss/gain account if actual output was 860 units (so that actual loss is 140 units).

(b) Complete the process account and the abnormal loss/gain account if actual output was 920 units (so that actual loss is 80 units).

Solution

Before we demonstrate the use of the 'four-step framework' we will summarise the way that the losses are dealt with.

*   Normal loss is given no share of cost.
*   **Abnormal loss** is given a cost, which is written off to the statement of profit or loss (debit entry) via an abnormal loss/gain account.
*   **Abnormal gain** is treated in the same way, except that being a gain rather than a loss, it appears as a **debit** entry in the process account and a **credit** entry in the statement of profit or loss.
*   The cost of output is therefore based on the **expected** units of output, which in our example amount to 90% of 1,000 = 900 units.

(a) **Output is 860 units**

Step 1 **Determine output and losses.**

If actual output is 860 units and the actual loss is 140 units:

	Units
Actual loss	140
Normal loss (10% of 1,000)	100
Abnormal loss	40

Normal loss is 10% of input, this means expected output is 90% of input (0.9 × 1,000) = 900 on this case.

Step 2 **Calculate cost per unit of output and losses.**

The cost per unit of output and the cost per unit of abnormal loss are based on **expected** output.

$$\frac{\text{Costs incurred}}{\text{Expected output}} = \frac{\$4,500}{900 \text{ units}} = \$5 \text{ per unit}$$

Step 3 **Calculate total cost of output and losses.**

Normal loss is not assigned any cost.

	$
Cost of output (860 × $5)	4,300
Normal loss	0
Abnormal loss (40 × $5)	200
	4,500

Step 4 **Complete accounts**.

PROCESS ACCOUNT

	Units	$		Units		$
Cost incurred	1,000	4,500	Normal loss	100		0
			Output (finished goods a/c)	860	(× $5)	4,300
			Abnormal loss	40	(× $5)	200
	1,000	4,500		1,000		4,500

ABNORMAL LOSS/GAIN ACCOUNT

	Units	$		Units	$
Process a/c	40	200	Statement of profit or loss	40	200

(b) **Output is 920 units**

Step 1 **Determine output and losses**.

If actual output is 920 units and the actual loss is 80 units:

	Units
Actual loss	80
Normal loss (10% of 1,000)	100
Abnormal gain	20

As before expected output is 900 units.

Step 2 **Calculate cost per unit of output and losses**.

The cost per unit of output and the cost per unit of abnormal gain are based on **expected** output.

$$\frac{\text{Costs incurred}}{\text{Expected output}} = \frac{\$4,500}{900\ \text{units}} = \$5 \text{ per unit}$$

(Whether there is abnormal loss or gain does not affect the valuation of units of output. The figure of $5 per unit is exactly the same as in the part (a), when there were 40 units of abnormal loss.)

Step 3 **Calculate total cost of output and losses**.

	$
Cost of output (920 × $5)	4,600
Normal loss	0
Abnormal gain (20 × $5)	(100)
	4,500

Step 4 **Complete accounts**.

PROCESS ACCOUNT

	Units	$		Units	$
Cost incurred	1,000	4,500	Normal loss	100	0
Abnormal gain a/c	20 (× $5)	100	Output (finished goods a/c)	920 (× $5)	4,600
	1,020	4,600		1,020	4,600

ABNORMAL LOSS/GAIN

	Units	$		Units	$
Statement of profit or loss	20	100	Process a/c	20	100

If there is a closing balance in the abnormal loss or gain account when the profit for the period is calculated, this balance is taken to the statement of profit or loss: an **abnormal gain** will be a **credit** and an **abnormal loss** will be a **debit** to the statement of profit or loss.

3 Accounting for scrap

Loss may have a **scrap value**. Revenue from scrap is treated as a reduction in costs. It is conventional for the **scrap value of normal loss to be deducted from the cost of materials** before a cost per equivalent unit is calculated.

3.1 Basic rules

Loss may have a scrap value. The following basic rules are applied in accounting for this value in the process accounts.

(a)   **Revenue from scrap** is treated, not as an addition to sales revenue, but as a **reduction in costs**.

(b)   The scrap value of **normal loss** is therefore used to reduce the material costs of the process.

Debit	Scrap account
Credit	Process account

with the scrap value of the normal loss.

(c)   The scrap value of **abnormal loss** is used to reduce the cost of abnormal loss.

Debit	Scrap account
Credit	Abnormal loss account

with the scrap value of abnormal loss, which therefore reduces the write-off of cost to the statement of profit or loss at the end of the period.

(d)   The scrap value of **abnormal gain** arises because the actual units sold as scrap will be less than the scrap value of normal loss. Because there are fewer units of scrap than expected, there will be less revenue from scrap as a direct consequence of the abnormal gain. The abnormal gain account should therefore be debited with the scrap value.

Debit	Abnormal gain account
Credit	Scrap account

with the scrap value of abnormal gain.

(e)   The **scrap account** is completed by recording the **actual cash received** from the sale of scrap.

Debit	Cash received
Credit	Scrap account

with the cash received from the sale of the actual scrap.

The same basic principle therefore applies that only **normal losses** should affect the cost of the good output. The scrap value of **normal loss only** is credited to the process account. The scrap values of abnormal losses and gains are analysed separately in the abnormal loss or gain account.

3.2 Example: Scrap value of loss

Let's return to the example in Paragraph 2.7, but assume this time that all scrap has a value of $0.90 per unit.

1,000 units at a cost of $4,500 are input to a process. Normal loss is 10% and there are no opening or closing inventories. Scrap has a value of $0.90 per unit.

Required

(a)   Complete the process account and the abnormal loss/gain account if actual output was 860 units (so that actual loss is 140 units).

(b)   Complete the process account and the abnormal loss/gain account if actual output was 920 units (so that actual loss is 80 units).

Solution

(a)   **Output is 860 units, normal loss is 100 units and abnormal loss is 40 units.**

The cost per unit of output and the cost per unit of abnormal loss are based on:

*   Costs incurred minus the scrap value of normal loss (normal loss only!)
*   Expected output

$$\frac{\text{Costs incurred less scrap value of normal loss}}{\text{Expected output}} = \frac{\$4,500 - (100 \times \$0.90)}{900 \text{ units}} = \$4.90 \text{ per unit}$$

PROCESS ACCOUNT

	Units	$		Units	$
Cost incurred	1,000	4,500	Normal loss	100	90
			Output (finished goods a/c) at $4.90 per unit	860	4,214
			Abnormal loss at $4.90 per unit	40	196
	1,000	4,500		1,000	4,500

ABNORMAL LOSS/GAIN ACCOUNT

	Units	$		Units	$
Process a/c	40	196	Scrap a/c	40	36
			Statement of profit or loss		160
					196

(b)   **Output is 920 units, normal loss is 100 units and abnormal gain is 20 units.**

The cost per unit is the same as above, $4.90 per unit.

PROCESS ACCOUNT

	Units	$		Units	$
Cost incurred	1,000	4,500	Normal loss	100	90
Abnormal gain a/c at $4.90 per unit	20	98	Output (finished goods a/c) at $4.90	920	4,508
	1,020	4,598		1,020	4,598

ABNORMAL LOSS/GAIN

	Units	$		Units	$
Scrap a/c	20	18	Process a/c	20	98
Statement of profit or loss		80			
		98			

4   Joint products and by-products

> **Joint products** are two or more products separated in a process, each of which has a significant value. A **by-product** is an incidental product from a process which has an insignificant value compared to the main product.

BPP
LEARNING
MEDIA

EXAM FOCUS POINT

There is an article on accounting for joint products on the ACCA website (ACCA, 2012). Make sure you read this article.

4.1 Introduction

We have studied process costing up to the point where we have calculated, say, output of process 3 as 50,000 units costing $400,000. This is all very well so long as the process produces 50,000 identical items, but what do we do if the next stage is to send some of the output through one kind of process and the rest through another, resulting in two different sorts of product? The end results may be of two basic types.

- **Joint products** are two or more products which are output from the same processing operation, but which are indistinguishable from each other (because they are the same commonly processed materials) up to their point of separation. Joint products have a substantial sales value (or a substantial sales value after further, separate processing has been carried out to make them ready for sale).

- A **by-product** is a product which is similarly produced at the same time and from the same common process as the main product or joint products. The distinguishing feature of a by-product is its relatively low sales value.

The problem, if joint products or by-products are involved, is to split the common costs of processing between the various end products.

4.2 Problems in accounting for joint products

Joint products are not separately identifiable until a certain stage is reached in the processing operations. This stage is the **'split-off point'**, sometimes referred to as the **separation point**. Costs incurred prior to this point of separation are **common** or **joint costs**, and these need to be apportioned between the joint products.

Joint products are not separately identifiable until a certain stage is reached in the processing operations. This stage is the **'split-off point'**, sometimes referred to as the **separation point**. Costs incurred prior to this point of separation are **common** or **joint costs**, and these need to be apportioned in some manner to each of the joint products.

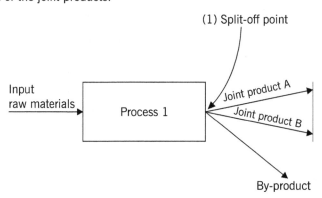

The **problems in accounting for joint products** are basically of two different sorts.

(a)   How common costs should be apportioned between products, in order to put a value to closing inventories and to the cost of sale (and profit) for each product

(b)   Whether it is more profitable to sell a joint product at one stage of processing, or to process the product further and sell it at a later stage

4.3 Dealing with common costs

The problem of costing for joint products concerns **common costs**, that is those common processing costs shared between the units of eventual output up to their 'split-off point'. Some method needs to be devised for sharing the common costs between the individual joint products for the following reasons.

(a)   To put a value to closing inventories of each joint product
(b)   To record the costs and therefore the profit from each joint product
(c)   Perhaps to assist in pricing decisions

Here are some examples of the common costs problem.

(a)   How to spread the common costs of oil refining between the joint products made (petrol, naphtha, kerosene and so on)

(b)   How to spread the common costs of iron and steel production between sheet steel and cast iron

Methods that might be used to establish a basis for apportionment for common costs to each product are as follows.

(a)   Physical measurement

(b)   Net realisable value at the split off point (sales value of end product less further processing costs after split-off point)

4.3.1 Dealing with common costs: Physical measurement

With physical measurement, **the common cost is apportioned to the joint products on the basis of the proportion that the output of each product bears by weight or volume to the total output.** An example of this would be the case where two products, product 1 and product 2, incur common costs to the point of separation of $3,000 and the output of each product is 600 tons and 1,200 tons respectively.

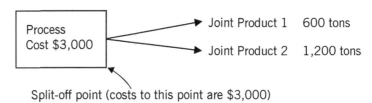

Split-off point (costs to this point are $3,000)

Product 1 sells for $4 per ton and product 2 for $2 per ton.

The division of the common costs ($3,000) between product 1 and product 2 could be based on the tonnage of output.

	Product 1		Product 2	Total
Output	600 tons	+	1,200 tons	1,800 tons
Proportion of common cost	$\left(\dfrac{600}{1,800}\right)$		$\left(\dfrac{1,200}{1,800}\right)$	
	$		$	$
Apportioned cost	1,000		2,000	3,000
Sales	2,400		2,400	4,800
Profit	1,400		400	1,800
Profit/sales ratio	58.3%		16.7%	37.5%

Physical measurement has the following limitations:

(a)   Where the products separate during the processes into different states, for example where one product is a gas and another is a liquid, this method is unsuitable.

(b)   This method does not take into account the relative income-earning potentials of the individual products, with the result that one product might appear very profitable and another appear to be incurring losses.

4.3.2 Dealing with common costs: Net realisable value at split-off point

The **net realisable value** of a joint product is its sales value minus its further processing costs after the point of separation.

An example of this would be where three joint products are produced from a common process:

Product A: 30,000 litres

Product B: 7,500 kg

Product C: 15,000 kg

The joint costs of processing up to the point of separation are $249,000.

Product C can be sold immediately after separation for $22.50 per kg. Product A needs further processing, at a cost of $12 per litre, before it is sold for $30 per litre. Product B also needs further processing, at a cost of $3 per kg, before it is sold for $10.50 per kg.

Under this method the common cost is apportioned to each product in the proportion that the net realisable value of that product bears to the total net realisable value of all products produced from the process.

	Product A 30,000 litres $	Product B 7,500 kg $	Product C 15,000 kg $	Total $
Final sales value	900,000	78,750	337,500	
Further processing costs	360,000	22,500	0	
Net realisable value	540,000	56,250	337,500	933,750
Pre-separation costs	144,000*	15,000	90,000	249,000
Profit	396,000	41,250	247,500	684,750
Profit per unit	13.20	5.50	16.50	

* $540,000 / $933,750 × $249,000 = $144,000

Apportionment basis = Common costs / Net realisable value

$\qquad$ = $249,000 / $933,750

$\qquad$ = $0.267 of cost per $1 net realisable value

4.3.3 The usefulness of costing for joint products

Costing information from joint product costing is of limited value. The apportionment of common costs between two or more joint products is necessary for the purpose of inventory valuation. However, joint product costs tell us very little about product profitability.

For example, suppose that two joint products are made in a process and when common costs are apportioned between them, one joint product shows a profit and the other shows a loss. It would be impossible to stop making the loss-making joint product without ceasing to manufacture the profitable joint product too, because they are made at the same time and in the same process. The only realistic measure of profit is the combined profit from both products. For the purpose of decision making and cost control, the entire process must be considered, not individual products.

5 Accounting for by-products

There are a number of methods to account for by-products and the choice of method will be influenced by the **circumstances of production** and **ease of calculation**.

The by-product has some commercial value and its accounting treatment of income is commonly as follows.

The **net realisable value of the by-product may be deducted from the cost of production of the main product**. The net realisable value is the final saleable value of the by-product minus any post-separation costs. Any closing inventory valuation of the main product or joint products would therefore be reduced.

6 The further processing decision

A joint product should be processed further **only** if final sales value minus further processing costs is greater than sales value at the split-off point.

The further processing decision problem is best explained by a simple example.

6.1 Example: Further processing

Alice Co manufactures two joint products, A and B. The costs of common processing are $15,000 per batch, and output per batch is 100 units of A and 150 units of B. The sales value of A at split-off point is $90 per unit, and the sales value of B is $60 per unit.

An opportunity exists to process product A further, at an extra cost of $2,000 per batch, to produce product C. One unit of joint product A is sufficient to make one unit of C which has a sales value of $120 per unit.

Should the company sell product A, or should it process A and sell product C?

Solution

The problem is resolved on the basis that product C should be sold if the sales value of C minus its further processing costs exceeds the sales value of A.

	$	
Sales value of C, per batch (100 × $120)	12,000	
Sales value of A, per batch (100 × $90)	9,000	
Incremental revenue from further processing	3,000	
Further processing cost	2,000	
Benefit from further processing in order to sell C	1,000	per batch

If the further processing cost had exceeded the incremental revenue from further processing, it would have been unprofitable to make and sell C. It is worth noting that the apportionment of joint processing costs between A and B is irrelevant to the decision, because the total extra profit from making C will be $1,000 per batch whichever method is used.

QUESTION

Further processing decision

PCC Co produces two joint products, Pee and Cee, from the same process. Joint processing costs of $150,000 are incurred up to split-off point, when 100,000 units of Pee and 50,000 units of Cee are produced. The selling prices at split-off point are $1.25 per unit for Pee and $2.00 per unit for Cee.

The units of Pee could be processed further to produce 60,000 units of a new chemical, Peeplus, but at an extra fixed cost of $20,000 and variable cost of 30c per unit of input. The selling price of Peeplus would be $3.25 per unit.

Required

Ascertain whether the company should sell Pee or Peeplus.

ANSWER

The only relevant costs/incomes are those which compare selling Pee against selling Peeplus. Every other cost is irrelevant: they will be incurred regardless of what the decision is.

	Pee $1.25				*Peeplus* $3.25
Selling price per unit					
	$			$	$
Total sales	125,000				195,000
Post-separation processing costs	–	Fixed	20,000		
	–	Variable	30,000		50,000
Sales minus post-separation (further processing) costs	125,000				145,000

It is $20,000 more profitable to convert Pee into Peeplus.

CHAPTER ROUNDUP

↳ **Process costing** is a costing method used where there are continuous processes. Process costs are attributed to the units produced in a period.

↳ During a production process, a **loss** may occur due to wastage, spoilage, evaporation, and so on.

↳ Loss may have a **scrap value**. Revenue from scrap is treated as a reduction in costs. It is conventional for the **scrap value of normal loss to be deducted from the cost of materials** before a cost per equivalent unit is calculated.

↳ **Joint products** are two or more products separated in a process, each of which has a significant value. A **by-product** is an incidental product from a process which has an insignificant value compared to the main product.

↳ Joint products are not separately identifiable until a certain stage is reached in the processing operations. This stage is the **'split-off point'**, sometimes referred to as the **separation point**. Costs incurred prior to this point of separation are **common** or **joint costs**, and these need to be apportioned between the joint products.

↳ There are a number of methods to account for by-products and the choice of method will be influenced by the **circumstances of production** and **ease of calculation**.

↳ A joint product should be processed further **only** if final sales value minus further processing costs is greater than sales value at the split-off point.

QUICK QUIZ

1   Process costing is centred around four key steps.

Step 1	....
Step 2	....
Step 3	....
Step 4	....

2   Abnormal gains result when actual loss is less than normal or expected loss.
    ○   True
    ○   False

3   During Period 1, 10,000 units of material were input to a process. Actual output was 8,500 units and process costs in the period were $22,950. Normal loss is 10% of input. What was the abnormal loss or gain in Period 1?
    ○   Abnormal loss 500 units
    ○   Abnormal gain 500 units
    ○   Abnormal loss 1,500 units
    ○   Abnormal gain 1,500 units

4   Using the data in Question 3, what was the cost of finished output in Period 1?
    ○ $19,508
    ○ $20,534
    ○ $21,675
    ○ $22,950

5   During Period 2, 10,000 units of material were input to a process. Actual output was 9,400 units and process costs were $33,840. Normal loss is 10% of input. How should abnormal gain be accounted for?

   O   Debit Abnormal Gain account $1,440, Credit Process account $1,440
   O   Debit Process account $1,440, Credit Abnormal gain account $1,440
   O   Debit Abnormal Gain account $1,504, Credit Process account $1,504
   O   Debit Process account $1,504, Credit Abnormal gain account $1,504

6   Normal loss (no scrap value) ⎤   ⎡ Same value as good output (positive cost)

     Abnormal loss   ⎥   ?   ⎢ No value

     Abnormal gain   ⎦   ⎣ Same value as good output (negative cost)

7   How is revenue from the scrap value of normal loss treated?

   O   As an addition to sales revenue
   O   As a reduction in costs of processing
   O   As a bonus to employees
   O   All of the above

8   What is the difference between a joint product and a by-product?

9   What is meant by the term 'split off' point?

10   Costs incurred in a process totalled $216,720 for a period. 24,000 units of finished product were manufactured including 1,200 units which were rejected on inspection and disposed of. The level of rejects in the period was normal. Rejects are sold for $2.00 per unit.

     What was the cost per unit for the process?

   O $8.93
   O $9.03
   O $9.40
   O $9.51

ANSWERS TO QUICK QUIZ

1

Step 1	Determine output and losses
Step 2	Calculate cost per unit of output, losses and WIP
Step 3	Calculate total cost of output, losses and WIP
Step 4	Complete accounts

2   True

3   Abnormal loss 500 units
    Expected normal loss = 1,000 units. Actual loss (10,000 – 8,500) = 1,500 units. Abnormal loss = 500 units.

4   $21,675
    Cost per unit of expected output = $22,950/9,000 = $2.55. Cost of 8,500 units produced (× $2.55) = $21,675.

5   Debit Process account $1,504, Credit Abnormal gain account $1,504
    Cost per unit of expected output = $33,840/9,000 = $3.76. Value of 400 units of abnormal gain (× $3.76) = $1,504. The Process account is debited and the Abnormal gain account is credited.

6   Normal loss (no scrap value)   → Same value as good output (positive cost)

    Abnormal loss   → No value

    Abnormal gain   → Same value as good output (negative cost)

7   As a reduction in costs of processing

8   A **joint product** is regarded as an important saleable item whereas a by-product is not.

9   The **split-off point** (or the point of separation) is the point at which joint products become separately identifiable in a processing operation.

10   $9.40 [$216,720 – (1,200 units × $2/unit)] ÷ (24,000 – 1,200 units) = $9.40

Now try ...

Attempt the questions below from the **Practice Question Bank**

Number

Q63

Q64

Q65

Q66

Q67

BPP LEARNING MEDIA

part

Decision making

CHAPTER

15

The previous chapters have described how costing systems are used to record costs and measure costs, using absorption costing or marginal costing, and the different cost measurement methods used in job costing, batch costing, process costing and service costing.

This chapter and the two chapters that follow describe techniques that are used to provide financial information to management that should help them with decision making. This chapter **explains cost-volume-profit analysis**, which is based on marginal costing concepts, and which can **be used to measure how costs and profits vary with the volume of sales**, and so establish what volume of sales might be needed to break even or achieve a target level of profit.

Cost-volume-profit (CVP) analysis

TOPIC LIST	SYLLABUS REFERENCE
1 CVP analysis and breakeven point	D1 (b)
2 The contribution/sales (C/S) ratio	D1 (a), (b), (c)
3 The margin of safety	D1 (b), (c)
4 Breakeven arithmetic and target profits	D1 (d), (e)
5 Breakeven charts and profit/volume charts	D1 (f)
6 Limitations of CVP analysis	D1 (f)

Study Guide	Intellectual level
D Decision making	
1 Cost-volume-profit analysis	
(a) Calculate contribution per unit and the contribution/sales ratio	S
(b) Explain the concept of breakeven and margin of safety	K
(c) Use contribution per unit and contribution/sales ratio to calculate breakeven point and margin of safety	S
(d) Analyse the effect on breakeven point and margin of safety of changes in selling price and costs	S
(e) Use contribution per unit and contribution/sales ratio to calculate the sales required to achieve a target profit	S
(f) Interpret breakeven and profit/volume charts for a single product or business	S

Technical performance objective 13 is to 'record and analyse information relating to costs, revenues and profit'. The knowledge you gain in this chapter will help you demonstrate your competence in this area.

1 CVP analysis and breakeven point

Cost-volume-profit (CVP) analysis is the study of the interrelationships between costs, volume and profit at various levels of activity.

1.1 Introduction

The management of an organisation usually wishes to know the profit likely to be made if the aimed-for production and sales for the year are achieved. Management may also be interested to know the following.

(a) The **breakeven** point which is the activity level at which there is neither profit nor loss
(b) The **amount** by which actual **sales can fall** below anticipated sales, **without** a **loss** being incurred

The breakeven point (BEP) can be calculated arithmetically.

$$\text{Breakeven point} = \frac{\text{Total fixed costs}}{\text{Contribution per unit}} = \frac{\text{Contribution required to break even}}{\text{Contribution per unit}}$$

$$= \text{Number of units of sale required to break even.}$$

1.2 Example: Breakeven point

Expected sales	10,000 units at $8 = $80,000
Variable cost	$5 per unit
Fixed costs	$21,000

Required

Compute the breakeven point.

Solution

The contribution per unit is $(8 – 5)	=	$3
Contribution required to break even	=	fixed costs = $21,000
Breakeven point (BEP)	=	21,000 ÷ 3
	=	7,000 units
In revenue, BEP	=	(7,000 × $8) = $56,000

Sales above 7,000 units will result in profit of $3 per unit of additional sales. For example, profit at 10,000 units is $9,000 [(10,000 – 7,000) × 3] and sales below 7,000 units will mean a loss of $3 per unit for each unit by which sales fall short of 7,000 units. In other words, profit will improve or worsen by the amount of contribution per unit.

	7,000 units		7,001 units
	$		$
Revenue	56,000		56,008
Less variable costs	35,000		35,005
Contribution	21,000		21,003
Less fixed costs	21,000		21,000
Profit	0	(= breakeven)	3

2 The contribution/sales (C/S) ratio

The **C/S ratio** is a measure of how much contribution is earned from each $1 of sales.

The C/S ratio is calculated as follows.

$$\text{C/S ratio} = \frac{\text{Contribution}}{\text{Sales}} \times 100\%$$

2.1 Example: C/S ratio

Expected sales	10,000 units @ $8 = $80,000
Variable cost	$5 per unit
Fixed costs	$21,000

Required

Calculate the C/S ratio.

Solution

Contribution = Selling price – variable costs
   = $8 – $5
   = $3

$$\text{C/S ratio} = \frac{\text{Contribution}}{\text{Sales}} \times 100\%$$

$$= \frac{\$3}{\$8} \times 100\%$$

$$= 37.5\%$$

A C/S ratio of 37.5% means that for every $1 of sales, a contribution of 37.5c is earned.

2.2 An alternative method to calculate breakeven

An alternative way of calculating the breakeven point to give an answer in terms of sales revenue is as follows.

BPP
LEARNING
MEDIA

$$\frac{\text{Required contribution}}{\text{C / S ratio}} = \frac{\text{Fixed costs}}{\text{C / S ratio}} = \text{Sales revenue at breakeven point}$$

In the example above, the C/S ratio is $\dfrac{\$3}{\$8} = 37.5\%$

Breakeven is where sales revenue equals $\dfrac{\$21,000}{37.5\%} = \$56,000$

At a price of $8 per unit, this represents 7,000 units of sales.

Thus, in order to earn a total contribution of $21,000 and if contribution increases by 37.5c per $1 of sales, sales must be:

$$\frac{\$1}{37.5c} \times \$21,000 = \$56,000$$

QUESTION

C/S ratio

The C/S ratio of product W is 20%. IB Co, the manufacturer of product W, wishes to make a contribution of $50,000 towards fixed costs. How many units of product W must be sold if the selling price is $10 per unit?

ANSWER

$$\frac{\text{Required contribution}}{\text{C / S ratio}} = \frac{\$50,000}{20\%} = \$250,000$$

∴ Number of units = $250,000 ÷ $10 = 25,000

---

3 The margin of safety

The **margin of safety** is the difference in units between the **expected sales volume** and the **breakeven sales volume** and it is sometimes expressed as a percentage of the expected sales volume.

The margin of safety may also be expressed as the difference between the expected/actual sales revenue and breakeven sales revenue, expressed as a percentage of the expected/actual sales revenue.

3.1 Example: Margin of safety

Mal de Mer Co makes and sells a product which has a variable cost of $30 and which sells for $40. Budgeted fixed costs are $70,000 and expected sales are 8,000 units.

Required

Calculate the breakeven point and the margin of safety.

Solution

(a) Breakeven point $= \dfrac{\text{Total fixed costs}}{\text{Contribution per unit}} = \dfrac{\$70,000}{\$(40-30)}$

$\qquad\qquad\qquad\qquad = 7,000\ \text{units}$

(b) Margin of safety $= 8,000 - 7,000\ \text{units} = 1,000\ \text{units}$

which may be expressed as $\dfrac{1,000\ \text{units}}{8,000\ \text{units}} \times 100\% \times 100\% = 12\frac{1}{2}\%$ of budget

(c)   The margin of safety indicates to management that actual sales can fall short of budget by 1,000 units or 12½% before the breakeven point is reached and no profit at all is made.

4   Breakeven arithmetic and target profits

At the **breakeven point**, sales revenue = total costs and there is no profit. At the breakeven point, total contribution = fixed costs.

4.1 Introduction

At **the breakeven point**, $S = V + F$

V = Total variable costs

F = Total fixed costs

Subtracting V from each side of the equation, we get:

$S - V = F$, that is, **total contribution = fixed costs**

4.2 Example: Breakeven arithmetic

Butterfingers Co makes a product which has a variable cost of $7 per unit.

Required

If fixed costs are $63,000 per annum, calculate the selling price per unit if the company wishes to break even with a sales volume of 12,000 units.

Solution

			$
Contribution required to break even (= Fixed costs)	=	$63,000	
Volume of sales	=	12,000 units	
Required contribution per unit $(S - V)$	=	$63,000 ÷ 12,000 =	5.25
Variable cost per unit (V)	=		7.00
Required sales price per unit (S)	=		12.25

4.3 Target profits

A similar formula may be applied where a company wishes to achieve a certain profit during a period. To achieve this profit, sales must cover all costs and leave the required profit.

The **target profit** is achieved when: $S = V + F + P$,

   where P = required profit

Subtracting V from each side of the equation, we get:

   $S - V = F + P$, so

   Total contribution required $= F + P$

4.4 Example: Target profits

Riding Breeches Co makes and sells a single product, for which variable costs are as follows.

	$
Direct materials	10
Direct labour	8
Variable production overhead	6
	24

The sales price is $30 per unit, and fixed costs per annum are $68,000. The company wishes to make a profit of $16,000 per annum.

Required

Determine the sales required to achieve this profit.

Solution

Required contribution = fixed costs + profit = $68,000 + $16,000 = $84,000

Required sales can be calculated in one of two ways.

(a) $\dfrac{\text{Required contribution}}{\text{Contribution per unit}} = \dfrac{\$84,000}{\$(30-24)} = 14,000$ units, or $420,000 in revenue

(b) $\dfrac{\text{Required contribution}}{\text{C / S ratio}} = \dfrac{\$84,000}{20\%^{*}} = \$420,000$ of revenue, or 14,000 units

$* \text{ C/S ratio} = \dfrac{\$30-\$24}{\$30} = \dfrac{\$6}{\$30} = 0.2 = 20\%.$

QUESTION
Target profit

Seven League Boots Co wishes to sell 14,000 units of its product, which has a variable cost of $15 to make and sell. Fixed costs are $47,000 and the required profit is $23,000.

Required

Calculate the sales price per unit.

ANSWER

Required contribution = fixed costs plus profit
                      = $47,000 + $23,000
                      = $70,000
Required sales   14,000 units

	$
Required contribution per unit sold	5
Variable cost per unit	15
Required sales price per unit	20

4.5 Decisions to change sales price or costs

You may come across a problem in which you will be expected to offer advice as to the effect of altering the selling price, variable cost per unit or fixed cost. Such problems are slight variations on basic breakeven arithmetic.

4.5.1 Example: Change in selling price

Stomer Cakes Co bake and sell a single type of cake. The variable cost of production is 15c and the current sales price is 25c. Fixed costs are $2,600 per month, and the annual profit for the company at current sales volume is $36,000. The volume of sales demand is constant throughout the year.

The sales manager, Ian Digestion, wishes to raise the sales price to 29c per cake, but considers that a price rise will result in some loss of sales.

Required

Ascertain the minimum volume of sales required each month to raise the price to 29c.

Solution

The minimum volume of demand which would justify a price of 29c is one which would leave total profit at least the same as before, ie $3,000 per month. Required profit should be converted into required contribution, as follows.

	$
Monthly fixed costs	2,600
Monthly profit, minimum required	3,000
Current monthly contribution	5,600
Contribution per unit (25c – 15c)	10c
Current monthly sales	56,000 cakes

The minimum volume of sales required after the price rise will be an amount which earns a contribution of $5,600 per month, no worse than at the moment. The contribution per cake at a sales price of 29c would be 14c.

$$\text{Required sales} = \frac{\text{required contribution}}{\text{contribution per unit}} = \frac{\$5,600}{14c} = 40,000 \text{ cakes per month.}$$

4.5.2 Example: Change in production costs

Close Brickett Co makes a product which has a variable production cost of $8 and a variable sales cost of $2 per unit. Fixed costs are $40,000 per annum, the sales price per unit is $18, and the current volume of output and sales is 6,000 units.

The company is considering whether to have an improved machine for production. Annual hire costs would be $10,000 and it is expected that the variable cost of production would fall to $6 per unit.

Required

(a) Determine the number of units that must be produced and sold to achieve the same profit as is currently earned, if the machine is hired.

(b) Calculate the annual profit with the machine if output and sales remain at 6,000 units per annum.

Solution

The current unit contribution is $(18 – (8 + 2)) = $8

(a)

	$
Current contribution (6,000 × $8)	48,000
Less current fixed costs	40,000
Current profit	8,000

With the new machine fixed costs will go up by $10,000 to $50,000 per annum. The variable cost per unit will fall to $(6 + 2) = $8, and the contribution per unit will be $10.

	$
Required profit (as currently earned)	8,000
Fixed costs	50,000
Required contribution	58,000
Contribution per unit	$10
Sales required to earn $8,000 profit	5,800 units

BPP
LEARNING
MEDIA

(b)   **If sales are 6,000 units**

		$	$
Sales (6,000 × $18)			108,000
Variable costs: production (6,000 × $6)		36,000	
sales (6,000 × $2)		12,000	
			48,000
Contribution (6,000 × $10)			60,000
Less fixed costs			50,000
Profit			10,000

Alternative calculation	$
Profit at 5,800 units of sale (see (a))	8,000
Contribution from sale of extra 200 units (× $10)	2,000
Profit at 6,000 units of sale	10,000

4.6 Sales price and sales volume

It may be clear by now that, given no change in fixed costs, **total profit is maximised when the total contribution is at its maximum**. Total contribution in turn depends on the unit contribution and on the sales volume.

An increase in the sales price will increase unit contribution, but sales volume is likely to fall because fewer customers will be prepared to pay the higher price. A decrease in sales price will reduce the unit contribution, but sales volume may increase because the goods on offer are now cheaper. The **optimum combination** of sales price and sales volume is arguably the one which **maximises total contribution**.

4.6.1 Example: Profit maximisation

C Co has developed a new product which is about to be launched on to the market. The variable cost of selling the product is $12 per unit. The marketing department has estimated that at a sales price of $20, annual demand would be 10,000 units.

However, if the sales price is set above $20, sales demand would fall by 500 units for each 50c increase above $20. Similarly, if the price is set below $20, demand would increase by 500 units for each 50c stepped reduction in price below $20.

Required

Determine the price which would maximise C Co's profit in the next year.

Solution

At a price of $20 per unit, the unit contribution would be $(20 − 12) = $8. Each 50c increase (or decrease) in price would raise (or lower) the unit contribution by 50c. The total contribution is calculated at each sales price by multiplying the unit contribution by the expected sales volume.

	Unit price $	Unit contribution $	Sales volume Units	Total contribution $
	20.00	8.00	10,000	80,000
(a) **Reduce price**				
	19.50	7.50	10,500	78,750
	19.00	7.00	11,000	77,000
(b) **Increase price**				
	20.50	8.50	9,500	80,750
	21.00	9.00	9,000	81,000
	21.50	9.50	8,500	80,750
	22.00	10.00	8,000	80,000
	22.50	10.50	7,500	78,750

The total contribution would be maximised, and therefore profit maximised, at a sales price of $21 per unit, and sales demand of 9,000 units.

QUESTION

Breakeven

Betty Battle Co manufactures a product which has a selling price of $20 and a variable cost of $10 per unit. The company incurs annual fixed costs of $29,000. Annual sales demand is 9,000 units.

New production methods are under consideration, which would cause a $1,000 increase in fixed costs and a reduction in variable cost to $9 per unit. The new production methods would result in a superior product and would enable sales to be increased to 9,750 units per annum at a price of $21 each.

If the change in production methods were to take place, the breakeven output level would be:

O   400 units higher
O   400 units lower
O   100 units higher
O   100 units lower

ANSWER

	Current	Revised	Difference
	$	$	
Selling price	20	21	
Variable costs	10	9	
Contribution per unit	10	12	
Fixed costs	$29,000	$30,000	
Breakeven point (units)	2,900	2,500	400 lower

$$\text{Breakeven point} = \frac{\text{Total fixed costs}}{\text{Contribution per unit}}$$

$$\text{Current BEP} = \frac{\$29,000}{\$10} = 2,900 \text{ units}$$

$$\text{Revised BEP} = \frac{\$30,000}{\$12} = 2,500 \text{ units}$$

The correct answer is therefore 400 units lower.

---

5 Breakeven charts and profit/volume charts

- The breakeven point can also be determined graphically using a **breakeven chart** or a **contribution breakeven chart**.

- The **profit/volume (PV) chart** is a variation of the breakeven chart which illustrates the relationship of profits to sales.

5.1 Breakeven charts

The breakeven point can also be determined graphically using a breakeven chart. This is a chart which shows approximate levels of profit or loss at different sales volume levels within a limited range.

A breakeven chart has the following axes.

- A **horizontal** axis showing the **sales/output** (in value or units)
- A **vertical axis** showing $ for **sales revenues** and **costs**

The following lines are drawn on the breakeven chart.

(a) The **sales line**

- Starts at the origin
- Ends at the point signifying expected sales

(b) The **fixed costs line**

- Runs parallel to the horizontal axis
- Meets the vertical axis at a point which represents total fixed costs

(c) The **total costs line**

- Starts where the fixed costs line meets the vertical axis
- Ends at the point which represents anticipated sales on the horizontal axis and total costs of anticipated sales on the vertical axis

The **breakeven point** is the **intersection** of the **sales line** and the **total costs line**.

The distance between the **breakeven point** and the **expected (or budgeted) sales**, in units, indicates the **margin of safety**.

5.1.1 Example: A breakeven chart

The budgeted annual output of a factory is 120,000 units. The annual fixed overheads amount to $40,000 and the variable costs are 50c per unit. The sales price is $1 per unit.

Required

Construct a breakeven chart based on annual output up to 120,000.

Solution

Breakeven chart (1) is shown on the following page.

The chart is drawn as follows:

(a) The **vertical axis** represents **money** (costs and revenue) and the **horizontal axis** represents the **level of activity** (production and sales).

(b) The fixed costs are represented by a **straight line parallel to the horizontal axis** (in our example, at $40,000).

(c) The **variable costs** are added 'on top of' fixed costs, to give **total costs**. It is assumed that fixed costs are the same in total and variable costs are the same per unit at all levels of output.

The line of costs is therefore a straight line and only two points need to be plotted and joined up. Perhaps the two most convenient points to plot are total costs at zero output, and total costs at the budgeted output and sales.

- At zero output, costs are equal to the amount of fixed costs only, $40,000, since there are no variable costs.

- At the budgeted output of 120,000 units, costs are $100,000.

	$
Fixed costs	40,000
Variable costs 120,000 × 50c	60,000
Total costs	100,000

(d) The sales line is also drawn by plotting two points and joining them up.

- At zero sales, revenue is nil.
- At the budgeted output and sales of 120,000 units, revenue is $120,000.

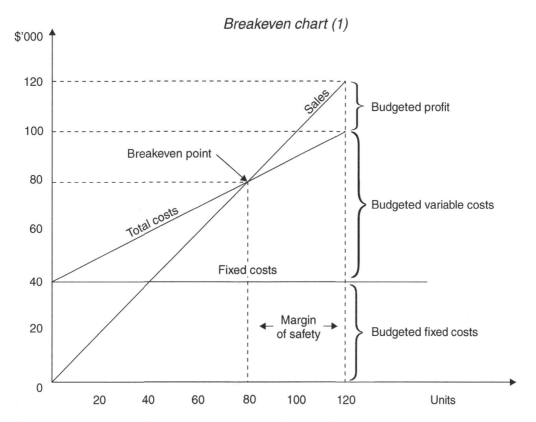

Breakeven chart (1)

The breakeven point is where total costs are matched exactly by total revenue. From the chart, this can be seen to occur at output and sales of 80,000 units, when revenue and costs are both $80,000. This breakeven point can be proved mathematically as:

$$\frac{\text{Required contribution (= fixed costs)}}{\text{Contribution per unit}} = \frac{\$40,000}{50c\,\text{per unit}} = 80,000 \text{ units}$$

The margin of safety can be seen on the chart as the difference between the budgeted level of activity and the breakeven level.

Budgeted profit

The profit can be calculated at the output of 120,000 units as follows:

	$
Sales (120,000 units)	120,000
Variable costs	60,000
Contribution	60,000
Fixed costs	40,000
Profit	20,000

5.2 Example: Variations in the use of breakeven charts

Breakeven charts can be used to **show variations** in the possible **sales price**, **variable costs** or **fixed costs**. Suppose that a company sells a product which has a variable cost of $2 per unit. Fixed costs are $15,000. It has been estimated that if the sales price is set at $4.40 per unit, the expected sales volume would be 7,500 units; whereas if the sales price is lower, at $4 per unit, the expected sales volume would be 10,000 units.

Required

Draw a breakeven chart to show the budgeted profit, the breakeven point and the margin of safety at each of the possible sales prices.

BPP LEARNING MEDIA

Solution

Workings	Sales price $4.40 per unit $		Sales price $4 per unit $
Fixed costs	15,000		15,000
Variable costs (7,500 × $2.00)	15,000	(10,000 × $2.00)	20,000
Total costs	30,000		35,000
Budgeted revenue (7,500 × $4.40)	33,000	(10,000 × $4.00)	40,000
Expected profit	3,000		5,000

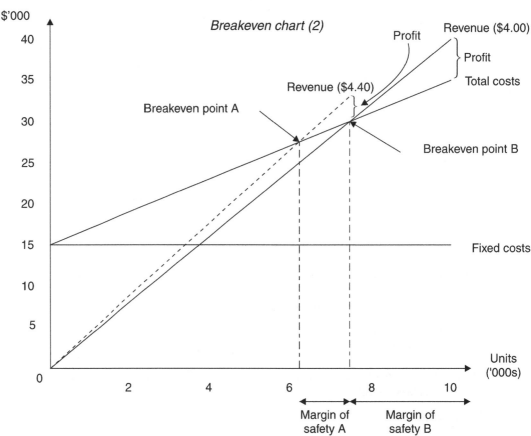

(a) **Breakeven point A** is the breakeven point at a sales price of $4.40 per unit, which is 6,250 units or $27,500 in costs and revenues.

(check: $\dfrac{\text{Required contribution to break even}}{\text{Contribution per unit}}$ $\dfrac{\$15,000}{\$2.40\,\text{per unit}} = 6{,}250$ units)

The margin of safety (A) is 7,500 units − 6,250 units = 1,250 units or 16.7% of expected sales.

(b) **Breakeven point B** is the breakeven point at a sales price of $4 per unit which is 7,500 units or $30,000 in costs and revenues.

(check: $\dfrac{\text{Required contribution to break even}}{\text{Contribution per unit}}$ $\dfrac{\$15,000}{\$2\,\text{per unit}} = 7{,}500$ units)

The margin of safety (B) = 10,000 units − 7,500 units = 2,500 units or 25% of expected sales.

Since a price of $4 per unit gives a higher expected profit ($5,000 compared to $3,000) and a wider margin of safety, this price will probably be preferred even though the breakeven point is higher than at a sales price of $4.40 per unit.

5.3 Contribution (or contribution breakeven) charts

As an alternative to drawing the fixed cost line first, it is possible to start with that for variable costs. This is known as a **contribution chart**. An example is shown below using the earlier example.

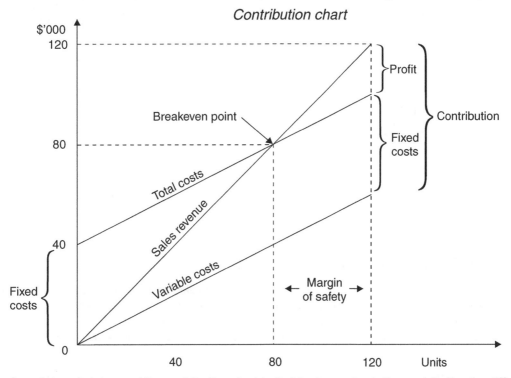

Contribution chart

One of the **advantages** of the contribution chart is that is shows clearly the **contribution** for **different levels of production** (indicated here at 120,000 units, the budgeted level of output) as the 'wedge' shape between the sales revenue line and the variable costs line. At the **breakeven point**, the **contribution equals fixed costs** exactly. At levels of output **above** the **breakeven** point, the **contribution** is **larger**, and not only covers fixed costs, but also leaves a profit. **Below** the **breakeven** point, the **loss** is the amount by which contribution fails to cover fixed costs.

5.4 The profit/volume (P/V) chart

The profit/volume (P/V) chart is a variation of the breakeven chart which illustrates the relationship of profit to sales.

A P/V chart is constructed as follows (look at the chart in the example that follows as you read the explanation).

(a)   'P' is on the y axis and actually comprises not only 'profit' but contribution to profit (in monetary value), extending above and below the x axis with a zero point at the intersection of the two axes, and the negative section below the x axis representing fixed costs. This means that at zero production, the firm is incurring a loss equal to the fixed costs.

(b)   'V' is on the x axis and comprises either volume of sales or value of sales (revenue).

(c)   The profit-volume line is a straight line drawn with its starting point (at zero production) at the intercept on the y axis representing the level of fixed costs, and with a gradient of contribution/unit (or the C/S ratio if sales value is used rather than units). The P/V line will cut the x axis at the breakeven point of sales volume. Any point on the P/V line above the x axis represents the profit to the firm (as measured on the vertical axis) for that particular level of sales.

5.4.1 Example: P/V chart

Let us draw a P/V chart for our example. At sales of 120,000 units, total contribution will be 120,000 × $(1 − 0.5) = $60,000 and total profit will be $20,000.

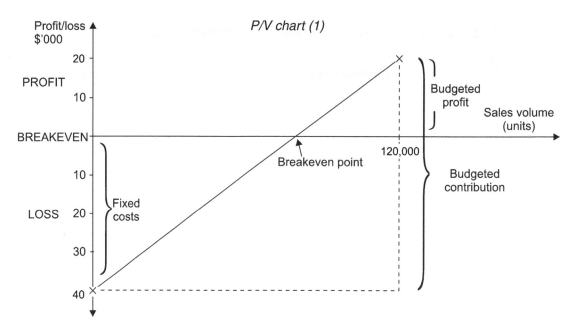

5.5 The advantage of the P/V chart

The P/V chart shows clearly the effect on profit and breakeven point of any changes in selling price, variable cost, fixed cost and/or sales demand. If the budgeted selling price of the product in our example is increased to $1.20, with the result that demand drops to 105,000 units despite additional fixed costs of $10,000 being spent on advertising, we could add a line representing this situation to our P/V chart.

At sales of 105,000 units, contribution will be 105,000 × $(1.20 − 0.50) = $73,500 and total profit will be $23,500 (fixed costs being $50,000).

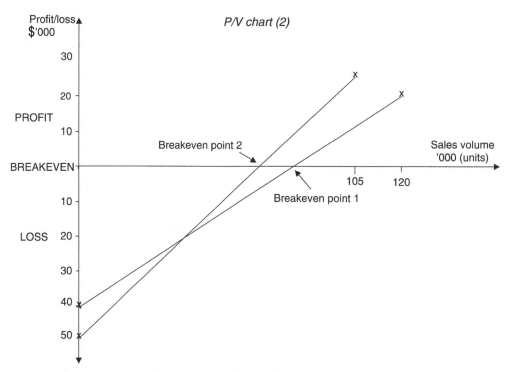

The diagram shows that if the selling price is increased, the breakeven point occurs at a lower level of sales revenue (71,429 units instead of 80,000 units), although this is not a particularly large increase when viewed in the context of the projected sales volume. It is also possible to see that for sales above 50,000 units, the profit achieved will be higher (and the loss achieved lower) if the price is $1.20. For sales volumes below 50,000 units the first option will yield lower losses.

The P/V chart is the clearest way of presenting such information; two conventional breakeven charts on one set of axes would be very confusing.

Changes in the variable cost per unit or in fixed costs at certain activity levels can also be easily incorporated into a P/V chart. The profit or loss at each point where the cost structure changes should be calculated and plotted on the graph so that the profit/volume line becomes a series of straight lines.

For example, suppose that in our example, at sales levels in excess of 120,000 units the variable cost per unit increases to $0.60 (perhaps because of overtime premiums that are incurred when production exceeds a certain level). At sales of 130,000 units, contribution would therefore be 130,000 × $(1 − 0.60) = $52,000 and total profit would be $12,000.

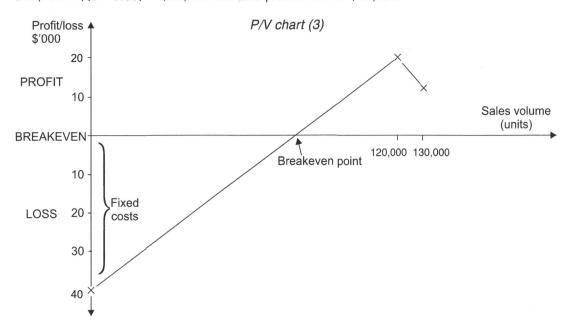

6 Limitations of CVP analysis

Breakeven analysis is a useful technique for managers. Breakeven arithmetic can provide **simple** and **quick** estimates. **Breakeven charts** provide a **graphical representation** of breakeven arithmetic. Breakeven analysis has a number of limitations.

- It **can only apply to a single product** or a single mix of a group of products.
- A breakeven chart may be **time-consuming** to prepare.
- It **assumes** fixed costs are constant at all levels of output.
- It **assumes** that **variable costs** are the **same** per unit at all levels of output.
- It **assumes** that **sales prices** are **constant** at all levels of output.
- It assumes **production** and **sales** are the **same** (inventory levels are ignored).
- It **ignores** the **uncertainty** in the estimates of fixed costs and variable cost per unit.

CHAPTER ROUNDUP

- **Cost-volume-profit (CVP) analysis** is the study of the interrelationships between costs, volume and profit at various levels of activity.

- The **C/S ratio** is a measure of how much contribution is earned from each $1 of sales.

- The **margin of safety** is the difference in units between the **expected sales volume** and the **breakeven sales volume** and it is sometimes expressed as a percentage of the expected sales volume.

- At the **breakeven point**, sales revenue = total costs and there is no profit. At the breakeven point, total contribution = fixed costs.

- The breakeven point can also be determined graphically using a **breakeven chart** or a **contribution breakeven chart**.

- The **profit/volume (P/V) chart** is a variation of the breakeven chart which illustrates the relationship of profits to sales.

QUICK QUIZ

1   The **breakeven point** is the ....
    ....

2   Use the following to make up three formulae which can be used to calculate the breakeven point.

| Contribution per unit |
| Fixed costs |
| Contribution required to breakeven |
| C/S ratio |

(a)   Breakeven point (sales units)   =   [   ]

    or   [   ]

(b)   Breakeven point (sales revenue)   =   [   ]

    or   [   ]

3   The C/S ratio is a measure of how much profit is earned from each $1 of sales.
    ○   True
    ○   False

4   The **margin of safety** is the difference in units between the expected sales volume and the breakeven sales volume. How is it sometimes expressed?

5   Profits are maximised at the breakeven point.
    ○   True
    ○   False

6   At the breakeven point, total contribution = ...

7   The total contribution required for a **target profit** = ...

8   Give three uses of breakeven charts.

9   Breakeven charts show approximate levels of profit or loss at different sales volume levels within a limited range. Which of the following are true?

1   The sales line starts at the origin.
2   The fixed costs line runs parallel to the vertical axis.
3   Breakeven charts have a horizontal axis showing the sales/output (in value or units).
4   Breakeven charts have a vertical axis showing $ for revenues and costs.
5   The breakeven point is the intersection of the sales line and the fixed cost line.

O   1 and 2
O   2 only
O   1, 3 and 4
O   3, 4, and 5

10   On a breakeven chart, the distance between the breakeven point and the expected (or budgeted) sales, in units, indicates the ....

11   5,400 units of a company's single product were sold for a total revenue of $140,400. Fixed costs in the period were $39,420 and net profit was $11,880.

What was the contribution per unit?

O $7.30
O $9.50
O $16.50
O $18.70

ANSWERS TO QUICK QUIZ

1   The **breakeven point** is the number of units of sale required to breakeven or the sales revenue required to break even.

2   (a)   Breakeven point (sales units)   = $\dfrac{\text{Fixed costs}}{\text{Contribution per unit}}$

                                    or $\dfrac{\text{Contribution required to breakeven}}{\text{Contribution per unit}}$

    (b)   Breakeven point (sales revenue)   = $\dfrac{\text{Fixed costs}}{\text{C / S ratio}}$

                                      or $\dfrac{\text{Contribution required to breakeven}}{\text{C / S ratio}}$

3   False. The C/S ratio is a measure of how much **contribution** is earned from each \$1 of sales.

4   As a **percentage** of the budgeted sales volume

5   False. At the breakeven point there is no profit.

6   At the breakeven point, total contribution = fixed costs.

7   Fixed costs + required profit

8   • To plan the production of a company's products
    • To market a company's products
    • To give a visual display of breakeven arithmetic

9   1, 3 and 4

10   Margin of safety

11   \$9.50 (\$39,420 + \$11,880) ÷ 5,400 units = \$9.50

Now try ...

Attempt the questions below from the **Practice Question Bank**

Number

Q68

Q69

Q70

Q71

Q72

Short-term decisions

Managers need to have an idea of what the financial implications of a decision might be, and how costs and revenues will change if a particular decision is taken. Information for decision making, both short-term and long-term decisions, should be based on the concept of relevant costs.

The concept of **relevant costs** is very important in cost and management accounting. This chapter explains the **nature of relevant costs and how they are measured**. It also explains the application of relevant costs to decision making in a particular situation, when there is **limited availability of a key resource (a 'limiting factor')** and management want to establish the optimal use of resources so as to **maximise profits**.

	SYLLABUS REFERENCE
TOPIC LIST	
1 Relevant costs	D2 (e), (f)
2 Limiting factors	D2 (a), (b), (c)
3 Make/buy-in problems	D2 (d)

Technical performance objective 13 is to 'record and analyse information relating to costs, revenues and profit'. The knowledge you gain in this chapter will help you demonstrate your competence in this area.

1 Relevant costs

Relevant costs are future cash flows arising as a direct consequence of a decision.

Relevant costs are **future costs**, **cashflows** and **incremental costs**.

1.1 Relevant costs

A **relevant cost** is a cost that is incurred incrementally as a result of a possible future course of action that would not be incurred if the course of action is not chosen.

Decision making should be based on relevant costs.

(a) **Relevant costs are future incremental costs**. A decision is about the future and it cannot alter what has been done already. Costs that have been incurred in the past are totally irrelevant to any decision that is being made 'now'. Such costs are **past costs** or **sunk costs**.

An example of a sunk cost is development costs which have already been incurred. Suppose that a company has spent $250,000 in developing a new service for customers, but the marketing department's most recent findings are that the service might not gain customer acceptance and could be a commercial failure. The decision whether or not to abandon the development of the new service would have to be taken, but the $250,000 spent so far should be ignored by the decision makers because it is a sunk cost.

Costs that have been incurred include not only costs that have already been paid, but also costs that have been **committed**. A **committed cost** is a future cash flow that will be incurred anyway, regardless of the decision taken now.

(b) **Relevant costs are cash flows**. Only cash flow information is required. This means that costs or charges which do not reflect **additional cash spending** (such as depreciation and notional costs) should be ignored for the purpose of decision making.

Other terms are sometimes used to describe relevant costs.

An **opportunity cost** is the value of the benefit sacrificed when one course of action is chosen, in preference to an alternative.

Suppose for example that there are three options, A, B and C, only one of which can be chosen. The net profit from each would be $80, $100 and $70 respectively.

Since only one option can be selected option B would be chosen because it offers the biggest benefit.

	$
Profit from option B	100
Less opportunity cost (ie the benefit from the most profitable alternative, A)	80
Differential benefit of option B	20

The decision to choose option B would not be taken simply because it offers a profit of $100, but because it offers a differential profit of $20 in excess of the next best alternative.

EXAM FOCUS POINT

Unless you are given an indication to the contrary, you should assume the following.

- Variable costs will be relevant costs.
- Fixed costs are irrelevant to a decision.

This need not be the case, however, and you should analyse variable and fixed cost data carefully. Do not forget that 'fixed' costs may only be fixed in the short term.

1.2 Non-relevant variable costs

There might be occasions when a variable cost is in fact a sunk cost (and therefore a **non-relevant variable cost**). For example, suppose that a company has some units of raw material in inventory. They have been paid for already, and originally cost $2,000. They are now obsolete and are no longer used in regular production, and they have no scrap value. However, they could be used in a special job which the company is trying to decide whether to undertake. The special job is a 'one-off' customer order, and would use up all these materials in inventory.

(a) In deciding whether the job should be undertaken, the relevant cost of the materials to the special job is nil. Their original cost of $2,000 is a **sunk cost**, and should be ignored in the decision.

(b) However, if the materials did have a scrap value of, say, $300, then their relevant cost to the job would be the **opportunity cost** of being unable to sell them for scrap, ie $300.

1.3 Attributable fixed costs

There might be occasions when a fixed cost is a relevant cost, and you must be aware of the distinction between **'specific'** or **'directly attributable' fixed costs**, and general fixed overheads.

Directly attributable fixed costs are those costs which, although fixed within a relevant range of activity level are relevant to a decision for either of the following reasons.

(a) They could increase if certain extra activities were undertaken. For example, it may be necessary to employ an extra supervisor if a particular order is accepted. The extra salary would be an **attributable fixed cost**.

(b) They would decrease or be eliminated entirely if a decision were taken either to reduce the scale of operations or shut down entirely.

General fixed overheads are those fixed overheads which will be unaffected by decisions to increase or decrease the scale of operations, perhaps because they are an apportioned share of the fixed costs of items which would be completely unaffected by the decisions. General fixed overheads are unlikely to be relevant in decision making.

1.4 Absorbed overhead

Absorbed overhead is a **notional** accounting cost and hence should be ignored for decision-making purposes. It is **overhead incurred** which may be relevant to a decision.

1.5 The relevant cost of materials

The relevant cost of raw materials is generally their **current replacement cost**, **unless** the materials have already been purchased and would not be replaced once used. In this case the relevant cost of using them is the **higher** of the following.

* Their current resale value
* The value they would obtain if they were put to an alternative use

If the materials have no resale value and no other possible use, then the relevant cost of using them for the opportunity under consideration would be nil.

QUESTION

Relevant cost of materials

O'Reilly Co has been approached by a customer who would like a special job to be done for him, and who is willing to pay $22,000 for it. The job would require the following materials.

Material	Total units required	Units already in inventory	Book value of units in inventory $/unit	Realisable value $/unit	Replacement cost $/unit
A	1,000	0	–	–	6
B	1,000	600	2	2.50	5
C	1,000	700	3	2.50	4
D	200	200	4	6.00	9

Material B is used regularly by O'Reilly Co, and if units of B are required for this job, they would need to be replaced to meet other production demand.

Materials C and D are in inventory as the result of previous over-buying, and they have a restricted use. No other use could be found for material C, but the units of material D could be used in another job as substitute for 300 units of material E, which currently costs $5 per unit (of which the company has no units in inventory at the moment).

Required

Calculate the relevant costs of material for deciding whether or not to accept the contract.

ANSWER

(a) **Material A** is not yet owned. It would have to be bought in full at the replacement cost of $6 per unit.

(b) **Material B** is used regularly by the company. There are existing inventories (600 units) but if these are used on the contract under review a further 600 units would be bought to replace them. Relevant costs are therefore 1,000 units at the replacement cost of $5 per unit.

(c) 1,000 units of **material C** are needed and 700 are already in inventory. If used for the contract, a further 300 units must be bought at $4 each. The existing inventories of 700 will not be replaced. If they are used for the contract, they could not be sold at $2.50 each. The realisable value of these 700 units is an opportunity cost of sales revenue forgone.

(d) The required units of **material D** are already in inventory and will not be replaced. There is an opportunity cost of using D in the contract because there are alternative opportunities either to sell the existing inventories for $6 per unit ($1,200 in total) or avoid other purchases (of material E), which would cost 300 × $5 = $1,500. Since substitution for E is more beneficial, $1,500 is the opportunity cost.

(e) **Summary of relevant costs**

	$
Material A (1,000 × $6)	6,000
Material B (1,000 × $5)	5,000
Material C (300 × $4) plus (700 × $2.50)	2,950
Material D	1,500
Total	15,450

1.6 The relevant cost of labour

The relevant cost of labour, in different situations, is best explained by means of an example.

1.6.1 Example: Relevant cost of labour

LW Co is currently deciding whether to undertake a new contract. 15 hours of labour will be required for the contract. LW Co currently produces product L, the standard cost details of which are shown below.

STANDARD COST CARD
PRODUCT L

	$/unit
Direct materials (10 kg @ $2)	20
Direct labour (5 hrs @ $6)	30
	50
Selling price	72
Contribution	22

(a) What is the relevant cost of labour if the labour must be hired from outside the organisation?

(b) What is the relevant cost of labour if LW Co expects to have five hours' spare capacity?

(c) What is the relevant cost of labour if labour is in short supply?

Solution

(a) Where labour must be hired from outside the organisation, the relevant cost of labour will be the variable costs incurred.

Relevant cost of labour on new contract = 15 hours @ $6 = $90

(b) It is assumed that the 5 hours' spare capacity will be paid anyway, and so if these 5 hours are used on another contract, there is no additional cost to LW plc.

Relevant cost of labour on new contract

	$
Direct labour (10 hours @ $6)	60
Spare capacity (5 hours @ $0)	0
	60

(c) Contribution earned per unit of Product L produced = $22

If it requires 5 hours of labour to make one unit of product L, the contribution earned per labour hour = $22/5 = $4.40.

Relevant cost of labour on new contract

	$
Direct labour (15 hours @ $6)	90
Contribution lost by not making product L ($4.40 × 15 hours)	66
	154

It is important that you should be able to identify the relevant costs which are appropriate to a decision. In many cases, this is a fairly straightforward problem, but there are cases where great care should be taken.

2 Limiting factors

> A **limiting factor** is a factor which limits the organisation's activities. In a **limiting factor situation**, contribution will be maximised by earning the biggest possible contribution per unit of limiting factor.

One of the more common decision-making problems is a situation where there are not enough resources to meet the potential sales demand, and so a decision has to be made about what mix of products to produce, using what resources there are as effectively as possible.

A limiting factor is a factor which limits the organisation's activities.

A **limiting factor** could be sales if there are sufficient production resources to meet the sales demand, but any one of the organisation's resources (labour, materials and so on) may be insufficient to meet the level of production demanded.

2.1 Optimal production solution

It is assumed in limiting factor analysis that management wishes to maximise profit and that **profit will be maximised when contribution is maximised** (given no change in the fixed cost expenditure incurred). In other words, **marginal costing ideas are applied**.

Contribution will be maximised by earning the biggest possible contribution from each unit of limiting factor. For example if grade A labour is the limiting factor, contribution will be maximised by earning the biggest contribution from each hour of grade A labour worked.

The limiting factor decision therefore involves the determination of the contribution earned by each different product from each unit of the limiting factor.

The **optimal production** solution can be determined by following this five-step approach.

Step 1	Identify the limiting factor.
Step 2	Calculate contribution per unit of output for each product.
Step 3	Calculate contribution per unit of limiting factor for each product.
Step 4	Rank products (make product with highest contribution per unit of limiting factor first).
Step 5	Make products in rank order until scarce resource is used up **(optimal production solution)**.

QUESTION

Limiting factor

LF Co makes a single product for which the cost details are as follows.

	$ per unit
Direct material ($3 per kg)	12
Direct labour ($8 per hour)	72
Production overhead	18
Total production cost	102

Demand for next period will be 20,000 units. No inventories are held and only 75,000 kg of material and 190,000 hours of labour will be available. What will be the limiting factor next period?

O   Material only
O   Labour only
O   Material and labour
O   There will be no limiting factor next period

ANSWER

Material required = 20,000 units × ($12/$3) = 80,000 kg.

Material is therefore a limiting factor, since only 75,000 kg are available. This eliminates option D.

Labour required = 20,000 units × ($72/$8) = 180,000 hours.

Labour is not a limiting factor, since 190,000 labour hours are available. This eliminates the second and third options.

Therefore the correct answer is Material only.

2.1.1 Example: Optimal production solution

AB Co makes two products, the Ay and the Be. Unit variable costs are as follows.

	Ay $	Be $
Direct materials	1	3
Direct labour ($3 per hour)	6	3
Variable overhead	1	1
	8	7

The sales price per unit is $14 per Ay and $11 per Be. During July 20X2 the available direct labour is limited to 8,000 hours. Sales demand in July is expected to be 3,000 units for Ays and 5,000 units for Bes.

Required

Determine the optimal production solution, assuming that monthly fixed costs are $20,000, and that opening inventories of finished goods and work in progress are nil. Also calculate the profit from this solution.

Solution

Step 1 Confirm that the limiting factor is something other than sales demand.

	Ays	Bes	Total
Labour hours per unit	2 hrs	1 hr	
Sales demand	3,000 units	5,000 units	
Labour hours needed	6,000 hrs	5,000 hrs	11,000 hrs
Labour hours available			8,000 hrs
Shortfall			3,000 hrs

Labour is the limiting factor on production.

Step 2 Identify the unit contribution earned by each product.

	Ays $	Bes $
Sales price	14	11
Variable cost	8	7
Unit contribution	6	4

Step 3 **Calculate the contribution** per unit of limiting factor, that is per labour hour worked.

	Ays $	Bes $
Sales price	14	11
Variable cost	8	7
Unit contribution	6	4
Labour hours per unit	2 hrs	1 hr
Contribution per labour hour (= unit of limiting factor)	$3	$4

Step 4　　Although Ays have a higher unit contribution than Bes, two Bes can be made in the time it takes to make one Ay. Because labour is in short supply it is more profitable to make Bes than Ays.

Step 5　　Determine the **optimal production solution**. Sufficient Bes will be made to meet the full sales demand, and the remaining labour hours available will then be used to make Ays.

(a)

Product	Demand	Hours required	Hours available	Priority of manufacture
Bes	5,000	5,000	5,000	1st
Ays	3,000	6,000	3,000 (bal)	2nd
		11,000	8,000	

(b)

Product	Units	Hours needed	Contribution per unit $	Total $
Bes	5,000	5,000	4	20,000
Ays	1,500	3,000	6	9,000
		8,000		29,000
Less fixed costs				20,000
Profit				9,000

In conclusion:

(a)　　Unit contribution is **not** the correct way to decide priorities. This is shown in the calculation following showing the effect if Ays had been ranked before Bes.

Product	Units	Hours needed	Contribution per unit $	Total $
Bes	2,000	2,000	4	8,000
Ays	3,000	6,000	6	18,000
		8,000		26,000
Less fixed costs				20,000
Profit				6,000

(b)　　Labour hours are the scarce resource, and therefore contribution **per labour hour** is the correct way to decide priorities.

(c)　　The Be earns $4 contribution per labour hour, and the Ay earns $3 contribution per labour hour. Bes therefore make more profitable use of the scarce resource, and should be manufactured first.

An important factor to consider when making a limiting factor decision is whether the lost sales / dissatisfied customers whose demand has not been met will have a significant impact on future sales.

3 Make/buy-in problems

In a **make/buy-in problem** with no limiting factors, the relevant costs for the decision are the **differential costs** between the two options.

3.1 Introduction

A **make/buy-in problem** involves a decision by an organisation about whether it should make a product/carry out an activity with its own internal resources, or whether it should pay another organisation to make the product/carry out the activity. Examples of make/buy-in problems would be as follows.

(a)　　Whether a company should manufacture its own components, or buy the components from an outside supplier

(b)　　Whether a construction company should do some work with its own employees, or whether it should subcontract the work to another company

If an organisation has the freedom of choice about whether to make internally or buy externally and has no scarce resources that put a restriction on what it can do itself, the relevant costs for the decision will be the **differential costs** between the two options.

3.1.1 Example: Make/buy-in problem

Buster Co makes four components, W, X, Y and Z, for which costs in the forthcoming year are expected to be as follows.

	W	X	Y	Z
Production (units)	1,000	2,000	4,000	3,000
Unit marginal costs	$	$	$	$
Direct materials	4	5	2	4
Direct labour	8	9	4	6
Variable production overheads	2	3	1	2
	14	17	7	12

Directly attributable fixed costs per annum and committed fixed costs are as follows.

	$
Incurred as a direct consequence of making W	1,000
Incurred as a direct consequence of making X	5,000
Incurred as a direct consequence of making Y	6,000
Incurred as a direct consequence of making Z	8,000
Other fixed costs (committed)	30,000
	50,000

A subcontractor has offered to supply units of W, X, Y and Z for $12, $21, $10 and $14 respectively.

Required

Decide whether Buster Co should make or buy-in the components.

Solution

(a) **The relevant costs are the differential costs between making and buying**, and they consist of differences in unit variable costs plus differences in directly attributable fixed costs. Subcontracting will result in some fixed cost savings.

	W	X	Y	Z
	$	$	$	$
Unit variable cost of making	14	17	7	12
Unit variable cost of buying	12	21	10	14
	(2)	4	3	2
Annual requirements (units)	1,000	2,000	4,000	3,000
Extra variable cost of buying (per annum)	(2,000)	8,000	12,000	6,000
Fixed costs saved by buying	1,000	5,000	6,000	8,000
Extra total cost of buying	(3,000)	3,000	6,000	(2,000)

(b) The company would save $3,000 pa by subcontracting component W (where the purchase cost would be less than the marginal cost per unit to make internally) and would save $2,000 pa by subcontracting component Z (because of the saving in fixed costs of $8,000).

(c) In this example, relevant costs are the variable costs of in-house manufacture, the variable costs of subcontracted units, and the saving in fixed costs.

3.2 Other factors to consider in the make/buy-in problem

(a) If components W and Z are subcontracted, how will the company most profitably use the spare capacity? Would the company's workforce resent the loss of work to an outside subcontractor?

(b) Would the subcontractor be reliable with delivery times, and would he supply components of the same quality as those manufactured internally?

(c) Does the company wish to be flexible and maintain better control over operations by making everything itself?

BPP
LEARNING
MEDIA

(d)   Are the estimates of fixed cost savings reliable? In the case of Product W, buying is clearly cheaper than making in-house. In the case of product Z, the decision to buy rather than make would only be financially beneficial if the fixed cost savings of $8,000 could really be 'delivered' by management.

(e)   Is the buy-in price sustainable? A supplier will need to be willing and able to supply the products at the prices used in the analysis in the long term.

3.3 Make/buy-in problems and limiting factors

In a situation where a company must subcontract work to make up a shortfall in its own production capability, its total costs are minimised if those components/products subcontracted are those with the lowest extra variable cost of buying per unit of limiting factor saved by buying.

3.3.1 Example: make/buy-in problems and limiting factors

Green Co manufactures two components, the Alpha and the Beta, using the same machines for each. The budget for the next year calls for the production and assembly of 4,000 of each component. The variable production cost per unit of the final product, the gamma, is as follows.

	Machine hours	Variable cost
		$
1 unit of Alpha	3	20
1 unit of Beta	2	36
Assembly		20
		76

Only 16,000 hours of machine time will be available during the year, and a sub-contractor has quoted the following unit prices for supplying components: Alpha $29; Beta $40. Advise Green Co and calculate the total variable cost of the optimal solution.

The assembly costs are not relevant costs because they are unaffected by the make/buy-in problem. The units subcontracted should be those which will add least to the costs of Green Co. Since 4,000 hours of work must be sub-contracted, the cheapest policy is to subcontract work which adds the least extra costs (the least extra variable costs) per hour of own-time saved.

Solution

(a)   There is a shortfall in machine hours available, and some products must be sub-contracted.

Product	Units		Machine hours
Alpha	4,000		12,000
Beta	4,000		8,000
		Required	20,000
		Available	16,000
		Shortfall	4,000

(b)

	Alpha	Beta
	$	$
Variable cost of making	20	36
Variable cost of buying	29	40
Extra variable cost of buying	9	4
Machine hours saved by buying	3 hrs	2 hrs
Extra variable cost of buying, per hour saved	$3	$2

It is cheaper to buy Betas than to buy Alphas and so the priority for making the components in-house will be in the reverse order to the preference for buying them from a subcontractor.

(c)

Component	Hrs per unit to make in-house	Hrs required in total	Cumulative hours
Alpha	3 hrs	12,000	12,000
Beta	2 hrs	8,000	20,000
		20,000	
Hours available		16,000	
Shortfall		4,000	

There are enough machine hours to make all 4,000 units of Alpha and 2,000 units of Beta. 4,000 hours production of Beta must be sub-contracted. This will be the cheapest production policy available.

(d)

Component	Machine hours	Number of units	Unit variable cost $	Total variable cost $
Make				
Alpha	12,000	4,000	20	80,000
Beta (balance)	4,000	2,000	36	72,000
	16,000			152,000
Buy	Hours saved			
Beta (balance)	4,000	2,000	40	80,000
		Total variable costs of components		232,000
		Assembly costs (4,000 × $20)		80,000
		Total variable costs		312,000

The five-step approach can be modified for this type of problem.

Step 1	Identify the limiting factor (if not already identified) and the resource shortfall.
Step 2	Calculate the differential variable costs of buying-in per unit of component.
Step 3	Calculate the differential variable costs of buying-in per unit of limiting factor.
Step 4	Rank components.
Step 5	Determine optimal production/buy-in solution.

CHAPTER ROUNDUP

- ↳ **Relevant costs** are future cash flows arising as a direct consequence of a decision.

- ↳ Relevant costs are **future costs, cashflows** and **incremental costs**.

- ↳ A **limiting factor** is a factor which limits the organisation's activities. In a **limiting factor situation**, contribution will be maximised by earning the biggest possible contribution per unit of limiting factor.

- ↳ In a **make/buy-in problem** with no limiting factors, the relevant costs for the decision are the **differential costs** between the two options.

QUICK QUIZ

1   Sunk costs are directly relevant in decision making.

    ○   True
    ○   False

2   A limiting factor is a factor which ....

3   When there is a limiting factor, what five steps are involved to determine the optimal production solution?

Step 1	....
Step 2	....
Step 3	....
Step 4	....
Step 5	....

4   A sunk cost is:

    ○   A cost committed to be spent in the current period
    ○   A cost which is irrelevant for decision making
    ○   A cost connected with oil exploration in the North Sea
    ○   A cost unaffected by fluctuations in the level of activity

5   A company manufactures and sells four products. Details are as follows:

Product	P	Q	R	S
	$	$	$	$
Contribution per unit	16.0	14.5	17.6	19.0
Net profit per unit	4.6	4.8	5.2	5.0
Contribution per machine hour	5.0	4.8	4.4	3.8
Net profit per machine hour	1.4	1.6	1.3	1.0

Machine hours available in the next period will not be sufficient to meet production requirements. There are no product-specific fixed costs.

What should be the order of priority for production in order to maximise profit?

O   Product P, Product Q, Product R, Product S
O   Product Q, Product P, Product R, Product S
O   Product R, Product S, Product Q, Product P
O   Product S, Product R, Product P, Product Q

6   A company has incurred development costs of $25,000 to date on a proposed new product. Further costs of $18,000 would be required to complete the development of the product.

In deciding whether to continue with the new product development which of the following is correct regarding development costs?

	Sunk cost	Incremental cost
O	$0	$43,000
O	$18,000	$25,000
O	$25,000	$18,000
O	$43,000	$0

ANSWERS TO QUICK QUIZ

1   False

2   Limits the organisation's activities

3

Step 1	Identify the limiting factor.
Step 2	Calculate contribution per unit for each product.
Step 3	Calculate contribution per unit of limiting factor.
Step 4	Rank products (make product with highest contribution per unit of limiting factor first).
Step 5	Make products in rank order until scare resource is used up **(optimal production plan)**.

4   A cost which is irrelevant for decision making

5   Product P, Product Q, Product R, Product S.   Contribution per machine hour needs to be maximised.

6   Sunk cost: $25,000   Incremental cost: $18,000

Now try ...

Attempt the questions below from the **Practice Question Bank**

Number

Q73

Q74

Q75

Q76

Q77

CHAPTER

17

Decision making for the long term is similar in many respects to short term decision making, and relevant costs must be used to assess whether a proposed investment should go ahead or not (assuming that the decision will be made on financial considerations only). In addition, however, the financial assessment of long-term investments should also take into consideration the **time value of money**. Investments should be expected to **earn a return**, and the size of the return should be expected to increase with time. **Cash flow considerations** may also be important, and a business may not want to invest in a project where it may take a long time to earn the investment returns.

This chapter explains how long-term decisions should take into consideration the **time value of money**, and possibly also the **cash payback period**. It introduces the technique of **discounted cash flow**, which is extremely important in financial management.

Capital investment appraisal

1 Introduction to capital investment appraisal

Long-term investments include the purchase of buildings, machinery and equipment. Management will need to have estimates of the initial investment and future costs and revenues of a project in order to make any **long-term decisions**.

Long-term decisions generally involve looking at the options available when a company (or an individual) puts money into an investment.

If a company invests in a project, it will expect some sort of financial return (or more money) at some point in the future. If the project runs for a number of years then whether or not to invest in the project will involve taking a long-term decision.

One of the things companies will need to consider when investing in long-term projects is the **time value of money**.

Think about the following question.

'If I have $5 in my pocket **now**, how much will it be worth in four years' time?'

This is a difficult question to answer, but we will be looking at ways in which companies use the concept of the **time value of money** when they are appraising projects and making long-term decisions.

Note. When going through the rest of this chapter, where interest rates, discount rates, the rate of return and the cost of capital are given, these should be assumed to be **per annum**, unless otherwise stated.

2 Interest

Interest is the amount of money which an investment earns over time. **Simple interest** is interest which is earned in equal amounts every year assuming no change in the interest rate. If interest earned also earns interest itself in later periods, this is known as **compound interest**.

2.1 Simple interest

- **Interest** is the amount of money which an investment earns over time.
- **Simple interest** is interest which is earned in equal amounts every year (or month), assuming no change in the interest rate, and which is a given proportion of the original investment (the principal).

If a sum of money is invested for a period of time, then the amount of simple interest which accrues is equal to the number of periods × the interest rate × the amount invested. We can write this as a formula.

The formula for **simple interest** is as follows:

$S = P + nrP$

where P	=	The original sum invested
r	=	The interest rate (expressed as a proportion, so 10% = 0.1)
n	=	The number of periods (normally years)
S	=	The sum invested after n periods, consisting of the original capital (P) plus interest earned (future value)

2.1.1 Example: Simple interest

Fred invests $1,000 at 10% simple interest per annum.

Required

Calculate how much Fred will have after five years.

Solution

Using the formula $S = P + nrP$

where P	=	$1,000
r	=	10%
n	=	5

$\therefore S = \$1,000 + (5 \times 0.1 \times \$1,000) = \$1,500$

2.2 Compound interest

Interest is normally calculated by means of **compounding**.

If a sum of money is invested and the interest earned each period is added to the investment, then the **interest earned in earlier periods will also earn interest in later periods**.

2.2.1 Example: Compound interest

Suppose that Fred invests $2,000 at 10% interest per annum. After one year, the original principal plus interest will amount to $2,200.

	$
Original investment	2,000
Interest in the first year (10%)	200
Total investment at the end of one year	2,200

(a) **After two years** the total investment will be $2,420.

	$
Investment at end of one year	2,200
Interest in the second year (10%)	220
Total investment at the end of two years	2,420

The second year interest of $220 represents 10% of the original investment, and 10% of the interest earned in the first year.

(b)   Similarly, **after three years**, the total investment will be $2,662.

	$
Investment at the end of two years	2,420
Interest in the third year (10%)	242
Total investment at the end of three years	2,662

Instead of performing the calculations shown above, we could have used the following formula.

The basic formula for **compound interest** is $S = P(1 + r)^n$

where	P	=	the original sum invested
	r	=	the interest rate, expressed as a proportion (so 5% = 0.05)
	n	=	the number of periods (normally years)
	S	=	the sum invested after n periods (future value)

You will need a scientific calculator with a power button ($x^{\blacksquare}$, y^x or x^y)

Using the formula for compound interest, $S = P(1 + r)^n$

where	P	=	$2,000
	r	=	10% = 0.1
	n	=	3
	S	=	$2,000 \times 1.10^3$
		=	$2,000 \times 1.331$
		=	$2,662

The interest earned over three years is $662, which is the same answer that was calculated in the example above.

If today's date is 31 May 20X3, note the following timings of cash flows.

- Time 0 = now (31 May 20X3)
- Time 1 = one year's time (31 May 20X4)
- Time 2 = two year's time (31 May 20X5)

QUESTION   Compound interest

If Fred invests $5,000 now (28 February 20X3) how much will his investment be worth:

(a)   On 28 February 20X6, if the interest rate is 20% per annum?
(b)   On 28 February 20X7, if the interest rate is 15% per annum?
(c)   On 28 February 20X6, if the interest rate is 6% per annum?

ANSWER

(a)   At 28 February 20X6, n = 3, $5,000 \times 1.20^3 = \$8,640$
(b)   At 28 February 20X7, n = 4, $5,000 \times 1.15^4 = \$8,745.03$
(c)   At 28 February 20X6, n = 3, $5,000 \times 1.06^3 = \$5,955.08$

2.3 Nominal interest rates

In the previous examples, interest has been calculated **annually**, but this isn't always the case. Interest may be compounded **daily**, **weekly**, **monthly** or **quarterly**.

Most interest rates are expressed as **per annum figures** even when the interest is compounded over periods of less than one year. In such cases, the given interest rate is called a **nominal rate**. We can, however, work out the **effective rate**. It is this effective rate (shortened to one decimal place) which is quoted in advertisements as the **annual percentage rate (APR)**, sometimes called the **compound annual rate (CAR)**.

EXAM FOCUS POINT

Students often become confused about the various rates of interest.

- The **nominal rate** is the interest rate expressed as a per annum figure, even though interest may be compounded over periods of less than one year. For example, 5% interest payable every six months is expressed as 10% p.a. nominal.
- The **effective rate** is the adjusted nominal rate expressed as a per annum figure. For example, if a bank offers customers 10% per annum nominal rate, with interest payable every six months, this is an effective rate of 10.25% p.a. (see 2.5 below).

2.4 Effective interest rates

The **equivalent annual** rate of interest, when interest is compounded at shorter intervals, is known as an **effective annual rate of interest**.

FORMULA TO LEARN

Effective interest rate $= [(1+r)^{\frac{12}{n}} - 1]$ or $[(1+r)^{\frac{365}{y}} - 1]$

where r is the rate of interest for each time period
n is the number of months in the time period
y is the number of days in the time period

2.4.1 Example: Effective interest rates

Calculate the effective annual rate of interest of:

(a)   1.5% per month, compound
(b)   4.5% per quarter, compound
(c)   9% per half year, compound

Solution

(a) $(1.015)^{12} - 1 = 0.1956 = 19.56\%$
(b) $(1.045)^4 - 1 = 0.1925 = 19.25\%$
(c) $(1.09)^2 - 1 = 0.1881 = 18.81\%$

2.5 Example: Nominal and effective rates of interest

A building society may offer investors 10% per annum interest payable half-yearly. If the 10% is a nominal rate of interest, the building society would in fact pay 5% every 6 months, compounded so that the effective annual rate of interest would be:

$[(1.05)^2 - 1] = 0.1025 = 10.25\%$ per annum.

Similarly, if a bank offers depositors a nominal 12% per annum, with interest payable quarterly, the effective rate of interest would be 3% compound every 3 months, which is:

$[(1.03)^4 - 1] = 0.1255 = 12.55\%$ per annum.

An important point to note is that the more frequent the compounding, the greater the effective annual rate of interest. For example a nominal interest rate of interest may be 18%, but this could mean interest at 1.5% every month, interest at 4.5% every three months, interest at 9% every six months or interest at 18% every year. The effective annual interest rate when interest is compounded at 1.5% each month is 19.56%. This is more than the effective annual interest rate when interest is compounded at 4.5% every three months (19.25%), which is more than the effective annual rate for interest at 9% every six months (18.8%) and interest payable annually at 18%.

BPP
LEARNING
MEDIA

QUESTION

Effective rates

Calculate the effective annual rate of interest of:

(a)   15% nominal per annum compounded quarterly
(b)   24% nominal per annum compounded monthly

ANSWER

(a)   15% per annum (nominal rate) is 3.75% per quarter. The effective annual rate of interest is:

$$[1.0375^4 - 1] = 0.1587 = 15.87\%$$

(b)   24% per annum (nominal rate) is 2% per month. The effective annual rate of interest is:

$$[1.02^{12} - 1] = 0.2682 = 26.82\%$$

---

3 The principles of discounted cash flow

- The basic principle of **discounting** involves calculating the **present value** of an investment (ie the value of an investment **today** at time 0).

- The term **present value** means the cash equivalent now of a sum to be received or to be paid in the future.

The basic principle of **discounting** is that if we wish to have $S in n years' time, we need to invest a certain sum **now** (year 0) at an interest rate of r% in order to obtain the required sum of money in the future. In day-to-day terms, we could say that if we wish to have $1,000 in 5 years' time, how much would we need to invest now at an interest rate of 4%?

3.1 Compounding

Suppose that a company has $10,000 to invest, and wants to earn a return of 10% (compound interest) on its investments. This means that if the $10,000 could be invested at 10%, the value of the investment with interest would build up as follows.

(a)   After 1 year $10,000 × (1.10)   = $11,000
(b)   After 2 years $10,000 × (1.10)^2   = $12,100
(c)   After 3 years $10,000 × (1.10)^3   = $13,310 and so on

This is **compounding**. The formula for the future value of an investment plus accumulated interest after n time periods is:

$$FV = PV \times (1 + r)^n$$

where   FV   is the future value of the investment with interest
        PV   is the initial or 'present' value of the investment
        r   is the compound rate of return per time period, expressed as a proportion
             (so 10% = 0.10, 5% = 0.05 and so on)
        n   is the number of time periods

3.2 Discounting

Discounting starts with the future value, and converts a future value to a present value. For example, if a company expects to earn a (compound) rate of return of 10% on its investments, how much would it need to invest now to have the following investments?

(a) $11,000 after 1 year
(b) $12,100 after 2 years
(c) $13,310 after 3 years

The answer is $10,000 in each case, and we can calculate it by discounting. The discounting formula to calculate the present value of a future sum of money at the end of n time periods is:

$$PV = FV \frac{1}{(1+r)^n}$$

(a)   After 1 year, $11,000 $\times \dfrac{1}{1.10}$ = $10,000

(b)   After 2 years, $12,100 $\times \dfrac{1}{1.10^2}$ = $10,000

(c)   After 3 years, $13,310 $\times \dfrac{1}{1.10^3}$ = $10,000

Discounting can be applied to both money receivable and also to money payable at a future date. By discounting all payments and receipts from a capital investment to a present value, they can be compared on a common basis at a value which takes account of when the various cash flows will take place.

3.3 Present values

The term **'present value'** simply means the cash equivalent now of a sum to be received or to be paid in the future.

The **discounting formula** is:

$$PV = FV \times \frac{1}{(1+r)^n}$$

where   FV   is the future value of the investment with interest
        PV   is the present value (PV) of that sum
        r   is the rate of return, expressed as a proportion
        n   is the number of time periods (usually years)

The rate r is sometimes called the **cost of capital**.

Note. That this equation is just a rearrangement of the compounding formula.

3.3.1 Example: Present values

(a)   Calculate the present value of $60,000 received at the end of year 6, if interest rates are 15% per annum.
(b)   Calculate the present value of $100,000 received at the end of year 5, if interest rates are 6% per annum.

Solution

The discounting formula, $PV = FV \times \dfrac{1}{(1+r)^n}$ is required.

(a)   FV   = $60,000
        n   =   6
        r   =   0.15

        PV   = $60,000 \times \dfrac{1}{1.15^6}$
             =   60,000 × 0.432
             = $25,920

(b)   FV   = $100,000
        n   =   5
        r   =   0.06

$$PV = 100,000 \times \frac{1}{1.06^5}$$
$$= 100,000 \times 0.747$$
$$= \$74,700$$

3.4 Present value tables

Now that you understand the principles of discounting and you are able to calculate present values, you will be happy to hear that you do not need to remember the formula for discounting.

Refer to the **present value tables** in the Appendix to this Text.

The use of present value tables is best explained by means of an example.

3.4.1 Example: Present value tables

(a) Using tables, calculate the present value of $60,000 at year 6, if interest rates are 15% per annum.

(b) Using tables, calculate the present value of $100,000 at year 5, if interest rates are 6% per annum.

Solution

(a) Looking at the present value tables, look along the row n = 6 (year 6) and down column r = 15% (interest rates are 15% per annum). The required discount rate is 0.432.

The present value of $60,000 at year 6, when interest rates are 15% is therefore:

$60,000 × 0.432 = $25,920

(b) Looking at the present value tables, look along the row n = 5 (year 5) and down column r = 6% (interest rates are 6% per annum). The required discount rate is 0.747.

The present value of $100,000 at year 5, when interest rates are 6% is therefore:

$100,000 × 0.747 = $74,700

Do either of these present values look familiar? Well, both of them should be as they are the same present values that we calculated in the previous example using the discounting formula!

QUESTION

Present values

Today's date is 30 April 20X3. If Fred wishes to have $16,000 saved by 30 April 20X8, how much should he invest if interest rates are 5%? Use the present value tables at the back of this text.

ANSWER

30 April 20X3   = Now

30 April 20X4   = time period 5

   ∴ n = 5

   r   = 5%

Present value = $16,000 × discount rate (where n = 5 and r = 5%)

        = $16,000 × 0.784

        = $12,544

4 Annuities and perpetuities

- An **annuity** is a constant sum of money received or paid each year for a given number of years.
- A **perpetuity** is an annuity which lasts forever.

4.1 Annuities

KEY TERM

An annuity is a constant sum of money received or paid each year for a given number of years.

For example, the present value of a three year annuity of $100 which begins in one year's time when interest rates are 5% is calculated as follows.

Time	Cash flow $	Discount factor 5%	Present value $
1	100	0.952	95.20
2	100	0.907	90.70
3	100	0.864	86.40
		2.723	272.30

There is a rather long and complicated formula which can be used to calculate the present value of an annuity. Fortunately there are also **annuity tables** which calculate all of the **annuity factors** that you might ever need for MA2. These are included at the end of this Interactive Text.

In order to calculate the present value of a constant sum of money, we can multiply the annual cash flow by the sum of the discount factors for the relevant years. These total factors are known as **cumulative present value factors or annuity factors**.

In the example above this is $100 × 2.723 = $272.30 which is the present value already calculated.

Present value of an annuity = annuity × annuity factor

KEY TERM

4.1.1 Example: Annuity tables

What is the annuity factor (cumulative present value factor) of $1 per annum for 5 years at 11% interest?

Solution

Refer to the annuity tables at the back of this Interactive Text.

Read across to the column headed 11% (r = 11%) and down to period 5 (n = 5). The annuity factor = 3.696.

Now look back at the present value tables and look in the column n = 11%. The cumulative present value rates for n = 1 to 5 = 0.901 + 0.812 + 0.731 + 0.659 + 0.593 = 3.696. Can you see now why these annuity tables are also called cumulative present value tables?

4.1.2 Example: Present value of an annuity

Fred has to make an annual payment of $1,000 to a car hire company each year from 30 June 20X3 to 30 June 20X8.

Required

Calculate the present value of Fred's total payments if today's date is 1 July 20X2. Use a discount rate of 7%.

Solution

The first payment will be in one year's time ie time 1.

There will be six annual payments.

Annuity factor (where n = 6, r = 7%) = 4.767

Present value of payments = $1,000 × annuity factor
= $1,000 × 4.767
= $4,767

4.2 Perpetuities

A **perpetuity** is an annuity which lasts forever.

The **present value of a perpetuity** = $\dfrac{\text{annuity}}{\text{interest rate *}}$

*expressed as a proportion eg 20% = 0.2

4.2.1 Example: A perpetuity

Fred is to receive $35,000 per annum in perpetuity starting in one year's time. If the annual rate of interest is 9% what is the present value of this perpetuity?

Solution

$PV = \dfrac{\text{annuity}}{\text{interest rate}}$

$\therefore PV = \dfrac{\$35,000}{0.09}$

$= \$388,889$

5 Cash flows and profits

To be successful in business, organisations must make profits. Profits are needed in order to pay dividends to shareholders and to allow partners to make drawings.

Performance objective 14 requires you to 'manage and control cash receipts, payments and balances'. You can apply the knowledge you obtain from this chapter of the Text to help to demonstrate this competence.

If an organisation makes a loss, the value of the business falls and if there are long-term losses, the business may eventually collapse.

Net profit measures how much the capital of an organisation has increased over a period of time. Profit is calculated by applying the **matching concept**, that is to say by matching the costs incurred with the sales revenue generated during a period.

5.1 The importance of cash

In addition to being **profitable**, an organisation needs to have enough cash in order to pay for the following:

- Goods and services
- Capital investment (plant, machinery and so on)
- Labour costs
- Other expenses (rent, rates, taxation and so on)
- Dividends

Net cash flow measures the difference in the payments leaving an organisation's bank account and the receipts that are paid into the bank account.

5.2 Net profit and net cash flow

Reasons why net profit and net cash flow differ are mainly due to timing differences.

(a) **Purchase of non-current assets**

Suppose an asset is purchased for $20,000 and depreciation is charged at 10% of the original cost.

(i) Cash payment during the year = $20,000 (and this does not affect the statement of profit or loss).

(ii) Depreciation charge = 10% × $20,000 = $2,000. This is charged to the statement of profit or loss and will reduce overall profits.

(b) **Sale of non-current assets**

When an asset is sold there is usually a profit or loss on sale. Suppose an asset with a carrying value of $15,000 is sold for $11,000, giving rise to a loss on disposal of $4,000.

(i) Increase in cash flow during the year = $11,000 sale proceeds. There will be no effect on the statement of profit or loss.

(ii) Loss on sale of non-current assets = $4,000. This will be recorded in the firm's statement of profit or loss and will reduce overall profits.

(c) **Matching receipts from receivables and sales invoices raised**

If goods are sold on credit, the cash receipts will be the same as the value of the sales (ignoring early settlement discounts and bad debts). However, receipts may occur in a different period as a result of the timing of payments.

(d) **Matching payments to payables and cost of sales**

If materials are bought on credit, the cash payments to suppliers will be the same as the value of materials purchased. Again the payments may be in different periods due to timing. Materials purchase are matched against sales in a particular period to calculate profit, demonstrating that profit and cash flow will differ in a particular period.

5.3 Cash flow in capital investment appraisal

In a capital investment appraisal situation, the driver of long-term value is cash flow. In particular the timing and amount of cash received or paid is used in the evaluation rather than an assessment of profit (or loss) which is a short-term measure often used to assess value.

EXAM FOCUS POINT

It is very important that you fully understand the difference between cash and profit. The key differences are covered by points (a) and (b) above. Points (c) and (d) are relevant to the examination of short-term differences such as cash budgeting/forecasting.

6 Capital investment appraisal – net present value method

- **Discounted cash flow** involves discounting future cash flows from a project in order to decide whether the project will earn a satisfactory rate of return.

- The two main discounted cash flow **methods** are the **net present value** (NPV) method and the **internal rate of return** (IRR) method.

Discounted cash flow methods can be used to appraise capital investment projects.

Discounted cash flow (DCF) involves the application of discounting arithmetic to the estimated future cash flows (receipts and expenditures) from a capital investment project in order to decide whether the project is expected to earn a satisfactory rate of return.

The two main discounted cash flow methods are as follows.

- The net present value (NPV) method
- The internal rate of return (IRR) method

6.1 The net present value (NPV) method

The **net present value (NPV) method** calculates the present values of all items of income and expenditure related to an investment at a given rate of return, and then calculates a net total. If it is positive, the investment is considered to be acceptable. If it is negative, the investment is considered to be unacceptable.

6.2 The cost of capital

The **cost of capital** has two aspects to it.

(a) It is the **cost of funds** that a company raises and uses.

(b) The return that investors expect to be paid for putting funds into the company. It is therefore the **minimum return** that a company should make from its own investments, to earn the cash flows out of which investors can be paid their return.

The cost of capital can therefore be measured by studying the returns required by investors, and used to derive a **discount rate** for discounted cash flow analysis and investment appraisal.

6.2.1 Example: The net present value of a project

Dog Co is considering whether to spend $5,000 on an item of equipment which will last for 2 years. The excess of cash received over cash expenditure from the equipment would be $3,000 in the first year and $4,000 in the second year.

Required

Calculate the net present value of the investment in the equipment at a discount rate of 15%.

Solution

In this example, an outlay of $5,000 now promises a net cash inflow of $3,000 **during** the first year and $4,000 **during** the second year. It is a convention in DCF, however, that cash flows spread over a year are assumed to occur **at the end of the year**, so that the cash flows of the project are as follows. The initial cost occurs at time 0, now, and therefore the discount factor is 1.00 as $5,000 is the present value of the expenditure now.

	$
Year 0 (now)	(5,000)
Year 1 (at the end of the year)	3,000
Year 2 (at the end of the year)	4,000

A net present value statement is drawn up as follows.

Year	Cash flow $	Discount factor 15%	Present value $
0	(5,000)	1.000	(5,000)
1	3,000	0.870	2,610
2	4,000	0.756	3,024
	Net present value		+ 634

The project has a positive net present value, so it is acceptable.

6.3 The timing of cash flows

Note that annuity tables and the formulae both assume that the first payment or receipt is a year from now. **Always check examination and assessment questions for when the first payment falls**.

For example, if there are five equal annual payments starting now, and the interest rate is 8%, we should use a factor of 1 (for today's payment) + 3.312 (for the other four payments) = 4.312.

6.4 Cash versus profit

Remember that it is **cash flow figures** that must be included in your calculations. If depreciation has been deducted to arrive at a profit figure, it must be **added back** to give the net cash inflow.

QUESTION
NPV (1)

Daisy Co is considering whether to make an investment costing $28,000 which would earn a profit of $2,400 per annum for each of the next 5 years, after charging depreciation at the straight-line rate over five years, to a residual value of $0.

Required

What is the net present value of the investment at a cost of capital of 11%?

ANSWER

Year	Profit	Depreciation	Cash flow $	Discount factor 11%	Present value $
0			(28,000)	1.000	(28,000)
1	2,400	5,600	8,000	0.901	7,208
2	2,400	5,600	8,000	0.812	6,496
3	2,400	5,600	8,000	0.731	5,848
4	2,400	5,600	8,000	0.659	5,272
5	2,400	5,600	8,000	0.593	4,744
				NPV	1,568

Working

Cash flow = $2,400 profit per annum + $5,600 depreciation per annum* = $8,000 per annum.

* Depreciation = $28,000/5 years = $5,600 per annum.

The important point to note is that depreciation is a non-cash expense. The actual cash spending occurs in Year 0, when the investment is made.

Alternatively, you could treat the cash inflows of $8,000 for 5 years as an annuity.

Year	Cash flow $	Discount factor 11%	Present value $
0	(28,000)	1.000	(28,000)
1–5	8,000	3.696	29,568
			1,568

QUESTION

NPV (2)

Mostly Co is considering a project which would cost $50,000 now and yield $9,000 per annum every year in perpetuity, starting a year from now. The cost of capital is 15%.

Required

Calculate the net present value of the project.

ANSWER

Year	Cash flow $	Discount factor 15%	Present value $
0	(50,000)	1.0	(50,000)
1 - ∞	9,000	1/0.15	60,000
			NPV 10,000

The net present value of the project is $10,000.

6.5 What does a net present value mean?

The net present value is a measure of the value in terms of 'today's money' of the net benefits from a proposed investment. The discount rate is the rate of return that will be sufficient to cover the cost of the organisation's capital.

If an investment with a positive NPV goes ahead it will add value to the organisation, because the value of its net returns will be more than are needed to satisfy the providers of capital to the organisation.

In theory, the value of the organisation should increase by the amount of the NPV if the investment goes ahead.

7 Capital investment appraisal – internal rate of return (IRR) method

The **IRR method** determines the rate of interest (internal rate of return) at which the NPV = 0. The internal rate of return is therefore the rate of return on an investment.

The **internal rate of return (IRR) method** of evaluating investments is an alternative to the NPV method. The NPV method of discounted cash flow determines whether an investment earns a **positive or a negative NPV when discounted at a given rate of interest**. If the NPV is zero (that is, the present values of costs and benefits are equal) the return from the project would be exactly the rate used for discounting.

The **IRR method of discounted cash flow** is a method which determines the rate of interest (the internal rate of return) at which the NPV is 0. The internal rate of return is therefore the rate of return on an investment.

The IRR method will indicate that a project is viable **if the IRR exceeds the minimum acceptable rate of return**. Thus if the company expects a minimum return of, say, 15%, a project would be viable if its IRR is more than 15%.

7.1 Example: The IRR method over one year

If $500 is invested today and generates $600 in one year's time, the internal rate of return (r) can be calculated as follows.

PV of cost $=$ PV of benefits

$$500 = \frac{600}{(1+r)}$$

$$500\,(1+r) = 600$$

$$1+r = \frac{600}{500} = 1.2$$

$$r = 0.2 = 20\%$$

The arithmetic for calculating the IRR is more complicated for investments and cash flows extending over a period of time longer than one year. An approximate IRR can be calculated using either a **graphical method** or by a technique known as the **interpolation** method.

7.2 Graphical approach

A useful way to **estimate** the IRR of a project is to **find the project's NPV at a number of discount rates** and **sketch a graph of NPV against discount rate**. You can then use the sketch to estimate the **discount rate at which the NPV is equal to zero** (the point where the curve cuts the discount rate (horizontal) axis).

7.2.1 Example: Graphical approach

A project might have the following NPVs at the following discount rates.

Discount rate %	NPV $
5	5,300
10	400
15	(1,700)
20	(2,900)

This could be sketched on a graph as follows.

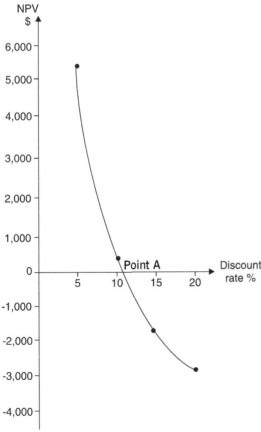

Reading from the graph, the IRR can be **estimated as 11%** (ie point A at which the curve cross the horizontal axis).

BPP
LEARNING
MEDIA

The graphical approach is a useful way of illustrating how the NPV of a project changes as the discount rate used varies.

7.3 The interpolation method

Using the interpolation method, the IRR is calculated by first of all finding the NPV at each of two interest rates. Ideally, one interest rate should give a small positive NPV and the other a small negative NPV.

The IRR would then be somewhere between these two interest rates: above the rate where the NPV is positive, but below the rate where the NPV is negative. However, it is possible to use two positive values or two negative values to extrapolate the IRR.

The IRR, where the NPV is zero, can be calculated as follows.

$$IRR = a\% + \left[\frac{NPV_A}{NPV_A - NPV_B} \times (b-a) \right] \%$$

where a is one interest rate
b is the other interest rate
NPV_A is the NPV at rate a
NPV_B is the NPV at rate b

Using the information from the graphical approach example above.

a   =   10%
b   =   15%
NPV_A = $400
NPV_B = $(1,700)

$$IRR = 10\% + \frac{400}{(400+1,700)} \times (15-10) \ \%$$

$$= 10\% + 0.95\%$$
$$= 10.95\%$$

QUESTION   IRR

The net present value of an investment at 16% is + $50,000 and at 20% is + $10,000. The internal rate of return of this investment (to the nearest whole number) is:

- ○   19%
- ○   20%
- ○   21%
- ○   22%

ANSWER

The IRR in this example is greater than 20% because the NPV is still positive when discounted at 20% per annum. It can be estimated using extrapolation, rather than interpolation. The techniques are similar.

$$IRR = a\% + \left[\frac{NPV_B}{NPV_A - NPV_B} \times (a-b) \right] \%$$

Where a   =   20%
      b   =   16%
      NPV_A =   NPV at rate a = $50,000
      NPV_B =   NPV at rate b = $10,000

$$IRR = 20\% + \left[\frac{\$10,000}{\$50,000-10,000} \times (20-16) \right] \% \quad \text{or} \quad = 16\% + \left[\frac{\$50,000}{\$50,000-10,000} \times (20-16) \right]$$

$$= 20\% + 1\% \qquad\qquad\qquad\qquad\qquad = 16\% + 5\%$$
$$= 21\% \qquad\qquad\qquad\qquad\qquad\qquad = 21\%$$

The correct answer is therefore 21%.

QUESTION

The net present value of an investment at 18% is – $14,000 and at 14% is – $5,000. The internal rate of return of this investment (to the nearest whole number) is:

O   13%
O   12%
O   11%
O   10%

ANSWER

The IRR in this example is less than 14% because the NPV is still negative when discounted at 14% per annum. It can be estimated using extrapolation.

$$IRR = a\% - \left[\frac{NPV_A}{NPV_B - NPV_A} \times (b-a) \right]\%$$

Where   a   =   14%
         b   =   18%
        NPV_A =   NPV at rate a = – $5,000
        NPV_B =   NPV at rate b = – $14,000

$$IRR = 14\% - \left[\frac{\$5,000}{\$14,000 - \$5,000} \times (18-14) \right]\% \quad \text{or} \quad = 18\% - \left[\frac{\$14,000}{\$14,000 - \$5,000} \times (18-14) \right]$$

      = 14% – 2.2%   = 18% – 6.2%
      = 11.8%   = 11.8%

Rounding to the nearest % is sensible given the uncertainty generally about estimating cash flows several years ahead and given also the use of annual intervals in discounting.

The correct answer is therefore 12%.

7.4 The interpolation method, constant annual cash flows and annuity factors

When the cash flows from a project are a constant amount each year, the IRR can be calculated (approximately) using the interpolation method and annuity factors. (Annuity factors are the value of $1 per annum at a discount rate of x% for each year from year 1 to year n.)

An example will be used to illustrate the technique.

QUESTION

An investment will cost $75,000 and is expected to provide a cash return of $20,000 each year for the next six years. What is the IRR of the investment?

The present value of $1 per annum at 14% for years 1–6 = $3.889

The present value of $1 per annum at 16% for years 1–6 = $3.685

ANSWER

When the NPV of the investment is $0, the cumulative discount factor for $20,000 each year from year 1 to year 6 = $75,000/$20,000 = 3.750.

The NPV at a discount rate of 14% would be positive, because the annuity factor at 14% (3.889) is higher than 3.750.

The NPV at a discount rate of 16% would be negative, because the annuity factor at 16% (3.685) is lower than 3.750.

The IRR can be calculated using the following formula, which is based on interpolation:

$$\textbf{IRR} = a\% + \left[\frac{CDFa - CDFirr}{CDFa - CDFb} \times (b - a)\right]\%$$

where a is the lower discount rate
   b is the higher discount rate
   CDFa is the cumulative discount factor (annuity factor) at the lower discount rate
   CDFb is the cumulative discount factor (annuity factor) at the higher discount rate
   CDFirr is the cumulative discount factor (annuity factor) where the NPV = 0

Applying this formula:

$$\textbf{IRR} = 14\% + \left[\frac{3.889 - 3.750}{3.889 - 3.685} \times (16 - 14)\right]\%$$

= 14% + [0.139/0.204] × 2%

= 15.36%.

Note. The calculation of the IRR in this example has used the interpolation method. In practice, the exact IRR could be obtained using a mathematical calculator.

7.5 What does the IRR of an investment mean?

It was explained previously that in theory, the value of an organisation should increase by the NPV of the investments that it undertakes (assuming that only investments with a positive NPV are selected). The IRR of an investment is a measure of the return that the investment is expected to achieve. If the IRR is more than the organisation's cost of capital, the investment should go ahead.

However unlike the NPV of investments, the IRR does not provide a measure of how much value the investment will create. A project with an NPV of + $1 million and an IRR of 15% is more valuable than a project with a NPV of + $100,000 and an IRR of 25%. The project with the higher NPV will create more value (by $900,000), even though it has a lower IRR.

EXAM FOCUS POINT

You will need to learn the IRR formula so that you can calculate the IRR if required.

8 Capital investment appraisal – payback method

The **payback period** is the time that is required for the cash inflows from a capital investment project to equal the cash outflows.

8.1 What is the payback period?

The **payback period** is the time that is required for the total of the cash inflows of a capital investment project to equal the total of the cash outflows.

Before the payback period can be calculated, management must have details of the following.

- The initial cash outflow for the project under consideration
- Estimates of any future cash inflows or savings

8.2 Example: Payback method

Ruby Co is considering a new project which will require an initial investment $60,000. The estimated profits before depreciation are as follows:

Year	Estimated net cash inflows
	$
1	20,000
2	30,000
3	40,000
4	50,000
5	60,000

The payback period is calculated by considering the cumulative estimated profits before depreciation.

Year	Estimated net cash inflows	Cumulative net cash inflows
	$	$
1	20,000	20,000
2	30,000	50,000
3	40,000	90,000
4	50,000	140,000
5	60,000	200,000

The investment of $60,000 is paid back in year 3. If the cash flows accrue evenly throughout the year, we can calculate the payback period as follows.

At the end of year 2, $50,000 of the cash invested has been paid back, leaving $10,000 outstanding.

The net cash inflow in year 3 is $40,000.

The point at which the $60,000 investment has been paid back is:

2 years + ($10,000/$40,000 × 12 months) = 2 years and 3 months

If, on the other hand, the cash flows are received at the end of the year then the payback period would be 3 years.

8.3 Using the payback period to appraise capital investment projects

There are two ways in which the payback period can be used to appraise projects.

(a)　If two or more mutually exclusive projects are under consideration, the usual decision is to accept the project with the **shortest payback period**.

(b)　If the management of a company have a **payback period limit**, then only projects with payback periods which are less than this limit would be considered for investment.

8.4 Example: Project appraisal – payback method

Suppose Ruby Co has a payback period limit of two years, and is considering investing in one of the following projects, both of which require an initial investment of $400,000. Cashflows accrue evenly throughout the year.

Project A			**Project B**	
Year	Cash inflow		Year	Cash inflow
	$			$
1	100,000		1	200,000
2	200,000		2	180,000
3	100,000		3	120,000
4	150,000		4	100,000
5	150,000		5	100,000

Required

Which project is acceptable from the point of view of the payback period?

BPP
LEARNING
MEDIA

Solution

Firstly, we need to calculate the payback periods for Projects A and B.

Project A

Year	Cash inflow $	Cumulative cash inflow $
1	100,000	100,000
2	200,000	300,000
3	100,000	400,000
4	150,000	550,000
5	150,000	700,000

Project A has a payback period of 3 years.

Project B

Year	Cash inflow $	Cumulative cash inflow $
1	200,000	200,000
2	180,000	380,000
3	120,000	500,000
4	100,000	600,000
5	100,000	700,000

Project B has a payback period of between 2 and 3 years.

Payback period   = 2 years + ($20,000/$120,000 × 12 months)
                         = 2 years + 2 months

Since Ruby Co has a payback period limit of two years, neither project should be invested in (as both payback periods are greater than two years). If, however, Ruby Co did not have a payback limit, or it was three years or longer, it should invest in Project B because it has the shorter payback period of the two projects.

QUESTION   IRR

A company is considering a project to purchase an item of equipment costing $900,000. This would be depreciated over six years to a residual value of $0, using the straight line method. The expected additional profit from using the equipment in each of the six years would be:

Year 1 $40,000

Year 2 $80,000

Year 3 $100,000

Year 4 $150,000

Year 5 $100,000

Year 6 $40,000

What is the expected payback period, assuming that cash flows accrue at an even rate during each year?

O   3 years 3 months
O   3 years 4 months
O   3 years 8 months
O   3 years 9 months

BPP
LEARNING
MEDIA

ANSWER

Annual depreciation will be $900,000/6 years = $150,000.

Year	Annual cash inflows $	Cumulative cash inflows $
0	(900,000)	(900,000)
1	190,000	(710,000)
2	230,000	(480,000)
3	250,000	(230,000)
	300,000	70,000

(There is no need to calculate cumulative cash flows after Year 3.)

Payback = 3 years + (230,000/300,000) × 12 months

= 3 years 9 months.

8.5 What does payback mean?

The payback for an investment is a measure of how long it will take to recover the initial cash spending on an investment. If an organisation has cash flow difficulties, payback may be an important consideration. Similarly, payback may be a way of avoiding investments in projects where the expected cash flows are difficult to estimate reliably, especially more than a few years into the future.

However, payback does not measure the value of an investment, or the expected return on investment that it will provide. It ignores all cash flows and returns after payback has been achieved.

Payback is often used as an initial step in appraising a project. However, a project should not be evaluated on the basis of payback alone. If a project passes the 'payback test' ie if it has a payback period that is less than the payback period limit of the company then it should be evaluated further with a more sophisticated project appraisal technique (such as the NPV or IRR methods).

8.6 Discounted payback

Payback can be combined with DCF, and a discounted payback period calculated.

The **discounted payback period** is the time it will take before a project's cumulative NPV turns from being negative to being positive.

For example if we have a cost of capital of 10% and a project with the cash flows shown below, we can calculate a discounted payback period.

Year	Cash flow $	Discount factor 10%	Present value $	Cumulative NPV $
0	(100,000)	1.000	(100,000)	(100,000)
1	30,000	0.909	27,270	(72,730)
2	50,000	0.826	41,300	(31,430)
3	40,000	0.751	30,040	(1,390)
4	30,000	0.683	20,490	19,100
5	20,000	0.621	12,420	31,520
		NPV =	31,520	

The discounted payback period is early in year 4.

A company can set a target discounted payback period, and choose not to undertake any projects with a discounted payback period in excess of a certain number of years, say five years.

CHAPTER ROUNDUP

↳ **Long-term investments** include the purchase of buildings, machinery and equipment. Management will need to have estimates of the initial investment and future costs and revenues of a project in order to make any **long-term decisions.**

↳ **Interest** is the amount of money which an investment earns over time. **Simple interest** is interest which is earned in equal amounts every year assuming no change in the interest rate. If interest earned also earns interest itself in later periods, this is known as **compound interest.**

↳ The basic principle of **discounting** involves calculating the **present value** of an investment (ie the value of an investment **today** at time 0).

↳ The term **present value** means the cash equivalent now of a sum to be received or to be paid in the future.

↳ An **annuity** is a constant sum of money received or paid each year for a given number of years.

↳ A **perpetuity** is an annuity which lasts forever.

↳ To be successful in business, organisations must make profits. Profits are needed in order to pay dividends to shareholders and to allow partners to make drawings.

↳ **Discounted cash flow** involves discounting future cash flows from a project in order to decide whether the project will earn a satisfactory rate of return.

↳ The two main discounted cash flow methods are the **net present value** (NPV) method and the **internal rate of return** (IRR) method.

↳ The **net present value (NPV) method** calculates the present values of all items of income and expenditure related to an investment at a given rate of return, and then calculates a net total. If it is positive, the investment is considered to be acceptable. If it is negative, the investment is considered to be unacceptable.

↳ The **IRR method** determines the rate of interest (internal rate of return) at which the NPV = 0. The internal rate of return is therefore the rate of return on an investment.

↳ The **payback period** is the time that is required for the cash inflows from a capital investment project to equal the cash outflows.

QUICK QUIZ

1   What does the term present value mean?

2   An annuity is a sum of money received every year.

   O   True
   O   False

3   What is a perpetuity?

4   What are the two usual methods of capital expenditure appraisal using discounted cash flow methods?

5   What is the payback period?

6   A company is proposing to launch a new product. Incremental net cash inflows of $36,000 per annum for five years are expected, starting at Time 1.

   An existing machine, with a carrying value of $85,000, would be used to manufacture the new product. The machine could otherwise be sold now, Time 0, for $60,000. The machine, if used for the manufacture of the new product, would be depreciated on a straight line basis over five years, starting at Time 1.

What are the relevant amounts that should be used, at Time 0 and Time 1, in the discounted cash flow appraisal of the project?

	Time 0	Time 1
O	$0	$19,000
O	$0	$24,000
O	($60,000)	$36,000
O	($85,000)	$36,000

7   What is the present value, at a discount rate of 12% of a cash inflow of $80,000?

(a)   At the end of Year 6

(b)   At the beginning of Year 6

8   A project would have a NPV of + $34,400 at a discount rate of 8% and an NPV of – $10,250 at a discount rate of 11%. Using interpolation, what is the approximate IRR?

9   An investment project has net present values as follows:

Discount rate 11% per annum: net present value $35,170 positive

Discount rate 15% per annum: net present value $6,040 positive

What is the best estimate of the internal rate of return?

    O   14.5%

    O   15.8%

    O   19.5%

    O   19.8%

1   The amount of money which must be invested now for n years at an interest rate of r% to give a future sum of money at the time it will be due

2   False

It is a **constant** sum of money **received** or **paid** each year for a **given number** of years.

3   An annuity which lasts forever

4   The net present value (NPV) method

The internal rate of return (IRR) method

5   The payback period is the time that is required for the cash inflows of a capital investment project to equal the cash outflows.

6

Time 0	Time 1
($60,000)	$36,000

7   (a) $\$80,000 \times 1/1.12^6 = \$80,000 \times 0.50663 = \$40,530$.

(b)   The beginning of Year 6 is the end of Year 5.

$\$80,000 \times 1/1.12^5 = \$80,000 \times 0.56743 = \$45,394$.

8   $IRR = a\% + \left[\dfrac{NPV_a}{NPV_a - NPV_b} \times (b-a)\right]\%$

$= 8\% + [34,400/34,400 - - 10,250] \times (11 - 8)\%$
$= 8\% + [34,400/44,650] \times 3\%$
$= 8\% + 2.3\%$
$= 10.3\%$

9   15.8%$IRR = a\% + \left[\dfrac{NPV_a}{NPV_a - NPV_b} \times (b-a)\right]\%$

$= 11\% + \left[\dfrac{35,170}{35,170 - 6,040} \times (15-11)\right]\%$

$= 11\% + 4.8\%$
$= 15.8\%$

Now try ...

Attempt the questions below from the **Practice Question Bank**

Number

Q78

Q79

Q80

Q81

Q82

part

E

Cash management

18

Cash and cash flows

Previous chapters have described how costs and profits are measured, and how estimates of cost are used to provide information for decision making. This is the first of several chapters on **cash management**, which is a completely different aspect of the management of finances.

It explains the nature of **cash inflows and outflows**, and how the cycle of cash inflows and outflows is related to the **working capital cycle** of purchasing, **payments for purchases**, **sales and receipts from sales**.

It also explains the **important differences between net cash flows and profitability**. A business may be profitable, but could fail because of a shortage of cash (or liquidity). This is why cash flows must be managed, as well as profitability.

Study Guide	Intellectual level
E Cash management	
1 Nature of cash and cash flow	
(a) Define cash and cash flow	K
(b) Outline the various sources of cash receipts and payments (including regular/exceptional asset/expenses receipts and payments, and drawings)	K
(c) Describe the relationship between cash flow accounting and accruals accounting	K
(d) Distinguish between the cash flow pattern of different types of organisations	S
(e) Explain the importance of cash flow management and its impact on liquidity and company survival (note: calculation of ratios is not required)	K

1 Introduction

You will have encountered the difference between **cash** and **accruals** accounting in your previous studies for financial accounting, but the distinction is important in this exam as well.

This chapter provides an introduction to cash and credit management. You need to appreciate the links between them, and in particular how the key objectives of **liquidity, profitability** and **security** influence management.

You also need to understand how different types of cash flows have **different patterns**. Some cashflows will be **regular**, but others will be less frequent, or **unpredictable**, and these can have a major influence on an organisation's cash position.

- For management accounting purposes **cash** includes petty cash, bank account balances and marketable securities. It also includes the un-used portion of any overdraft facility.

- **Cash flow** is the movement of funds into and out of a business. It is the cycle of cash inflows and outflows that determine a business's solvency.

2 The cash flow cycle

A **business** which **fails to make profits will go under in the long term**. However, a business which runs out of cash, even for a couple of months, will fail, despite the fact that it is basically profitable.

You will probably already have learned about **cash** and **credit**, for example in earlier studies. For MA2 *Managing Costs and Finance* however, you need to have familiarity with the planning aspects of cash and credit, and how cash and credit are inter-related.

A **business** which **fails to make profits will go under in the long term**. However, a business which runs out of cash, even for a couple of months, will fail, despite the fact that it is basically profitable. Why?

2.1 Example: David Co

David Co, a small business, has won a contract worth $1 million from Goliath, which will be paid in equal annual instalments of $200,000 over five years at the end of each year. David Co has a maximum bank overdraft of $200,000. The work on the contract is completed at the end of year 2: a total of $750,000 was incurred on expenses, $200,000 in year 1 and $550,000 in year 2. The cash position of David Co over these five years as a result of this contract is as follows.

Year	1 $	2 $	3 $	4 $	5 $
Brought forward (surplus/ overdraft)	–	–	(200,000)	(150,000)	50,000
Received from Goliath	200,000	200,000	200,000	200,000	200,000
Payments to suppliers	(200,000)	(400,000)	(150,000)	–	–
Cash surplus/(overdraft)	–	(200,000)	(150,000)	50,000	250,000
Accounts payable outstanding		150,000	–		

We can see that at the end of year 2, David Co is in trouble.

(a) David Co has run up the **maximum overdraft**, but some suppliers have to wait over a year – until the end of year 3 – in order to get paid. Many will be unwilling to wait that long. **Suppliers** will refuse to supply goods until they are paid for previous supplies. This will prevent the business functioning at all. David Co cannot pay its bills on time, and suppliers can start legal proceedings for the business to be wound up.

(b) If the bank overdraft lasts for long enough, the bank may take a similar view, although the overdraft will have been paid off by the end of year 4. **Employees** who are not paid can sue for breach of contract. They might also find alternative employment. The bank may worry about the length of exposure.

Although the contract is profitable, cash outflows and inflows are differently timed. David Co could have avoided this demise if it had planned things differently.

(a) David Co could have negotiated improved payment terms with Goliath. For example, annual instalments of $275,000 at the end of year 1 and year 2, followed by instalments of $150,000 at the end of years 3, 4 and 5. This would have enabled the company to 'match' receipts against payments to suppliers whilst utilising the overdraft facility, to ensure that all suppliers were paid on a timely basis.

Year	1 $	2 $	3 $	4 $	5 $
Brought forward (surplus/ overdraft)	–	75,000	(200,000)	(50,000)	100,000
Received from Goliath	275,000	275,000	150,000	150,000	150,000
Payments to suppliers	(200,000)	(550,000)	–	–	–
Cash surplus/(overdraft)	75,000	(200,000)	(50,000)	100,000	250,000
Accounts payable outstanding	–	–	–	–	–

(b) David Co could also have attempted to negotiate improved credit terms with suppliers based on the agreed timing of receipts from Goliath.

2.2 Working capital

Working capital is the difference between a firm's current assets and current liabilities. These are assets or liabilities which are, or can be turned into, cash.

The management of cash, receivables and payables is essentially a **cycle**, a flow of funds in and out of the business.

BPP
LEARNING
MEDIA

Working capital is the net difference between **current assets** (mainly inventory, receivables and cash) and **current liabilities** (such as payables and a bank overdraft).

(a)   **Current assets** are items which are either cash already, or which will soon lead to the receipt of cash. Inventories will be sold to customers and create receivables; and customers will soon pay in cash for their purchases.

(b)   **Current liabilities** are items which will soon have to be paid for with cash. Payables will have to be paid and bank overdrafts are usually regarded as short-term borrowing which may need to be repaid fairly quickly (or on demand, ie immediately). In statements of financial position, the word 'current' is applied to inventories, receivables, short-term investments and cash (current assets) and amounts due for payment within one year's time (current liabilities).

2.3 The working capital cycle

The **working capital cycle** measures the period of time between cash outflows for materials and cash inflows from customers.

The **working capital cycle** measures the period of time between the time cash is paid out for raw materials and the time cash is received in from customers for goods sold.

(a)   A firm buys raw materials, probably on credit.

(b)   It holds the raw materials for some time in stores before being issued to the production department and turned into an item of finished goods.

(c)   The finished goods might be kept in a warehouse for some time before they are eventually sold to customers.

(d)   By this time, the firm will probably have paid for the raw materials purchased.

(e)   If customers buy the goods on credit, it will be some time before the cash from the sales is eventually received.

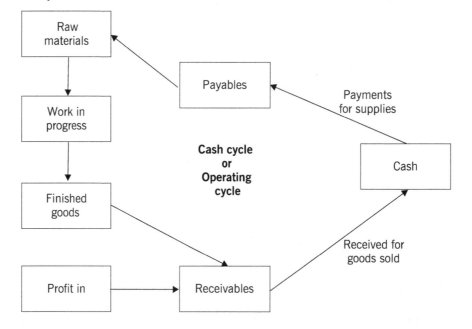

2.3.1 Example: Working capital cycle

Suppose that a firm buys raw materials on 1½ months' credit, holds them in store for 1 month and then issues them to the production department. The production cycle is very short, but finished goods are held for 1 month before they are sold. Customers take two months' credit. The working capital cycle would be:

	Months
Raw material inventory holding period	1.0
Less: payables payment period	(1.5)
Finished goods inventory holding period	1.0
Receivables collection period	2.0
Working capital cycle	$\underline{\underline{2.5}}$

There would be a gap of $2\frac{1}{2}$ months between paying cash for raw materials and receiving cash (including profits) from customers.

Suppose the firm purchases its raw materials on 1 January. The sequence of events would then be:

	Date
Purchase of raw materials	1 Jan
Issue of materials to production (one month after purchase)	1 Feb
Payment made to suppliers (1½ months after purchase)	15 Feb
Sale of finished goods (one month after production begins)	1 Mar
Receipt of cash from customers (two months after sale)	1 May

The working capital cycle is the period of 2½ months from 15 February, when payment is made to suppliers, until 1 May, when cash is received from customers.

2.4 Different types of business

Different types of business have their own working capital cycle characteristics.

In a **retailing business**, most sales are for cash or by credit card and debit card, and the company therefore receives most of its cash income at the time of sale. Large supermarket chains which sell goods within a few days of purchase might not pay their suppliers until after the goods have been sold and the cash received.

In a **manufacturing business**, many sales will be on credit, as will many purchases. The working capital cycle will therefore be more conventional, with payments preceding receipts.

EXAM FOCUS POINT

In later chapters we shall also discuss ways in which businesses can reduce various components of the working capital cycle – something that is frequently tested in exams.

3 Types of cash transaction

Cash transactions can be **asset** or **expense**, **exceptional** or **unexceptional** and **regular** or **irregular**.

Previously, we concentrated on **working capital**, in other words cash or near-cash aspects of a business's trading operations. There are many types of cash transaction. They differ in their purpose, form and frequency.

(a) **Asset and expense items**

    (i) Asset items generally relate to the long-term functioning of the business, such as acquiring non-current assets.

    (ii) Expense items generally relate to day-to-day operations, as in the operating cycle, including other matters such as overdraft interest.

BPP
LEARNING
MEDIA

(b) **Exceptional and unexceptional items**

    (i)   Exceptional items are unusual. For example the costs of closing down part of a business.

    (ii)   Unexceptional items include everything else. You have to be careful using this distinction, as the phrase 'exceptional item' has a precise meaning in the preparation of a company's financial statements.

(c) **Regular and irregular items**

    (i)   Regular items occur at predictable intervals. Such intervals might be frequent such as the payment of wages every week or month, or relatively infrequent, such as the payment of dividends twice a year.

    (ii)   Irregular items do not occur at regular intervals eg purchase of new machinery, disaster recovery expenses.

3.1 Cash outflows

Cash outflows can occur for a number of reasons. Here are some examples.

(a)   Payments to:

    (i)   **Suppliers** for goods purchased
    (ii)   **Employees** for wages and bonuses

    These are expense items.

(b)   Payments to government for taxes owing. The payment of corporation tax may be an **annual disbursement**.

(c)   Payments to suppliers of finance:

    (i)   **Dividends** to shareholders
    (ii)   **Interest** to debentureholders, bondholders, banks
    (iii)   **Drawings** by sole traders or partners

    The regularity of these payments will vary. Dividends are normally paid twice a year.

(d)   Payments to cover the purchase cost of non-current assets, such as buildings and equipment. These are **asset payments** in that they are purchased for long-term use in the business. They may be irregular.

(e)   Payments to acquire investments:

    (i)   **New businesses** or **takeovers of companies** (capital)
    (ii)   **Short-term financial instruments** to use surplus cash to turn a quick profit

(f)   Purchases of foreign currency for trading overseas.

3.2 Cash inflows

Cash inflows also come in many kinds.

(a)   Cash received for sales:

    (i)   Immediately from cash customers
    (ii)   From customers for sales made **on credit**

    These are expenses receipts.

(b)   Long-term grants from government institutions. The use of such 'exceptional' receipts will depend on the terms of the grant.

(c)   Cash received from providers of finance:

(i)   **Equity share capital** invested in the business
(ii)   **Long-term loans** provided by banks and other financial institutions

These are **asset receipts**, as they are for long-term investment in the business. Only rarely do companies raise share capital.

(d)   Cash received from:

(i)   **Sale of non-current assets** after their useful life
(ii)   The **liquidation** (ie conversion into cash) of **short-term investments**

4   Profits and cash flow

Accounts showing **trading profits** are not the same as statements of cash flow.

A company can make losses but still have a net cash income from trading. A company can also make profits but have a net cash deficit on its trading operations.

4.1 Differences between trading profits and cash flows

We considered some of the differences between **trading profits** and **cash flows** earlier in your studies. The main differences are summarised below.

(a)   Cash may be obtained from a transaction which has **nothing to do** with **profit or loss**. For example, an issue of shares or loan stock for cash has no effect on profit but is obviously a source of cash. Similarly, an increase in bank overdraft provides a source of cash for payments, but it is not reported in the statement of profit or loss (income statement).

(b)   Cash may be paid for the **purchase of non-current assets.** The charge in the statement of profit or loss is depreciation, which is only a part of an asset's cost, and which is **not** included in the cash statement as it is not a movement of cash.

(c)   When a **non-current asset is sold** there is a profit or loss on sale equal to the difference between the sale proceeds and the 'carrying value' of the asset in the statement of financial position at the time it is sold.

(d)   **Profit** is sales minus the cost of sales. **Operational cash flow** is the difference between **cash received** and **cash paid** from trading. Cash received differs from sales because of changes in the amount of receivables. Cash paid differs from the cost of sales because of changes in the amount of inventory and payables. Operational cash flow therefore differs from profit.

The statement of profit or loss reports the total value of sales in a year. If goods are sold on credit, the cash receipts will differ from the value of sales as customers will pay after the year end.

	$
Customers owing money at the start of the year	X
Sales during the year	X
Total money due from customers	X
Less customers owing money at the end of the year	(X)
Cash receipts from customers during the year	X

Similarly, the statement of profit or loss reports the cost of goods sold during the year, but some goods are purchased on credit, and some remain in store over the year end.

The relationship between the cost of materials in the materials cost of sales and cash payments for materials purchased is as follows:

	$
Cost of sales	X
Closing inventory at the end of the year	X
	X
Opening inventory at the start of the year	(X)
Purchases during the year	Y
Payments still owing to suppliers at the start of the year	X
Purchases during the year	Y
	X
	$
Less payments still owing to suppliers at the end of the year	(X)
Equals cash payments to suppliers during the year	X

You therefore need to watch out carefully for timing differences between sales being made and cash being received, and purchases/expenditure and cash payments.

Suppose that a company buys and re-sells products. Gross profit from trading and operational cash flows from trading can be compared as follows.

Profit
Sales – Cost of sales = Profit

Operational cash flow
Cash in – Cash out = Operational cash flow

Notes
Cash in = Sales + Opening receivables – Closing receivables
Purchases = Cost of sales + Closing inventory – Opening inventory
Cash out = Purchases + Opening payables – Closing payables

QUESTION   Operational cash flow

Assume that Beta achieved sales turnover in a particular year of $200,000 and the cost of sales was $170,000. Inventories were $12,000, payables $11,000 and receivables $15,000 at the start of the year. At the end of the year, inventories were $21,000, payables were $14,000 and receivables $24,000. Find out the profits and the operational cash flow resulting from the year's trading.

ANSWER

	Profits $	Operational cash flow $
Sales	200,000	200,000
Opening receivables (∴ received in year)		15,000
Closing receivables (outstanding at year end)		(24,000)
Cash in		191,000
Cost of sales	170,000	170,000
Closing inventory (bought, but not yet used, in year)		21,000
Opening inventory (used, but not bought, in year)		(12,000)
Purchases in year		179,000
Opening payables (∴ paid in year)		11,000
Closing payables (outstanding at year end)		(14,000)
Cash out		176,000
Profit/operational cash flow	30,000	15,000

Reconciliation

	$	$
Profit		30,000
Less increase in receivables	(9,000)	
Less increase in inventory	(9,000)	
Plus increase in payables	3,000	(15,000)
Operational cash inflow		15,000

EXAM FOCUS POINT

Don't try to memorise whether you need to add or subtract receivables, payables or inventories as this will lead to mistakes in the exam. Rather, try to understand the purpose of what you are doing and it will come naturally to you in the exam.

4.2 Negative cash flows

A company that trades profitably should earn **cash surpluses**, at least in the longer term. However, a profitable company can also suffer from negative cash flows.

(a) It might spend cash on **non-current asset purchases** and **extra working capital investments**.

(b) It might use cash to pay for **business acquisitions**.

(c) High inflation rates might force a company to **increase its funding** of business assets in money terms, even when there is no real growth in the business.

(d) **Dividends** might **exceed cash surpluses** for the year. In recession, for example, profits fall but there will be pressure from shareholders to maintain or increase the dividend. Furthermore, the terms of funding arrangements such as business loans may require the company to pay out large sums in interest.

(e) **Debt repayments** may mean that a profitable company has a negative cash flow.

The difference between profit and cash flow has important implications.

(a) If a company is profitable but short of cash, one reason could be an increase in the other elements of working capital. If a company were to seek credit from a bank to finance the growth in working capital, the bank might ask the management whether **operational cash flows could be improved** by squeezing working capital, and:

(i) Reducing receivables;
(ii) Reducing inventories; or
(iii) Taking more credit from suppliers.

Better control over working capital could remove the need to borrow.

(b) If a company is making losses, it could try to maintain a positive operational cash flow by taking **more credit** (ie by increasing its payables and so reducing working capital).

4.2.1 Negative operational cash flows: implications

Negative cash flows from operations would normally be an indicator of **financial distress**, unless the company is in a period of rapid (and profitable) growth and is having to invest heavily in additional working capital (inventories and receivables). If a company has negative cash flows from operations for at least two of the previous three years, it will probably be safe to conclude that its financial position is deteriorating significantly.

5 Cash accounting and accruals accounting

> **Cash budgets** are not prepared according to the accruals concept, which tries to ensure income and expenditure are matched. Instead they are prepared on a cash (receipts and payments) basis.

The distinction between profits and cash flow has been a theme of this chapter so far, but it is best to state it boldly. You must understand the principle, which is applied in nearly all businesses' accounts, that **accounts** are not prepared on a **cash basis** but on an **accruals (or earnings) basis**. That is, a sale or purchase is dealt with in the year in which it is made, even if cash changes hands in a later year. Revenue must be matched against the costs incurred in earning it.

Most businesses, even if they do not sell on credit, make purchases on credit. If cash accounting is used, then accounts do not present a true picture of the business's activities in any given period.

5.1 Example: Accruals concept

Brenda has a business importing and selling model Corgi dogs. In May 20X7 she makes the following purchases and sales.

Invoice date	Numbers bought/sold	Amount	Date paid
Purchases		$	
7.5.X7	20	100	1.6.X7
Sales			
8.5.X7	4	40	1.6.X7
12.5.X7	6	60	1.6.X7
23.5.X7	10	100	1.7.X7

What is Brenda's profit for May?

Solution

	$
Cash basis	
Revenue	0
Purchases	0
Profit/Loss	0
Accruals basis	
Sales ($40 + $60 + $100)	200
Purchases	(100)
Profit	100

Obviously, the accruals basis gives a 'truer' picture than the cash basis. Brenda has no cash to show for her efforts until June but her customers are legally bound to pay her and she is legally bound to pay for her purchases.

The accruals concept states that, in **computing profit**, revenue earned must be matched against the expenditure incurred in earning it. This is illustrated in the example of Brenda; profit of $100 was computed by matching the revenue ($200) earned from the sale of 20 Corgis against the cost ($100) of acquiring them.

If, however, Brenda had only sold 18 Corgis, it would have been incorrect to charge her statement of profit or loss with the cost of 20 Corgis, as she still has 2 Corgis in stock. If she intends to sell them in June she is likely to make a profit on the sale. Therefore, only the purchase cost of 18 Corgis ($90) should be matched with her sales revenue, leaving her with a profit of $90.

Her statement of financial position would therefore look like this.

	$
Current assets	
Inventory (at cost, ie 2 × $5)	10
Receivables (18 × $10)	180
	190
Equity	
Retained earnings	90
Current liabilities	
Payables	100
	190

In this example, the concepts of **going concern** and accruals are linked. Because the business is assumed to be a going concern it is possible to carry forward the cost of the unsold Corgis as a charge against profits of the next period.

If Brenda decided to give up selling Corgis, then the going concern concept would no longer apply and the value of the two Corgis in the statement of financial position would be a break-up valuation rather than cost. Similarly, if the two unsold Corgis were now unlikely to be sold at more than their cost of $5 each (say, because of damage or a fall in demand) then they should be recorded on the statement of financial position at their net realisable value (ie the likely eventual sales price less any expenses to be incurred to make them saleable, eg paint) rather than cost.

5.1.1 The accruals concept defined

Accruals basis of accounting. The effects of transactions are recognised when they occur (rather than when cash is received or paid) and they are recorded in the periods to which they relate.

Company legislation gives legal recognition to the accruals concept. This has the effect of requiring businesses to take account of sales and purchases when made, rather than when paid for, and also to carry unsold stock forward in the statement of financial position rather than to deduct its cost from profit for the period.

5.1.2 Relevance of accruals basis of accounting

The accruals basis of accounting is a way of letting investors know how much profit a business has made by matching income and expenditure. It has **no relevance whatsoever** to day to day cash management.

5.2 The importance of cash flow information

Survival in business depends on the ability to generate cash. Cash flow information directs attention towards this critical issue.

Advantages of cash flow accounting being employed in financial reporting are as follows:

(a) Potential lenders will be more interested in an entity's ability to **repay** them than in its profitability.

(b) Cash flow reporting satisfies the needs of other financial report users better:

   (i) For management, it provides the sort of information on which **decisions** should be taken: (in management accounting, 'relevant costs' to a decision are future cash flows); traditional profit accounting does not help with decision making.

   (ii) For shareholders and auditors, cash flow accounting can provide a satisfactory basis for **stewardship accounting**.

(c) Cash flow forecasts are easier to prepare, as well as more useful, than profit forecasts.

6 | Cash flow management and liquidity management

Cash flow management involves ensuring that the organisation has sufficient cash to meet its obligations to settle liabilities when payment becomes due. It involves careful management of working capital.

Organisations should be able to settle their liabilities when these become due for payment. Failure to pay suppliers on time could lead to their refusal to grant credit terms in the future. Banks expect to receive interest and capital repayments on time from their borrowers, and may take action against borrowers who are in default.

Cash flow management involves monitoring cash flows (inflows and outflows) to ensure that there will be sufficient cash to meet payment obligations when they fall due, or to take measures in advance to obtain the cash that will be needed (for example by negotiating a bank overdraft facility). This aspect of cash flow management is also known as liquidity management.

Cash flow problems can occur when an organisation has excessive amounts of working capital, in particular excessive inventories and trade receivables.

(a)   Inventories have to be paid for, and the larger the amount of inventories, the more cash is tied up. An increase in inventory will reduce cash flows.

(b)   Trade receivables are amounts of money owed to the organisation. Cash inflows are delayed by giving credit to customers and giving them time to pay.

(c)   Payments to suppliers take cash out of the business. Paying suppliers earlier than necessary, or failing to negotiate favourable credit terms from suppliers, means that cash payments occur sooner than they need to. This affects cash flows and liquidity.

An organisation should monitor its working capital cycle – its investment in inventory and trade receivables, and the credit that it takes from suppliers – to ensure that cash flows into the business reasonably quickly and that:

- The time between acquiring materials or incurring payments to make finished goods (less the credit period taken from suppliers); and

- The time that cash is eventually received from customers after the goods have been sold is kept to a reasonable level and is not excessively long.

Customers should not be allowed to take more credit than agreed in their credit terms. If they are late making payments, measures should be taken to chase payments – by sending written or telephone reminders, and so on. An organisation should monitor its trade receivables closely, to identify late payers and take action. Inventory should not be allowed to become more than is necessary for efficient operations.

CHAPTER ROUNDUP

⤷ You will have encountered the difference between **cash** and **accruals** accounting in your previous studies for financial accounting, but the distinction is important in this exam as well.

⤷ A **business** which **fails to make profits will go under in the long term**. However, a business which runs out of cash, even for a couple of months, will fail, despite the fact that it is basically profitable.

⤷ **Working capital** is the difference between a firm's current assets and current liabilities. These are assets or liabilities which are, or can be turned into, cash.

⤷ The **working capital cycle** measures the period of time between cash outflows for materials and cash inflows from customers.

⤷ **Cash transactions** can be **asset** or **expense**, **exceptional** or **unexceptional** and **regular** or **irregular**.

⤷ Accounts showing **trading profits** are not the same as statements of cash flow.

⤷ **Cash budgets** are not prepared according to the accruals concept, which tries to ensure income and expenditure are matched. Instead they are prepared on a cash (receipts and payments) basis.

⤷ **Cash flow management** involves ensuring that the organisation has sufficient cash to meet its obligations to settle liabilities when payment becomes due. It involves careful management of working capital.

QUICK QUIZ

1 Which of the following is not an element of working capital?

    O   Inventories
    O   Cash
    O   Trade payables
    O   Non-current assets

2 What period of time is measured by the working capital cycle?

3 The difference between asset and expense flows is that asset flows relate to the long-term functioning of the business; expense flows relate to day-to-day operations.

    O True
    O False

4 Why are profits and cash flows different?

5 Name the three main focuses of cash and credit management.

6 The .... is the matching of revenues and costs to the period to which they relate.

7 Payments to suppliers of finance include:

    1   Dividends
    2   Interest
    3   Repayments of trade credit
    4   Drawings

    O   1 and 3 only
    O   2 and 3 only
    O   1, 2 and 4 only
    O   2, 3 and 4 only

ANSWERS TO QUICK QUIZ

1   Non-current assets. Working capital is current assets less current liabilities.

2   The time between payment of cash for raw materials and receipt of cash from customers

3   True. Asset relates to the long term, expense the short term.

4   Profits are calculated using various non-cash items, whereas cash flows include receipts and payments and relate to activities that happened in other periods.

5   Profitability, liquidity and security/safety

6   The **accruals concept** is the matching of revenues and costs to the period to which they relate.

7   1, 2 and 4 only. Dividends, interest and drawings are examples of payments to suppliers of finance. Payments to trade suppliers are not.

Now try ...

Attempt the questions below from the **Practice Question Bank**

Number

Q83

Q84

Q85

Q86

19

This fairly short chapter continues with the explanation of **cash management within a business or public sector organisation**. It outlines the functions of a **treasury department** and describes techniques of **cash handling**.

There is also some assessment of how cash management, and in particular cash balances and borrowing, may be affected by changes in the **economic or financial environment**.

Cash and treasury management

TOPIC LIST	
1 Treasury management	E2 (a)
2 Cash handling procedures	E2 (b)
3 The economic and financial environment	E2 (d)

Study Guide	Intellectual level
E Cash management	
2 Cash management	
(a) Outline the basic treasury functions	K
(b) Describe cash handling procedures	K
(d) Describe how trends in the economic and financial environment can affect management of cash balances	K

1 Treasury management

Treasury management in a modern enterprise covers various areas, and in a large business may be a **centralised** function.

Large companies rely heavily on the financial and currency markets. These markets are volatile, with interest rates and foreign exchange rates changing continually and by significant amounts. To manage cash (funds) and currency efficiently, many large companies have set up a separate treasury department.

1.1 The role of the treasurer

The Association of Corporate Treasurers has listed the experience it will require from its student members before they are eligible for full membership of the Association (ACT, 2016). This list of required experience gives a good indication of the core roles of treasurership.

(a) **Corporate financial objectives**

    (i)   Financial aims and strategies
    (ii)   Financial and treasury policies
    (iii) Financial and treasury systems

(b) **Liquidity management**

    (i)   Working capital and money transmission management
    (ii)   Banking relationships and arrangements
    (iii) Money management

Cash management and liquidity management involve making sure that the organisation has the **liquid funds** it **needs** and invests any surplus funds, even for very short terms. In cash-rich companies, the treasurer will be heavily involved in the investment of surplus funds to earn a good yield until they are required again for another purpose. A good relationship with one or more banks is desirable.

(c) **Funding management**

    (i)   Funding policies and procedures
    (ii)   Sources of funds
    (iii) Types of funds

The treasurer needs to know where funds are obtainable; for how long; at what interest rate; whether security would be required or not and whether interest rates would be fixed or variable.

(d) **Currency management**

    (i)   Exposure policies and procedures

    (ii)   Exchange dealing, including futures and options

    (iii)   International monetary economics and exchange regulations

A company (such as a multinational) which is involved in international transactions faces the possibility of exposure to foreign exchange risk: the values of assets and liabilities denominated in one currency will change with fluctuations in the exchange rate against another.

(e) **Corporate finance**

Corporate finance is concerned with matters such as:

    (i)   Raising share capital

    (ii)   Its form (ordinary or preference, or different classes of ordinary shares)

    (iii)   Obtaining a stock exchange listing, dividend policy

    (iv)   Financial information for management

    (v)   Mergers

    (vi)   Acquisitions

    (vii) Business sales

(f) **Related subjects**

    (i)   Corporate taxation (domestic and foreign tax)

    (ii)   Risk management (swaps, options) and insurance

    (iii)   Pension fund investment management

2 Cash handling procedures

Cash handling procedures should prevent fraud or theft.

2.1 Objectives

The most important objectives of cash handling procedures relating to cash receipts and payments are:

- All **monies received** are **recorded**
- All **monies received** are **banked**
- **Cash** and **cheques** are **safeguarded** against loss or theft
- All **payments** are **authorised, made** to the **correct recipients** and **recorded**
- **Payments** are **not made twice** for the same liability

Segregation of duties is particularly important here. The person responsible for receiving and recording cash when it arrives in the post should not be the same as the person responsible for banking it. Ideally the cash book should be written up by a further staff member, and a fourth staff member should reconcile the various records of amounts received.

Records of cash are obviously also at the heart of a company's accounting records; therefore if these accounting records are to fulfil legal requirements, cash must be recorded **promptly**.

2.2 Key procedures

Cash handling procedures relating to **receipts** include:

- Proper **post-opening** arrangements
- **Prompt recording**
- **Prompt banking**
- **Reconciliation** of records of cash received and banked

The following detailed matters should be considered.

BPP LEARNING MEDIA

2.2.1 Cash at bank and in hand – receipts

Segregation of duties between the various functions listed below is particularly important.

Recording of receipts by post

- **Safeguards** to **prevent interception of mail** between receipt and opening
- Appointment of **responsible person** to supervise mail
- **Protection** of **cash and cheques** (restrictive crossing)
- **Amounts received listed** when post opened
- **Post stamped** with date of receipt

Recording of cash sales and collections

- **Restrictions** on **receipt of cash** (by cashiers only, or by salesmen etc)
- **Evidencing** of receipt of cash
    - Serially numbered receipt forms
    - Cash registers incorporating sealed till rolls
- **Clearance** of cash offices and registers
- **Agreement** of **cash collections** with **till rolls**
- **Agreement** of **cash collections** with **bankings** and cash and sales records
- **Investigation** of cash shortages and surpluses

General controls over recording

- **Prompt maintenance** of records (cash books, ledger accounts)
- **Limitation** of **duties** of receiving cashiers
- **Holiday arrangements**
- **Giving** and **recording** of **receipts**
    - Retained copies
    - Serially numbered receipts books
    - Custody of receipt books
    - Comparisons with cash book records and bank paying in slips

Banking

- **Daily bankings**
- Make-up and comparison of paying-in slips against initial receipt records and cash book
- Banking of receipts intact/control of disbursements

Safeguarding of cash and bank accounts

- **Restrictions** on **opening new bank accounts**
- **Limitations** on **cash floats** held
- **Restrictions** on **payments** out of **cash received**
- **Restrictions** on **access** to cash registers and offices
- **Independent checks** on cash floats
- **Surprise cash counts**
- **Custody** of **cash outside office hours**
- **Custody** over **supply** and issue of cheques
- **Preparation** of **cheques** restricted (person responsible should be separate from purchase ledger)

Safeguarding of cash and bank accounts

- **Safeguards** over **mechanically signed cheques**/cheques carrying printed signatures
- **Restrictions** on issue of **blank** or **bearer** cheques
- **Safeguarding** of **IOUs**, cash in transit
- **Insurance arrangements**
- **Bank reconciliations**
  - Issue of bank statements
  - Frequency of reconciliations by independent person
  - Reconciliation procedures
  - Treatment of longstanding unpresented cheques
  - Stop payment notice on unpresented cheques
  - Sequence of cheque numbers is confirmed as complete
  - Comparison of reconciliation with cash books

2.2.2 Cash at bank and in hand – payments

Cash handling procedures over **payments** include:

- **Restriction of access** to cash and cheques
- Procedures for preparation and authorisation of payments

The arrangements for controlling payments will depend to a great extent on the nature of business transacted, the volume of payments involved and the size of the company.

The cashier should generally not be concerned with keeping or writing-up books of account other than those recording disbursements nor should he have access to, or be responsible for the custody of, securities, title deeds or negotiable instruments belonging to the company.

The person responsible for preparing cheques or traders' credit lists should not himself be a cheque signatory. Cheque signatories in turn should not be responsible for recording payments.

Cheque payments

- **Cheque requisitions**

  - Appropriate supporting documentation
  - Approval by appropriate staff
  - Presentation to cheque signatories
  - Cancellation (crossing/recording cheque number)

- **Authority** to sign cheques

  - Signatories should not also approve cheque requisitions
  - Limitations on authority to specific amounts
  - Number of signatories (all cheques/larger cheques require more than one signature)
  - Prohibitions over signing of blank cheques

- **Prompt despatch** of signed **cheques**

- **Obtaining** of paid **cheques** from **banks**

- Payments **recorded promptly** in **cash book** and **ledger**

Cash payments

- **Authorisation** of **expenditure**
- **Cancellation** of **vouchers** to ensure cannot be paid
- **Limits** on **disbursements**
- **Rules** on **cash advances** to employees, IOUs and cheque cashing

Also, remember that **segregation of duties** is a very important objective throughout the cash system.

BPP
LEARNING
MEDIA

3 The economic and financial environment

┌───┐
│ Trends in the economic and financial environment can affect management of cash balances. │
└───┘

(a) The economic environment refers to economic conditions, and in particular the **rate of growth** or decline in a national economy or the global economy. Economies go through periods of high growth, lower growth and sometimes negative growth (recession).

(b) Major factors in the financial environment are the level of **interest rates** and the relative ease or difficulty in **borrowing** or **raising capital**.

When the growth rate in the economy is slowing down, or when the economy is entering a period of recession, profitability will fall for many businesses, and some may start to incur losses. When economic conditions are unfavourable, interest rates will often fall and be relatively low. Businesses may therefore:

- Try to preserve their cash, and build up cash balances, in the expectation that the money will soon be needed

- Be reluctant to borrow

A different attitude to cash balances may be prevalent when the economy is in a period of high growth. Business managers may be very confident about the future prospects for their business, and they may be much more **willing to invest and take risks**. In doing this, they may be prepared to operate with relatively low cash balances and to borrow from their bank in order to invest for growth.

In a period of growth, some successful businesses should generate **large net cash inflows**, and build up their cash balances. Interest rates tend to increase when the economy is expanding rapidly, and if a large cash balance builds up, a company may be willing to invest it short term, perhaps anticipating an opportunity to use their cash to make an acquisition.

CHAPTER ROUNDUP

↳ **Treasury management** in a modern enterprise covers various areas, and in a large business may be a **centralised** function.

↳ Cash handling procedures should prevent fraud or theft.

↳ Cash handling procedures relating to **receipts** include:

– Proper **post-opening** arrangements
– **Prompt recording**
– **Prompt banking**
– **Reconciliation** of records of cash received and banked

↳ Cash handling procedures over **payments** include:

– **Restriction of access** to cash and cheques
– Procedures for preparation and authorisation of payments

↳ Trends in the economic and financial environment can affect management of cash balances.

QUICK QUIZ

1   Under what headings do the functions of a treasurer fall?

2   Which of the following are functions carried out by a treasury department?

1   Negotiating arrangements with bankers
2   Dealing in foreign exchange
3   Preparing the corporate budget and business plan
4   Involvement in business acquisitions and sales

O   1 and 2 only
O   3 and 4 only
O   1, 2 and 4 only
O   All of the above

3   List three key cash handling procedures.

1   The main categories are: corporate financial objectives; liquidity management; funding management; currency management; corporate finance.

2   1, 2 and 4 only. While the treasury department will be involved in the preparation of the cash budget, it is unlikely to have a major role in the wider budgeting and planning process.

3   Key cash handling procedures include:

- Segregation of duties
- Physical security
- Accountability
- Bank reconciliations

Now try ...

Attempt the questions below from the **Practice Question Bank**

Number

Q87

Q88

Q89

Q90

Q91

CHAPTER

20

An important part of cash management is **cash forecasting** or **cash budgeting**, to establish whether the organisation will have the cash that it needs to carry on in business.

Cash forecasts may be used to identify any **shortage or surplus of cash that will occur in the future**, so that measures can be taken to obtain cash from other sources to cover any expected shortage (or to cut back on spending or defer planned major expenditures), or to **invest cash** for the period of time that a surplus is expected to continue.

This chapter describes how cash budgets are prepared and used for planning and control purposes, and how statistical techniques such as indexing for inflation may be used to prepare cash forecasts.

Forecasting cash flows

Study Guide

Intellectual level

E   Cash management

3   Cash budgets

(a)   Explain the objectives of cash budgeting   K

(b)   Explain and illustrate statistical techniques used in cash   S
        forecasting including moving averages and allowance for
        inflation

(c)   Prepare a cash budget/forecast   S

(d)   Explain and illustrate how a cash budget can be used as a   S
        mechanism for monitoring and control

 Performance objective 14 requires you to 'manage and control cash receipts, payments and balances'. You can apply the knowledge you obtain from this chapter of the Text to help to demonstrate this competence.

1   Introduction

 The main purpose of preparing cash budgets is to forecast whether there are likely to be **cash shortages** or **large surpluses**.

Don't however spend all your time on the mechanics of budget preparation. The main purpose of preparing budgets is to measure whether there are likely to be **cash shortages** (or large surpluses). When looking at a cash flow forecast, you need to recognise if the business is likely to have problems, and recommend what can be done to rectify them.

EXAM FOCUS POINT

Preparing cash budgets is a vital skill for the exam. Practise as often as you can.

2   The purpose of cash budgets and forecasts

 Cash flow forecasts provide an early warning of liquidity problems and funding needs.

Cash forecasting is vital to ensure that sufficient funds will be available when they are needed to sustain the activities of an enterprise, at an acceptable cost.

Forecasts provide an early warning of liquidity problems, by estimating:

- How much cash is required
- When it is required
- How long it is required for
- Whether it will be available from anticipated sources

A company must know **when** it might need to borrow and for how long, not just **what amount** of funding could be required.

 BPP LEARNING MEDIA

Banks have increasingly insisted that customers provide cash forecasts (or a business plan that includes a cash forecast) as a precondition of lending. A newly established company wishing to open a bank account will also normally be asked to supply a **business plan**. The cash and sales forecasts will also allow the bank to **monitor** the **progress** of the new company, and **control** its **lending** more effectively.

2.1 Deficiencies

Any forecast **deficiency** of cash will have to be funded.

(a)   **Borrowing**. If borrowing arrangements are not already secured, a source of funds will have to be found. If a company cannot fund its cash deficits it could be wound up.

(b)   The firm can make arrangements to **sell any short-term financial investments** to raise cash.

(c)   The firm can delay payments to suppliers, or pull in payments from customers. This is sometimes known as **leading and lagging**.

Because cash forecasts cannot be entirely accurate, companies should have **contingency funding**, available from a surplus cash balance and liquid investments, or from a bank facility. The approximate size of contingency margin will vary from company to company, according to the cyclical nature of the business and the approach of its cash planners.

Forecasting gives management time to **arrange** its **funding**. If planned in advance, instead of a panic measure to avert a cash crisis, a company can more easily choose when to borrow, and will probably obtain a lower interest rate.

2.2 Forecasting cash surpluses

Many **cash-generative** businesses are less reliant on high quality cash forecasts. If a cash surplus is forecast, having an idea of both its size and how long it will exist could help decide how best to invest it.

In some cases, the amount of **interest** earned from surplus cash could be significant for the company's earnings. The company might then need a forecast of its interest earnings in order to indicate its prospective earnings per share to stock market analysts and institutional investors.

QUESTION   Changes affecting cash flow

Give examples of unforeseen changes which may affect cash flow patterns.

ANSWER

Your list might have included some of the following:

(a)   A **change** in the general **economic environment** – an economic recession will cause a slump in trade

(b)   A **new product**, launched by a competitor, which takes business away from a company's traditional and established product lines

(c)   **New cost-saving product technology**, which forces the company to invest in the new technology to remain competitive

(d)   **Moves by competitors** which have to be countered (for example a price reduction or a sales promotion)

(e)   **Changes in consumer preferences**, resulting in a fall in demand

(f)   **Government action** against certain trade practices or against trade with a country that a company has dealings with

(g)   **Strikes** or other industrial action

(h)   **Natural disasters**, such as floods or fire damage, which curtail an organisation's activities

2.3 Receipts and payments forecasts

Cash budgets and **forecasts** can be used for **control reporting**. A forecast can be prepared of cash receipts and payments, and net cash flows. This is known as a **cash flow based forecast**.

A **cash budget** is a detailed forecast of cash receipts, payments and balances over a planning period. It is formally adopted as part of the business plan or master budget for the period.

Cash flow based forecasts (**receipts** and **payments**) are forecasts of the **amount** and timing of cash receipts and payments, net cash flows and changes in cash balances, for each time period covered by the forecast. Cash flow based forecasts include cash budgets up to a year or so ahead and short-term forecasts of just a few days.

A cash budget (or cash flow budget) is a detailed forecast of expected cash receipts, payments and balances over a budget period.

The cash budget is formally adopted as a **planning target** for the budget period. It is part of the annual master budget. It is usually prepared by taking a profits budget for the period and adjusting the figures for sales, and costs of sales, into cash flows (receipts and payments).

In companies that use cash flow reporting for **control purposes**, there will probably be:

- A cash budget divided into monthly or quarterly periods
- A statement comparing actual cash flows against the monthly or quarterly budget
- A revised cash forecast
- A statement comparing actual cash flows against a revised forecast

2.3.1 Revised and rolling forecasts

Revised forecasts should be prepared to keep forecasts relevant and up-to-date. Examples would be a revised three-month forecast every month for the next three-month period, or a revised forecast each month or each quarter up to the end of the annual budget period.

A **rolling forecast** is a forecast that is **continually updated**. A rolling forecast can be a 12-month forecast which is updated at the end of every month, with a further month added to the end of the forecast period and with figures for the intervening 11 months revised if necessary.

Cash flow control with budgets and revised forecasts

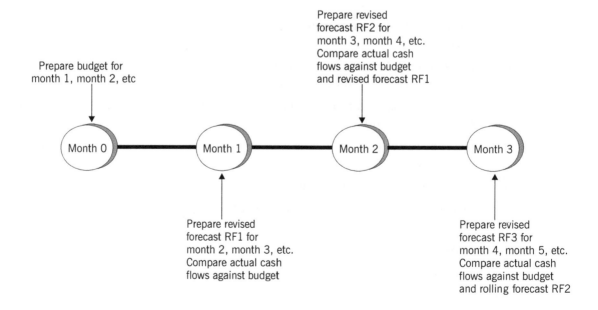

2.4 Guidelines on preparing a forecast

The cash flow forecast should be broken down into the shortest time periods for which reasonably accurate information can be assembled.

(a) For short-term cash forecasts of up to one month or so, **weekly periods** are appropriate. In the very short term, up to one week or so, **daily cash forecasts** may be requested.

(b) For longer-term cash forecasts, periods of a month, a quarter or longer will be suitable. The more distant the time horizon becomes, the longer the forecasted periods should be.

Even fairly predictable items of income and spending (eg salary payments, and tax/national insurance deductions) cannot usually be forecast with **total** accuracy. Any forecast should therefore include a clear statement of the **assumptions** on which the figures are based. With clearly-stated assumptions, a forecast can be tested for **reasonableness**.

3 Cash budgets in receipts and payments format

Cash budgets are prepared by taking **operational budgets** and converting them into forecasts as to when receipts and payments occur. The forecast should indicate the highest and lowest cash balance in a period as well as the balance at the end.

A **cash budget** (or **cash flow budget**) is prepared from budgets and capital funding and spending programmes. A budget normally covers one year, and is divided into shorter time periods of a month or a quarter.

A cash budget is prepared by taking the budgets for sales, costs of sales and profit, and converting the income and expenditure items in these budgets into cash flows by allowing for credit periods, prepayments, accruals and so on. Adjustments are then made for:

- Cash flow items not appearing in the statement of profit or loss (income statement); or
- Items in the statement of profit or loss which do not have a cash effect.

Broad guidelines to the preparation of a cash budget is shown below.

Step 1	Sort out cash receipts from customers.
	• Establish budgeted sales month by month.
	• Establish the credit period(s) taken by customers.
	• From these, calculate when the budgeted sales revenue will be received as cash.
	• Deduct any discount allowed for early payment.
	• Deduct any allowance for bad debts.
	• Establish when the outstanding receivables at the start of the budget period will be collected.
Step 2	Establish whether any other cash income will be received, and when. Put these sundry items of cash receipts into the budget.
Step 3	Review existing funding arrangements such as bank overdrafts and loans. Ensure that the repayment of debt is included in the budget.

Step 4   Sort out cash payments to suppliers.

- Establish purchase quantities each month.
- Establish the credit period(s) taken from suppliers.
- From these, calculate when the cash payments to suppliers will be made.
- Establish when the outstanding payables at the start of the budget period will be paid.

Step 5   Establish other cash payments in the month.

These will include:

- Payments of wages and salaries
- Payments for sundry expenses
- Other one-off expenditures, such as non-current asset purchases, tax payments
- Dividend or interest payments

Items of cost not involving cash payments (eg depreciation) must be excluded. Payments should be scheduled into the month when they will actually occur. For example, rental costs of $120,000 per annum might be charged to the statement of profit or loss at $10,000 per month. The cash budget should identify in which month or months the $120,000 will actually be paid. Watch out for changes to certain figures during the period covered by the question.

Step 6   Set out the cash budget month by month. A commonly used general layout is as follows.

Receipts	X
Less payments	(X)
Net cash flow in month	X
Closing cash balance	X or (X)
	X

The closing cash balance in one month becomes the opening cash balance the next month.

3.1 Time periods and overdraft size

Forecasts are divided into time periods. Dividing the forecast period into daily flows, weekly flows or monthly flows should coincide as closely as possible with **significant cash flow events**, to provide management with information about the **high or low points for cash balances**. In other words, as well as predicting the **month end surplus or overdraft**, the maximum overdraft **during** the month should also be predicted.

3.2 Example: timing of cash flows

Oak Tree Villa Co operates a retail business. Purchases are sold at cost plus $33\frac{1}{3}$%. Or put another way, purchases are 75% of sales.

(a)

	Budgeted sales $	Labour costs $	Expenses incurred $
January	40,000	3,000	4,000
February	60,000	3,000	6,000
March	160,000	5,000	7,000
April	120,000	4,000	7,000

(b)   It is management policy to have sufficient inventory in hand at the end of each month to meet sales demand in the next half month.

(c)   Suppliers for materials and expenses are paid in the month after the purchases are made or the expenses incurred. Labour is paid in full by the end of each month.

(d)   Expenses include a monthly depreciation charge of $2,000.

(e)   (i)   75% of sales are for cash.
       (ii)   25% of sales are on one month's interest-free credit.

(f)   The company will buy equipment for cash costing $18,000 in February and will pay a dividend of $20,000 in March. The opening cash balance at 1 February is $1,000.

Required

(a)   A statement of profit or loss (income statement) for February and March
(b)   A cash budget for February and March

Solution

(a)   Statement of profit or loss (Income statement)

	February		March		Total	
	$	$	$	$	$	$
Revenue		60,000		160,000		220,000
Cost of sales						
(75% of revenue)		45,000		120,000		165,000
Gross profit		15,000		40,000		55,000
Less: labour	3,000		5,000		8,000	
expenses	6,000		7,000		13,000	
		9,000		12,000		21,000
		6,000		28,000		34,000

(b)   *Workings*

1   *Receipts*

		$
In February	75% of Feb revenue (75% × $60,000)	45,000
	+25% of Jan revenue (25% × $40,000)	10,000
		55,000
In March	75% of Mar revenue (75% × $160,000)	120,000
	+25% of Feb revenue (25% × $60,000)	15,000
		135,000

2

	Purchases in January $		Purchases in February $
Purchases:			
For Jan sales (50% of $30,000)	15,000		
For Feb sales (50% of $45,000)	22,500	(50% of $45,000)	22,500
For March sales	–	(50% of $120,000)	60,000
	37,500		82,500

These purchases are paid for in February and March.

3   Expenses: cash expenses in January ($4,000 – $2,000) and February ($6,000 – $2,000) are paid for in February and March respectively. Depreciation is not a cash item.

Cash budget

	February $	March $	Total $
Receipt from sales	55,000	135,000	190,000
Payments			
Payables	37,500	82,500	120,000
Expenses payables	2,000	4,000	6,000
Labour	3,000	5,000	8,000
Equipment purchase	18,000	–	18,000
Dividend	–	20,000	20,000
Total payments	60,500	111,500	172,000
Receipts less payments	(5,500)	23,500	18,000
Opening cash balance b/f	1,000	(4,500)*	1,000
Closing cash balance c/f	(4,500)*	19,000	19,000

* The cash balance at the end of February is carried forward as the opening cash balance for March.

Notes

1   The profit in February and March does mean that there is sufficient cash to operate the business as planned.

2   Steps should be taken either to ensure that an overdraft facility is available for the cash shortage at the end of February, or to defer certain payments so that the overdraft is avoided.

3.3 Example: Receivables and payables

For example, suppose that a statement of financial position as at 31 December 20X4 shows that a company has the following receivables and payables.

	$
Receivables	150,000
Payables	60,000

You are informed of the following:

(a)   Customers are allowed two months to pay.
(b)   1½ months' credit is taken from suppliers.
(c)   Sales and materials purchases were both made at an even monthly rate in 20X4.

Required

Determine in which months of 20X5 the customers will eventually pay and the suppliers will be paid.

Solution

(a)   Since customers take two months to pay, the $150,000 of receivables in the statement of financial position represent credit sales in November and December 20X4, who will pay in January and February 20X5 respectively. Since sales in 20X4 were at an equal monthly rate, the cash budget should plan for receipts of $75,000 each month in January and February from the customers in the opening statement of financial position.

(b)   Similarly, since suppliers are paid after 1½ months, payments will be made in January and the first half of February 20X5, which means that budgeted payments will be as follows.

	$
In January (purchases in second half of November and first half of December 20X4)	40,000
In February (purchases in second half of December 20X4)	20,000
Total payables in the statement of financial position	60,000

Payables represent 1½ months' purchases. Since sales and purchases are made evenly, $60,000 represents $20,000 per half month.

3.4 Example: A month-by-month cash budget in detail

Now you have some idea as to the underlying principles, let us put these to work. From the following information which relates to George and Zola Co you are required to prepare a month by month cash budget for the second half of 20X5 and to append such brief comments as you consider might be helpful to management.

(a)   The company's only product, a calfskin vest, sells at $40 and has a variable cost of $26 made up as follows.

	$
Materials	20
Labour	4
Variable overheads	2

(b)   Fixed costs of $6,000 per month are paid on the 28th of each month.

(c)   *Quantities sold/to be sold on credit*

May	*June*	*July*	*Aug*	*Sept*	*Oct*	*Nov*	*Dec*
1,000	1,200	1,400	1,600	1,800	2,000	2,200	2,600

(d)   *Production quantities*

May	*June*	*July*	*Aug*	*Sept*	*Oct*	*Nov*	*Dec*
1,200	1,400	1,600	2,000	2,400	2,600	2,400	2,200

(e)   Cash sales at a discount of 5% are expected to average 100 units a month.

(f)   Customers are expected to settle their accounts by the end of the second month following sale.

(g)   Suppliers of material are paid two months after the material is used in production.

(h)   Wages are paid in the same month as they are incurred.

(i)   70% of the variable overhead is paid in the month of production, the remainder in the following month.

(j)   Corporation tax of $18,000 is to be paid in October.

(k)   A new delivery vehicle was bought in June, the cost of which, $8,000 is to be paid in August. The old vehicle was sold for $600, the buyer undertaking to pay in July.

(l)   The company is expected to be $3,000 overdrawn at the bank at 30 June 20X5. The overdraft is charged at 2% per month on any brought forward balance.

(m)   The opening and closing inventories of raw materials, work in progress and finished goods are budgeted to be the same.

Solution

CASH BUDGET FOR 1 JULY TO 31 DECEMBER 20X5

	July $	Aug $	Sept $	Oct $	Nov $	Dec $	Total $
Receipts							
Credit sales	40,000	48,000	56,000	64,000	72,000	80,000	360,000
Cash sales	3,800	3,800	3,800	3,800	3,800	3,800	22,800
Sale of vehicles	600						600
	44,400	51,800	59,800	67,800	75,800	83,800	383,400
Payments							
Materials	24,000	28,000	32,000	40,000	48,000	52,000	224,000
Labour	6,400	8,000	9,600	10,400	9,600	8,800	52,800
Variable overhead (W1)	3,080	3,760	4,560	5,080	4,920	4,520	25,920
Fixed costs	6,000	6,000	6,000	6,000	6,000	6,000	36,000
Overdraft interest (W2)	60		2		83		145
Corporation tax				18,000			18,000
Purchase of vehicle		8,000					8,000
	39,540	53,760	52,162	79,480	68,603	71,320	364,865
Excess of receipts over payments	4,860	(1,960)	7,638	(11,680)	7,197	12,480	18,535
Balance b/f	(3,000)	1,860	(100)	7,538	(4,142)	3,055	(3,000)
Balance c/f	1,860	(100)	7,538	(4,142)	3,055	15,535	15,535

Workings

1 *Variable overhead*

	June $	July $	Aug $	Sept $	Oct $	Nov $	Dec $
Variable overhead production cost	2,800	3,200	4,000	4,800	5,200	4,800	4,400
70% paid in month		2,240	2,800	3,360	3,640	3,360	3,080
30% in following month		840	960	1,200	1,440	1,560	1,440
		3,080	3,760	4,560	5,080	4,920	4,520

2 *Overdraft interest*
   (2% on b/f)   60   2   83

Comments

(a) There will be a small overdraft at the end of August but a much larger one at the end of October. It may be possible to delay payments to suppliers for longer than two months or to reduce purchases of materials or reduce the volume of production by running down existing inventory levels.

(b) If neither of these courses is possible, the company may need to negotiate extended overdraft facilities with its bank.

(c) The cash deficit is only temporary and by the end of December there will be a comfortable surplus. The use to which this cash will be put should ideally be planned in advance.

4 Control and corrective action

As a part of **short-term planning,** budgeting should be seen in the context of the overall **business plan**. This will include a **long-term financial plan** for the enterprise.

A forecast is of no use unless actual outcome is compared with the forecast so that corrective action can be taken. An objective of **cash flow control** is to **achieve net cash flows** or cash balances that **satisfy a target or budget** that management has set. The cash flow target could be to avoid borrowing, or to keep the amount borrowed within a specified overdraft limit. Targets could also be imposed on a company by a bank.

4.1 Uncertainties in forecast cash flows

Why might a forecast differ from the actual flows?

(a) **Poor forecasting techniques**

(b) **Unpredictable events** or **developments**, eg:

    (i)   Loss of a major customer
    (ii)   Insolvency of a major customer who owes the company money
    (iii) Changes in interest rates
    (iv) Inflation, which may affect various costs and revenues differently

4.2 Cash flow control reports

Cash flow control reports should be prepared regularly for managers with responsibility for cash receipts, payments and balances.

(a) In many companies, reports could be **restricted** to the treasury department or financial controller's department. Reporting can be informal, perhaps a daily check on cleared funds in the company's bank accounts.

(b) Reports can also be distributed more widely, to operational managers as well as to treasurers and financial controllers. Widespread reporting of cash flows will only be useful, however, if operational managers are conscious of a responsibility to control their cash flows as well as their costs and profits.

Control reports could be prepared for operational cash flows. The frequency, format and structure of a control report can be designed to suit management requirements, but the purpose of the report should be to compare either:

- **Actual cash flows** against a **budget** or target (as illustrated below); or
- A **current forecast** of cash flows against an **original budget** or target.

Reports could be discussed at monthly management meetings (or board meetings) and managers asked to explain **differences** or **variances** that exceed a certain control limit (perhaps a percentage of the budgeted cash flow figure).

In the example below, the managers responsible could be asked to explain the high payments for teaching costs in March ($106,000 or 27% above the budget amount) and advertising ($28,000 or 33% above budget). The financial controller or director might be asked to comment on the company's borrowing limits, and whether these are now expected to be sufficient.

CASH FLOW CONTROL REPORT

Alpha Language Schools: UK Division
Month: March
Currency: USD ($'000)

	Month			Cumulative: year to date		
	*Budget $'000	Actual $'000	Difference $'000	*Budget $'000	Actual $'000	Difference $'000
Cash receipts						
Tuition	1,100	1,150	50	2,900	2,980	80
Books	70	25	(45)	210	155	(55)
Cassettes	340	355	15	650	692	42
Sale of non-current assets	0	24	24	30	24	(6)
Other income	15	7	(8)	45	44	(1)
	1,525	1,561	36	3,835	3,895	60
Cash payments						
Staff costs: teaching	390	496	106	1,000	1,270	270
Staff costs management	250	248	(2)	650	624	(26)
Book purchases	60	32	(28)	155	81	(74)
Materials printing	25	28	3	65	62	(3)
Origination	15	19	4	40	35	(5)
Commissions	60	61	1	155	158	3
Advertising	85	113	28	210	275	65
Marketing expenses	72	69	(3)	185	170	(15)
Travel and entertaining	216	235	19	520	499	(21)
Equipment	60	72	12	150	144	(6)
Establishment	150	146	(4)	450	435	(15)
Office expenses	42	37	(5)	100	96	(4)
Other payments	30	24	(6)	75	72	(3)
	1,455	1,580	125	3,755	3,921	166
Net cash flow	70	(19)	(89)	80	(26)	(106)
Opening cash balance	22	5	(17)	12	12	–
Closing cash balance	92	(14)	(106)	92	(14)	(106)

Of course, the difference in previous periods might have led to a **revised forecast**, and it might be this revised forecast that is used for control purposes.

4.3 Cash flow problems

Cash flow problems can arise in various ways.

(a) **Making losses**

If a business is continually making losses, it will eventually have cash flow problems.

(b) **Inflation**

In a period of inflation, a business needs ever-increasing amounts of cash just to replace used-up and worn-out assets. A business can be making a profit in historical cost accounting terms, but still not be receiving enough cash to buy the replacement assets it needs.

(c) **Growth**

When a business is growing, it needs to acquire more non-current assets, and to support higher amounts of inventories and receivables. These additional assets must be paid for somehow.

(d) **Seasonal business**

When a business has seasonal or cyclical sales, it may have cash flow difficulties at certain times of the year, when (i) cash inflows are low, but (ii) cash outflows are high, perhaps because the business is building up its inventories for the next period of high sales.

(e) **One-off items of expenditure**

There might occasionally be a single non-recurring item of expenditure that creates a cash flow problem, such as:

(i) The repayment of loan capital on maturity of the debt

(ii) The purchase of an exceptionally expensive item, for example, freehold property

4.4 Corrective action

Cash deficits can arise out of **basic trading factors** underlying the business such as falling sales or increasing costs. Clearly, the way to deal with these items is to take normal business measures, rectifying the fall in sales by marketing activities or, if this cannot be achieved, by cutting costs.

4.4.1 Controlling the working capital cycle: short-term deficiencies

Cash deficits can also arise out of the business's management of the working capital cycle and from timing differences.

(a) **Short-term borrowing** from the bank is only a temporary measure. The bank might convert an overdraft into a long-term loan, or perhaps agree to new overdraft limits.

(b) **Sale of short-term investments** could provide liquidity.

(c) **Raising share capital** is expensive and should be generally used for long-term investment, not short-term cash management.

(d) The **nature** and **timing** of **discretionary flows** might alter.

(e) **Different sources of finance** (such as leasing) might alter.

(f) **Inventory levels** could also decrease to reduce the amount of money that is 'tied up' in their production cost.

(g) The technique of **leading and lagging.** Effectively this means shortening the working capital cycle, by:

(i) **Obtaining money** from **customers** as soon as possible, in other words reducing the collection period

(ii) **Taking as much credit** as possible, delaying payment until there is less need for borrowing from the bank

4.5 Example: leading and lagging

Assume that Gilbert Gosayne Co sells Nullas. Each Nulla costs $50 to make and is sold for $100. The bank has refused an overdraft to Gilbert Gosayne. Suppliers are normally paid at the end of Month 1; the Nullas are sold on the 15th of Month 2. Payment is received on the first day of Month 4.

(a) Under this system we have the following forecast.

	Inflows $	Outflows $	Balance $
Month 1 (end)	–	50	(50)
Month 2	–	–	(50)
Month 3 (end)	100	–	50

In other words the cash cycle means that the firm is in deficit for all of Months 2 and 3. As the bank has refused an overdraft, the payables will not be paid.

(b) If, however, Gilbert Gosayne Co persuades its payables to wait for two weeks until the 15th of Month 2 and offers a settlement discount of $5 to customers to induce them to pay on the 15th of Month 2, the situation is transformed.

	Inflows $	Outflows $	Balance $
Month 1	–	–	–
Month 2	95	50	45
Month 3	–	–	45

In practice, however, a firm's customers and suppliers might be 'leading and lagging' themselves.

(a) Suppliers can object to their customers taking extra credit; and it can also harm their businesses, thus jeopardising their ability to make future supplies. The customer also loses the possibility of taking advantage of trade discounts.

(b) Customers might refuse to pay early, despite the inducement of a discount.

A firm might be in a position to choose which of its suppliers should be paid now rather than later. Certain suppliers have to be paid early, if they are powerful. The bank is a powerful supplier, it is worth keeping the bank happy even if the firm loses out on a few trade discounts in the process.

4.6 Longer-term methods of easing cash shortages

Shortening the operating cycle is helpful in dealing with **short-term deficiencies** and saving interest costs, but it is not necessarily a long-term solution to the business's funding problems. A shorter operating cycle time will **reduce the amount of cash** that a company needs to invest in its operating activities.

The steps that are usually taken by a company when a need for cash arises can be summarised as follows:

(a) **Postponing capital expenditure**

Some capital expenditure items are more important and urgent than others.

(i) It might be imprudent to postpone expenditure on non-current assets which are needed for the **development and growth** of the business.

(ii) On the other hand, some capital expenditures are routine and might be postponable without serious consequences. The **routine replacement** of **motor vehicles** is an example. If a company's policy is to replace company cars every two years, but the company is facing a cash shortage, it might decide to replace cars every three years.

(b) **Accelerating cash inflows which would otherwise be expected in a later period**

The most obvious way of bringing forward cash inflows would be to offer tighter terms to customers, in order to obtain earlier payment. Often, this policy will result in a loss of goodwill and can cause problems. There will also be very little scope for speeding up payments when the credit period currently allowed to customers is no more than the norm for the industry. It might be possible to encourage customers to pay more quickly by offering discounts for earlier payment.

(c) **Reversing past investment decisions by selling assets previously acquired**

Some assets are less crucial to a business than others and so, if cash flow problems are severe, the option of selling investments or property might have to be considered.

(d) **Negotiating a reduction in cash outflows, so as to postpone or even reduce payments**

There are several ways in which this could be done.

(i) **Longer credit periods** might be negotiated with **suppliers**. However, if the credit period allowed is already generous, suppliers might be very reluctant to extend credit even further.

(ii) **Loan repayments** could be **rescheduled** by agreement with a bank.

(iii) A **deferral** of the **payment of corporation tax** could be agreed with the tax authority.

(iv) **Dividend payments** could be **reduced**. Dividend payments are discretionary cash outflows, although a company's directors might be constrained by shareholders' expectations.

EXAM FOCUS POINT

A typical question on cash forecasts might ask you to explain how an organisation might deal with a predicted cash shortfall.

4.7 Quality control of forecasts

When actual results differ from budget, it can be tempting to conclude that plans never work out in practice. However, as planning is a vital management activity, and if actual results differ from the plan, it is important to find out whether the **planning processes** can be improved.

Accuracy of cash flow forecasts can be enhanced by:

(a) **Reviewing actual cash flows** against the **forecasts**, learning from past mistakes; and

(b) **Preparing updated rolling forecasts** or **revised forecasts**, where useful, to replace earlier, less reliable forecasts.

A constant monthly amount for receipts and payments will often indicate either **sloppy cash forecasting practice**, or a **high degree of uncertainty** in the forecast, since it is rare for a specific receivables and payables to remain unchanged except when there is a formal arrangement.

As a financial year progresses, the actual cash flows for the past months could show **large variances** from budget, but a **rolling forecast** indicates that the original budget for the end-of-year cash balance will still be achieved. This could occur if the rolling forecast has been prepared by adjusting the forecast for the unexpired months of the year, in order to keep the annual budget (on paper at least) for the end-of-year cash position. Where this occurs, suspicion must arise that the rolling forecast has been prepared with little thought.

Unchanged figures over a number of months of revised forecast submissions are also an indication of a **weak forecasting system**. It could be that business expectations have not changed; however there are few businesses that do not fluctuate with market conditions. A more likely explanation is that the rolling cash forecast has been prepared by copying the figures from the previous forecast or that a new revised forecast has not been prepared at all.

5 Cash budgeting with inflation

5.1 Index numbers

An **index** is a measure over a period of time of the average changes in prices of items or a group of items.

If a business achieves an increase in revenue of 10% in monetary (cash) terms over a year, this result becomes less impressive if we are told that there was general price inflation of 15% over the year. The business is now selling less at the new higher prices.

When results of a business are being compared over a period of time for internal management purposes, managers of the business should agree and use an appropriate method of allowing for changing price levels. The usual method is to use a series of **index numbers**.

An index is a measure, over a period of time, of the average changes in the values (prices or quantities) of a group of items.

An index may be a price index or a quantity index.

(a) A **price index** measures the change in the money value of a group of items over a period of time. Perhaps the most well-known price index in the UK is the **Retail Prices Index** (RPI) which measures changes in the costs of items of expenditure of the average household, and which used to be called the 'cost of living' index.

(b) A **quantity index** measures the change in the non-monetary values of a group of items over a period of time. A well-known example is a productivity index, which measures changes in the productivity of various departments or groups of workers.

As we shall see, a suitable **price index** provides a method of allowing for changing price levels when comparing costs or revenues over time.

PART E: CASH MANAGEMENT

5.2 Index points

'**Points**' measure the difference in the index value in one year with the value in another year.

Points measure changes in an index because they provide an easy method of arithmetic. The alternative is to use percentages, because indices are based on percentages.

5.3 The base period, or base year

Index numbers are normally expressed as percentages, taking the value for a **base date** as 100. The choice of a base date or base year is not significant, except that it should normally be '**representative**' – that is preferably not one in which there were abnormally high or low prices for any items in the 'basket of goods' making up the index.

5.4 Example: Calculation of an index

Suppose revenue for a company over the last five years were as follows.

Year	Revenue $'000
20X5	35
20X6	42
20X7	40
20X8	45
20X9	50

The managing director decided that he wanted to set up a revenue index (ie an index which measures how revenue has done from year to year), using 20X5 as the base year. The $35,000 of revenue in 20X5 is given the index 100%. What are the indices for the other years?

Solution

If $35,000 = 100%, then:

$$20X6 \quad \$42,000 = \frac{42,000}{35,000} \times 100\% = 120\%$$

The same calculation can be applied to other figures, and the table showing sales for the last five years can be completed, taking 20X5 as the base year.

Year	Revenue $'000	Index
20X5	35	100
20X6	42	120
20X7	40	114
20X8	45	129
20X9	50	143

5.5 Indices in practice

In practice, indices generally consist of **more than one item**. For example, suppose that the cost of living index is calculated from only three commodities: bread, tea and caviar, and that the prices for 20X1 and 20X5 were as follows.

	20X1	20X5
Bread	20c a loaf	40c a loaf
Tea	25c a packet	30c a packet
Caviar	450c an ounce	405c an ounce

Note that the prices above are in different units, and there is no indication of the **relative importance** of each item. In formulating index numbers, these aspects can be overcome by **weighting**. To determine the weighting, we need information about the **relative importance** of each item.

BPP LEARNING MEDIA

For the purpose of **internal management reporting**, results recorded over a number of periods can be adjusted using an appropriate price index to convert the figures from money terms to 'real' terms.

5.5.1 The use of index numbers in cash forecasting and budgeting

How are index numbers useful in **cash budgeting and forecasting**? The person preparing the cash budget is not particularly interested in prices in 'real terms': instead, it is the **exact monetary amount** that he or she is interested in.

Index numbers are still useful, however.

(a)   We can use index numbers to **predict future cash inflows**. For example, if 500,000 units will be sold in three or four month's time, an estimate of future monetary prices gives some idea of the amount of sales **in cash**.

(b)   Similarly, with cash outflows, an **estimated future price index** can suggest the likely size of cash payments.

(c)   Their use in forecasting can also suggest a **need for increased borrowing** limits, which might be fixed in monetary terms.

Where inflation is very high, the value of financial assets, such as debt, declines.

(a)   Companies will try and **collect their debts** even **more quickly**, so that the cash can be reinvested.

(b)   Delaying payments to suppliers **reduces** the **underlying value** of the debt.

(c)   A company's forecasts become **out of date** very quickly.

(d)   Interest rates might be **very high**, in the short term, and so a treasurer will invest cash on short-term deposit.

Different items, such as capital items, costs of various kinds, and revenues, are likely to be subject to differing rates of inflation, and **different indices** may therefore be appropriate for different items.

QUESTION   RPI

Explain the general principles and methods involved in the compilation and construction of the UK General Index of Retail Prices (RPI) under the following headings: base year; weights; items included; data collection; calculation.

ANSWER

(a)   **Base year.** Currently the base date for the RPI is January 1987, which was given an index of 100. The index for later months is then given in terms of the January 1987 level. For example the index for November 1999 is 166.7, indicating that prices in November 1999 were on average 66.7% higher than in January 1987.

(b)   **Weights.** The weights used in calculating the RPI are designed to reflect the relative importance of the different sorts of expenditure of households.

(c)   **Items included.** The items included in the calculation of the index are designed to be a representative selection of goods and services bought in the UK. Items are combined in sections, which in turn are combined in groups.

(d)   **Data collection.** The collection of data on prices is carried out for each of the items monthly. Officials visit a sample of shops, geographically spread across the UK, to record the prices actually being charged.

(e)   **Calculation.** The first step to calculate the RPI for a month is to calculate each of the price relatives (being the ratio of the current price for one item to the price at the base date). These price relatives are then weighted using the weights explained in (b) to give each of the section indices. The section indices are in turn combined using section weights to give the group indices. The group indices are combined to give the final RPI figure for the month.

BPP
LEARNING
MEDIA

QUESTION

Index and budgets

You are assisting with the work on a maintenance department's budget for the next quarter of 20X4. The maintenance department's budget for the current quarter (just ending) is $200,000.

A base weighted index for the next quarter stands at 103.5, compared to 100 for this quarter, for the price of input quantities.

On the basis of the index, what will the budget be for the next quarter?

O $193,000   O $207,000
O $200,000   O $270,000

ANSWER

$207,000.

The index suggests prices will increase by 3.5%. This produces a budget of $200,000 × 1.035 = $207,000.

6 Time series analysis

When preparing a **cash budget** a number of figures must be estimated. These include sales, purchases, wages, overheads and exceptional receipts or payments. One method of estimating sales and costs figures is to look at the past and determine any **pattern there might be in these figures over time** in order to estimate the likely future figures.

One method of analysing past or historic figures is to use the technique of **time series analysis**.

6.1 Time series

A **time series** is a series of figures or values recorded over time.

There are four components to a time series: **trend**, **seasonal variations**, **cyclical variations** and **random variations**.

A **time series** is a series of figures or values recorded over time.

The following are examples of time series.

(a)   Output at a factory each day for the last month
(b)   Monthly sales over the last two years
(c)   Total annual costs for the last ten years
(d)   Retail Prices Index each month for the last ten years
(e)   The number of people employed by a company each year for the last 20 years

A graph of a time series is called a **historigram**. (Note the 'ri'; this is not the same as a histogram.) For example, consider the following time series.

Year	Sales $'000
1	20
2	21
3	24
4	23
5	27
6	30
7	28

The historigram is as follows.

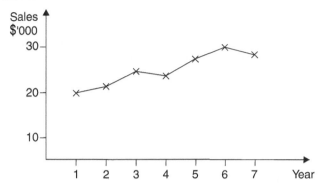

The horizontal axis is always chosen to represent time, and the vertical axis represents the values of the data recorded.

There are several features of a time series which it may be necessary to analyse in order to prepare forecasts.

(a)   A **trend**.

(b)   **Seasonal variations** or fluctuations.

(c)   **Cycles**, or cyclical variations.

(d)   **Non-recurring, random variations**. These may be caused by unforeseen circumstances, such as a change in the government of the country, a war, the collapse of a company, technological change or a fire.

6.2 The trend

A **trend** of a series of figures in a time series is the way in which the figures are moving in general despite various fluctuations caused by seasonality.

The **trend** is the underlying long-term movement over time in the values of the data recorded.

TERM

In the following examples of time series, there are three types of trend.

Year	Output per labour hour Units	Cost per unit $	Number of employees
4	30	1.00	100
5	24	1.08	103
6	26	1.20	96
7	22	1.15	102
8	21	1.18	103
9	17	1.25	98
	(A)	(B)	(C)

(a)   In time series (A) there is a downward trend in the output per labour hour. Output per labour hour did not fall every year, because it went up between years 5 and 6, but the long-term movement is clearly a downward one.

(b)   In time series (B) there is an upward trend in the cost per unit. Although unit costs went down in year 7 from a higher level in year 6, the basic movement over time is one of rising costs.

(c)   In time series (C) there is no clear movement up or down, and the number of employees remained fairly constant around 100. The trend is therefore a static, or level one.

6.3 Seasonal variations

Seasonal variations are short-term fluctuations in recorded values, due to different circumstances which affect results at different times of the year, on different days of the week, at different times of day, or all of the above.

TERM

Here are two examples of seasonal variations:

(a)   Sales of ice cream will be higher in summer than winter.

(b)   The telephone network may be heavily used at certain times of the day (such as mid-morning and mid-afternoon and much less used at other times (such as in the middle of the night).

QUESTION

Seasonal variations

Can you think of some more examples of seasonal variations?

ANSWER

Here are some suggestions.

(a)   Sales of overcoats will be higher in autumn than in spring.
(b)   Shops might expect higher sales shortly before Christmas, or in their winter and summer sales.
(c)   Sales might be higher on Friday and Saturday than on Monday.

'Seasonal' is a term which may appear to refer to the seasons of the year, but its meaning in time series analysis is somewhat broader, as the examples given above show.

6.4 Example: A trend and seasonal variations

The number of customers served by a company of travel agents over the past four years is shown in the following historigram.

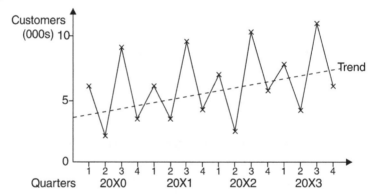

In this example, there would appear to be large seasonal fluctuations in demand, but there is also a basic upward trend.

6.5 Cyclical variations

Cyclical variations are **fluctuations which take place over a longer time period** than seasonal variations. It may take several years to complete the cycle. For example the sales of fashion items such as flared trousers could be said to be cyclical. The last cycle took approximately 30 years (mid 1960s to mid 1990s) to complete.

7 Finding the trend

One method of finding the trend is by the use of **moving averages**. A moving average is an average value that is revised as new information is received.

Remember that when finding the moving average of an even number of results, a second moving average has to be calculated so that trend values can relate to specific actual figures.

The **moving average method** of cash forecasting is relatively simple. The most recent observations are used to compute an average which is **continually updated** as new information becomes available.

Look at these monthly sales figures.

Year 6	Sales $'000
August	0.02
September	0.04
October	0.04
November	3.20
December	14.60

It looks as though the business is expanding rapidly – and so it is, in a way. But when you know that the business is a Christmas card manufacturer, then you see immediately that the January sales will no doubt slump right back down again.

It is obvious that the business will do better in the Christmas season than at any other time – that is the seasonal variation with which the statistician has to contend. Using the monthly figures, how can he tell whether or not the business is doing well overall – whether there is a rising sales trend over time other than the short-term rise over Christmas?

One possibility is to compare figures with the equivalent figures of a year ago. However, many things can happen over a period of twelve months to make such a comparison misleading – for example, new products might now be manufactured and prices will probably have changed.

In fact, there are a number of ways of overcoming this problem of distinguishing trend from seasonal variations. One such method is called **moving averages**. This method attempts to **remove seasonal (or cyclical) variations from a time series by a process of averaging so as to leave a set of figures representing the trend**.

7.1 Finding the trend by moving averages

A **moving average** is an average of the results of a fixed number of periods. Since it is an average of several time periods, it is **related to the mid-point of the overall period**.

7.2 Example: Moving averages

Year	Sales Units
20X0	390
20X1	380
20X2	460
20X3	450
20X4	470
20X5	440
20X6	500

Required

Take a moving average of the annual sales over a period of three years.

Solution

(a)   Average sales in the three year period 20X0–20X2 were

$$\left(\frac{390+380+460}{3}\right) = \frac{1,230}{3} = 410$$

This average relates to the middle year of the period, 20X1.

(b)   Similarly, average sales in the three year period 20X1–20X3 were

$$\left(\frac{380+460+450}{3}\right) = \frac{1,290}{3} = 430$$

This average relates to the middle year of the period, 20X2.

(c)   The average sales can also be found for the periods 20X2–20X4, 20X3–20X5 and 20X4–20X6, to give the following.

Year	Sales	Moving total of 3 years' sales	Moving average of 3 years' sales ($\div$ 3)
20X0	390		
20X1	380	1,230	410
20X2	460	1,290	430
20X3	450	1,380	460
20X4	470	1,360	453
20X5	440	1,410	470
20X6	500		

Note the following points:

(i)   The **moving average series has five figures** relating to the years from 20X1 to 20X5. The **original series had seven figures** for the years from 20X0 to 20X6.

(ii)   There is an upward trend in sales, which is more noticeable from the series of moving averages than from the original series of actual sales each year.

7.3 Moving averages of an even number of results

In the previous example, moving averages were taken of the results in an **odd** number of time periods, and the average then related to the mid-point of the overall period.

If a moving average were taken of results in an even number of time periods, the basic technique would be the same, but the mid-point of the overall period would not relate to a single period. For example, suppose an average were taken of the following four results.

Spring	120	
Summer	90	
Autumn	180	average 115
Winter	70	

The average would relate to the mid-point of the period, between summer and autumn.

The trend line average figures need to relate to a particular time period; otherwise, seasonal variations cannot be calculated. To overcome this difficulty, we **take a moving average of the moving average**. An example will illustrate this technique.

7.4 Example: Moving averages over an even number of periods

Calculate a moving average trend line of the following results of Linden Co.

Year	Quarter	Volume of sales '000 units
20X5	1	600
	2	840
	3	420
	4	720
20X6	1	640
	2	860
	3	420
	4	740
20X7	1	670
	2	900
	3	430
	4	760

Solution

A moving average of four will be used, since the volume of sales would appear to depend on the season of the year, and each year has four quarterly results. The moving average of four does not relate to any specific period of time; therefore a second moving average of two will be calculated on the first moving average trend line.

Year	Quarter	Actual volume of sales '000 units (A)	Moving total of 4 quarters' sales '000 units (B)	Moving average of 4 quarters' sales '000 units (B ÷ 4)	Mid-point of 2 moving averages Trend line '000 units (C)
20X5	1	600			
	2	840			
	3	420	2,580	645.0	650.00
	4	720	2,620	655.0	657.50
20X6	1	640	2,640	660.0	660.00
	2	860	2,640	660.0	662.50
	3	420	2,660	665.0	668.75
	4	740	2,690	672.5	677.50
20X7	1	670	2,730	682.5	683.75
	2	900	2,740	685.0	687.50
	3	430	2,760	690.0	
	4	760			

By taking a mid point (a moving average of two) of the original moving averages, we can relate the results to specific quarters (from the third quarter of 20X5 to the second quarter of 20X7).

QUESTION

Trend in sales

What can you say about the trend in sales of Linden Co above?

ANSWER

The trend in sales is upward.

7.5 Moving averages on graphs

One way of displaying the trend clearly is to show it by plotting the moving average on a graph.

7.5.1 Example: Moving averages on graphs

Actual sales of Slap-It-On suntan lotion for 20X5 and 20X6 were as follows.

	Sales	
	20X5	20X6
	$'000	$'000
January	100	110
February	120	130
March	200	220
April	200	210
May	240	230
June	250	240
July	210	250
August	210	300
September	200	150
October	110	110
November	90	80
December	50	40
	1,980	2,070

Required

Calculate the trend in the suntan lotion sales and display it on a graph.

Hint. Calculate an annual moving total.

Solution

20X6	Sales	Moving total	Moving average (trend)
	$'000	$'000	$'000
January	110	1,990	165.83
February	130	2,000	166.67
March	220	2,020	168.33
April	210	2,030	169.17
May	230	2,020	168.33
June	240	2,010	167.50
July	250	2,050	170.83
August	300	2,140	178.33
September	150	2,090	174.17
October	110	2,090	174.17
November	80	2,080	173.33
December	40	2,070	172.50

There is one very important point not immediately obvious from the above table, and that is to do with the time periods covered by the moving total and moving average.

(a)   The moving total, as we have seen, is the total for the previous 12 months. The figure of $1,990, for instance, represents total sales from February 20X5 to January 20X6.

(b)   The moving average is the average monthly sales over the previous 12 months. The figure of $165.83, for instance, represents average monthly sales for each month during the period February 20X5 to January 20X6.

When **plotting a moving average on a graph**, it is therefore important to remember that the **points should be located at the mid-point of the period to which they apply**. For example, the figure of $165.83 (moving average at end of January 20X6) relates to the 12 months ending January 20X6 and so it must be plotted in the **middle** of that period (31 July 20X5).

The moving data on suntan lotion sales could be drawn on a graph as follows.

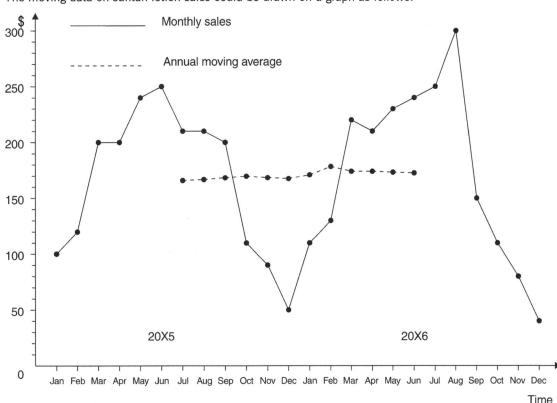

Points to note about this graph are as follows.

(a)   The annual moving average can only be plotted from July 20X5 to May 20X6 as we have no data prior to January 20X5 or after December 20X6.

(b)   The moving average has the effect of smoothing out the seasonal fluctuations in the ordinary sales graph (which is the reason why moving averages are used in the first place).

8   Finding the seasonal variations

> **Seasonal variations** are the difference between actual and trend figures **(additive model)**, or the actual figures expressed as a proportion of the trend **(multiplicative model)**.
>
> An average of the seasonal variations for each time period within the cycle must be determined and then adjusted so that the total of the seasonal variations sums to zero.

Once a trend has been established, we can find the **seasonal variations**. There are two models which are used in time series analysis – the **additive model** and the **multiplicative model**.

The additive model is where each actual figure in the time series is made up as follows.

*   **A = T + S**

        Where: A = Actual figure

                   T = Trend figure

                   S = Seasonal variation

*   Therefore the seasonal variation is calculated as S = A – T

TERM

The **multiplicative model** is where each actual figure in the time series is made up as follows.

- **A = T × S**

  Where: A = Actual figure

  T = Trend figure

  S = Seasonal variation

- Therefore the **seasonal variation** is calculated as $S = \dfrac{A}{T}$

8.1 Additive model

The actual and trend sales for Linden Co (as calculated in Example 7.4) are set out below. The **difference between the actual results for any one quarter and the trend figure for that quarter** will be the seasonal variation for that quarter.

Year	Quarter	Actual	Trend	Seasonal variation
20X5	1	600		
	2	840		
	3	420	650.00	–230.00
	4	720	657.50	62.50
20X6	1	640	660.00	–20.00
	2	860	662.50	197.50
	3	420	668.75	–248.75
	4	740	677.50	62.50
20X7	1	670	683.75	–13.75
	2	900	687.50	212.50
	3	430		
	4	760		

The variation between the actual result for any one particular quarter and the trend line average is not the same from year to year, but an **average of these variations can be taken**.

	Q_1	Q_2	Q_3	Q_4
20X5			–230.00	62.50
20X6	–20.00	197.50	–248.75	62.50
20X7	–13.75	212.50		
Total	–33.75	410.00	–478.75	125.00
Average (÷ 2)	–16.875	205.00	–239.375	62.50

Our estimate of the 'seasonal' or quarterly variation is almost complete, but there is one more important step to take. Variations around the basic trend line should cancel each other out, and add up to zero. At the moment, they do not. We therefore **spread the total of the variations** (11.25) **across the four quarters** (11.25 ÷ 4) **so that the final total of the variations sum to zero.**

	Q_1	Q_2	Q_3	Q_4	Total
Estimated quarterly variations	– 16.8750	205.0000	–239.3750	62.5000	11.250
Adjustment to reduce variations to 0	–2.8125	–2.8125	–2.8125	–2.8125	–11.250
Final estimates of quarterly variations	–19.6875	202.1875	–242.1875	59.6875	0
These might be rounded as follows	Ql: –20,	Ql: 202,	Ql:-242,	Ql: 60,	Total: 0

8.2 Multiplicative model

The method of estimating the seasonal variations in the above example was to use the differences between the trend and actual data. This model **assumes that the components of the series are independent** of each other, so that an increasing trend does not affect the seasonal variations and make them increase as well, for example.

The alternative is to use the **multiplicative model** whereby each actual figure is expressed as a proportion of the trend.

Refer back to our example, Linden Co taking the first two years of data only. We can use the equation here to work out the seasonal variations. The trend is calculated in exactly the same way as before. So if $A = T \times S$ then $S = A/T$ and we can calculate $\mathbf{S = A/T}$ for the multiplicative model.

Year	Quarter	Actual (A)	Trend (T)	Seasonal percentage (A/T)
20X5	1	600		
	2	840		
	3	420	650.00	0.646
	4	720	657.50	1.095
20X6	1	640	660.00	0.970
	2	860	662.50	1.298
	3	420		
	4	740		

Suppose that seasonal variations for the next four quarters are 0.628, 1.092, 0.980 and 1.309 respectively. The summary of the seasonal variations expressed in proportional terms is therefore as follows.

Year	Q_1 %	Q_2 %	Q_3 %	Q_4 %
20X5			0.646	1.095
20X6	0.970	1.298	0.628	1.092
20X7	0.980	1.309		
Total	1.950	2.607	1.274	2.187
Average	0.975	1.3035	0.637	1.0935

Instead of summing to zero, as **with the additive approach**, the **averages should sum (in this case) to 4.0, 1.0 for each of the four quarters.** They actually sum to 4.009 so 0.00225 has to be deducted from each one.

	Q_1	Q_2	Q_3	Q_4
Average	0.97500	1.30350	0.63700	1.09350
Adjustment	−0.00225	−0.00225	−0.00225	−0.00225
Final estimate	0.97275	1.30125	0.63475	1.09125
Rounded	0.97	1.30	0.64	1.09

Note that the **proportional model is better than the additive model when the trend is increasing or decreasing over time.** In such circumstances, seasonal variations are likely to be increasing or decreasing too. The additive model simply adds absolute and unchanging seasonal variations to the trend figures whereas the proportional model, by multiplying increasing or decreasing trend values by a constant seasonal variation factor, takes account of changing seasonal variations.

9 Using time series analysis in cash budgeting

Time series analysis in **budgeting** is used in order to **estimate future figures** based upon the past trend and seasonal variations that have been calculated. This process of using historical information to estimate future figures is known as extrapolation.

Previously, we have looked at how to calculate a trend using moving averages, and how to find seasonal variations using both the **additive** and **multiplicative** models. Now we will consider how this information can be used together in the **cash budgeting process**.

9.1 Example: Time series analysis in cash budgeting

The sales (in $'000) of swimwear by a large department store for each period of three months are as follows.

Quarter	20X4 $'000	20X5 $'000	20X6 $'000	20X7 $'000
First		8	20	40
Second		30	50	62
Third		60	80	92
Fourth	24	20	40	

The management accountant wishes to use the **additive model** to predict sales for the last quarter of 20X7 and the first quarter of 20X8.

Solution

The requirement can be tackled in three stages.

(a) **Find the centred moving average trend**

	Quarter	4 quarter moving total	Centred moving total	Moving average (÷4)
20X4	4			
20X5	1	122		
	2	118	120	30
	3	130	124	31
	4	150	140	35
20X6	1	170	160	40
	2	190	180	45
	3	210	200	50
	4	222	216	54
20X7	1	234	228	57
	2			
	3			

The centred moving average trend is shown in the right hand column of the table.

(b) **Find the average seasonal variation for each quarter**

		Quarter 1	2	3	4	Total
Year	20X5		0.00	+29.00	−15.00	
	20X6	−20.00	+5.00	+30.00	−14.00	
	20X7	−17.00				
Total		−37.00	+5.00	+59.00	−29.00	
Average		−18.50	+2.50	+29.50	−14.50	−1
Adjust total variation to nil		+0.25	+0.25	+0.25	+0.25	+1
Average seasonal variation		−18.25	+2.75	+29.75	−14.25	

(c) **Calculate predicted sales**

We might guess that the trend line is rising steadily, by (57 − 40)/4 = 4.25 per quarter in the period 1st quarter 20X6 to 1st quarter 20X7 (57 being the prediction in 1st quarter 20X7 and 40 the prediction in 1st quarter 20X6).

Since the trend may be levelling off a little, a quarterly increase of +4 in the trend will be assumed.

		Trend	Seasonal variation	Forecast
1st quarter	20X7	57		
4th quarter	20X7 (+ (3 × 4))	69	−14.25	54.75
1st quarter	20X8 (+ (4 × 4))	73	−18.25	54.75

Rounding to the nearest thousand dollars, the forecast sales are $55,000 for each of the two quarters.

QUESTION

Forecast sales

Sales of product X each quarter for the last three years have been as follows (in thousands of units). Trend values, found by a moving averages method, are shown in brackets.

Year	1st quarter	2nd quarter	3rd quarter	4th quarter
1	18	30	20 (18.75)	6 (19.375)
2	20 (20)	33 (20.5)	22 (21)	8 (21.5)
3	22 (22.125)	35 (22.75)	25	10

Average seasonal variations for quarters 1 to 4 are −0.1, +12.4, +1.1 and −13.4 respectively.

Required

Use the trend line and estimates of seasonal variations to forecast sales in each quarter of year 4.

ANSWER

The trend line indicates an increase of about 0.6 per quarter. This can be confirmed by calculating the average quarterly increase in trend line values between the third quarter of year 1 (18.75) and the second quarter of year 3 (22.75). The average rise is

$$\frac{22.75-18.75}{7} = \frac{4}{7} = 0.57, \text{ say } 0.6$$

Taking 0.6 as the quarterly increase in the trend, the forecast of sales for year 4, before seasonal adjustments (the trend line forecast) would be as follows.

Year	Quarter			Trend line
3	*2nd	(actual trend)	22.75, say	22.8
	3rd			23.4
	4th			24.0
4	1st			24.6
	2nd			25.2
	3rd			25.8
	4th			26.4

*last known trend line value.

Note. That you could actually plot the trend line figures on a graph, extrapolate the trend line into the future and read off forecasts from the graph using the extrapolated trend line.

Seasonal variations should now be incorporated to obtain the final forecast.

	Quarter	Trend line forecast '000 units	Average seasonal variation '000 units	Forecast of actual sales '000 units
Year 4	1st	24.6	−0.1	24.5
	2nd	25.2	+12.4	37.6
	3rd	25.8	+1.1	26.9
	4th	26.4	−13.4	13.0

9.2 Problems with using time series for forecasting

Time series analysis can be a useful method of attempting to forecast future sales and cost figures. However you should also be aware that the technique does have its limitations.

- The less historic data available the less reliable the results will be.

- The further into the future we forecast the less reliable the results will be.

- There is an assumption that the trend and seasonal variations from the past will continue into the future.

- Cyclical and random variations have been ignored.

CHAPTER ROUNDUP

- ⤷ The main purpose of preparing cash budgets is to forecast whether there are likely to be **cash shortages** or **large surpluses**.

- ⤷ **Cash flow forecasts** provide an early warning of liquidity problems and funding needs.

- ⤷ **Cash budgets** and **forecasts** can be used for **control reporting**. A forecast can be prepared of cash receipts and payments, and net cash flows. This is known as a **cash flow based forecast**.

- ⤷ A **cash budget** is a detailed forecast of cash receipts, payments and balances over a planning period. It is formally adopted as part of the business plan or master budget for the period.

- ⤷ **Cash budgets** are prepared by taking **operational budgets** and converting them into forecasts as to when receipts and payments occur. The forecast should indicate the highest and lowest cash balance in a period as well as the balance at the end.

- ⤷ As a part of **short-term planning,** budgeting should be seen in the context of the overall **business plan**. This will include a **long-term financial plan** for the enterprise.

- ⤷ An **index** is a measure over a period of time of the average changes in prices of items or a group of items.

- ⤷ When preparing a **cash budget** a number of figures must be estimated. These include sales, purchases, wages, overheads and exceptional receipts or payments. One method of estimating sales and costs figures is to look at the past and determine any **pattern there might be in these figures over time** in order to estimate the likely future figures.

- ⤷ A **time series** is a series of figures or values recorded over time. There are four components of a time series: **trend**, **seasonal variations**, **cyclical variations** and **random variations**.

- ⤷ A **trend** of a series of figures in a time series is the way in which the figures are moving in general despite various fluctuations caused by seasonality.

- ⤷ One method of finding the trend is by the use of **moving averages**. A moving average is an average value that is revised as new information is received. Remember that when finding the moving average of an even number of results, a second moving average has to be calculated so that trend values can relate to specific actual figures.

- ⤷ **Seasonal variations** are the difference between actual and trend figures **(additive model)**, or the actual figures expressed as a proportion of the trend **(multiplicative model)**. An average of the seasonal variations for each time period within the cycle must be determined and then adjusted so that the total of the seasonal variations sums to zero.

- ⤷ Time series analysis in **budgeting** is used in order to **estimate future figures** based upon the past trend and seasonal variations that have been calculated. This process of using historical information to estimate future figures is known as extrapolation.

QUICK QUIZ

1   What do cash forecasts estimate?

2   What might be the significance of forecast surpluses?

3   A .... forecast is a forecast that is continually updated.

4   Why should the assumptions in a cash forecast be clearly stated?

5   List the steps in preparing a cash flow budget.

6   How can you estimate when sales receipts will occur?

7   What is the purpose of a cash flow control report?

8 'Shortening the working capital cycle by obtaining money from customers as soon as possible, **and** taking as much credit from suppliers as possible.' What technique does this describe?

9 Heavy Metal Co is preparing its cash flow forecast for the next quarter. Which of the following items should be excluded from the calculations?

O The receipt of a bank loan that has been raised for the purpose of investment in a new rolling mill
O Depreciation of the new rolling mill
O A tax payment that relates to profits in a previous accounting period
O Disposal proceeds from the sale of the old mill

10 A company had sales of $800,000 in December, and budgeted sales are $500,000 in January and $300,000 in February. 40% of customers pay after one month, 40% pay after two months and 20% pay in cash. What are the budgeted cash receipts from sales for February?

11 A company budgets to purchase $500,000 in materials in April, $800,000 in May and $700,000 in June. 10% of purchases are paid for in the month of purchase, in order to benefit from a discount of 2% for immediate payment. One half of the remaining purchases are paid for in the following month and the rest are paid for after two months. What are budgeted payments to materials suppliers in June?

O $653,600
O $655,000
O $656,400
O $718,600

12 A company budgets that its fixed costs for next year will be $1,800,000. These include annual rental costs, for which there are six-monthly payments of $120,000 in March and September, and depreciation charges of 300,000. All other fixed costs occur at an even monthly rate throughout the year, and are paid for in the month that they occur. What are the budgeted cash payments for fixed cost expenses in March?

O $215,000
O $225,000
O $245,000
O $270,000

13 Which of the following are limitations of time series analysis?

1 Cyclical and random variations are ignored.

2 The further into the future we forecast, the less reliable the results will be.

3 Time series data is often presented graphically.

4 There is an assumption that the trend and seasonal variations from the past will continue into the future.

O 1 and 4
O 2, 3 and 4
O 1 and 2
O 1, 2 and 4

1   How much cash is required, when, for how long, and whether it will be available

2   The surplus could be invested to earn interest.

3   A **rolling** forecast is a forecast that is continually updated.

4   It allows the forecast to be tested for reasonableness.

5   Sort out cash receipts from customers; other cash income received; cash payments to suppliers; other cash payments; set out month-by-month cash budget.

6   Make assumptions based on past experience

7   To help ensure that net cash flows or cash balances satisfy targets set by management

8   Leading and lagging

9   Depreciation of the new rolling mill. This is a non-cash item and should therefore be excluded.

10   (20% × $300,000) + (40% × $500,000) + (40% × $800,000) = $580,000.

11   $653,600. (10% × 98% × $700,000) + (45% × $800,000) + (45% × $500,000) = $653,600.

12   $225,000. Fixed cost cash expenses each year = $1,800,000 – $300,000 = $1,500,000.

   Subtract rent costs: $1,500,000 – (2 × $120,000) = $1,260,000.

   Cash payments each month, excluding rent = $1,260,000/12 = $105,000.

   Total cash payments for fixed costs in March = $105,000 + Rent $120,000 = $225,000.

13   1, 2 and 4. Time series data can be used to produce a graph with time plotted along the horizontal axis and figures on the vertical axis. This can give a useful visual presentation of the figures over a time period. 1, 2 and 4 are all limitations of time series analysis.

Now try ...

Attempt the questions below from the **Practice Question Bank**

Number

Q92

Q93

Q94

Q95

Q96

21

Investing surplus funds

An organisation may have a surplus of cash. This may be temporary, or it may be expected to last for a long time. In practice, cash surpluses are often temporary, and management will eventually want to use the money to **invest** or **pay dividends** or make **tax payments**.

Cash in an ordinary business bank account earns no interest, and when there is a cash surplus, management should consider investing the money to earn some return.

This chapter describes the various types of investment that may be chosen for the **investment of short-term cash surpluses**.

Study Guide	Intellectual level
E	**Cash management**	
2	**Cash management**	
(c)	Outline guidelines and legislation in relation to the management of cash balances in public sector organisations	K
4	**Investing and financing**	
(a)	Explain how surplus cash and cash deficit may arise	K
(b)	Explain the following types of short term investments and the associated risks/returns:	K
	(i) bank deposits	
	(ii) money-market deposits	
	(iii) certificates of deposit	
	(iv) government stock	
	(v) local authority stock	

1 Cash deficit and surplus cash

> Companies may face situations where they have a **cash deficit**. In such a scenario, appropriate action must be taken if the company is to continue to trade on a day-to-day basis.
>
> Companies may sometimes have **cash surpluses**. The surplus needs to be used in the best way, and this will often mean **investing** it.

1.1 What is a deficit?

A cash deficit is a shortage of available funds to satisfy current obligations.

A **cash deficit** may arise for a number of reasons.

(a) **Current funding arrangements** may be insufficient. A business may need to enter into additional overdraft or loan agreements to access necessary funds.

(b) **Seasonal factors** may mean that a company has cash tied up in inventory that it is unable to sell due to seasonal demand. For example, an ice cream company could experience a cash deficit in the winter months.

(c) Companies who **are reliant on one or two large customers** are more likely to experience a cash deficit if the customer does not pay for goods within the agreed payment period.

1.2 What is a surplus?

A cash surplus is the value of cash over and above what is reqired to satisfy current obligations.

Businesses will sometimes have surplus cash because of improvements **in working capital management**, **sales of non-current assets**, or because unexpectedly large amounts of cash have been **generated from operations**.

Cash surpluses may arise from **seasonal factors**, so that surpluses generated in good months are used to cover shortfalls later. In this case, the management of the business needs to ensure that the surpluses are big enough to cover the later deficits. The mere existence of a surplus in one or two months in a row is no guarantee of liquidity in the long term.

1.2.1 Example: Surpluses

(a) Drif Co receives money every month from cash sales and from customers for credit sales of $1,000. It makes payments, in the normal course of events of $800 a month.
In January, the company uses an overdraft facility to buy a car for $4,000.

	Jan $	Feb $	March $
Brought forward	–	(3,800)	(3,600)
Receipts	1,000	1,000	1,000
Payments	(800)	(800)	(800)
Car	(4,000)	0	0
Overdrawn balance	(3,800)	(3,600)	(3,400)

The company has been left with a persistent overdraft, even though, in operating terms it makes a monthly surplus of $200.

(b) Guide Co on the other hand has monthly cash receipts of $1,200 and monthly cash payments of $1,050. The company sets up a special loan account: it borrows $5,000 to buy a car. This it pays off at the rate of $80 a month.

	Jan $	Feb $	March $
Brought forward	–	70	140
Receipts	1,200	1,200	1,200
Payments	(1,050)	(1,050)	(1,050)
Car	(80)	(80)	(80)
Overdrawn balance	70	140	210

Which do you consider has the healthier finances? Clearly Drif Co produces an operating surplus (before the motor purchase) of $200 ($1,000 – $800) a month, which is more than Guide ($150, ie $1,200 – $1,050). Furthermore Guide Co has a much higher net debt, the loan for the car being $5,000 as opposed to $4,000.

Yet, in effect the financing arrangements each has chosen has turned the tables. Drif Co is relying on normal overdraft finance which will be **repayable on demand**. Its normal **operating surplus** of receipts from cash sales and credit customers, over payments to suppliers and other payables has been completely swamped by the long-term financing of a car.

On the other hand, Guide Co, by arranging a separate term loan, which is more secure from Guide Co's point of view, is able to run an **operating surplus** of $70 a month. It has effectively separated an operating surplus arising out of month to month business expenses from its cash requirements for capital investment (in the car), a **financial inflow**.

This goes to show therefore that:

(a) A 'surplus' can sometimes be created by the **way** in which **financial information is presented**
(b) It is often necessary to **distinguish different kinds of cash transaction** (eg capital payments)
(c) **Different types of debt** have **different risks** for the company attached to them

BPP
LEARNING
MEDIA

2 Budgeting for surpluses

> A company has a variety of opportunities for using its **cash surpluses**, but the choice of obtaining a
> return is determined by considerations of **profitability**, **liquidity** and **safety**.

2.1 What should be done with a cash surplus?

In asking what a business should do with a cash surplus, we should ask why a business needs cash.

(a)   Firstly, a business needs cash to meet its **regular commitments** of paying its suppliers, its
       employees' wages, its taxes, its annual dividends to shareholders and so on. This reason for
       holding cash is called the **transactions motive**.

(b)   Cash is also needed to create a safety buffer to cover unforeseen contingencies. He names this
       the **precautionary motive**. In the context of a business, this buffer may be provided by an
       overdraft facility, which has the advantage that it will cost nothing until it is actually used.

(c)   The third motive for holding cash is the **speculative motive**. However, most businesses do not
       hold surplus cash as a speculative asset (eg in the hope that interest rates will rise).

The **cash management policy** of a business will reflect its **strategic position**. Thus, if a company is
planning future major **non-current asset purchases**, or if it is planning to **acquire another business**, it
will consider whether any cash surplus should be retained and invested in marketable securities until it
is needed. If a company has no plans to grow or to invest, then surplus cash not required for
transactions or precautionary purposes should be returned to shareholders.

Surplus cash may be returned to shareholders by:

*   Increasing the usual level of the **annual dividends** which are paid
*   Making a one-off **special dividend payment**
*   Using the money to **buy back its own shares** from some of its shareholders

2.1.1 How much cash will a business require for transactions and precautionary purposes?

A number of mathematical cash management models have been developed to try to establish a
theoretical basis to the idea of an optimal cash balance. Many larger companies use such models in
practice. For the medium-sized or smaller business, deciding how to manage cash balances is more
often a matter left to the judgement and skill of the financial manager, in the light of the cashflow
forecast. Once an 'optimal' cash balance is established, the remainder of a surplus should be invested in
marketable securities.

2.1.2 Investing surplus cash

A business's management of cash should be conducted with **liquidity**, **safety** and **profitability** as the
three considerations in mind. Cash is an asset of a business; if it is to be invested, and it must be
invested profitably, the investment must be secure.

Banks provide one avenue for investment, but larger firms can invest in other forms of financial
instrument in the money markets. Types of short-term investments and the associated risks/returns are
considered within the remaining sections of this chapter.

EXAM FOCUS POINT

Specific types of investment are likely to be examined:

*   Bank deposits
*   Money-market deposits
*   Certificates of deposit
*   Government stock
*   Local authority stock

QUESTION   Profitability

Compare the following two situations. Nisar and Debbie are both in the car repair business. Both own equipment worth $4,000 and both owe $200 to suppliers. Nisar, however, has accumulated $1,000 in cash which is deposited in a non interest bearing current account at his bank. Debbie has $100 in petty cash.

	Nisar	Debbie
	$	$
Non-current assets	4,000	4,000
Cash at bank	1,000	100
Payables	(200)	(200)
Net assets	4,800	3,900
Profit for the year	1,200	1,200

Which would you say is the more profitable?

ANSWER

Both obviously have made the **same amount of profit** in the year in question. In absolute terms they are equal.

However, if we examine more closely, we find that the relative performance of Nisar and Debbie differs.

	Nisar	Debbie
Profit	$1,200	$1,200
Net assets	$4,800	$3,900
%	25	30.7

In other words, Debbie is making the same amount out of more limited resources. Nisar could have easily increased his profit if he had invested his spare cash and earned interest on it.

2.2 Guidelines for investing

Any business will normally have a number of guidelines as to how the funds are invested. A firm will try and maximise the **return** for an **acceptable level** of **risk**. What is acceptable depends on the preferences of the firm in question.

There is generally held to be a relationship between **risk** and **return**. Generally speaking, a **higher return** involves a **higher risk**. A risk of an investment is its propensity to fluctuate in value.

(a)   **Shares**. The price of shares on the stock market can 'go down as well as up'. For example, on Day 1 you might have paid $100 for shares which on Day 2 had fallen in value to $90, whereas on Day 3 their value might have increased to $120.

(b)   **Deposit**. The amount of money you deposit in your bank account will not change, ie $100 will still be $100, and there will be an amount of accrued interest.

To maintain liquidity, it is often company policy that the surplus funds should be invested in financial instruments which are easily converted into cash; in effect, enough of the surplus funds should be invested to **maintain liquidity**. Some investments are much more liquid than others – one that is highly liquid will generally attract a lower return.

There have been a number of reported incidents where a firm's corporate treasury department took too many risks with the firm's funds, investing them in risky financial instruments to gain a profit. These went sour, and firms have been left with large losses, arising solely out of treasury operations, with little relevance to the firm's main business.

Another consideration is the **maturity** (length or duration) of the investment. A longer maturity will generally provide a higher return.

Guidelines can cover issues such as the following:

(a)   Surplus funds can only be invested in **specified types of investment** (eg no equity shares).

(b)   All investments must be **convertible** into cash within a set number of days.

(c)   Investments should be **ranked**: surplus funds to be invested in higher risk instruments when only a sufficiency has been invested in lower risk items (so that there is always a cushion of safety).

(d)   If a firm invests in certain financial instruments, a **credit rating** should be obtained. Credit rating agencies, discussed in a later chapter, issue gradings according to risk.

2.3 Legal restrictions on investments

The type of investments an organisation can make is restricted by law in certain special cases:

(a)   Where public (ie taxpayers') money is invested by a **public sector** (central or local government) institution

(b)   Where the money is invested by a company on behalf of personal investors in cases such as **pension schemes**

(c)   In the case of **trusts**

2.4 Investment by public sector organisations

Public sector organisations are subject to various rules affecting the ways in which they can handle cash, and how they can invest any surplus funds that they have.

One example of UK legislation is *The Local Authorities (Capital Finance) (Approved Investments) Regulations 2015* which govern the investment policy of **local authorities**. These regulations ensure that local authorities choose investments that give **safe and easy access** to cash rather than high interest. This used to mean that authorities were restricted to **government securities** and **high-street bank** and **building societies**. Recent changes in the rules have also allowed authorities access to a **deposit facility** run by the treasury and commercially run **money market funds** with the highest level of creditworthiness.

3   Cash investments: bank deposit accounts

Surplus funds can be deposited in **interest bearing accounts** offered by banks, finance houses or building societies. Generally speaking:

*   These are for a fixed period of time
*   Withdrawal may not be permitted, or may result in a penalty
*   The principal does not decline in monetary value

Before looking at different forms of cash investment, let us be clear on the point about comparing rates of interest.

(a)   If interest on an account is paid more frequently than annually, the annual return is higher than available from an account paying interest at the same rate at the end of each year. This is because some interest can be earned in the year on the interest which is paid before the end of the year.

(b)   A comparison can be made between such accounts by calculating the **compound annual rate of interest** (CAR).

If x% interest is paid n times per year, then the compound annual rate of interest is given by the following.

$$CAR = \left(\left(1+\frac{x}{n}\right)^n -1\right) \times 100$$

For example, Account A offers 5.3% gross payable annually, while Account B offers 5.25% gross, payable quarterly. The CAR for B is:

$$\left(\left(1+\frac{0.0525}{4}\right)^4 - 1\right) \times 100 = 5.35\%$$

This is higher than the annual return on Account A.

Interest rates on cash investments may or may not vary, depending on the terms of the account.

3.1 High street bank deposits

All of the retail 'High Street' banks offer a wide range of different types of interest earning account, the variety having increased in recent years in competition with the building societies. The main clearers and many building societies also pay interest on some types of current account.

For someone who wishes to invest a small sum for a short period, **deposit account** facilities are available from the banks. However, the interest rate is relatively low, and many of these accounts are now being discontinued.

High interest deposit accounts and high interest cheque accounts. If you have a larger amount of money to invest, you can place the money in a high interest account. Access is usually still immediate, but the rate of interest offered will be higher.

Option deposits. These arrangements are for predetermined periods of time ranging from two to seven years with minimum deposits. The interest rates, which may be linked to base rates, reflect the longer term nature of the arrangement and the corresponding lack of withdrawal facilities before the expiry of the agreed term. For businesses, these might be of limited relevance.

3.2 Finance company deposits

All of the larger finance companies will accept cash deposits for varying periods from seven days upwards. Most of them insist on a minimum deposit but they do pay a higher rate of interest than for basic bank deposits. Finance companies are involved in lending of above average risk.

QUESTION
Risk and return

Lending by finance companies is of above average risk. What level of return would you expect from depositing money with a finance company?

○   A slightly lower return than average
○   An average return
○   A slightly higher return than average
○   A significantly higher return than average

ANSWER

A slightly higher return than average, ie a slightly higher return than offered by a bank: risk and reward are related.

3.3 Risks and returns

Bank deposits are considered to be **low risk**. The investor's initial capital is secure and the company can not receive back less than it puts in. For this reason, interest rates are not attractive to companies that regularly have surplus cash as returns are low.

4 Money-market deposits

Money-market deposit accounts are either **fixed term** or **notice** accounts. The customer agrees to deposit money either for a fixed period, or a notice period and the money is then invested in stocks and bonds.

A **money-market deposit account** (MMDA) is a deposit account offered by a bank which invests in stocks and bonds. The bank pays the depositor interest based on current interest rates in the money markets.

4.1 A background to money-market deposits

Money-market deposit accounts are either fixed term or notice accounts which pay interest based on current interest rates in the money markets. The customer agrees to deposit money either for a **fixed period**, or a **notice period**. These accounts typically pay a higher rate of interest and require a higher minimum balance.

4.2 Risks and returns

Money-market deposits can offer a reasonable return. Investments in **money-market notice accounts** are typically liquid meaning that funds can usually be withdrawn within a few business days. Investors can also take advantage of rising interest rates by keeping funds in an investment that will adjust to the money markets.

There are a number of risks associated with money-market deposits. Most MMDAs require the depositor to deposit a minimum amount.

Money-market deposit rates are variable. In other words, companies do not know how much they will earn on their investment from month to month.

There may be restrictions on the number of transactions that can be made in a month.

A final risk with money-market deposits is due to inflation. Because money-market deposits are considered to be safer than other investments like stocks, long term average returns on money-market deposits tends to be less than long term average returns on riskier investments. Over long periods of time, inflation can eat away at returns.

5 Certificates of deposit

A **certificate of deposit** is a certificate indicating that a sum of money has been deposited with a bank and will be repaid at a later date. As CDs can be bought and sold, they are a liquid type of investment.

A **certificate of deposit (CD)** is a negotiable instrument in bearer form. In other words, it is a certificate which can be bought and sold. Title belongs to the holder and ownership is transferred by physical delivery from buyer to seller.

Certificates of deposit (CDs) are issued by an institution (bank or building society), certifying that a specified sum has been deposited with the issuing institution, to be repaid on a specific date. The term may be as short as seven days, or as long as five years. Most are for a term of six months.

Since CDs are negotiable, if the holder of a CD cannot wait until the end of the term of the deposit and wants cash immediately, the CD can be sold. The certificates of deposit market is one of the London money markets, and there is no difficulty for a CD holder to sell if the wish to do so arises.

5.1 Risks and returns

The appeal of a CD is that it offers an **attractive rate of interest, and** can be **easily sold**. CDs are sold on the market at a discount which reflects prevailing interest rates.

The document recognises the obligation of the amount to the **bearer** (with or without interest) at a future date. The holder of a certificate is therefore entitled to the money on deposit, usually with **interest**, on the stated date. Payment is obtained by presenting the CD on the appropriate date to a recognised bank (which will in turn present the CD for payment to the bank or building society that issued it).

CDs have one major advantage over a **money-market fixed deposit** with the same bank or building society, namely **liquidity**. Unlike a money market fixed deposit which cannot be terminated until it matures, CDs can be liquidated **at any time** at the prevailing market rate.

There is a large and active **secondary market** in bank and building society CDs. Hence they are an ideal way to invest funds in the short term while retaining the flexibility to convert into cash at short notice if the need arises.

Buyers of CDs in the secondary market are banks and other companies or institutions wishing to invest at money market rates. They are attracted by the competitive rates of interest on a CD, the comparatively low credit risk (of the bank failing to repay the deposit with interest at maturity) and the continuing liquidity of CDs, which can be resold any number of times before maturity.

6   UK government stock

Gilts are securities issued by the UK government.

The term **gilts** is short for 'gilt-edged securities' and refers to marketable British Government securities. These **stocks**, although small in number (around 100), dominate the fixed interest market. Most gilts have a face value of £100, at which the government promises to buy the gilt back on a specific future date.

The *Financial Times* classifies gilts as follows.

(a)   Shorts – lives up to 5 years.

(b)   Mediums – lives from 5 to 15 years.

(c)   Longs – lives of more than 15 years.

(d)   Undated stocks. Issued many years ago these are sometimes known as irredeemable or one-way option stocks. These include War Loan $3^1/_2$%, Conversion Loan $3^1/_2$%, Consolidated Stock $2^1/_2$%. Each has certain other peculiarities.

(e)   Index-linked stocks.

By 'life' is meant the number of years before the issuer repays the principal amount.

6.1 Fixed interest gilts

Most gilts are fixed interest, and their prices and yields follow the principles outlined above. There are some other types of gilt, outlined below.

6.2 Index-linked stocks

There are various **index-linked Treasury stocks** in issue. Both the interest and the eventual redemption value are linked to inflation.

The half yearly interest payment is calculated on the basis of the value of the Retail Prices Index eight months before the interest payment date. Thus if a 2% index-linked stock was issued 8 months after the index had stood at 100 and the index stood at 150 eight months before a particular interest payment date, then the interest payable would be:

BPP
LEARNING
MEDIA

Interest payable = ½ × $\frac{150}{100}$ × 2% = 1.5%

The ½ is needed as the **interest is payable half-yearly**. The redemption value is similarly indexed.

These gilts offer a **guaranteed real return** equal to the coupon rate. Many investment fund managers would have considered such a return highly satisfactory over the last 15 years.

6.3 Risks and returns

Government stocks are about as safe an investment as you can get. There is no risk of default and their relatively short maturity means that the prices are relatively stable. Whilst interest can be fixed (fixed interest gilts), returns are ultimately low.

7 UK local authority stocks

> **Local authority stocks** may be issued by any size of authority from County Councils to Borough Councils.

We have already mentioned that it is possible for investors to deposit their money with local authorities. In addition to these investments there are a very large number of marketable local authority securities. Stocks may be issued by any size of authority from County Councils to Borough Councils.

Some of the **local authority stocks** are issued with long lives and there are several one way option stocks and even a handful of genuinely irredeemable stocks.

7.1 Risks and returns

Local authority stocks may, in most respects, be considered as being very similar to British Government Stocks. The main differences are that:

(a) The **security** of a local authority is **not** considered quite **as good** as that of the central government; and

(b) The **market** in most of the stocks is much **thinner** (ie there are not many transactions) than for gilts, since the amounts involved are smaller and the stocks tend to be held by just a few institutions.

As a result of the points listed above, the return on local authority stocks tends to be rather higher than on gilts.

In addition to the longer term loan stocks, many local authorities issue bonds which are redeemable after one or two years. These are commonly known as **yearlings**.

8 Risk and exposure

> The relative attractiveness of any of these investments derives from their **return** and the **risk**. **Diversification** across a range of separate investments can reduce risk for the investor.

All investments possess some degree of **risk**. In some cases this may be very small indeed.

(a) Those **investments with the lowest risk** are, perhaps, fixed interest National Savings plans. Any chance that the British government might default on the payment of interest or capital is exceedingly remote. For all practical purposes, such investments are risk-free in money terms. There is, however, a real risk that both income and capital values may be eroded by inflation.

(b) At the other extreme many forms of investment are **highly speculative**. Indeed some tactics such as selling shares you do not own, have a theoretically **unlimited downside potential**.

8.1 Effects of risk

We have considered the risks and returns relating to short-term investments in the previous sections. Risk may be considered in terms of its effect on income, capital or both.

(a)   **Income only**

For most cash investments there is virtually no risk that the **capital** invested will not be repaid. Also while there may be little doubt that the interest will be paid, those cash investments which carry a **variable rate of interest** also carry the risk that the rate will fall in line with conditions prevailing in the market.

(b)   **Capital only**

With an investment in gilts or other 'undoubted' marketable fixed interest stocks, there is always a risk of a capital loss if prices fall, even though the payment of interest may be considered completely secure.

(c)   **Capital and income**

For many investments both income and capital are at risk. Often a loss of income will precede a loss of capital. A company may reduce its ordinary share dividend, precipitating a fall in the share price.

Risk may be caused by general factors, or by factors specific to an individual security or sector.

(a)   **General factors**

All investments are affected, to some extent, by changes in the political and economic climate.

(b)   **Inflation**

A fall in the value of money may affect both income and capital. Cash and other non-equity investments are particularly susceptible, although the high yield may provide some compensation.

(c)   **Special factors**

The results of an individual company will be affected not only by general economic conditions but also by:

(i)   Its type of products or services
(ii)   Its competitive position within the industry
(iii)   Management factors

8.2 The relationship between risk and return

The return expected by an investor will depend on the level of risk. The higher the risk, the higher the required return. This can be illustrated as in the diagram below.

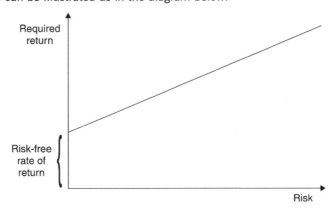

Marketable UK securities can be ranked in order of increasing risk and increasing expected return.

- Government stocks
- Local authority stocks
- Other 'public' corporation stocks
- Company mortgage loan stocks
- Other secured loans
- Unsecured loans
- Convertible loan stocks
- Preference shares
- Equities

Low risk

High risk

The riskiness of certificates of deposit varies with the **creditworthiness of the issuers**. They are riskier than government (and probably local government) securities, but less risky than shares.

What combination of risk and return is appropriate? Given that an investor is faced with a range of investments with differing risk/return combinations, what sort of investment should he choose? This is very difficult question to answer. Whilst most investors are risk-averse (they prefer less risk to more risk, given the same return), the intensity of that aversion varies between individuals. Some are quite happy to take a bit of a gamble in the hope of achieving a higher return.

CHAPTER ROUNDUP

⤷ Companies may face situations where they have a **cash deficit**. In such a scenario, appropriate action must be taken if the company is to continue to trade on a day-to-day basis.

⤷ Companies may sometimes have **cash surpluses**. The surplus needs to be used in the best way, and this will often mean **investing** it.

⤷ A company has a variety of opportunities for using its **cash surpluses**, but the choice of obtaining a return is determined by considerations of **profitability**, **liquidity** and **safety**.

⤷ Surplus funds can be deposited in **interest bearing accounts** offered by banks, finance houses or building societies. Generally speaking:

– These are for a fixed period of time.
– Withdrawal may not be permitted, or may result in a penalty.
– The principal does not decline in monetary value.

⤷ Money-market deposit accounts are either **fixed term** or **notice** accounts. The customer agrees to deposit money either for a fixed period, or a notice period and the money is then invested in stocks and bonds.

⤷ A **certificate of deposit** is a certificate indicating that a sum of money has been deposited with a bank and will be repaid at a later date. As CDs can be bought and sold, they are a liquid type of investment.

⤷ **Gilts** are securities issued by the UK government.

⤷ **Local authority stocks** may be issued by any size of authority from County Councils to Borough Councils.

⤷ The relative attractiveness of any of these investments derives from their **return** and the **risk**. **Diversification** across a range of separate investments can reduce risk for the investor.

QUICK QUIZ

1 Which of the following UK securities is considered the least risky?

○ Government securities
○ Secured loans
○ Convertible loan notes
○ Preference shares

2 What are gilts?

3 What is meant by a yearling?

4 What advantage does a certificate of deposit have over a time deposit?

○ Profitability
○ Maturity
○ Security
○ Liquidity

5 What factors affect the riskiness of investments?

6 Local authority stocks are considered riskier than equities.

○ True
○ False

 BPP LEARNING MEDIA

ANSWERS TO QUICK QUIZ

1   Government securities. Government securities are considered to be the least risky.

2   Marketable British Government securities

3   A local authority bond redeemable after one or two years

4   Liquidity. A CD can be liquidated at any time at the prevailing market rate.

5   (a)   Market sentiment about the general political and economic climate
    (b)   The rate of inflation, and the future outlook for inflation
    (c)   Factors relating to the products, competitive position and management of the enterprise

6   False.

Now try ...

Attempt the questions below from the **Practice Question Bank**

Number

Q97

Q98

Q99

For many businesses, **banks** are an important source of cash to meet **operational cash flow needs** and also a **source of finance for medium-term investments**.

Banks will only lend money when they are satisfied that they will be repaid with interest. There is risk for the banks, **and banks will assess the risk before deciding whether to agree to lend, and what the interest rate should be**.

This chapter describes the lending criteria that management should consider when they ask for bank finance, and compares the main forms of bank lending, overdrafts, revolving credit and loans.

Raising finance from a bank

Study Guide	Intellectual level
E **Cash management**	
4 **Investing and financing**	
(c) Explain different ways of raising finance from a bank and the basic terms and conditions associated with each financing	K

1 Introduction

Short- and **medium-term finance** may come from a **variety of sources**. It is important to decide which is most appropriate for a given situation.

In this chapter we shall be looking at how businesses obtain money for their short- and medium-term needs.

The bank is a **key provider of finance.** We therefore concentrate on the attitude the bank might take to requests for funds and the most important features of bank overdraft and loan financing. Comparison of overdraft and loan financing will be very important for exam purposes.

As well as understanding what finance a bank can provide, you also need to know about the **legal relationship** between a bank and its customers.

Remember when you're reading this chapter, that as well as describing what finance sources are available, you need to consider their **suitability**. You must therefore be aware of the advantages and disadvantages, and with these in mind, be able to **recommend** the best source of finance in a specific set of circumstances.

Like other chapters, we look at the UK as exemplar of other systems around the world.

2 Budgeting for borrowings

Companies often have to rely on **bank finance**; the right type of finance should be obtained.

As far as borrowing is concerned, there are three aspects to the **maintenance of liquidity**.

(a) The firm needs enough money to **function operationally**, pay salaries, suppliers and so on. Of course, eventually it will receive funds from customers, but the length of the cash cycle can mean reliance on **overdraft finance** at times.

(b) The firm also needs to **minimise the risk** that some of its sources of finance will be removed from it.

(c) The firm also needs to **provide** against the **contingency** of any sudden movements in cash. Contingency measures can take the form of special arrangements with the bank, insurance policies and so on.

Some of these needs are more pressing than others.

(a) **Working capital**. Working capital is often financed by overdraft – this is a result of lagged payments and receipts as discussed earlier and the willingness of businesses to offer credit.

(b) **Long-term finance** is used for major investments. Capital expenditure is easier to put off than, say, wages in a crisis, but a long-term failure to invest can damage the business and reduce its capacity.

(c) Thirdly, the borrowing might be required to **finance assets overseas**, in which case the **currency** of the borrowing might be important.

Bank borrowing can be obtained in the following ways:

- **Overdraft**. A company, through its current account, can borrow money on a short-term basis up to a certain amount. Overdrafts are repayable on demand.

- **Term loan**. The customer borrows a fixed amount and pays it back with interest over a period or at the end of it.

- **Committed facility**. The bank undertakes to make a stipulated amount available to a borrower, on demand.

- **Revolving facility**. A facility that is renewed after a set period. Once the customer has repaid the amount, the customer can borrow again.

- **Uncommitted facility**. The bank, if it feels like it, can lend the borrower a specified sum. The only purpose of this is that all the paperwork has been done up front. The bank has no obligation to lend.

- **Banker's acceptance facilities**. This relates to bills of exchange that a bank agrees to accept. Bills of exchange, when accepted, are a legal obligation to make a payment. A bank may agree to accept bills drawn on it by the payables of a customer, and it then undertakes to make the payment of the bill on behalf of the customer. The customer must then repay the bank (with interest/charges). Bank bills are often used in foreign trade, when foreign suppliers will agree to payment by means of a bank bill arrangement, when they are not prepared to give trade credit to the buyer.

3 The bank/customer relationship

Several types of **contractual relationship** may exist between bank and customer.

3.1 Receivable/payable relationship

The customer deposits his/her money with the bank. These funds go into the customer's account and can be withdrawn at any time. **The bank is the receivable** (for the money owed to the customer) and the **customer is the payables**. However, there are circumstances where this relationship can be reversed. If a customer borrows from a bank, for example if the customer's account is overdrawn, then the customer owes money to the bank and is a receivable of the bank.

3.2 Mortgagor/mortgagee relationship

This relationship can come into being when the bank asks a customer to secure a loan by a charge or mortgage over assets such as property. If the customer defaults, and fails to pay interest or repay the loan capital when payment is due, the bank may have the right to take control of the secured asset(s), and possibly sell them off in order to repay the money it is owed. When a loan is secured, the borrower is the **mortgagor**, giving security for the loan, while the bank is the **mortgagee**, lending on the basis of the security provided.

3.3 Fiduciary relationship

If one of the parties in a relationship based on trust is in an influential position, then that person could exert **undue influence** to make the other party enter into a contract. The law therefore expects the 'superior' party in the relationship to act in **good faith**. It is said to be a **fiduciary relationship**. The law expects banks to act with **utmost good faith**, particularly where the bank is advising the customer.

3.4 Maintaining a good relationship with the bank

The Treasury department of a firm should maintain appropriate relationships with the firm's bank (or banks, if the firm maintains more than one bank account). Maintaining a good relationship involves the following:

(a) **Maintaining** the **value of any security** which is pledged to secure a loan

(b) **Informing the bank** as to the **progress of the business**, especially its demands for cash (Forecasts of expected future cash flow are often required for credit to be advanced.)

(c) **Only using the overdraft for appropriate financial needs** and within authorised limits

---

4 Banks' criteria for lending

> The principles of good lending (called the **canons of lending**) guide a bank's decision about whether or not to lend money. The bank wishes to ensure that the borrower will be able to make the scheduled repayments, in full and within the required period of time.

If the bank makes a loan which is not repaid, a bank's profits suffer in a number of ways:

- The expected interest from the loan is not earned.
- The amount advanced and not recoverable is written off as a bad debt.
- The costs of administering the account are much increased.
- There are legal costs in chasing the debt.

4.1 Lending criteria

When a business is trying to borrow from a bank, it is useful to think about what factors will influence the lending decision of the bank.

A bank's decision whether or not to lend will be based on several factors. These may be remembered by the mnemonic is **CAMPARI**.

Character of the customer
Ability to borrow and repay
Margin of profit
Purpose of the borrowing
Amount of the borrowing
Repayment terms
Insurance against the possibility of non-payment

EXAM FOCUS POINT

Lending criteria are a popular exam topic. Ensure that you remember the 'CAMPARI' mnemonic.

4.1.1 Character of the borrower

A bank will be more willing to lend to a customer whose character it trusts, because of the long-established history of the borrower, or the character of its top managers. The **character of the borrower** can be established and judged.

(a) The borrower's **past record** with the bank is examined.

(b) **Personal interviews** are mainly used for business lending.

(c) Personal lending is more often **credit scored** (by computer).

(d) In the case of a company, the bank may look at **key ratios** which indicate the company's performance.

4.1.2 Ability to borrow and repay

A bank will usually expect repayment of a business loan (or an overdraft to a business customer) from the normal operational cash flows of the business. If the net cash flows of a borrower are considered insufficient to meet the interest payments and capital repayments, the bank will usually not lend, even when there is good security for the loan. The bank will look at a business customer's **financial performance** as an indication of **future trends**. Hopefully the loan will be invested in such a way as to generate profit.

Re-investment of retained profits is a sign of the owner's faith in the business. (In other words, the owner does not take out all profits as dividends or drawings.)

Bankers scour financial statements for signs of: low/declining profitability; increased dependence on borrowing; overtrading; inadequate control over working capital; sudden provisions or allowances; delays.

Although a bank will use published accounts and management accounts, it will not lend *solely* on that basis: in other words the viability of the loan itself will be assessed.

A business wanting to borrow from a bank should be able to provide believable cash flow forecasts or profit forecasts that demonstrate its ability to repay the borrowed money.

4.1.3 Margin of profit

Remember, banks want to lend money to make money! The rate of interest that is charged will depend on the assessment of risk by the bank. The basic ruler is that if a bank is prepared to lend money, it will charge a higher rate of interest on loans or overdrafts that it considers to be more risky.

(a) **Fixed rates**

The lending policies of most banks stipulate different rates for different purposes to customers.

(b) **Discretionary rates**

The bank will decide on the return which it requires from the lending. A loan for a risky venture (such as a new business) will be offered at a higher rate of interest, so as to compensate the bank for the risk it takes that the lending will not be repaid, than a loan perceived to be of low risk.

4.1.4 Purpose of the borrowing

The borrower must specify the **purpose of the borrowing**, and the bank must be satisfied that the purpose of borrowing is satisfactory. Loans for certain purposes will normally not be granted at all. Some will be granted only on certain conditions.

(a) **Illegal loans**

A loan which is for an illegal purpose such as drug smuggling obviously must be refused.

(b) **Lending to finance working capital**

Lending money (usually on overdraft) to finance some of the working capital of a business is quite normal. However when the intended purpose of an advance is to finance a big increase in inventory or receivables, the bank will consider the liquidity of the business, and whether the customer will need more and more financial assistance from the bank as time goes on.

(c) **Loans for new business ventures**

A loan to set up a new business venture should be viewed in the context that all new ventures are risky; while many do succeed a considerable number of them fail to make profits and survive.

The purpose of the loan will also help to determine the nature of the lending and its term. For example if a company needs to borrow in order to have cash to meet its day-to-day operational needs, the bank may be prepared to offer an overdraft facility, but not a medium-term loan.

BPP
LEARNING
MEDIA

4.1.5 Amount of the borrowing

The lending proposition must state exactly **how much** the customer wants to borrow. This might seem self-evident, but there are two important points to consider.

(a) The banker will check that the borrower is **not asking for too much**, or **more than is needed** for the particular purpose. This is especially important with requests for an overdraft facility. Clearly this consideration is linked in with the borrower's ability to repay.

(b) The banker checks that the borrower has not asked for **less than it** really **needs**. Otherwise the bank may later have to lend more, purely to safeguard the original advance.

The bank's lending policy will indicate limits on the amount of certain loans and the amount which must be paid 'up front' by the borrower. For example, a bank may be willing to lend $2 million to help a company buy new premises, but only if the customer will contribute $1 million of its own money towards the full cost of $3 million.

4.1.6 Repayment terms

The likelihood that the **advance** will be **repaid** is the most important requirement for a loan. A bank should not lend money to a person or business who has not got the resources to repay it with interest, even if it also has **security** for the loan. Security for the loan gives the lender the right to take certain assets if the borrower defaults. Security is only a **safety net**, to be called upon only in the event of an unfortunate and unexpected inability to repay.

The timescale for repayment is very important. Overdrafts are technically repayable **on demand** (though it is rare for a bank to insist on this without first having discussed a different timescale for repayment). Other loans might be payable in instalments, especially medium-term loans to acquire assets.

4.1.7 Insurance against the possibility of non-payment

If a bank **needs** to take **insurance** against the possibility that the loan will not be repaid (in the form of security, such as title deeds or a life policy) then the loan should not be made – as stated above, **security** is only a safety net.

4.2 Security for lending

The **security for a loan** should have the following characteristics.

(a) **Easy to take**

The bank will want to have, or to obtain easily, title to the secured property so that it may be sold and the loan repaid.

(b) **Easy to value**

The security should have an **identifiable value** which:

(i) Is stable or increasing; and
(ii) Fully covers the lending plus a margin.

You can see this most clearly when banks and building societies refuse to lend more than, say, 95% of the value of a house. It has (at the time of lending) a margin of safety of 5%.

(c) **Easy to realise**

The ideal security is one which can readily be sold and converted to cash. Banks prefer readily realisable security because:

(i) The **administrative costs** are thereby **kept** to a **minimum**

(ii) There is **less danger of deterioration** (say, of premises) between the time of default and that of realisation

(iii) A **quick pay-off reduces the length of time** over which **interest accrues** on the unpaid advance

For business borrowers, security may take the form of a fixed charge over specific assets of the borrower, or a 'floating charge' over all its assets.

4.3 Personal guarantees

A business is a separate entity from the person who owns it for accounting purposes. It is also a principle of company law that in most cases the liability of shareholders for the debts of a company is limited to the capital they contributed. The debts of a business clearly include bank loans and overdrafts. However, in practice, it is often the case that, in its search for security, the bank will ensure that a business loan is supported by a **personal guarantee** from the owner of the business. Such requirements are therefore mainly a concern of smaller or medium sized businesses, largely run by their owners.

For example, Mr Badger is Managing Director of Setts Co. Setts Co has an overdraft arrangement with the bank, but Mr Badger has to give a personal guarantee of the overdraft. This means that if Setts Co fails to pay its debt **to the bank**, the bank can call in the guarantee, and Mr Badger will have to pay the debt out of his own resources.

QUESTION

Loan application

Grog Co is a wholesaler, selling alcoholic beverages to shopkeepers for resale to the general public. Grog Co has a large warehouse at Ponders End, North London. Its cash cycle is such that most of the time it makes a cash surplus but recently a number of thefts and unexplained account movements have reduced the size of the surplus. The managing director, Lil Drop, has recently decided that she wants to move house. Rather than take out a mortgage, she suggests to the bank that the company borrows money, on overdraft, to buy her a house. She will personally guarantee the loan, although at the moment her only asset she can pledge as security is a port wine making firm in Portugal, which she inherited from a great aunt: other members of the family are suing her for a share. What chance do you think Grog Co has of obtaining the loan?

ANSWER

The banker will pour himself a glass of CAMPARI, as it were, and say no. Lil Grog can pledge **no security**, and the purpose of the loan is **not for business reasons**. Furthermore, Grog Co's ability to repay looks increasingly in doubt.

5 Overdrafts and revolving credit facilities

Overdrafts are subject to an agreed limit, and are repayable on demand. The customer has a flexible means of short-term borrowing. An overdraft is best considered as **support for normal working capital**. A customer's account can be expected to swing between surplus and overdraft. Banks will look cautiously at overdrafts which are used to purchase non-current assets.

Where payments from a current account exceed income to the account for a temporary period, the bank finances the deficit by means of an **overdraft**. It is very much a form of **short-term lending**, available to both personal and business customers.

5.1 Overdraft considerations

Factors associated with an overdraft are as follows.

(a) **Amount**

The debit amount should not exceed a certain limit agreed between the bank and the borrower, usually with reference to known income.

(b) **Margin**

Interest is charged on the amount overdrawn, usually as a margin over base rate. Interest is calculated on the daily amount overdrawn and is charged to the account quarterly. A fee may also be levied where the bank has agreed a large facility with the customer, even where this facility is not fully used.

(c) **Purpose**

Overdrafts are usually required to cover short-term deficits: for instance, many people run short at the end of each month before their salaries are paid in.

(d) **Repayment**

Overdrafts are technically repayable on demand and it is usual in the facility letter to make this plain to the customer.

(e) **Security**

Depending on the size of the facility open to the customer, security may be required by the bank.

(f) **Benefits**

The borrower has a flexible means of short term borrowing; the bank has to accept the fluctuation in the account.

By providing an overdraft facility to a customer, the bank is committing itself to provide an overdraft to the customer whenever the customer wants it, up to the agreed limit.

5.1.1 The cost of an overdraft facility

The bank will charge interest on the lending, but only to the extent that the customer **uses the facility** and goes into overdraft. If the customer does not go into overdraft, the bank cannot charge interest.

However the bank will usually charge a **commitment fee** when a customer is granted an overdraft facility or an increase in the overdraft facility. This is a fee for granting an overdraft facility and agreeing to provide the customer with funds if and whenever they need them. It may be set at a percentage amount of the total overdraft facility.

5.2 Overdrafts and the working capital cycle

Many businesses require their bank to provide financial assistance for normal trading over the working capital **cycle**.

For example, suppose that a business has the following working capital cycle.

	$	$
Inventories and receivables		10,000
Bank overdraft	1,000	
Payables	3,000	
		4,000
Working capital		6,000

It now buys inventories costing $2,500 for cash, using its overdraft. Working capital remains the same, $6,000, although the bank's financial stake has risen from $1,000 to $3,500.

	$	$
Inventories and receivables		12,500
Bank overdraft	3,500	
Payables	3,000	
		6,500
Working capital		6,000

A bank overdraft provides support for normal trading finance. In this example, finance for normal trading rises from $(10,000 – 3,000) = $7,000 to $(12,500 – 3,000) = $9,500 and the bank's contribution rises from $1,000 out of $7,000 to $3,500 out of $9,500.

A feature of bank lending to support normal trading finance is that the amount of the overdraft required at any time will depend on the **cash flows of the business** – the timing of receipts and payments, seasonal variations in trade patterns and so on. The purpose of the overdraft is to bridge the gap between cash payments and cash receipts.

When a business customer has an overdraft facility, and the account is always in overdraft, then it has a **solid core** (or **hard core**) instead of swing. For example, suppose that the account of Blunderbuss Co has the following record for the previous year:

Quarter to	Average balance $	Range $		$	Debit turnover $
31 March 20X5	40,000 debit	70,000 debit	–	20,000 debit	600,000
30 June 20X5	50,000 debit	80,000 debit	–	25,000 debit	500,000
30 September 20X5	75,000 debit	105,000 debit	–	50,000 debit	700,000
31 December 20X5	80,000 debit	110,000 debit	–	60,000 debit	550,000

These figures show that the account has been permanently in overdraft, and the hard core of the overdraft has been rising steeply over the course of the year.

If the hard core element of the overdraft appears to be becoming a long-term feature of the business, the bank might wish, after discussions with the customer, to convert the hard core of the overdraft into a medium-term loan, thus giving formal recognition to its more permanent nature. Otherwise annual reductions in the hard core of an overdraft would typically be a requirement of the bank.

5.3 The purpose of an advance for day-to-day trading

The purpose of a bank overdraft for normal day-to-day trading is to help with the financing of current assets. However, there are a number of different reasons why a business might need an overdraft facility. Only **some** of these reasons will be sound and acceptable to a bank.

Borrowing by a business will either **increase the assets of the business**; or **decrease its liabilities**.

5.4 Increasing business assets

If borrowing is to increase the business assets, a bank will first check whether the purpose is to acquire more **non-current assets** or more **current assets**. There is nothing wrong with asking a bank for financial assistance with the purchase of non-current assets. But borrowing to purchase a non-current asset reduces the liquidity of the business, and might even make it illiquid.

An overdraft facility for **day-to-day trading** should therefore be:

- Either to **increase total current assets**
- Or to **reduce other current liabilities**

5.5 Increasing total current assets

A request for an overdraft facility to increase total current assets can be pinpointed more exactly, to a wish by the company:

- To increase its inventory levels
- To increase its overall receivables
- To increase its overall sales turnover

The underlying guide to a bank's attitude to lending (in addition to avoiding risk) is whether the finance will be temporary (and 'swinging') or longer term.

There might be a number of reasons for a business **increasing its inventory levels** without increasing its total sales.

(a) The business might have received a large, firm order from a customer, and must produce goods to order before the customer will pay for them. The need for finance is only **temporary**, and a bank overdraft would be suitable.

BPP
LEARNING
MEDIA

(b)   The business might wish to build up inventories in anticipation of a seasonal peak demand. Again the business will need **temporary** finance to support the cost of the inventories, and again, an overdraft would be a suitable form of finance.

(c)   The business might want to make a **speculative** purchase of inventories – for example to take advantage of an opportunity to purchase a consignment of raw materials at a favourable price. Provided that the 'speculative' nature of the inventory build-up is not unacceptably risky, and provided that the build-up is **temporary**, an overdraft would again be a suitable form of finance.

(d)   The business might be building up its inventory levels **permanently**, without increasing its sales turnover. In such a situation, there would be a danger that some inventories are becoming **slow-moving or unsaleable** through deteriorating quality or obsolescence. A build-up of inventory also implies a need for a review of finance facilities, and an overdraft may **not** be suitable.

Reasons for a business wanting to **increase its total receivables** without increasing its sales turnover might be:

(a)   A **loss of efficiency** in the **credit control**, invoicing and debt collection procedures of the business
(b)   The **inability** of existing customers **to pay** without being allowed more credit.

In both cases, the bank will be cautious about agreeing to an increased overdraft facility. Delays in invoicing should be eliminated by the business; however, if more credit must be allowed to maintain sales, a bank might agree to an overdraft facility for this purpose.

When a business **increases its sales turnover**, it will almost certainly have to increase its investment in inventories and receivables. It will probably be able to obtain more credit from suppliers, but the balance of the extra finance required will have to be provided out of extra proprietors' capital or other lending. A danger with business expansion is **overtrading**, and a bank will be wary of requests to support ambitious expansion schemes.

5.6 Using an overdraft to reduce other current liabilities

A bank might be asked to provide an overdraft facility to enable a business to pay its tax bills, or to reduce its volume of payables. The payment of tax might be sales tax/VAT (generally every quarter) or year end corporation tax. An overdraft facility to help a business to pay tax when it falls due is a 'legitimate' and acceptable purpose for an overdraft, although the bank might wish to know why the business had not set funds aside to pay the tax. A bank should be able to expect that the overdraft would soon be paid off out of profits from future trading.

An **extension** to an overdraft in order to pay suppliers must be for the purpose of **reducing the overall average volume of payables**, which in turn implies a significant change in the trade credit position of the business, all other things being equal. Why might such a reduction in total payables be required?

(a)   **To take advantage of attractive purchase discounts offered by suppliers for early settlement of debts**. This should be an acceptable purpose for an extra overdraft to a bank, because taking the discount would reduce the costs and so increase the profits of the business.

(b)   **To pay suppliers who are pressing for payment**. A bank will deal cautiously with such a request. It might be because the supplier is desperate for money. If the **business customer** is getting into difficulties, and is falling behind with paying their debts, a bank would take the view that agreeing to an increased overdraft would simply mean taking over debts that might one day never be paid, and so may not agree to such a proposition.

5.7 Revolving credit facility

A revolving credit facility is similar in many ways to a bank overdraft facility. The borrower agrees a maximum borrowing limit, and can borrow up to this limit. If a company has a revolving credit facility with a limit of $5 million, and it then borrows $2 million, it can borrow a further $3 million. If the company repays $500,000 of the borrowed $2 million, it can now borrow a further $3.5 million.

The main differences between an overdraft facility and a revolving credit facility are that:

(a) The borrowing limit is usually much higher for a revolving credit facility than for a bank overdraft, and a bank may therefore agree to provide revolving credit only to a large and well-established business.

(b) The revolving credit facility is for an agreed period of time (and may be renewed when it expires). In contrast an overdraft facility can be withdrawn at any time, at the option of the bank.

(c) With a revolving credit facility the bank charges interest on the amount borrowed and there is a facility fee or commitment fee charge on the amount of the facility that has not been borrowed.

6 Medium- and long-term loans

A **term loan** is drawn in full at the beginning of the loan period and repaid at a specified time or in defined instalments. Term loans are offered with a variety of **repayment schedules**. Often, the interest and capital repayments are predetermined. The term of the loan will be determined by the useful life of the asset purchased, the lending policies of the bank, and the outcome of any negotiations between the borrower and the bank.

Interest payments on a loan are based on the full amount borrowed. The loan is repayable not later than the date agreed in the loan agreement; or if the borrower breaks a 'loan covenant' at an earlier date.

6.1 The uses of loans

There are certain features about medium-term lending on loan account that make it different from lending on overdraft.

(a) The borrower knows what it will be **expected** to **pay back** at regular intervals and the bank can also predict its future income with more certainty (depending on whether the interest rate is fixed or floating).

(b) Once the loan is agreed, the **term of** the loan must be **adhered** to, provided that the borrower does not fall behind with its repayments. The amount borrowed (or outstanding amount yet to be repaid) is not repayable on demand by the bank.

(c) Bank loans may be for a period of several years, whereas overdraft facilities are usually renegotiated regularly, perhaps every year.

(d) Because the bank will be committing its funds to a borrower for a number of years, it may wish to insist on **building certain written safeguards** into the loan agreement, to prevent the borrower from becoming over-extended with their borrowing during the course of the loan. The most important safeguard is security. Many medium-term loans are secured against assets of the borrower, whereas overdrafts are normally unsecured.

(e) The interest rate on a bank loan may be fixed, whereas overdrafts are always charged at a variable rate of interest, so that the interest rate rises or falls with changes in the bank's base lending rate.

6.2 The term of the loan

The term of the loan will depend on four factors.

(a) The **length of the loan**, which should not exceed the **useful life of the asset** to be purchased, because the customer will presumably expect to repay the loan whilst he is still enjoying the use of the asset and any profits it might be earning

(b) The **internal guidelines** of the individual bank

(c) Government **regulations**, if any, on the maximum term for certain types of lending

(d) **Negotiations** between borrower and bank, which involve the opinion of the borrower about what term of loan it would like, and the bank's judgement about what term it is prepared to offer

6.3 Loan repayment profiles

Loans can be repaid in three ways.

(a) **Bullet**

The borrower does not repay any of the loan principal until the end of the loan period. The principal is then repaid in full. For example, if a five-year loan of $100,000 has a bullet repayment profile, the loan principal outstanding will be the full $100,000 to the end of the loan period.

(b) **Balloon**

Some of the loan principal is repaid during the term of the loan. At maturity, however, there is still a substantial proportion of loan principal outstanding, which is then repaid.

(c) **Amortising or straight repayment loan**

The loan principal is repaid gradually over the term of the loan. Loan repayments at regular intervals (usually every month, quarter or six months) consist of interest and a repayment of some of the principal. With the final loan payment, the principal outstanding falls to zero. Mortgage repayment loans operate on this principle.

A borrower should try to negotiate repayment terms that match the net cash flows that it expects to receive from using and investing the borrowed money. The key principle should be (as for the lending bank) that the borrower should be able to repay borrowing from the cash flows that the borrowed money generates.

6.4 Loan interest

The interest on a loan will either be paid back in fixed instalments with the capital as above; or be calculated at the set rate at the end of the balance period so that the bulk of the interest is paid early on (as in a repayment mortgage) or equally throughout the loan.

The interest rate on a loan can be:

(a) **Fixed** throughout the period of the loan

(b) **Variable**, depending on interest rates obtainable in the money markets. Variable rates are usually arranged as a specified number of percentage points above either base rate or above the benchmark rate at which banks lend to each other such as:

- SONIA (the Sterling overnight index average) in the UK

- ESTR (the Euro short-term rate) in Europe

- TONAR (Tokyo overnight average rate) in Japan

- SARON (Swiss overnight rate) in Switzerland

- SOFR (the secured overnight financing rate) in the US

In addition to the interest payable, a firm might have to pay:

- An **arrangement fee** to the bank, for considering the loan application
- **Legal costs**
- **Commitment fees**

QUESTION

Interest rate

What factors will a lender use to determine the interest rate charged to the borrower?

ANSWER

There are seven criteria used to determine the interest charge.

(a) The **level of risk** involved. Overdrafts tend to have higher rates than loans because there is uncertainty over the length of time the facility is required and when the debt will be repaid.

(b) The **level of interest rates in the economy.** Lenders rarely charge interest rates lower than the Bank of England base rate as this is the level of return they could receive elsewhere.

(c) The **status of the borrower**. Borrowers with poor credit histories are often charged a higher rate of interest.

(d) Any **security offered by the borrower**. Securing the loan on assets reduces the interest charge as the lender will take the asset as payment should the borrower default on the loan.

(e) The **amount of the loan**. Many lenders charge higher rates of interest when the loan advance is high as the repayments put a further financial burden on the borrower, increasing the risk of default.

(f) The **purpose of the loan**. Loans to finance working capital may attract different rates then those to finance new ventures due to the different perceived risk.

(g) The **duration of the loan**. Loans over longer periods tend to be viewed as more risky as there is a longer time span available for a borrower to default.

6.5 Loan covenants

Taking out a loan often entails certain obligations for the borrower over and above repaying the loan on demand. These obligations are called covenants.

(a) **Positive covenants** require a borrower to do something, for example:

   (i) Provide the bank with its annual financial statements
   (ii) Submit certificates that the company is keeping to the loan agreement
   (iii) Provide management accounts

(b) **Negative or restrictive covenants** are promises by a borrower not to do something, eg the company pledges not to borrow more money until the current loan is repaid.

(c) **Quantitative covenants** set limitations on the borrower's financial position. For example, the company might agree that its total borrowings shall not exceed 100% of shareholders' funds.

7 Overdrafts and loans compared

There are a number of **factors** to consider when deciding whether an overdraft or loan is more appropriate as the method of borrowing.

A borrower may ask the bank for an overdraft facility when the bank would wish to suggest a loan instead; alternatively, a borrower may ask for a loan when an overdraft would be more appropriate.

(a) In most cases, when a business borrower wants finance to help with **'day to day' trading** and cash flow needs, an **overdraft** is the appropriate method of financing. Cash needs fluctuate from day-to-day and season-to-season, and a business may need to borrow at some times of the day or week but not at others. The borrower should not be short of cash all the time, and should expect to be in credit on some days, but in need of an overdraft on others.

(b) When a borrower wants to **borrow** from a bank **for only a short period of time**, even for the purchase of a major non-current asset such as an item of plant or machinery, an overdraft facility might be more suitable than a loan, because the borrower will stop paying interest as soon as its account goes into credit. This situation is probably fairly uncommon in practice.

(c) When a borrower wants to borrow from a bank, but cannot see their way to repaying the bank except over the course of a few years, the **medium-term** nature of the financing is best catered for by the provision of a **loan** rather than an overdraft facility.

7.1 Advantages of an overdraft over a loan

(a)   The customer **only pays interest** when he is **overdrawn**.

(b)   The bank has the **flexibility** to review the customer's overdraft facility periodically, and perhaps agree to additional facilities, or insist on a reduction in the facility.

(c)   An overdraft can do the **same job** as a medium-term loan: a facility can simply be renewed every time it comes up for review.

Bear in mind, however, that overdrafts are normally repayable on demand.

7.2 Advantages of a medium-term loan for longer term lending

(a)   Both the borrower and the bank **know** exactly what the **repayments** of the loan will be and how much **interest** is payable, and when. This makes planning (budgeting) simpler for the borrower.

(b)   The borrower does **not** have to **worry** about the bank deciding to reduce or withdraw an overdraft facility before it is in a position to repay what is owed. There is an element of 'security' or 'peace of mind' in being able to arrange a loan for an agreed term.

(c)   Medium-term loans normally carry a **facility letter setting** out the precise terms of the agreement.

However, a **mix** of overdrafts and loans might be suggested in some cases. Consider a case where a business asks for a loan, perhaps to purchase a shop with a stock of goods included. The bank **might** wish to suggest a loan to help with the purchase of the shop, but that goods ought to be financed by an overdraft facility.

CHAPTER ROUNDUP

↳ **Short-** and **medium-term finance** may come from a **variety of sources**. It is important to decide which is most appropriate for a given situation.

↳ Companies often have to rely on **bank finance**; the right type of finance should be obtained.

↳ Several types of **contractual relationship** may exist between bank and customer.

↳ The principles of good lending (called the **canons of lending**) guide a bank's decision about whether or not to lend money. The bank wishes to ensure that the borrower will be able to make the scheduled repayments, in full and within the required period of time.

↳ **Overdrafts** are subject to an agreed limit, and are repayable on demand. The customer has a flexible means of short-term borrowing. An overdraft is best considered as **support for normal working capital**. A customer's account can be expected to swing between surplus and overdraft. Banks will look cautiously at overdrafts which are used to purchase non-current assets.

↳ A **term loan** is drawn in full at the beginning of the loan period and repaid at a specified time or in defined instalments. Term loans are offered with a variety of **repayment schedules**. Often, the interest and capital repayments are predetermined. The term of the loan will be determined by the useful life of the asset purchased, the lending policies of the bank, and the outcome of any negotiations between the borrower and the bank.

↳ There are a number of **factors** to consider when deciding whether an overdraft or loan is more appropriate as the method of borrowing.

QUICK QUIZ

1 Banks act as a link between borrowers and savers. What is this role called?

- O Financial intervention
- O Financial interposition
- O Financial intermediation
- O Financial interlineations

2 A bank's loan to a customer is secured by a charge on the customer's house. Who is the mortgagor and who is the mortgagee?

3 What is a fiduciary relationship?

4 List three rights and three duties of a banker.

5 A .... is a loan for a fixed amount for a specified period.

6 In the following mnemonic, concerning a bank's decision to lend (the 'canons of good lending'), what does each of the letters stand for?

C ....
A ....
M ....
P ....
A ....
R ....
I ....

7 How is the loan principal repaid in the case of a bullet repayment loan?

- O At the start of the loan period
- O By instalments that increase in value
- O By equal instalments during the loan period
- O At the end of the loan period

BPP LEARNING MEDIA

ANSWERS TO QUICK QUIZ

1   Financial intermediation

2   The customer is the mortgagor and the bank is the mortgagee.

3   A relationship based on trust in which the superior party must act in good faith

4   Examples of rights include: to levy reasonable charges and commissions; to use customer's money in a legal and morally acceptable way; and to be repaid overdrawn balances on demand. Examples of duties include: to honour customer's cheques; to receive customers' funds; to comply with customers' instructions; and to provide statements in a reasonable time.

5   A **term loan** is a loan for a fixed amount for a specified period.

6   **C**haracter of the customer
    Ability to borrow and repay
    Margin of profit
    Purpose of the borrowing
    Amount
    Repayment terms
    Insurance against possible repayment

7   At the end of the loan period

Now try ...

Attempt the questions below from the **Practice Question Bank**

Number

Q100

Q101

Q102

Q103

Q104

Mathematical tables

PRESENT VALUE TABLE

Present value of $1 ie $(1+r)^{-n}$

where r = interest rate,

n = number of periods until payment

Periods (n)	Discount rates (r)									
	1%	2%	3%	4%	5%	6%	7%	8%	9%	10%
1	0.990	0.980	0.971	0.962	0.952	0.943	0.935	0.926	0.917	0.909
2	0.980	0.961	0.943	0.925	0.907	0.890	0.873	0.857	0.842	0.826
3	0.971	0.942	0.915	0.889	0.864	0.840	0.816	0.794	0.772	0.751
4	0.961	0.924	0.888	0.855	0.823	0.792	0.763	0.735	0.708	0.683
5	0.951	0.906	0.863	0.822	0.784	0.747	0.713	0.681	0.650	0.621
6	0.942	0.888	0.837	0.790	0.746	0.705	0.666	0.630	0.596	0.564
7	0.933	0.871	0.813	0.760	0.711	0.665	0.623	0.583	0.547	0.513
8	0.923	0.853	0.789	0.731	0.677	0.627	0.582	0.540	0.502	0.467
9	0.914	0.837	0.766	0.703	0.645	0.592	0.544	0.500	0.460	0.424
10	0.905	0.820	0.744	0.676	0.614	0.558	0.508	0.463	0.422	0.386
11	0.896	0.804	0.722	0.650	0.585	0.527	0.475	0.429	0.388	0.350
12	0.887	0.788	0.701	0.625	0.557	0.497	0.444	0.397	0.356	0.319
13	0.879	0.773	0.681	0.601	0.530	0.469	0.415	0.368	0.326	0.290
14	0.870	0.758	0.661	0.577	0.505	0.442	0.388	0.340	0.299	0.263
15	0.861	0.743	0.642	0.555	0.481	0.417	0.362	0.315	0.275	0.239

(n)	11%	12%	13%	14%	15%	16%	17%	18%	19%	20%
1	0.901	0.893	0.885	0.877	0.870	0.862	0.855	0.847	0.840	0.833
2	0.812	0.797	0.783	0.769	0.756	0.743	0.731	0.718	0.706	0.694
3	0.731	0.712	0.693	0.675	0.658	0.641	0.624	0.609	0.593	0.579
4	0.659	0.636	0.613	0.592	0.572	0.552	0.534	0.516	0.499	0.482
5	0.593	0.567	0.543	0.519	0.497	0.476	0.456	0.437	0.419	0.402
6	0.535	0.507	0.480	0.456	0.432	0.410	0.390	0.370	0.352	0.335
7	0.482	0.452	0.425	0.400	0.376	0.354	0.333	0.314	0.296	0.279
8	0.434	0.404	0.376	0.351	0.327	0.305	0.285	0.266	0.249	0.233
9	0.391	0.361	0.333	0.308	0.284	0.263	0.243	0.225	0.209	0.194
10	0.352	0.322	0.295	0.270	0.247	0.227	0.208	0.191	0.176	0.162
11	0.317	0.287	0.261	0.237	0.215	0.195	0.178	0.162	0.148	0.135
12	0.286	0.257	0.231	0.208	0.187	0.168	0.152	0.137	0.124	0.112
13	0.258	0.229	0.204	0.182	0.163	0.145	0.130	0.116	0.104	0.093
14	0.232	0.205	0.181	0.160	0.141	0.125	0.111	0.099	0.088	0.078
15	0.209	0.183	0.160	0.140	0.123	0.108	0.095	0.084	0.074	0.065

BPP
LEARNING
MEDIA

ANNUITY TABLE

Present value of an annuity of 1 ie $\dfrac{1-(1+r)^{-n}}{r}$.

where r = interest rate,

n = number of periods

Periods					Discount rates (r)					
(n)	1%	2%	3%	4%	5%	6%	7%	8%	9%	10%
1	0.990	0.980	0.971	0.962	0.952	0.943	0.935	0.926	0.917	0.909
2	1.970	1.942	1.913	1.886	1.859	1.833	1.808	1.783	1.759	1.736
3	2.941	2.884	2.829	2.775	2.723	2.673	2.624	2.577	2.531	2.487
4	3.902	3.808	3.717	3.630	3.546	3.465	3.387	3.312	3.240	3.170
5	4.853	4.713	4.580	4.452	4.329	4.212	4.100	3.993	3.890	3.791
6	5.795	5.601	5.417	5.242	5.076	4.917	4.767	4.623	4.486	4.355
7	6.728	6.472	6.230	6.002	5.786	5.582	5.389	5.206	5.033	4.868
8	7.652	7.325	7.020	6.733	6.463	6.210	5.971	5.747	5.535	5.335
9	8.566	8.162	7.786	7.435	7.108	6.802	6.515	6.247	5.995	5.759
10	9.471	8.983	8.530	8.111	7.722	7.360	7.024	6.710	6.418	6.145
11	10.368	9.787	9.253	8.760	8.306	7.887	7.499	7.139	6.805	6.495
12	11.255	10.575	9.954	9.385	8.863	8.384	7.943	7.536	7.161	6.814
13	12.134	11.348	10.635	9.986	9.394	8.853	8.358	7.904	7.487	7.103
14	13.004	12.106	11.296	10.563	9.899	9.295	8.745	8.244	7.786	7.367
15	13.865	12.849	11.938	11.118	10.380	9.712	9.108	8.559	8.061	7.606

(n)	11%	12%	13%	14%	15%	16%	17%	18%	19%	20%
1	0.901	0.893	0.885	0.877	0.870	0.862	0.855	0.847	0.840	0.833
2	1.713	1.690	1.668	1.647	1.626	1.605	1.585	1.566	1.547	1.528
3	2.444	2.402	2.361	2.322	2.283	2.246	2.210	2.174	2.140	2.106
4	3.102	3.037	2.974	2.914	2.855	2.798	2.743	2.690	2.639	2.589
5	3.696	3.605	3.517	3.433	3.352	3.274	3.199	3.127	3.058	2.991
6	4.231	4.111	3.998	3.889	3.784	3.685	3.589	3.498	3.410	3.326
7	4.712	4.564	4.423	4.288	4.160	4.039	3.922	3.812	3.706	3.605
8	5.146	4.968	4.799	4.639	4.487	4.344	4.207	4.078	3.954	3.837
9	5.537	5.328	5.132	4.946	4.772	4.607	4.451	4.303	4.163	4.031
10	5.889	5.650	5.426	5.216	5.019	4.833	4.659	4.494	4.339	4.192
11	6.207	5.938	5.687	5.453	5.234	5.029	4.836	4.656	4.486	4.327
12	6.492	6.194	5.918	5.660	5.421	5.197	4.988	4.793	4.611	4.439
13	6.750	6.424	6.122	5.842	5.583	5.342	5.118	4.910	4.715	4.533
14	6.982	6.628	6.302	6.002	5.724	5.468	5.229	5.008	4.802	4.611
15	7.191	6.811	6.462	6.142	5.847	5.575	5.324	5.092	4.876	4.675

Practice question and answer bank

1 Management information

1   **Which of the following statements is NOT true?**

   O   Management accounts detail the performance of an organisation over a defined period and the state of affairs at the end of that period.

   O   There is no legal requirement to prepare management accounts.

   O   The format of management accounts is entirely at management discretion.

   O   Management accounts are both an historical record and a future planning tool.

   (2 marks)

2   **Which of the following statements is NOT correct?**

   O   Financial accounting information can be used for internal reporting purposes.

   O   Routine information can be used to make decisions regarding both the long term and the short term.

   O   Management accounting provides information relevant to decision making, planning, control and evaluation of performances.

   O   Cost accounting can be used to provide inventory valuations for internal reporting only.

   (2 marks)

3   **Which TWO of the following are characteristics of good information?**

   ☐   It is highly detailed.

   ☐   It is accurate.

   ☐   It is relevant.

   ☐   It is highly summarised.

   (2 marks)

4   **Which of the following is the best description of management control?**

   O   Formulating ways to proceed
   O   Choosing between various alternatives
   O   Monitoring something so as to keep it on course
   O   Ensuring subordinates are motivated to achieve organisational objectives

   (2 marks)

5   **Which TWO of the following describe a cost centre?**

   ☐   A unit of product or service in relation to which costs are ascertained

   ☐   An amount of expenditure attributable to an activity

   ☐   A production or service location, function, activity or item of equipment for which costs are accumulated

   ☐   A centre for which an individual manager is responsible

   (2 marks)

2 The role of information technology

6   **Which of the following is an output device?**

    O   Screen
    O   Keyboard
    O   CPU
    O   Disk

    (2 marks)

7   **A method of input which involves a machine that is able to read characters by using lasers to detect the shape of those characters is known as which of the following?**

    O   MICR
    O   OCR
    O   OMR
    O   CPU

    (2 marks)

8   **Which of the following factors may affect the choice of computer output medium?**

    (1)   Whether a hard copy of the output is required
    (2)   Whether the output requires further computer processing
    (3)   Whether a large volume of output is to be used for reference purposes

    O   (1) and (2) only
    O   (1) and (3) only
    O   (2) and (3) only
    O   (1), (2) and (3)

    (2 marks)

9   Data input has three stages. One of these is the origination of data.

    Which TWO of the following correctly describe the other stages?

    ☐   Translation of data
    ☐   Transcription of data
    ☐   Inputting of data
    ☐   Formatting of data

    (2 marks)

10 'A physically small external storage device usually connected via a USB port.'

    Which of the following choices does the above sentence describe?

    O   DVD
    O   CD-ROM
    O   Memory stick
    O   Zip disk

    (2 marks)

3 Cost classification

11   A company calculates the prices of jobs by adding overheads to the prime cost and adding 25% to total costs as a profit margin. Job number H123 was sold for $7,500 and incurred overheads of $3,000.

What was the prime cost of the job?

- O $2,625
- O $3,000
- O $6,000
- O $6,625

(2 marks)

12   **Which of the following correctly describes the prime cost?**

- O   All costs incurred in manufacturing a product
- O   The total of direct costs
- O   The material cost of a product
- O   The cost of operating a department

(2 marks)

13   **Which TWO of the following costs are part of the prime cost for a manufacturing company?**

☐ Cost of transporting raw materials from the supplier's premises

☐ Wages of factory workers engaged in machine maintenance

☐ Depreciation of lorries used for deliveries to customers

☐ Hire of machinery for a particular production job

(2 marks)

14   **Which TWO of the following are indirect costs?**

☐ The depreciation of maintenance equipment

☐ The overtime premium incurred at the specific request of a customer

☐ The hire of a tool for a specific job

☐ The cost of a supervisor's wages on a production line

(2 marks)

4 Cost behaviour

15   **Variable costs are conventionally deemed to:**

- O   Be constant per unit of output
- O   Vary per unit of output as production volume changes
- O   Be constant in total when production volume changes
- O   Vary, in total, from period to period when production is constant

(2 marks)

BPP
LEARNING
MEDIA

16 The following is a graph of cost against level of activity.

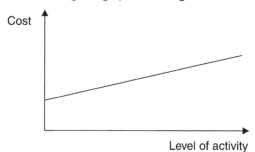

To which of the following costs does the graph correspond?

O   Electricity bills made up of a standing charge and a variable charge
O   Bonus payment to employees when production reaches a certain level
O   Salesman's commission payable per unit up to a maximum amount of commission
O   Bulk discounts on purchases, the discount being given on all units purchased

(2 marks)

---

17 A production worker is paid a salary of $650 per month, plus an extra 5 cents for each unit produced during the month.

How is this labour cost best described?

O   A variable cost
O   A fixed cost
O   A step cost
O   A semi-variable cost

(2 marks)

---

18 B Co has recorded the following data in the two most recent periods.

Total costs of production $	Volume of production Units
27,000	1,400
36,600	2,200

What is the best estimate of the company's fixed costs per period?

$ [   ]

(2 marks)

---

19 The following table relates to different levels of production of the alpha.

	1 alpha $	10 alphas $
Total variable cost	12.50	125.00
Total fixed cost	5,000	5,000

What is the total cost per unit when 5 alphas are produced (to two decimal places)?

$ [   ]

(2 marks)

5   Information for comparison

20   **Which is the correct description of a flexed budget?**

   O   A budget that can be changed according to circumstances
   O   A budget that is adjusted according to actual activity
   O   A budget that is open to negotiation
   O   A budget that is used for planning purposes only

   (2 marks)

21   **Which TWO of the following statements about the application of feedback and feedforward control are true?**

   ☐   Feedback and feedforward are both applied in budgetary planning and control.

   ☐   Feedback is used in the analysis of variances.

   ☐   Feedforward enables budgeted data for a period to be amended for the next period.

   ☐   Feedforward relates to the setting of performance standards

   (2 marks)

22   A product has a budgeted direct material cost of $5 per unit. In a specific period the production information was:

   Budget   9,000 units
   Actual   8,800 units

   $44,380 was incurred on direct materials for the period's production.

   What was the direct material variance, comparing actual with the flexed budget?

   $☐

   (2 marks)

23   The budgeted sales of SM Ltd were 800 units at a selling price of $20. The actual sales were 775 units at a total sales revenue of $17,050.

   What is the activity variance?

   $☐

   (2 marks)

24   **Which of the following would help to explain a favourable direct material usage variance?**

   (1)   The material purchased was of a higher quality than standard.
   (2)   Losses due to evaporation were less than expected.
   (3)   Activity levels were lower than budget therefore less material was used.

   O   All of them
   O   (1) and (2) only
   O   (2) and (3) only
   O   (1) and (3) only

   (2 marks)

BPP
LEARNING
MEDIA

6 Reporting management information

25 **Which TWO of the following are qualities of good management information?**

☐ Relevance

☐ Comparability

☐ Consistency

☐ Understandability

(2 marks)

26 **When communicating information, which of the following determine the choice of method used?**

(1) Comparative cost
(2) Degree of confidentiality
(3) Speed of delivery

○ (1) only
○ (3) only
○ (1) and (2) only
○ (1), (2) and (3)

(2 marks)

27 **In relation to effective communication of management information, which of the following statements is FALSE?**

○ An ad hoc report can be less concise than one that is regularly produced because its purpose is less clear.

○ Management reports should avoid swamping the reader with too much detail.

○ The use of visuals can enhance the clarity of the report and therefore make it easier to understand.

○ An executive summary, giving the main points of the report, both saves the time of the managers and makes the report more understandable.

(2 marks)

28 Different managers will require different information in order to facilitate decision making depending on the nature of the organisation and individual responsibilities.

Which of the following is least likely to be true?

○ Senior management will be interested in the financial statements, probably on a monthly basis to help make strategic decisions.

○ The human resources manager will require information on absenteeism analysed by department and reason for absence.

○ A factory supervisor will want details of order enquiries taken by the sales team each day in order to help plan production levels.

○ A sales manager will want a weekly report of orders achieved by each sales team to help assess their effectiveness.

(2 marks)

29   You are working in the finance department of a company. A colleague from the sales department
      has requested some accounting information that the sales department does not normally receive.
      They assure you that the head of the finance department is aware of the request.

      What should you do?

      O   Give them access to the information
      O   Print out the information and give it to them
      O   Ignore the request
      O   Refer the matter to the head of finance

                                                                                                    (2 marks)

7 Materials

30   **In a period of continual price inflation for material purchases, which of the following is true?**

      O   The LIFO method will produce lower profits than the FIFO method, and lower closing
            inventory values.

      O   The LIFO method will produce lower profits than the FIFO method, and higher closing
            inventory values.

      O   The FIFO method will produce lower profits than the LIFO method, and lower closing
            inventory values.

      O   The FIFO method will produce lower profits than the LIFO method, and higher closing
            inventory values.

                                                                                                    (2 marks)

31   A wholesaler buys and resells a range of items, one of which is the Kay. Each Kay is resold for
      $3 per unit and opening inventory for June was 400 units valued at $1.80 per unit. The
      wholesaler purchased a further 600 units on 10 June for $2.10 per unit, and sold 800 units on
      25 June.

      **What gross profit would be recorded for the sale of Kays during June, using the FIFO and the
      LIFO method of inventory valuation?**

	FIFO gross profit	LIFO gross profit
O	$780	$840
O	$840	$780
O	$1,560	$780
O	$1,560	$1,620

                                                                                                    (2 marks)

32   A wholesaler had opening inventory of 300 units of product Emm valued at $20 per unit at the
      beginning of January. The following receipts and sales were recorded during January.

Date	2 Jan	12 Jan	21 Jan	29 Jan
Receipts		400		
Sales	250		200	75

      The purchase cost of receipts was $22 per unit.

      **Using a periodic weighted average method of valuation, what is the value of closing inventory
      at the end of January?**

      $

                                                                                                    (2 marks)

33 600 units of component J, valued at a price of $6.20, were in inventory on 1 May. The following receipts and issues were recorded during May.

3 May	Received	800 units @ $6.88 per unit
13 May	Received	700 units @ $7.24 per unit
25 May	Issued	1,700 units

Using the LIFO method, what is the total value of the issues on 25 May?

$ _____

(2 marks)

34 XYZ Co had an opening inventory value of $352 (275 units valued at $1.28 each) on 1 April.

The following receipts and issues were recorded during April.

8 April	Receipts	600 units	$1.20 per unit
15 April	Receipts	400 units	$1.36 per unit
30 April	Issues	900 units	

Using the FIFO method, what is the total value of the issues on 30 April?

$ _____

(2 marks)

8 Labour

35 Gross wages incurred in department 1 in June were $54,000. The wages analysis shows the following summary breakdown of the gross pay.

	Paid to direct labour $	Paid to indirect labour $
Ordinary time	10,074	11,900
Overtime: basic pay	2,176	3,500
premium	544	875
Shift allowance	1,080	1,360
Sick pay	552	300
	14,426	17,935

What is the direct wages cost for department 1 in June?

$ _____

(2 marks)

36 **Which TWO of the following would be classed as indirect labour?**

☐ A coach driver in a transport company

☐ Machine operators in a milk bottling plant

☐ A maintenance assistant in a factory maintenance department

☐ On-call plumbers in a factory

(2 marks)

37   **Which of the following is included on a daily timesheet completed by an employee?**

    O   Time spent on a job for the entire job
    O   Number of pieces of work produced
    O   Hours worked on each job
    O   Cost of the job

                                                                                 (2 marks)

38   Triple Co pays overtime at time and a quarter. Jo's basic hours are 9 to 5 with an hour for lunch, but one particular Friday she worked until six o'clock. She is paid a basic wage of $10 per hour.

    How much did she earn on the Friday in question as overtime premium?

    $ [   ]

                                                                                 (2 marks)

39   An employee is paid $12.50 per piecework hour produced. In a 35 hour week they produce the following output.

	Piecework time allowed per unit
3 units of product A	3.75 hours
5 units of product B	11.00 hours

    What is the employee's pay for the week?

    $ [   ]

                                                                                  (2 marks)

9 Expenses

40   **Which of the following statements correctly describes asset items?**

    O   Items which relate to the long-term running of the business
    O   Items which relate to the day-to-day running of the business
    O   Items which are part of the business' working capital
    O   Items which are unusual, for example costs of closing down part of the business

                                                                                  (2 marks)

41   The management accounts of TopCo show the following expenses for May 20Y0.

Expense	Cost
Renault van	$20,000
Sign-painting of company name, logo and telephone number on van	$500
Diesel for van	$800
Breakdown cover for the van	$1,500

    What is the total asset expenditure for the month?

    $ [   ]

                                                                                  (2 marks)

42 Two assets are purchased for $8,000 each. Asset A is depreciated over four years using the straight line method and Asset B is depreciated at the rate of 25% per annum on the reducing balance method.

What is the value of each asset after four years?

	Value of asset after four years	
	$2,531	*$NIL*
Asset A	O	O
Asset B	O	O

(2 marks)

43 ____ is the process by which indirect expenses are charged to a cost centre.

What is the word missing in the sentence above?

O   Recharging
O   Recording
O   Allocation
O   Coding

(2 marks)

10 Overheads and absorption costing

44 Edison has the following data relating to overheads.

	Budget	*Actual*
Fixed overheads	$15,000	$14,000
Direct labour hours	20,000	19,500

Overheads are absorbed on the basis of labour hours.

Which of the following statements is true?

O   Overheads will be under-absorbed by $1,000 due to the lower than expected expenditure.

O   Overheads will be under-absorbed by $1,000 due to the unexpected decrease in labour hours.

O   Overheads will be under-absorbed by $625 due to lower than expected expenditure and lower than expected labour hours.

O   Overheads will be over-absorbed by $625 due to lower than expected labour hours more than offset by lower than expected expenditure.

(2 marks)

45 **Overhead apportionment is used to do which of the following?**

O   Charge whole items of costs to cost centres
O   Charge cost units with an appropriate share of overheads
O   Charge whole items of costs to cost units
O   Spread common costs over cost centres

(2 marks)

46 Data for cost centre Y for the latest period was as follows.

Budgeted direct labour hours	12,300
Actual direct labour hours	11,970
Production overhead absorption rate	$2.60 per direct labour hour
Production overhead under-absorbed	$5,670

What was the actual production overhead incurred during the period?

$ [   ]

(2 marks)

47 **Which TWO of the following statements about overhead absorption rates are true?**

☐ They are predetermined in advance for each period.

☐ They are used to charge overheads to products.

☐ They are based on actual data for each period.

☐ They are used to control overhead costs.

(2 marks)

---

48 A company absorbs overheads on the basis of machine hours. In a period, actual machine hours were $8,974, actual overheads were $198,600 and there was over-absorption of $25,750.

What was the budgeted overhead absorption?

$ ☐ per machine hour (to the nearest $).

(2 marks)

---

11 Marginal costing and absorption costing

49 **When comparing the profits reported under absorption costing and marginal costing during a period when the level of inventory increased, which of the following is true?**

O Absorption costing profits will be higher and closing inventory valuations lower than those under marginal costing.

O Absorption costing profits will be higher and closing inventory valuations higher than those under marginal costing.

O Marginal costing profits will be higher and closing inventory valuations lower than those under absorption costing.

O Marginal costing profits will be higher and closing inventory valuations higher than those under absorption costing.

(2 marks)

---

50 Summary results for H Co for June are shown below.

	$'000	Units
Sales revenue	820	
Variable production costs	300	
Variable selling costs	105	
Fixed production costs	180	
Fixed selling costs	110	
Production in March		1,000
Opening inventory		0
Closing inventory		150

Using marginal costing, what was the profit for June?

O $170,000
O $185,750
O $197,000
O $229,250

(2 marks)

51   A product has the following costs:

	$/unit
Variable production costs	9.60
Total production costs	15.00
Total variable costs	11.80
Total costs	20.00

14,400 units of the product were manufactured in a period during which 14,200 units were sold.

What is the profit difference using absorption costing rather than marginal costing?

$ [_____]

(2 marks)

52   .... is the difference between sales value and the marginal cost of sales.

What is/are the missing word(s) from the sentence above?

O   Marginal cost
O   Variable cost
O   Fixed cost
O   Contribution

(2 marks)

53   Marginal costing as a cost accounting system is significantly different from absorption costing.

How are fixed costs treated under each costing system?

	Period costs	Unit costs
Marginal costing	O	O
Absorption costing	O	O

(2 marks)

12 Cost bookkeeping

54   **Which of the following descriptions correctly describes a control account?**

O   An account for pooling costs before they are recharged
O   Contra to cash
O   An account which records total cost as opposed to individual costs
O   A type of suspense account

(2 marks)

55   There are two main cost bookkeeping systems used in business, integrated and interlocking systems.

Which system do the following features relate to?

	Integrated	Interlocking
Keeps one set of ledger accounts	O	O
Inventory may be valued differently in the financial accounts	O	O

(2 marks)

56 A company operates an integrated accounting system.

What would the accounting entries be for the issue to production of indirect materials from inventory?

	Debit	Credit
O	Work in progress account	Stores control account
O	Stores control account	Overhead control account
O	Overhead control account	Stores control account
O	Cost of sales account	Stores control account

(2 marks)

57 Delboy Co occupies a single factory location. In its cost accounts, it uses an absorption costing system. 60% of the building is taken up by the production divisions, with the remainder of the space taken up by general administration (30%) and marketing (10%). The rental cost for the premises in the year just ended was $30,000.

Which of the following bookkeeping entries would have been recorded in the company's integrated cost/financial accounts for the period?

O	Debit	Rent account	$18,000
	Credit	Production overhead control account	$18,000
O	Debit	Cash	$30,000
	Credit	Rent account	$30,000
O	Debit	Production overhead control account	$18,000
	Credit	Rent account	$18,000
O	Debit	Production overhead control account	$30,000
	Credit	Rent account	$30,000

(2 marks)

58 The production control account for R Co at the end of the period looks like this.

PRODUCTION OVERHEAD CONTROL ACCOUNT

	$		$
Stores control	57,000	Work in progress	1,012,000
Wages control	451,000	Statement of profit or loss (Income statement)	21,000
Expense payable	525,000		
	1,033,000		1,033,000

Which TWO of the following statements are correct?

☐ Indirect material issued from inventory was $57,000.

☐ Overhead absorbed during the period was $525,000.

☐ Overhead for the period was over-absorbed by $21,000.

☐ Indirect wages costs incurred were $451,000.

(2 marks)

13 Job, batch and service costing

59 **Which TWO of the following are characteristics of service costing?**

☐ High levels of indirect costs as a proportion of total service costs

☐ Output which includes by-products and joint products

☐ The work is relatively long in duration

☐ Use of composite cost units

(2 marks)

---

60 **Which of the following organisations should NOT be advised to use service costing?**

O Hotel
O Distribution service
O Clothing manufacturer
O Training firm

(2 marks)

---

61 **Which of the following is a feature of job costing?**

O Associated with continuous production of large volumes of low-cost items
O Establishes the costs of services rendered
O Production is carried out in accordance with the wishes of the customer
O Costs are aggregated and divided by units produced

(2 marks)

---

62 **Which of the following would be appropriate performance measures for a transport business?**

(1) Cost per tonne-kilometre
(2) Fixed cost per kilometre
(3) Maintenance cost of each vehicle per kilometre

O (1), (2) and (3)
O (1) only
O (2) only
O (1) and (3) only

(2 marks)

---

14 Process costing

63 In a particular process, the input for the period was 2,000 units. There were no inventories at the beginning or end of the process. Normal loss is 5% of input.

In which TWO of the following circumstances is there an abnormal gain?

☐ Actual output = 1,800 units

☐ Actual output = 1,890 units

☐ Actual output = 1,950 units

☐ Actual output = 2,000 units

(2 marks)

64   **Which TWO of the following statements in connection with process costing are correct?**

☐   A loss expected during the normal course of operations, for unavoidable reasons, is abnormal loss.

☐   An unexpected loss is an abnormal loss.

☐   An abnormal loss arises if the actual loss is greater than the expected loss.

☐   A normal loss is never less than actual loss.

(2 marks)

---

65   A company makes a product, which passes through a single process.

Details of the process for the last period are as follows:

Materials	2,000 kg at 20c per kg
Labour	$280
Production overheads	200% of labour

Normal losses are 10% of input in the process, and without further processing any losses can be sold as scrap for 8c per kg.

The output for the period was 1,680 kg from the process.

There was no work in progress at the beginning or end of the period.

What will be the value credited to the process account for the scrap value of the normal loss for the period?

$ [   ] (to the nearest $).

(2 marks)

---

66   Information for two processes is as follows:

Process	Normal loss as % of input	Input (litres)	Output (litres)
Mixing	5%	50,000	48,500
Filtering	6%	85,000	79,000

For each process was there an abnormal loss or an abnormal gain?

	Abnormal loss	Abnormal gain
Mixing	O	O
Filtering	O	O

(2 marks)

---

67   Costs incurred in a process totalled $514,800 for a period. 60,000 units of finished product were manufactured including 3,000 units which were rejected on inspection and disposed of. The level of rejects in the period was normal. Rejects are sold for $5.00 per unit.

What was the cost per unit for the process?

O $8.33
O $8.77
O $8.98
O $9.51

(2 marks)

15 Cost-volume-profit (CVP) analysis

68 A company makes a single product and incurs fixed costs of $12,000 per month. Variable cost per unit is $2 and each unit sells for $6. Monthly sales demand is 7,000 units.

What is the breakeven point in terms of monthly sales units?

O   2,000 units
O   3,000 units
O   4,000 units
O   6,000 units

(2 marks)

69 A company manufactures a single product for which cost and selling price data are as follows.

Selling price per unit	$4.80
Variable cost per unit	$3.20
Fixed costs per month	$38,400
Budgeted monthly sales	30,000 units

What is the margin of safety, expressed as a percentage of budgeted monthly sales (to the nearest whole number)?

 %

(2 marks)

70

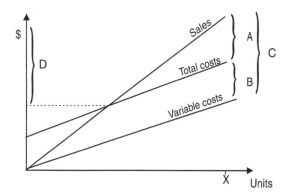

In the above breakeven chart, which of the following distances is the contribution at level of activity x?

O   Distance B
O   Distance D
O   Distance C
O   Distance A

(2 marks)

71

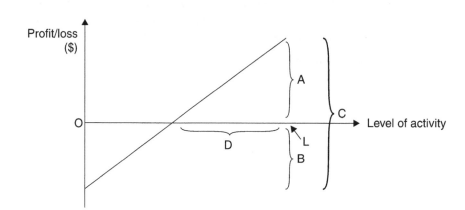

In the above profit-volume chart, which of the following distances is the contribution at level of activity L?

- O   Distance D
- O   Distance A
- O   Distance B
- O   Distance C

(2 marks)

---

72   A single product business has the following results for a period.

	$
Sales revenue	93,760 (@ $20 per unit)
Less variable costs	70,320
Contribution	23,440
Less fixed costs	9,792
Net profit	13,648

What is the breakeven point in units?

```
┌──────────┐
│          │
└──────────┘
```

(2 marks)

---

16 Short-term decisions

73   **Which of the following best describes opportunity cost?**

- O   The cost of taking up a business opportunity
- O   The cost of not taking up a business opportunity
- O   The benefit gained by taking up a business opportunity
- O   The benefit lost by taking up one business opportunity in favour of another

(2 marks)

---

74   **Which TWO of the following are relevant costs for decision making?**

- ☐   A sunk cost
- ☐   A committed cost
- ☐   A differential cost
- ☐   A future cost

(2 marks)

---

75   Ess Co manufactures four products but next month there is likely to be a shortage of labour. The following information is available.

	Q	R	S	T
	$	$	$	$
Contribution per unit	16.00	14.50	17.60	19.00
Net profit per unit	4.60	4.80	5.20	5.00
Contribution per labour hour	5.00	4.80	4.40	3.80
Net profit per labour hour	1.40	1.60	1.30	1.00

What order should the products be made in, in order to maximise profits?

- O   Q,R,S,T
- O   R,Q,S,T
- O   S,T,R,Q
- O   T,S,Q,R

(2 marks)

76 A company uses limiting factor analysis to calculate an optimal production plan given a scarce resource.

The following applies to the three products of the company:

Product	I	II	III
	$	$	$
Direct materials (at $2.40/kg)	14.40	9.60	6.00
Direct labour (at $4/hour)	16.00	10.00	4.00
Variable overheads ($0.80/hour)	3.20	2.00	0.80
	33.60	21.60	10.80
Maximum demand (units)	2,000	4,000	4,000
Optimal production plan	2,000	1,500	4,000

How many kg of material were available for use in production?

O 15,750 kg
O 28,000 kg
O 30,000 kg
O 38,000 kg

(2 marks)

77 Transco has incurred research and development costs of $32,000 to date on a proposed new product. Further costs of $8,000 would be required to complete the development of the product.

In deciding whether to continue with the new product development which of the following is correct regarding development costs?

	Sunk cost	Incremental cost
O	$0	$40,000
O	$8,000	$32,000
O	$32,000	$8,000
O	$40,000	$0

(2 marks)

17 Capital investment appraisal

78 **What is the present value of $5,000 in perpetuity at a discount rate of 10%?**

    O $500
    O $5,500
    O $4,545
    O $50,000

                                              (2 marks)

79 **Which of the following is a disadvantage of the payback method of investment appraisal?**

    O   It tends to maximise financial and business risk.
    O   It is a fairly complex technique and not easy to understand.
    O   It cannot be used when there are limited funds available.
    O   It doesn't account for the cost of capital in making investment decisions.

                                              (2 marks)

80 A company is considering investing in a manufacturing project that would have a three-year life span. The investment would involve an immediate cash outflow of $50,000. In each of the three years, 4,000 units would be produced and sold. The contribution per unit, based on current prices, is $5. The company has an annual cost of capital of 8%.

Year	Discount factor 8%
0	1.000
1	0.926
2	0.857
3	0.794

What is the net present value of the project?

$ [＿＿＿＿＿＿]   **(2 marks)**

81 A company is considering investing $100,000 now to receive five annual sums of $25,000, commencing in a year's time. The company has a cost of capital of 10%. The annuity factor for 10% over 5 years is 3.791.

What is the net present value of the investment?

$ [＿＿＿＿＿＿]

                                            (2 marks)

82 Top Co's accountant has worked out the following NPVs for an investment in machinery.

Using the data below, what is the internal rate of return for the investment?

NPV at 5%	$350
NPV at 10%	$(1,750)

[＿＿＿＿＿] %

                                            (2 marks)

BPP LEARNING MEDIA

18 Cash and cash flows

83   The following extracts are available from Peter Co's statement of financial position.

	$
Non-current assets	100,000
Inventory	12,000
Receivables	8,000
Payables	2,500
Overdraft	17,500
Long-term bank loan	75,000

What is Peter Co's working capital?

- O   Zero
- O $25,000
- O $40,000
- O $100,000

(2 marks)

84   The trainee accountant of Good Co has prepared the following cash flow.

	$
Sales	325,000
Opening receivables	(23,500)
Closing receivables	17,500
Bank loan received	125,000
Cash in	444,000
Purchases	193,500
Opening payables	27,000
Closing payables	(12,500)
Depreciation	(26,000)
Cash out	182,000
Cash flow	262,000

Has the trainee calculated the cash flow correctly?

- O   Yes, the total of $262,000 is correct.
- O   No, the total cash flow should be $137,000.
- O   No, the total cash flow should be $248,000.
- O   No, the total cash flow should be $277,000.

(2 marks)

85   **Which of the following is NOT classed as working capital?**

- O   Overdraft
- O   Bank loan
- O   Payables
- O   Inventory

(2 marks)

86   Cash transactions can be asset or expense, regular or irregular, exceptional or unexceptional.

Which of the following describes exceptional items?

- O   Relates to the long-term functioning of the business
- O   Unusual costs such as closure of part of the business
- O   Does not occur at regular intervals
- O   Capitalised in the accounts

(2 marks)

19 Cash and treasury management

87   Treasury management involves a wide range of activities under five basic functions.

Raising share capital and dividend policy fall under which function?

- O   Liquidity management
- O   Funding management
- O   Corporate finance
- O   Other activities of the treasurer

(2 marks)

---

88   **Which TWO of the following are important procedures to follow when handling cash receipts?**

- ☐   Ensuring prompt banking of cash
- ☐   Ensuring restriction of access to cash and cheques
- ☐   Ensuring proper procedures are in place for authorisation
- ☐   Ensuring cash received and banked is reconciled

(2 marks)

---

89   Trends in the economy can affect how businesses manage their cash.

When the economy is going through a period of high growth, a different attitude to cash balances is likely than when the economy is in recession.

For each choice, recession or high growth, select the likely attitude businesses will take toward managing their cash balances.

	Build up cash balances	Run down cash balances
Recession	O	O
High growth	O	O

(2 marks)

---

90   The segregation of duties is particularly important when handling cash.

Cashiers are responsible for which of the following duties relating to the receipt of cash?

- O   Receiving and recording cash when it arrives in the post
- O   Banking the cash
- O   Writing up the cash book
- O   Doing a reconciliation of the records of various amounts received

(2 marks)

---

91   Cheque signatories are authorised to sign cheques.

Which of the following activities should they be responsible for?

- O   Approving cheque requisitions
- O   Recording payments
- O   Preparing cheques
- O   Abiding by the limitation on authority to sign cheques up to a certain amount

(2 marks)

BPP
LEARNING
MEDIA

20 Forecasting cash flows

92 **Which of the following is NOT a valid reason for using forecasts as an early warning of liquidity problems?**

O   For estimating how much cash is required
O   For estimating the cost of borrowing for funds needed
O   For estimating when cash is required
O   For estimating whether the funds will be available from anticipated sources

(2 marks)

93 A company has the following receivables and payables according to its statement of financial position at 31 December 20X9.

	$
Receivables	375,000
Payables	150,000

Customers are allowed two months to pay. Sales were made at an even monthly rate in 20X9.

What are the planned receipts from customers in January 20Y0?

$ ☐

(2 marks)

94 Cash flow forecasts may differ from actual cash flows for a variety of reasons.

Which of the following is NOT a reason why this might happen?

O   A change in the cost of capital
O   Changes in interest rates
O   Inflation which may affect costs and revenues differently
O   Poor forecasting techniques

(2 marks)

95 A company has the following receivables and payables according to its statement of financial position at 31 December 20X9.

	$
Receivables	375,000
Payables	150,000

Suppliers give 1½ months credit. Materials were purchased at an even monthly rate in 20X9.

What are the planned payments to suppliers in January 20Y0?

O $50,000
O $75,000
O $100,000
O $250,000

(2 marks)

96   Suppose revenues for a company over the last five years were as follows.

Year	Revenue $'000
20X5	87.50
20X6	105.00
20X7	100.00
20X8	112.50
20X9	125.00

The company accountant decided that she wanted to set up a revenue index using 20X5 as the base year. The $87,500 of revenue in 20X5 is given the index 100%.

What is the index for 20X9?

[   ] %   **(2 marks)**

21 Investing surplus funds

97   **What are government bonds otherwise known as?**

○   Certificates of deposit
○   Bills
○   Gilts
○   Commercial paper

                                                                                 (2 marks)

98   **Which is the motive for holding cash that hopes that interest rates will rise?**

○   Transactions motive
○   Precautionary motive
○   Speculative motive
○   Inflationary motive

                                                                                 (2 marks)

99   There is generally believed to be a relationship between risk and return. Generally a higher risk earns a higher return.

For the following two examples, indicate whether the investment can lose value (its initial value goes down) or not.

	Lose value	Not lose value
Deposit account at a bank	○	○
Ordinary shares	○	○

                                                                                 (2 marks)

22 Raising finance from a bank

100   **Which TWO of the following factors apply to term loans?**

☐   Repayment is on demand.

☐   The length of the loan which should not exceed the useful life of the asset to be bought.

☐   The internal guidelines of the lender.

☐   Interest is calculated as a margin over base rate daily and charged quarterly.

                                                                                 (2 marks)

101 **A customer has which TWO of the following main duties in relation to a bank?**

☐ To use care and skill in their actions

☐ To be confidential in their dealings

☐ To exercise care (a duty of care)

☐ To advise the bank of any known forgeries (advice of forgery)

(2 marks)

102 A bank's decision on whether to lend is based on seven factors.

What is the handy mnemonic for these?

○ CARPARK
○ CAMPARI
○ CLAMPED
○ CALZONE

(2 marks)

103 Loans may be repaid in three ways. One of these is amortising over the term of the loan.

Which TWO of the following are the other ways?

☐ Bullet

☐ Dart

☐ Balloon

☐ Termination

(2 marks)

104 _____ covenants require a borrower to do something for instance provide management accounts.

What is the missing word from the sentence above?

○ Positive
○ Negative
○ Restrictive
○ Quantitative

(2 marks)

1 Management information

1   The correct answer is: Management accounts detail the performance of an organisation over a defined period and the state of affairs at the end of that period.

Financial accounts (not management accounts) detail the performance of an organisation over a defined period and the state of affairs at the end of that period. **Management accounts** are used to aid management record, plan and control the organisation's activities and to help the decision-making process.

2   The correct answer is: Cost accounting can be used to provide inventory valuations for internal reporting only.

Cost accounting can be used to provide inventory valuations for external reporting also.

3   The correct answers are: It is accurate. It is relevant.

Good information should be accurate and relevant. If the information is highly detailed, this may be too detailed for the user's needs so as to become 'irrelevant'. Similarly, information which is highly summarised may be insufficient for the user's needs. The information is then incomplete.

4   The correct answer is: Monitoring something so as to keep it on course.

Monitoring something so as to keep it on course is the best description of control. Option one refers to planning and option two refers to decision making. Option four describes assisting in employee motivation.

5   The correct answers are: A production or service location, function, activity or item of equipment for which costs are accumulated. A centre for which an individual manager is responsible.

The first option is the definition of a cost unit.

The second option describes the cost of an activity or cost centre.

2 The role of information technology

6   The correct answer is: Screen

A **screen** is an output device.

A **keyboard** is an input device.

The **CPU** performs the processing function.

A **disk** is a storage device.

7   The correct answer is: OCR

MICR is the recognition of characters by a machine that reads special formatted characters printed in magnetic ink.

OMR involves marking a pre-printed source document which is then read by a device which translates the marks on the document into machine code.

CPU is the central processing unit.

OCR is therefore correct.

8   The correct answer is: (1), (2), and (3)

All three factors affect the choice of computer output medium.

9   The correct answers are: Transcription of data. Inputting of data.

Transcription and inputting of data. Transcription is where data is put onto paper suitable for keying in by operators. Data input is by various means including direct entry using a keyboard.

BPP
LEARNING
MEDIA

10   The correct answer is: Memory stick

      A memory stick or pen drive is a small external storage device that can be connected to a
      computer through a USB drive.

3   Cost classification

11   The correct answer is: $3,000

      Selling price of a job $7,500

Less profit margin (25/125)	$1,500
Total cost of job	$6,000
Less overhead	$3,000
Prime cost	$3,000

12   The correct answer is: The total of direct costs

      Prime cost is the total of direct material, direct labour and direct expenses.

      The first option describes **total production cost**, including absorbed production overhead. The
      third option is only a part of prime cost. The fourth option is an **overhead** or indirect cost.

13   The correct answers are: Cost of transporting raw materials from the supplier's premises. Hire of
      machinery for a particular production job.

      The first option is a part of the cost of **direct materials**. The fourth option is a **direct expense** as
      the hire of equipment for a particular job.

      The second option is a **production overhead**. The third option is a **selling and distribution
      expense**.

14   The correct answers are: The depreciation of maintenance equipment. The cost of a supervisor's
      wages on a production line.

      Depreciation is an **indirect cost** because it does not relate directly to the number of units
      produced. A supervisor's wages cannot be traced to an individual production job.

      The second and third options can be traced directly to **specific cost units** therefore they are direct
      expenses.

4   Cost behaviour

15   The correct answer is: Be constant per unit of output

      Variable costs are conventionally deemed to increase or decrease in direct proportion to changes
      in output. Therefore the correct answer is the first option. The second and fourth options imply a
      changing unit rate, which does not comply with this convention. The third option relates to a
      fixed cost.

16   The correct answer is: Electricity bills made up of a standing charge and a variable charge

      The depicted cost has a **basic fixed element** which is payable even at zero activity. A **variable
      element** is then added at a constant rate as activity increases.

      Graphs for the other options would look like this.

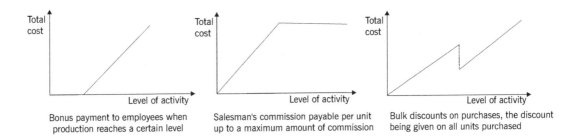

Bonus payment to employees when production reaches a certain level

Salesman's commission payable per unit up to a maximum amount of commission

Bulk discounts on purchases, the discount being given on all units purchased

17   The correct answer is: A semi-variable cost

The salary is **part fixed** ($650 per month) and **part variable** (5 cents per unit).

If you chose the first or second options, you were considering only part of the cost.

The third option, a step cost, involves a cost which remains constant up to a certain level and then increases to a new, higher, constant fixed cost.

18   The correct answer is: $10,200

	Units	$
High output	2,200	36,600
Low output	1,400	27,000
Variable cost of	800	9,600

Variable cost per unit $9,600/$800 = $12 per unit

Fixed costs = $36,600 − ($12 × 2,200) = $10,200

19   The correct answer is: $1,012.50

The cost of 5 alphas = ($12.50 × 5) + $5,000 = $5,062.50

Therefore the cost per unit = $5,062.50/5 = $1,012.50

5   Information for comparison

20   The correct answer is: A budget that is adjusted according to actual activity

A flexible budget is adjusted to actual activity levels.

21   The correct answers are: Feedback and feedforward are both applied in budgetary planning and control. Feedback is used in the analysis of variances.

Feedforward does not relate to the setting of performance standards or enable budgeted data to be amended for the next period.

22   The correct answer is: $380 A

	$
8,800 units should have cost	44,000
But did cost	44,380
	380 Adverse

23   The correct answer is: $550 A

	Units
Budgeted sales volume	800
Actual sales volume	775
Activity variance in units	25 (A)
× Budgeted sales price per unit	× $20
Activity variance	$500 (A)

BPP
LEARNING
MEDIA

24   The correct answer is: (1) and (2) only

Statement (1) is consistent with a favourable direct material usage variance, because higher quality material may lead to **lower wastage**.

Statement (2) is consistent with a favourable direct material usage variance, because lower losses would **reduce material usage**.

Statement (3) is not consistent with a favourable direct material usage variance. If activity levels were lower than budget this would not affect the materials used **per unit** of production. The usage variance would be calculated based on the **standard usage for the actual output**.

6   Reporting management information

25   The correct answer is: Relevance. Understandability.

Management information should be relevant and understandable.

26   The correct answer is: (1), (2) and (3)

All three items are important.

27   The correct answer is: An ad hoc report can be less concise than one that is regularly produced because its purpose is less clear.

The purpose of an ad hoc report should be agreed upfront which will make the purpose clear.

28   The correct answer is: A factory supervisor will want details of order enquiries taken by the sales team each day in order to help plan production levels.

Production should be based on sales orders not sales enquiries.

29   The correct answer is: Refer the matter to the head of finance

The matter should be referred to your superior, in this case the head of finance.

7   Materials

30   The correct answer is: The LIFO method will produce lower profits than the FIFO method, and lower closing inventory values.

With **LIFO**, if newer inventories cost more to buy from suppliers than older inventories, the costs of material issued and used will be higher. It follows that the cost of sales will be higher and the profit lower.

Closing inventories with **LIFO** will be priced at the purchase price of earlier items that were received into inventory. In a period of rising prices, this means that closing inventories will be valued at old, out-of-date and lower prices. Therefore the correct answer is the first option.

If you chose the second option you were correct about the profits but your reasoning concerning the inventory values was wrong.

31   The correct answers are: FIFO $840   LIFO $780

	FIFO		LIFO	
	$	$	$	$
Sales value $3 × 800		2,400		2,400
Less cost of sales:				
400 × $1.80	720			
400 × $2.10	840			
		1,560		
600 × $2.10			1,260	
200 × $1.80			360	
				1,620
Gross profit		840		780

32 The correct answer is: $3,811

		Units	$
Opening inventory	300 × $20	300	6,000
Issue on 2 Jan	250 × $20	(250)	(5,000)
		50	1,000
Receipt on 12 Jan		400	8,800
		450	9,800
Issues on 21 Jan and 29 Jan			
(9,800/450) × (200 + 75)		(275)	(5,989)
		175	3,811

33 The correct answer is: $11,812

Date of issue	Quantity issued units	Valuation units	$
25 May	1,700	700 × $7.24	5,068
		800 × $6.88	5,504
		200 × $6.20	1,240
			11,812

34 The correct answer is: $1,106

Date	Receipts Units	Issues Units	Balance	$
1 April			275 @ $1.28	352
8 April	600		600 @ $1.20	720
15 April	400		400 @ $1.36	544
				1,616
				$
30 April		900		
		275 @ $1.28 =		352
		600 @ $1.20 =		720
		25 @ $1.36 =		34
				1,106

8 Labour

35 The correct answer is: $12,250

The only **direct costs** are the **wages** paid to direct workers for ordinary time, plus the **basic pay for overtime**.

$10,074 + $2,176 = $12,250.

You need to include the basic pay for overtime of direct workers, which is always classified as a direct labour cost. The overtime premium and shift allowances are usually treated as indirect costs. However, if overtime and shiftwork are incurred specifically for a particular cost unit, then they are classified as direct costs of that cost unit. There is no mention of such a situation here. Sick pay is classified as an indirect labour cost.

36 The correct answers are: A maintenance assistant in a factory maintenance department. On-call plumbers in a factory.

The maintenance assistant is not working directly on the organisation's output but is performing an **indirect task**. The plumbers are part of the facilities staff looking after the factory so they would also be **indirect labour**. The other two options describe tasks that involve working **directly on the output**.

37 The correct answer is: Hours worked on each job.

Hours worked on each job. The first and second options refer to job cards and piecework tickets. The fourth option is the cost of the job rather than the hours spent on the job.

BPP
LEARNING
MEDIA

449

38   The correct answer is: $2.50

	$
Basic pay (8 × $10)	80.00
Overtime premium (1/4 × $10)	2.50
	82.50

For costing purposes all of the hours worked, whether in basic time or outside it, are costed at the basic rate. The premium is the extra amount paid on top of the basic rate for the hours worked over and above the basic hours. The **overtime premium** is thus $2.50. This is an important point because overtime premium is usually treated as an **indirect cost**.

39   The correct answer is: $828.13

Piecework hours produced are as follows.

Product A	3 × 3.75 hours	11.25 hours
Product B	5 × 11 hours	55.00 hours
Total piecework hours		66.25 hours

Therefore employee's pay = 66.25 hrs × $12.50 = $828.13 for the week.

9   Expenses

40   The correct answer is: Items which relate to the long-term running of the business.

Asset items relate to the long-term running of the business, such as the purchase of non-current assets. Items that relate to the day-to-day running of the business or which are included in the business's working capital are expense items. Unusual items are correctly known as exceptional items.

41   The correct answer is: $20,500

Asset expenditure relates to the purchase of non-current assets and the improvement in their capacity to earn. Expenses arise for the purpose of the trade or to maintain the earning capacity of existing assets.

42   The correct answers are: Asset A $NIL. Asset B $2,531

	Asset A (straight line)		Asset B (reducing balance)	
	Statement of financial position balance	Statement of profit or loss charge	Statement of financial position balance	Statement of profit or loss charge
	$	$	$	$
Cost	8,000		8,000	
Year 1 charge	(2,000)	2,000	(2,000)	2,000
c/f	6,000		6,000	
Year 2 charge	(2,000)	2,000	1,500	1,500
c/f	4,000		4,500	
Year 3 charge	(2,000)	2,000	(1,125)	1,125
c/f	2,000		3,375	
Year 4 charge	(2,000)	2,000	(844)	844
Value after four years	-		2,531	

43   The correct answer is: Allocation

Allocation is the process by which indirect expenses are charged to a cost centre. Indirect expenses are initially allocated to the appropriate cost centres before they are apportioned further.

10 Overheads and absorption costing

44 The correct answer is: Overheads will be over-absorbed by $625 due to lower than expected labour hours more than offset by lower than expected expenditure.

Overhead absorbed $= \dfrac{\$15,000}{20,000} \times 19,500$ 14,625

Overhead incurred   14,000
Over-absorbed overhead   625

The first option is untrue because lower expenditure is more likely to lead to over-absorption, unless there is a corresponding reduction in the actual labour hours.

The second option is incorrect because the decrease in labour hours in isolation would have resulted in an under-absorption of $375 (500 hours × $0.75 per hour).

If you selected the third option you performed the calculations correctly but misinterpreted the result as an under-absorption.

45 The correct answer is: Spread common costs over cost centres

Overhead apportionment involves sharing overhead costs as fairly as possible over a number of cost centres. Apportionment is used when it is not possible to allocate the whole cost to a single cost centre.

46 The correct answer is: $ | 36,792 |

	$
Production overhead absorbed (11,970 hours × $2.60)	31,122
Production overhead under-absorbed	5,670
Production overhead incurred	36,792

47 The correct answers are: They are predetermined in advance for each period. They are used to charge overheads to products.

Overhead absorption rates are determined in advance for each period, usually based on budgeted data. Therefore the first option is correct and the third option is incorrect. Overhead absorption rates are used in the final stage of overhead analysis, to absorb overheads into product costs.

Therefore the second option is correct. The fourth option is not correct because overheads are controlled using budgets and other management information.

48 The correct answer is: $ | 25 | per machine hour (to the nearest $).

	$
Actual overheads incurred	198,600
Over-absorbed overhead	25,750
Actual overheads absorbed	224,350

$\dfrac{\text{Actual overheads absorbed}}{\text{Actual machine hours}}$ = Amount absorbed per machine hour

224,350/8,974 = $25 per machine hour

11 Marginal costing and absorption costing

49 The correct answer is: Absorption costing profits will be higher and closing inventory valuations higher than those under marginal costing.

Closing inventory valuation under **absorption costing** will always be higher than under **marginal costing** because of the absorption of fixed overheads into closing inventory values.

BPP
LEARNING
MEDIA

The profit under absorption costing will be greater because the fixed overhead being carried forward in closing inventory is greater than the fixed overhead being written off in opening inventory.

50   The correct answer is: $170,000

Using **marginal costing**, the profit in June was:

	$	$
Sales revenue		820,000
Less variable production costs [$300,000 – ($\frac{150}{1,000}$) × $300,000)]		(255,000)
		565,000
Less: fixed production costs	180,000	
variable selling costs	105,000	
fixed selling costs	110,000	
		(395,000)
		170,000

51   The correct answer is: $1,080

200 units × ($15.00 – $9.60)/unit

52   The correct answer is: Contribution

Contribution is the difference between sales value and the marginal cost of sales.

53   The correct answers are: Marginal costing – Period costs. Absorption costing – Unit costs

12   Cost bookkeeping

54   The correct answer is: An account which records total cost as opposed to individual costs.

55   The correct answers are: Keeps one set of ledger accounts – Integrated. Inventory may be valued differently in the financial accounts – Integrated.

56   The correct answer is: Debit Overhead control account. Credit Stores control account.

The cost of indirect materials issued is **credited to the stores account** and 'collected' in the overhead control account **pending its absorption into work in progress**.

The first option represents the entries for the issue to production of **direct materials**.

If you selected the second option you identified the correct accounts but **your entries were reversed**.

The fourth option is not correct. The issue of materials should not be charged direct to cost of sales. The cost of materials issued should first be analysed as direct or indirect and charged to work in progress or the overhead control account accordingly.

57   The correct answer is:

	$
Debit Production overhead control account	$18,000
Credit Rent account	$18,000

The rent account for the period would look like this.

RENT ACCOUNT

	$		$
Cash	30,000	Production overhead	18,000
		Admin overhead	9,000
		Marketing overhead	3,000
	30,000		30,000

The debit balance in the rent account is analysed between the various functional classifications of overhead.

The first option uses the correct accounts but the entries are reversed. The second option is the reverse of the entries that would be used to record the original rent payment. The fourth option uses the correct accounts but only 60% of overhead should be charged to production.

58   The correct answers are: Indirect material issued from inventory was $57,000. Indirect wages costs incurred were $451,000.

The first option is correct. The cost of indirect material issued is 'collected' in the overhead control account **pending absorption into work in progress**.

The second option is incorrect. The overhead cost incurred was $525,000. The overhead **absorbed into work in progress** during the period was $1,012,000.

The third option is incorrect. The $21,000 is **debited to statement of profit or loss**, indicating an extra charge to compensate for the overhead **under-absorbed**.

The fourth option is correct. The indirect wage cost is 'collected' in the overhead control account **pending absorption into work in progress**.

13   Job, batch and service costing

59   The correct answers are: High levels of indirect costs as a proportion of total service costs. Use of composite cost units.

By-products and joint products are characteristics of **process costing**. Work of a relatively long duration is a characteristic of **contract costing**.

60   The correct answer is: Clothing manufacturer.

All of the options would use **service costing** except for the clothing manufacturer who would be providing products not services.

61   The correct answer is: Production is carried out in accordance with the wishes of the customer.

The first and fourth options are associated with **process costing**. The second option is associated with **service costing**.

62   The correct answer is: (1) and (3) only

Cost per tonne-kilometre (1) is appropriate for cost control purposes because it combines the distance travelled and the load carried, both of which affect cost. **The fixed cost per kilometre** (2) is not particularly useful for control purposes because it varies with the number of kilometres travelled. The **maintenance cost of each vehicle per kilometre** (3) can be useful for control purposes because it focuses on a particular aspect of the cost of operating each vehicle.

14   Process costing

63   The correct answers are: Actual output = 1,950 units. Actual output = 2,000 units.

Expected output = 2,000 units less normal loss (5%) 100 units = 1,900 units

In the first option there is an **abnormal loss** of 1,900 – 1,800 = 100 units
In the second option there is an **abnormal loss** of 1,900 – 1,890 = 10 units
In the third option there is an **abnormal gain** of 1,950 – 1,900 = 50 units
In the fourth option there is an **abnormal gain** of 2,000 – 1,900 = 100 units

64   The correct answers are: An unexpected loss is an abnormal loss. An abnormal loss arises if the actual loss is greater than the expected loss.

The first option is not correct; an **expected loss is a normal loss**. The fourth option is not correct. A normal loss could be less than actual loss if an abnormal loss occurred.

BPP
LEARNING
MEDIA

65   The correct answer is: $ [16] (to the nearest $)

Normal loss = 10% × input
               = 10% × 2,000 kg
               = 200 kg

When scrap has a value, normal loss is valued at the value of the scrap ie 8 cents per kg.

Normal loss = $0.08 × 200 kg
               = $16

66   The correct answer is: Mixing: Abnormal gain. Filtering: Abnormal loss

67   The correct answer is: $8.77

[$514,800 – (3,000 units × $5/unit)] ÷ (60,000 – 3,000 units) = $8.77

15   Cost-volume-profit (CVP) analysis

68   The correct answer is: 3,000 units

$$\text{Breakeven point} = \frac{\text{Total fixed costs}}{\text{Contribution per unit}} = \frac{\$12,000}{\$(6-2)} = 3{,}000 \text{ units}$$

If you selected 2,000 units you divided the fixed cost by the selling price, but remember that the selling price also has to cover the variable cost. 4,000 units is the margin of safety, and if you selected 6,000 units you seem to have divided the fixed cost by the variable cost per unit.

69   The correct answer is: [20] %

$$\text{Breakeven point} = \frac{\text{Total fixed costs}}{\text{Contribution per unit}} = \frac{\$38,400}{\$(4.80-3.20)} = 24{,}000 \text{ units}$$

Budgeted sales   30,000 units
Margin of safety   6,000 units

$$\text{Expressed as a \% of budget} = \frac{6{,}000}{30{,}000} \times 100\% = 20\%$$

70   The correct answer is: Distance C

Contribution at level of activity x = sales value less variable costs, which is indicated by distance C. Distance A indicates the profit at activity x, B indicates the fixed costs and D indicates the margin of safety in terms of sales value.

71   The correct answer is: Distance C

Above the **breakeven point**, contribution = fixed costs + profit, therefore distance C indicates the contribution at level of activity L.

Distance A indicates the profit at level of activity L, B indicates the fixed costs and D indicates the margin of safety.

72   The correct answer is: [1,958]

Total number of units   = $93,760/$20 = 4,688

Contribution per unit   = $23,440/4,688 = $5

Breakeven point   = Fixed costs/contribution per unit
                            = $9,792/$5
                            = 1,958

16 Short-term decisions

73   The correct answer is: The benefit lost by taking up one business opportunity in favour of another.

Opportunity cost is the benefit lost by taking up one business opportunity in favour of another.

74   The correct answers are: A differential cost. A future cost.

A differential cost is the difference in cost between two alternatives and is therefore a relevant cost for decision making. Relevant costs are also future costs. Costs incurred in the past are irrelevant to any decision being made now.

75   The correct answer is: Q,R,S,T

Profit is maximised by making the products with the highest contribution per limiting factor. The highest contribution per labour hour is given by product Q at $5.00 per hour. The lowest contribution per labour hour is given by product T at $3.80 per hour.

76   The correct answer is: 28,000 kg

	I	II	III	Total
Optimal production plan (units)	2,000	1,500	4,000	
Kgs required per unit	6	4	2.5	
Kgs material available	12,000	6,000	10,000	28,000

77   The correct answers are: Sunk cost: $32,000 Incremental cost: $8,000

The development costs of $32,000 are a **sunk cost** as they have already been incurred. The further costs of $8,000 are **incremental costs** and therefore relevant to the decision whether to continue.

17 Capital investment appraisal

78   The correct answer is: $50,000

The present value of $5,000 in perpetuity is calculated as $5,000/0.1.

If you selected **$500**, you might have calculated $5,000 × 10%.

If you selected **$5,500**, you might have calculated $5,000 × 110%.

If you selected **$4,545**, you might have calculated $5,000/110%.

79   The correct answer is: It doesn't account for the cost of capital in making investment decisions.

The first option is not a disadvantage because the fact that it tends to bias in favour of short-term projects means that it tends to minimise both financial and business risk.

The second option is untrue. It is simple to calculate the simple to understand, which may be important when management resources are limited.

The third option is not a disadvantage because it helps to identify those projects which generate additional cash for investment quickly.

The fourth option is a disadvantage because the firm needs to make a minimum return to cover the cost of raising funds and what investors are expecting as a return on their funds invested in the company.

BPP
LEARNING
MEDIA

80   The correct answer is: $1,540

Year	Annual cash flow	$	Discount factor 8%	PV $
0		(50,000)	1.000	(50,000)
1	(4,000 × $5)	20,000	0.926	18,520
2	(4,000 × $5)	20,000	0.857	17,140
3	(4,000 × $5)	20,000	0.794	15,880
				1,540

81   The correct answer is: $(5,225)

$100,000 – ($25,000 × 3.791) = $(5,225)

82   The correct answer is: 5.83%

$$\text{IRR} = 5\% + \frac{350}{(350+1,750)} \times (10-5)\%$$

$$= 5\% + 0.83\%$$

$$= 5.83\%$$

18   Cash and cash flows

83   The correct answer is: Zero

Working capital consists of current assets less current liabilities. In Peter Co's case it is inventory plus receivables less payables less overdraft (12,000 + 8,000 – 2,500 – 17,500) = zero.

84   The correct answer is: No, the total cash flow should be $248,000.

The trainee accountant has made two errors.

Firstly, opening receivables is cash received during the year and closing receivables is cash owing at the end of the year. Therefore the opening figure should be added to, and the closing figure deducted from, cash in.

Secondly, depreciation is not a cash item and should be ignored from the calculation.

The correct calculation for cash in is therefore (325,000 + 23,500 – 17,500 + 125,000) = $456,000.

The correct calculation for cash out is therefore (193,500 + 27,000 – 12,500) = $208,000.

Total cash flow is therefore (456,000 – 208,000) = $248,000.

85   The correct answer is: Bank loan

A **bank loan** is not classed as a current asset or liability and is therefore not a working capital item.

86   The correct answer is: Unusual costs such as closure of part of the business

Exceptional items are unusual. A good example is the closure of part of a business.

19   Cash and treasury management

87   The correct answer is: Corporate finance

Corporate finance is concerned with raising share capital and the dividend policy of the company. Funding management is directly concerned with the sources and types of funds and policies and procedures relating to funds. Liquidity management covers working capital, banking and money management. As the activities described fall into corporate finance, other activities don't apply.

88   The correct answers are: Ensuring prompt banking of cash. Ensuring cash received and banked is reconciled.

      Cash handling procedures relating to **receipts** include the prompt banking of cash

      received and the reconciliation between cash received and banked. The other two activities relate to cash payments.

89   The correct answers are: Recession: Build up cash balances. High growth: Run down cash balances.

90   The correct answer is: Banking the cash

      Cashiers handle money and in many businesses are responsible for banking cash received. They usually don't perform reconciliations or write up cash books. They may receive cash but generally their function is to bank cash.

91   The correct answer is: Abiding by the limitation on authority to sign cheques up to a certain amount.

      Cheque signatories are responsible for adhering to their limit on signing cheques. They are not responsible for any of the other activities which are usually carried out by finance or administration staff. The separate roles follow the segregation of duties.

20   Forecasting cash flows

92   The correct answer is: For estimating the cost of borrowing for funds needed

      A **forecast** is used to work out how much cash is needed, when it is needed, for how long and whether it will be available to borrow. However the forecast will not tell the company the actual cost of borrowing for the borrowing forecast.

93   The correct answer is: $187,500

      Since customers take two months to pay, the $375,000 of receivables in the statement of financial position represent credit sales from November and December 20X9. It is assumed these customers will pay in January and February 20Y0 at an equal monthly rate because sales were at an equal monthly rate. The cash budget should plan for receipts in these two months of $187,500 each.

94   The correct answer is: A change in the cost of capital

      A **change in the cost of capital**. Cash flow forecasting is not used for investment appraisal which is when the cost of capital would be relevant. Cash budgets are used to predict

      cash shortages or surpluses.

95   The correct answer is: $100,000.

      As suppliers are paid after 1½ months, payments will be made in January and the first half of February 20Y0. The $150,000 on the statement of financial position represents purchases in the second half of November and all of December 20X9. Therefore payment due in January is $150,000/3 = $50,000 × 2 = $100,000.

96   The correct answer is: 143%

      If $87,500 = 100%, then:

      20X9 $125,000 = $\dfrac{125,000}{87,500} \times 100\% = 143\%$

21 Investing surplus funds

97 The correct answer is: Gilts

Government bonds are otherwise known as gilts or gilt-edged securities.

98 The correct answer is: Speculative motive

A speculative motive hopes that interest rates will rise.

99 The correct answers are: Deposit at a bank: Not lose value. Ordinary shares: Lose value

The amount of money deposited in a bank account will not change and may earn interest.

However the value of traded shares can fluctuate depending on the stock market.

22 Raising finance from a bank

100 The correct answers are: The length of the loan which should not exceed the useful life of the asset to be bought. The internal guidelines of the lender.

The **length of the loan**, should not exceed the **useful life of the asset** to be purchased, because the customer will presumably expect to repay the loan whilst he is still enjoying

the use of the asset and any profits it might be earning. Banks will have **internal guidelines** for lending to customers. The other two choices apply to overdrafts.

101 The correct answers are: To exercise care (a duty of care). To advise the bank of any known forgeries (advice of forgery).

The customer has two main duties which are a duty of care in drawing cheques so that fraud is not enabled, and to advise on and known forgery.

102 The correct answer is: **CAMPARI**.

This is made up of the following factors.

Character of the customer
Ability to borrow and repay
Margin of profit
Purpose of the borrowing
Amount of the borrowing
Repayment terms
Insurance against the possibility of non-payment

103 The correct answers are: Bullet. Balloon.

Bullet payments are where the principal is repaid in full at the end of the term. **Balloon payments** are where some of the principal is repaid during the term but the main proportion is repaid at the end of the term.

104 The correct answer is: Positive

Positive covenants require the borrower to do something. Negative or restrictive covenants are a promise by the borrower **not** to do something. Quantitative covenants set limitations on the borrower's financial position.

Bibliography

Bibliography

ACT (2016) [Online]. Available from: www.treasurers.org/ [Accessed 17 November 2020].

Companies Act 2006. (2006). [Online]. Available from: www.legislation.gov.uk
[Accessed 17 November 2020]. www.nationalarchives.gov.uk/doc/open-government-licence/version/3/

Contains Parliamentary information licensed under the Open Parliament Licence v3.0.

Data Protection Act 2018. (2018). [Online]. Available from: www.legislation.gov.uk
[Accessed 17 November 2020].

Contains Parliamentary information licensed under the Open Parliament Licence v3.0.

The Local Authorities (Capital Finance) (Approved Investments) Regulations 2015 Available from:
www.legislation.gov.uk/uksi/2015/341/pdfs/uksi_20150341_en.pdf [Accessed 17 November 2020].

Index

BPP
LEARNING
MEDIA

Review form

Name: _____   Address: _____

_____

_____

How have you used this Interactive Text?
(Tick one box only)
☐ Home study (book only)
☐ On a BPP in-centre course _____
☐ On a BPP online course
☐ On a course with another college
☐ Other _____

Why did you decide to purchase this Interactive Text? *(Tick one box only)*
☐ Have used BPP Texts in the past
☐ Recommendation by friend/colleague
☐ Recommendation by a lecturer at college
☐ Saw advertising
☐ Other _____

Which BPP products have you used?
☑ Text   ☐ Kit   ☐ Passcards

During the past six months do you recall seeing/receiving any of the following?
(Tick as many boxes as are relevant)
☐ Our advertisement in *ACCA Student Accountant*
☐ Our advertisement in *Teach Accounting*
☐ Other advertisement _____
☐ Our brochure with a letter through the post
☐ ACCA E-Gain email
☐ BPP email
☐ Our website www.bpp.com

Which (if any) aspects of our advertising do you find useful?
(Tick as many boxes as are relevant)
☐ Prices and publication dates of new editions
☐ Information on Interactive Text content
☐ Facility to order books
☐ None of the above

Your ratings, comments and suggestions would be appreciated on the following areas.

	Very useful	Useful	Not useful
Introductory section (How to use this Interactive Text)	☐	☐	☐
Key terms	☐	☐	☐
Examples	☐	☐	☐
Questions and answers	☐	☐	☐
Fast forwards	☐	☐	☐
Quick quizzes	☐	☐	☐
Exam focus points	☐	☐	☐
Practice Question Bank	☐	☐	☐
Practice Answer Bank	☐	☐	☐
Index	☐	☐	☐
Structure and presentation	☐	☐	☐
Icons	☐	☐	☐

	Excellent	Good	Adequate	Poor
Overall opinion of this Interactive Text	☐	☐	☐	☐

Do you intend to continue using BPP products?   Yes ☐   No ☐

Please visit https://www.bpp.com/request-support to provide your feedback for this material.

Review form (continued)

Please note any further comments and suggestions/errors below.